T0294525

THE HUMANITARIAN DEVELOPMENT PARADIGM

Search for Global Justice

Wilfred L. David

University Press of America,® Inc.
Lanham · Boulder · New York · Toronto · Oxford

Copyright © 2004 by
University Press of America,® Inc.
4501 Forbes Boulevard
Suite 200
Lanham, Maryland 20706
UPA Acquisitions Department (301) 459-3366

PO Box 317
Oxford
OX2 9RU, UK

Library of Congress Control Number: 2003114130
ISBN 0-7618-2755-2 (clothbound : alk. ppr.)
ISBN 0-7618-2756-0 (paperback : alk. ppr.)

Contents

Tables and Figures

TABLES

FIGURES

Preface

Achievement of authentic development, or total upliftment of the entire human race, remains one of the foremost but intractable issues to be resolved during the new millennium. In the eyes of many influential leaders in the global community, it parallels resolution of the apocalyptic threat of a nuclear holocaust and, perhaps, prevention of sociospherical environmental collapse posed by disappearance of the ozone layer and attendant global warming. Yet, in many parts of the world, the very idea of "development" still conjures up images of a poor quality of life or the most parlous state of human ill-being and misery, mirroring an ongoing reality that most human beings are born without any realistic expectations of a life devoid of hunger, malnutrition, violence, and oppression. Billions of people, especially in the less developed sector of the world, have come to view development as an unfair "rat race" of giant proportions, a theoretical construct that is uniformly imposed from the capitals of North America and Europe, or as a metaphysical construct that is far removed from their daily lives of struggle for survival.

The growing disenchantment has found a forceful and visible expression in the confluence of anti-establishment ideas, perceptions, protests, and demonstrations. At one level, it is exemplified by widespread anti-American and anti-Western feelings in poor countries. The belief that Western policy is a primary source of poverty and underdevelopment has had a foundation in development reality itself. For example, the stark conditions facing many poor countries, especially in Africa, are traceable not only to the long-term impact of colonialism, but also generalized in terms of the more recent involvement of Western powers in globalization. It is widely viewed in the periphery as the latest stage in its exploitation by the West, with rich countries gaining at the expense of poor ones.

In an era of B-2 bombers, Evian water, and artificial hearts, more than 25,000 children worldwide die every year because they lack food, clean water, or basic medicines. Argentinians have been protesting in the streets of Buenos Aires about an economic collapse that has left their families in the dust. In the mid-1990s, fearing an influx of beggars into Caracas, the Venezuelan government decreed that hundreds of *Warao* Indians from the Orinoco river delta be transported back to their homes in the northeast jungles. They were camping in the parks and begging in the streets where they could make more money in a few days than most gainfully employed workers earned in a month. A Warao leader explained that his people desperately needed food and basic equipment in order to survive.

Such a jaundiced imagery is not confined to people living in poor countries. The perception is also shared by movements ostensibly championing global justice. Their members challenge Westernization (Americanization), the power of transnational corporations (TNCs), and are generally concerned about rising global inequality. The demonstrations that took place in Seattle, Washington, at the 1999 Ministerial Meetings of the World Trade Organization (WTO) have been widely reported. These were followed by equally impressive protests in Europe, Africa, Asia, and Latin America, and again in the spring of 2001 in Quebec against negotiators of a Free Trade Area for the Americas. The Seattle protests have also been a major forerunner to yearly challenges to the World Bank and International Monetary Fund (IMF) for imposing harsh austerity on the world's poor. Another major target has been the World Economic Forum, the annual meeting of the global elite, and especially corporate leaders, which takes place in Davos, Switzerland. As the Forum was meeting in January 2001, the first World Social Forum was convened at Porto Alegre, Brazil, in opposition to a world in which the domination of capital and financial markets perceptibly works against democracy and the need for long-term investments in basic social services.

Furthermore, the widening gap between the affluent few and impoverished majority seems to have created deep-rooted feelings of resentment and despair, prompting terrorist attacks on the World Trade Center and Pentagon on September 11, 2001. In the wake of this disaster, many in the West stared in disbelief as Palestinians celebrated the collapse of the World Trade Center and Indonesians marched behind banners bearing the likeness of Osama bin Laden. People, especially in North America and Europe, have become increasingly sensitized to the potential vulnerabilities that global terrorists can exploit, for example, poisoning of water supplies and spreading of deadly diseases. It is widely believed that global terrorism, networks of money laundering, the narcotics trade, and other forms of organized crime are all representative parts of the negative side of globalization.

Despite the emergence of such fault-lines in the global political economy, leading scholars in the West are still caught up in a hubristic interpretation of world affairs. Since the end of the Cold War, the march of intellectual and global history has witnessed a period in which a "one-world" global development ideology has come to rule the roost. In the ruling paradigm of "developmentocracy," everyone has to play by the "rich man's rules of the game" – liberalize, marketize, privatize, tighten their belts, promote hard currencies by adopting the IMF's weak currency mantra, and put the interests of Wall Street, TNCs, international financial institutions, and ruling elites above those of local populations. The derivative development discourse remains embedded in the imperialism of economics, thralldom of money, growth fetishism, and historical and cultural determinism.

This book makes a plea for a fundamental reorientation of, or "paradigm shift" in, the prevailing orthodoxy and its foundations in controlling sets of theoretical precepts, belief systems, images, ideologies, metaphors, and institutional orders. It reiterates a clarion call for a more participatory conversation of human liberation, or people-centered dialogue, in which human agency becomes the primary unit of interpretation and correlative human choices, capabilities, and freedoms are elevated to center stage of development theory, practice, and policy. A guiding preconception is that human life is created to serve a purpose greater than the market, state, or global economy. The book's paradigm-altering perspective of individual and collective human welfare rests on several interdependent building blocks that cut across traditional disciplines.

First, it promotes an idea of sustainable human well-being that is grounded in the primordial idea of *humanitarianism*. This connotes credible improvements in the life chances of all human beings, irrespective of particularistic or ascriptive attributes such as class, race, ethnicity, gender, and national origin. The governing dynamic is provided by the "overlapping consensus" encountered in major systems of thought and world religions. They collectively provide the bedrock for human security, people's empowerment, economic development, and social progress. At the same time, it is recognized that all humanity constantly lives in a unitary maelstrom of cooperation and conflict. The emergence of a dense cosmopolitan web of existence has been driven by a constant search for efficiency and advantage. In this process, humans have not only created complex social organizations generating wealth and power, but also the inequalities and societal antagonisms mentioned earlier.

Second, the quest for humanitarian development is anchored in a normative discourse that stresses core human values, global justice, and guaranteed human rights. Related to this are certain crucial *ground rules* or ethical questions that purportedly shape human conduct: "how people ought to live and behave in relation to others." Such ground rules and questions reflect the fact that the human life world is complex and interdependent. For example, the actions of individual Americans tend to reverberate throughout the entire sociosphere, constantly intermingling with the effects of actions of billions of other human beings. As noted earlier, many of us are advantaged participants in a global institutional order that is imposed on disadvantaged participants not by fate or nature but by the actions of other human agents. The important point is that the disadvantaged are perfectly capable of leading healthy and successful lives if allowed a meaningful chance to escape their generalized state of deprivation.

As a corollary, advocacy of a paradigm change involves philosophical reflection about the state of justice in the contemporary world, how we are all related in the existing structure of injustices and what constitutes a just world order. We hasten to add that this is not a call for more armchair philosophizing about development and underdevelopment. Rather, our idea of conversation is predicated on the intermeshing of theoretical and practical wisdom, the melding of theoretical and practical discourses, and ultimately creation of optimal synergy or reciprocity with the concrete social praxis of ordinary human beings.

Germane to this is a holistic interpretation of well-being that focuses on the totality of human welfare or the overall quality of life
people succeed in living. It connotes not only the availability and
distribution of material goods and services, but also values, employment, needs fulfillment, institutions, and knowledge. Satisfaction of
humanitarian development goals is intimately intertwined with endogenous processes of socio-cultural learning that are deeply embedded
in the structure of society, its history, and visions of the future. This
underscores the primordial significance of "moral resources" such as
social capital, trust, and norms in enabling people to live valued and
valuable lives. From this perspective, human beings can no longer be
construed as mere instrumental "means" or malleable resources that
can be constantly manipulated in the pursuit of material prosperity and
wealth creation.

Hence, the background edifice of the humanitarian enterprise is
grounded in multifaceted processes, interdependencies among
"wholes" and their constituent "parts," or a multiplicity of systemic interactions at the local (sub-national), national, and global (supranational) levels. At the methodological level, this calls for more interpretive pluralism, or what is termed *transdisciplinarity* (interdisciplinary interface). This eclectic approach highlights the need for flexibility and open-mindedness, attempts to synthesize insights drawn from
diverse areas of human experience, and is predicated on "intermingling" and "coalescence" of various academic disciplines, such as history, philosophy, economics, ecology, psychology, sociology, political
science, and anthropology. Not only are they integral parts of an
ongoing human project, but their knowledge claims and practical significance must always be located within the "totality," "interdependence," and "contextual" nature of human history and experience.

Correlatively, the book projects a new guidance system of global
populism or a synergistic system of developmental management that
must be pushed into two directions simultaneously: from "bottom to
top" or upwards above the nation-state; and from "top to bottom" or
downwards into several sub-national and programmatic levels. This
dualistic but organic trajectory rests on a policy orientation and decision-making environment based on institutional pluralism. At one
level, it underscores the fact that precision of formal economic models
often falls victim to the psychological motivations of human beings
and power differentials inherent in institutions. At another level, achievement of alternative goal-oriented human futures is predicated on

institutional "leap forward" or a complex dynamic based on symbiotic regimes – a reformed global system or sociosphere, reaching right up to the United Nations and beyond; a reconstituted developmental state; renewed organs of civil society; people-friendly markets; and the integrative power of community.

Finally, the book can be read with profit by different publics – students and teachers, policymakers and planners, generalists and specialists, alike. An overriding objective is to automatically place readers in a much better position to build theoretically and perspectivally from what they have already learnt from the social sciences, humanities, and/or practical experience. A primary audience comprises graduate and advanced undergraduate students with an interest in development studies. They may be enrolled in traditional disciplines and/or interdisciplinary programs such as international relations, political economy, environmental studies, as well as African, Asian, Latin American and Caribbean Studies. Depending on the nature of course requirements, the entire book may be chosen as a text or, alternatively, each chapter can be fruitfully used as a case study to sharpen problem-solving skills and stimulate discussion.

The menu may also whet the appetite of scholarly experts, development practitioners, and general readers who may be desirous of taking a fresh look at the human development problem as it unfolds in the 21st century, and/or to improve their knowledge and understanding of the complex humanitarian issues to be resolved at the global, regional, national, and local levels. In any event, the book's polemical thrust is intended to provoke argument, disagreement, and stimulate further research.

Acknowledgments

This book is an outgrowth of more than three decades of academic teaching, research, and active policy involvement in economic development in general, and the perspectival nature of interpretations, in particular. I have accumulated an endless succession of intellectual and personal debts during this odyssey, and acknowledging all of them is an impossible task. In this case, I simply thank in a general way those who over the years have encouraged my efforts either through exemplary published works or incisive criticism via personal contact. Nevertheless, some networks of personal obligations must be mentioned.

I would like to acknowledge a long standing gratitude to two inimicable institutional pillars of learning and scholarship – the Philosophy and Economics program at the University of London and the Modern Greats (PPE) - Politics, Philosophy, and Economics – concentration in the Faculty of Social Sciences at the University of Oxford. They originally kindled what was to mature into a lifelong interest in a transdisciplinarity, that is, an interdisciplinary methodology. They remain quintessential models of a broad, inclusive, and liberal education.

I am particularly thankful to numerous academic colleagues who patiently read earlier drafts of the manuscript, made detailed comments and/or suggested improvements, viz.: professors Ayo Langley, Abiy

Ford, John Cotman, and Patricia McCormick (Howard University); Ken Cole (University of East Anglia); Cedric Grant (Clark Atlanta University); Ewart Thomas (Stanford University); Edward Eule (Norfolk State University); Morris St. Pierre (Morgan State University), Alfredo Sfeir-Younis (United Nations and World Bank); and Leo Edwards (National Coalition of Caribbean Affairs). While the author must bear the ultimate responsibility for what he creates, I have drawn liberally from their critical interpretations and understandings.

Many of my past and present graduate students have coalesced into a willing laboratory, but at times dissenting audience, for my sometimes "strange" ideas about paradigms, conversations, and humanitarian development. I have benefited from endless discussions with Lamin Jangha, Ladimero Francisco, Xav Hagen, Rosangela King, Paul Pressley, Adryan Wallace, Alisa Wilder, June Bland, Angel Batiste, Gnaka, Naoko Takemoto, Grace Herrly, and Caroline Jeza.

I thank my colleagues at the University Press of America for the skill and care with which they brought the book to publication – especially Judith Rothman, Director; Stephen Ryan, Acquisitions Editor; and Beverly Baum, Production Editor.

An unpayable debt is owed to Wilfred David, Jr. and Ladimero Francisco and for lending their computing skills to the technical production of this work.

Last but certainly not least, I am forever grateful to my wife, Dr. Peggy David, for her daily encouragement and selfless support. Her editorial advice and critical overview of the project have been indispensable.

The usual caveat should be added that all errors remain the author's own responsibility.

Part One

Paradigms and People

Chapter 1

Why Are We So Rich and They So Poor?

> Revolutions usually begin with ideas and it is by our ideas that we
> change the way we live, the way we organize society, the way we
> manipulate material things.
>
> Barbara Ward (1962)

The sad reality of our times is that the broadening frontiers of
knowledge and global march of economic, technological, and scientific
progress have not been matched by equally significant advances in justice, fairness, basic human rights, and related correlates of sustainable
human or "authentic" development. This perceptible "failure of development" is visibly reflected in the despicable life chances and poor
quality of life facing the world's majority – billions of people living in
what we term "late development countries" (LDCs). Despite the emergence of global mega-trends favoring fast macroeconomic growth rates

and economic stability, domestic liberalization, deregulation, privatization, market-oriented economies, and other pillars of "economic adjustment," roughly 90 percent of the world's people still face parlous conditions of human deprivation and misery.

In the name of such economic adjustment and related notions of "material prosperity," "wealth-creation," "progress," and "development," masses of deprived people all over the world are forced to live under conditions of continuous upheaval and involuntary change. At the same time, they are denied access not only to real economic, social and political power, but even more importantly, to what essentially constitute the ordinary opportunities of life: access to meaningful jobs and critical resources such as land, capital, living space, and basic social services. In the eyes of several leaders of the global community and other people of good will throughout the globe, the increasing gap between the so-called "haves" and "have-nots" might have worsened from the mere "inequitable" to the "inhumane." Some now view "development" as a lost cause that cannot be salvaged.

More generally, the 20th and early 21st centuries are sometimes perceived as achieving new heights of humankind's capacity to inflict inhumane levels of cruelty, violence, destruction, and destitution. Underdevelopment, inequality, and their correlates are both causes and consequences of this inhumanity. The interpretation and understanding of such phenomena should not rely on an abstract conceptualization of humanity, but are inherently linked to the visible or concrete experiences of a humanity that is subject to and replete with many wrongs. The deepening crisis of human development is not necessarily reflected in aggregate statistics on the economic growth performance of countries, per capita income attainment, escalating inflation rates, or budget and balance of payments deficits.

Rather, it is manifested in a much more deep-seated feeling of disenchantment and hopelessness that now defines the lot of the poor majority in LDCs. Many in their midst have come to believe either in utter changelessness or that things might have changed for the worse. The very idea of "development" has been associated with a very low quality of life, psychological dependency, and related correlates of ill-being. In many parts of Africa, Asia, Latin America and the Caribbean, large numbers of people have come to view development as a giant intellectual chess game, a metaphysical abstraction, or imported theoretical construct that is far removed from their daily lives, situated experiences, or brutal struggles for survival. Hence, the notion constantly summons up images of massive disillusionment, surrealism, and confusion. Such sentiments are illustrated in Table 1.1 – a poem on development.

This raises a far more complex question about the nature of the guidance system, environment, or intellectual milieu defining alternative perceptions about the relationship between development reality and its interpretation.

Table 1.1: Poem on Development

DEVELOPMENT
Big word
Lotsa meanings
Staka Dollar
Magnetic circle
Entices Me
Urban drift
Empty villages
Customs forgotten
Loose living
Lost identity
Rat Race
Dollar talks
Values change
Wantoks* ignored
Every man for himself
I want to develop too!

* "Wantoks" means people of the same language group, literally "one talk".
Poem submitted by Jully Supolo, Solomon Islands, and sent to *CHOICES* by the UNDP office in Fiji.

Source: UNDP. *CHOICES*, 6, 1997, 29.

The problematique is implicit in the following question posed by the noted economic historian David Landes: "Why Are We So Rich and They So Poor?" – a query borrowed for the title of this chapter. Landes provides two alternative answers:

> One says that we are so rich and they so poor because we are so good and they so bad; that is, we are hardworking, knowledgeable, educated, well-governed, efficacious, and productive, and they are

the reverse. The other says that we are so rich and they so poor because we are so bad and they so good: we are greedy, ruthless, exploitative, aggressive, while they are weak, innocent, virtuous, abused, and vulnerable (Landes 1990, 1).

While the belief systems, images, and value-orientations under-lying the two alternative perspectives are by no means mutually ex-clusive, a reasonable judgment is that most observers or experts would prefer to stand on one side of the fence rather than on the other. The fo-cal point, however, is that insofar as a frontal attack has to be mounted against human deprivation, each line of explanation suggests a more or less different development trajectory, style, or path. Germane to this are some intractable philosophical considerations about the nature of the relationship between theoretical and practical discourses, knowledge and experience, or the discontinuities inherent in the historical interplay of controlling ideas, cosmological beliefs, and patterns of development and underdevelopment.

More generally, the lives and practical actions of human beings are continuously shaped and rearranged by dominant ideas, images, cognitive structures, and metaphors that typically coalesce into life-and-world visions or *paradigms*. The attendant belief systems, per-ceptions, and categories of thought can be construed as alternative in-terpretive systems or frameworks historically designed to acquire knowledge and truth. As such, they essentially represent modes of ana-lysis, explanation, interpretation, and understanding that are grounded in different philosophical preconceptions or ideologies. These, in turn, form the bases for generating competing academic practices, theore-tical models, and ultimately policy prescriptions and procedures of decision-making. Contextually, the development discourse is intima-tely bound up with fundamental conceptions and perspectives about individual behavior, human communities, nation states, markets, and other collectivities that guide our thoughts and actions.

Paradigms

The expansion of knowledge has been accompanied by a number of complementary changes in mental habits, conceptual systems, and ways in which academicians, policymakers, and ordinary people at-tempt to interpret and understand the multiple realities of human expe-rience. While not evident to the naked eye, the process is usually guided by an array of philosophical and cultural referents: (i) ontological commitments – belief systems or what we believe the world to be, as exemplified by questions such as: "what is Africa or Europe?"; (ii) epistemological presuppositions – how we come to know, or what it is we think that we know; (iii) axiologies – value-orientations, norms, or standards of behavior that tell us how we *ought* to behave; and (iv) logics – methods or patterns of reasoning. Such categories of interpretation and understanding tend to delimit the field of intellectual inquiry, shape the character and outlook of theoretical and policy discourse, and determine the significance of problems and ultimately the nature of acceptable solutions.

More often than not, disagreements among scholars, economists, policy analysts, development experts, and other producers of knowledge about alternative development trajectories do not stem from differences in the internal coherence or logical validity of their respective arguments or theories. Rather, contestations usually reflect fundamental variances in philosophical preconceptions. This suggests that the world being studied by social scientists is not just something "out there," in the sense of being "objectively" given. Rather, it displays characteristics that we project onto it.

While most spectators often plead objectivity in regard to the phenomena they observe, in reality no such objectivity exists. In order to gain knowledge at the most basic level, observers must view the swirl of events through the prejudicial lens of their sensed perceptions and experiences. Moreover, acquisition of this knowledge requires perception through the filter of change, since "facts" tend to refract or move in vectors away from a stationary position. In the final analysis, all this knowledge is then viewed and acted upon at a higher level through a socio-cultural framework – a belief system. However, as much as a camera's lens focuses on a particular picture, a bystander's filter of beliefs allows for a specific interpretation and description of phenomena or events being observed.

The upshot of the argument is that our knowledge claims, theories, and policy prescriptions normally rest on "assumptions," implying beliefs about human experience and how the world works. Our belief structures not only provide an understanding of experience and a sense of order, but also allow us to make choices about alternative options that can be utilized to fulfill our human development potentials.

The process involves a combination of beliefs and desires in making plans, predicting the consequences of our own behavior, and anti-

cipating the behavior of others (Cole 1995). As two other scholars re-
mark:

> Scientists, like other intellectuals, come to their work with a world
> view, a set of preconceptions that provides the framework for their
> analyses of the world. These preconceptions enter at both an expli-
> cit and an implicit level, but even when invoked explicitly, *unexa-
> mined and unexpressed assumptions* underlie them (Levins and
> Lewontin 1985, 267; emphasis added).

The persistence of conflicting or incompatible modes of analysis
and interpretation is usually reflected by differences in "paradigms"
within a field of inquiry. The notion of a paradigm emphasizes the
larger environment conditioning the creation and growth of knowledge.
This encapsulates the cultural, social, historical, and psychological
contexts in which theoretical systems emerge, mature, and change.
This contextualist or "externalist" perspective is usually contrasted
with the dominant "internalist" or evolutionary alternative. The latter
interprets the history of scientific inquiry as a gradual expansion of
knowledge based on a continuous process of theory formulation and
testing in accordance with experience, or a "trial-and-error" method. In
other words, it is believed that scientific progress can be rationally
constructed, in the sense that it comes within the purview of the "logic
of discovery," "conjectures and refutations," or "evolutionary epistemology" (Popper 1972, 159).

Thomas Kuhn (1970), a major protagonist of the contextualist approach, contends that scientists or researchers do not normally engage
in the rational formulation of hypotheses or theories. On the contrary,
they are primarily concerned with solving "puzzles" set by earlier researchers working in their field of inquiry. Furthermore, he depicts the
history of scientific thought in terms of a paradigm that is punctuated
by revolutionary theoretical changes. The paradigm is historically
grounded in well-respected theoretical traditions that generate substantial research programs. Specific scientific communities or "invisible colleges" usually coalesce around it. The socio-cultural milieu
provides the paradigm with its distinct cognitive structure, frame of reference for the intellectual discourse, and operational procedures.

Kuhn assigns two broad but related roles to a paradigm – "socio-
logical-psychological" and "exemplary." In the sociological sense, it
stands for the "entire constellation of beliefs, values, techniques, and so

on shared by members of a given [scientific] community" (Kuhn 1970, 175). This implies that analysts share a common vision of the world and how it functions based on the philosophical preconceptions mentioned earlier. In turn, these collectively facilitate the sedimentation of what is viewed as the "community-fine structure" of science. The leading "community of scholars" typically functions as a "management control system." The propagation of certain ideas and ideologies, theoretical constructs, empirical generalizations, and preferred types of policy prescriptions through this consensus-driven mechanism helps to explain why a dominant paradigm tends to maintain its tenacity and is difficult to overthrow.

At the psychological level, the diverse stimuli impinging on the differential vantage points of theorists or researchers may actually produce similar sensations when interpreted within the confines of the same paradigm. According to Kuhn,

> two groups, the members of which have systematically different sensations on receipt of the same stimuli, do in some sense live in different worlds. We posit the existence of stimuli to explain our perception of the world, and we posit their immutability to avoid both individual and social solipsism (1970, 193).

Solipsism is avoided because of a shared paradigm, that is, common values or parameters tend to buttress people's shared perceptions. As the field of knowledge grows and becomes more scientific, more and more researchers come to share the dominant vision or perspective. It is learned by practitioners and students in educational institutions and ultimately takes on the status of "expert" knowledge.

The learning process underscores the "exemplary" role of a paradigm. When viewed as an "exemplar" of past achievements within a specific academic discipline, a paradigm denotes

> the concrete puzzle solutions which, employed as models or examples, can replace explicit rules as a basis for the solution of the remaining puzzles of normal science [and] the student discovers a way to see his problem as like a problem he has already encountered (Kuhn 1970, 175, 189).

Exemplars are problem solutions or puzzles that reflect the empirical content of theories. They typically form the content of the scientific literature, and provide concrete examples in textbooks, academic journals, laboratories, and related tools for training students. As such, they represent a major form of group commitment and means of scientific communication.

One of the fundamental techniques by which members of a given scientific community develop the same vision when confronted with the same stimuli is by being shown examples of situations that their peers or predecessors have already learned to perceive as being similar or different from other construals of reality. In the Kuhnian schema, the intellectual activity involved in paradigm articulation is viewed as a cumulative process of clarification, extension and resolution of puzzles.

As research proceeds, a paradigm tends to limit the questions a researcher can meaningfully ask, thereby hindering the emergence of novel and challenging ideas. At the same time, many "anomalies" conflicting with the theoretical and cognitive structure of the dominant paradigm may emerge. These often result from the simple fact that experience always poses new problems, or from revelation of new or unsuspected phenomena. If such anomalies cannot be removed through more intensive research within the set parameters of the ruling paradigm, a crisis ensues and the community consensus is likely to crumble.

The end result is a "scientific revolution" based on a different conception of reality, and a new paradigm completely overthrows the old. Thus, Kuhn interprets scientific progress in revolutionary rather than evolutionary terms, or as taking place by leaps and jumps rather than incrementally. A pertinent question, therefore, is whether the new should totally displace the old, or whether they can coexist. Kuhn's iconoclastic idea of a scientific revolution is unrealistic and needs revision. A more plausible hypothesis is that normal scientific activity is defined by continuous tension among competing schools of thought or research programs. Rival ones can be introduced when they boast superior explanatory or interpretive power over predecessors or existing ones.

Useful insights into this more realistic alternative are provided by the "methodology of scientific research programs" (MSRP) of Imré Lakatos (1976). While the MSRP comes close to Kuhn's notion of a paradigm, there are some important differences. In the Lakatosian schema, schools of thought or scientific research programs represent clusters of interconnected theories that are thought to have "evolved," thereby providing the essential foundations for continuous development of scientific knowledge. The process is articulated in terms of what are termed the "hard core" and "protective belt" of a research strategy. The hard core consists of a set of purely metaphysical beliefs (ontological commitments) and a shared body of theoretical hypotheses that define and inspire the program's research strategy. The basic assumptions underlying the hard core are irrefutable and cannot be compromised, that is, they are not normally subject to question by the community of scholars.

The hard core is surrounded by a protective belt of auxiliary hypotheses that are malleable. Specific testable theories that give the research program its reputation are normally located in the protective belt. It is here that all empirical testing takes place, implications drawn out, and modifications made. This process, Lakatos contends, takes place over relatively long periods of time, and can be described in the following terms. When a series or succession of theories exists, each successive theory evolves from reinterpretations of previous ones in order to deal with anomalies. Since instances of falsification invariably occur during the testing of theories, scientific research programs have to be continuously amended in order to avoid refutation. Linked to this are two criteria for evaluating theoretical systems – termed *progressive* and *degenerating*.

A theoretically progressive system is one in which each new theory has an "excess of empirical content" over its rival or predecessor. Thus, it is able to predict some novel or hitherto unanticipated facts, some of which are corroborated. The system is also "empirically progressive" when its excess empirical content is also corroborated. Lakatos's conclusion is that a research program is progressive in both theoretical and empirical senses, and degenerating when these two conditions are not met. Degenerating programs tend to accommodate whatever new facts become available. They have to do so through endless modification of theories, and hence cannot be saved. A crisis develops when the dominant research program is degenerating and unsuccessful. This often leads to what Lakatos calls "problem shifts."

As indicated earlier, adequate assessment of the status of a scientific research program can be made only after a long period of time has elapsed. Some programs start out in a progressive mode, stagnate, and become progressive again. The important question remains whether a research program should be preserved until its heuristic power has been totally exhausted, or a rival program introduced only when the scientific community unanimously agrees that the previous or competing one is no longer viable. Lakatos answers in the negative, since "normal scientific activity" is construed as "nothing but a research program that has gained monopoly." To reiterate, the history of science is defined by a coexistence (even though fraught with tensions) of different research programs.

This is borne out by the history of social and economic thought, which amply demonstrates that social science disciplines are "multiple paradigmatic." For example, the evolution of economics has been punctuated by "paradigm" or "problem" shifts, "interpretive turns," and even "revolutionary" changes in theory and practice. As detailed elsewhere (David 1997a), these have ranged from classical political economy (liberal and Marxian), neo-classical "monoeconomics" and Keynesian "duoeconomics" to public choice theory and the so-called "new" classical political economy. The new and evolving research programs or theories have not been successful in erasing all traces of the old. This could be expected because even heretics within economics and its sub-disciplines remain bounded by traditional modes of thought in formulating their visions.

As a result, the corpus of modern economic thought represents a cumulation of all its successes and failures, but with a constantly revised neo-classical paradigm or research program still ruling the roost. In similar vein, the development discourse has experienced a number of "problem" or "paradigm" shifts – from perspectives of modernization through "growth-with-redistribution," basic needs fulfillment, and dependency (meliorist, reformist, and neo-Marxian varieties) to a now dominant neo-liberal paradigm (see David 1986; 1997a). The common tendency has been to emphasize the dichotomous nature of the field by separating orthodox or mainstream from heterodox or radical research programs and their supporting clusters of interconnected theories.

Evidence suggests that such a separation does not have much significance for interpretation and understanding of the deep-seated problems facing human development potentials in LDCs. From the humanistic perspective of this book, the enduring paradigmatic problem facing development studies revolves around the entrenched nature of what may be called "theory without reality," or even more fundamentally, "theory without humanity." The way forward inheres in a "back-to-forth" process based on the melding of pertinent theoretical and practical discourses in order to establish synergy with the concrete social praxis of human beings.

Orthodox Consensus: Western Cosmologies and Modernism

The paradigmatic nature of the discourse suggests that dominant groups constantly coalesce in advancing universal precepts about development, or what is essentially a global convergence of ideas, ideologies, and values – what we term the "orthodox consensus." The primary reference is to the closely-knit academic community of historians, economic theorists, development economists, policymakers, and practitioners who share a common belief in scientism, the universal applicability of economic principles, and the larger evolutionary possibilities of societies based on "modernization." This has produced a particularly deterministic and narrow perspective of development, its interpretation through heavy reliance on abstract models, historical generalizations, or "plausible typologies," and a technical vocabulary that is meant to circumscribe the parameters of the "scientific" discourse.

Such consensual procedures reflect the dominant set of cosmological beliefs that purportedly lie at the heart of Western culture. They variously project a strong ideological support for "high modernism," which signifies attempts to design society in accordance with what are perceived to be scientific laws, as distinct from the intelligence and practical consciousness of its members – ordinary citizens themselves (Scott 1997). The major protagonists are more or less convinced that society can be reshaped from outside in accordance with some rationalist, scientific, or modernist program. From this perspective, the apparent disorder of societies, or lack of human development in LDCs, can be construed as a sign that they are not yet modern, that is, governed by some overriding system of rationality.

A basic preconception lies in the idea of human progress encountered in Western civilization. In the history of ideas, the very notion of "civilization" connoted not only a concerted movement toward material prosperity, justice, and freedom, but also rested on an optimistic belief that human, intellectual, and moral development would continue unabated into the distant future. Such a sentiment, for example, was forcefully articulated by French philosophers of the European Enlightenment, such as Francois Guizot. The very word "civilization," he opined,

> awakens, when it is pronounced, the idea of a people which is in
> motion, not to change its place but to change its state, a people

> whose condition is expanding and improving. The idea of progress, development, seems to me the fundamental idea contained in the word civilization (quoted in Bury 1920, 272).

The Western perspective of civilization has also been buttressed by the global dissemination of economic standards, technology, knowledge, political, and social ideologies. As Deepak Lal reminds us, "it was a "package" of cosmological beliefs, political decentralization, and application of the "acquisitive spirit" that uniquely led to Promethean growth and ascendancy of the West" (1999, 173). Belief patterns pertaining to individualism and the free market have been successively diffused throughout the globe, and even forced upon other societies and cultures. The normative implication is that only those societies willing or able accept the West's material beliefs in science, the market economy, and technology will be able to prosper.

An essential linkage was propagated by the ideology of a Eurocentric global history. It rests on the implicit assumption that Europeans and their descendants "invented" modernity, and that this was not accidental, nor contingent (Landes 1998). A normative extension of this preconception is that the world will continue to get richer and that the poor will eventually catch up. This expectation about increase in wealth or "convergence" toward riches, what Adam Smith called the "natural order of progress" or opulence, has been adumbrated in several influential attempts to construct theories of world history based on a single or uniform process with a recognizable trend.

For example, Nobel Laureate Sir John Hicks (1969) provided a "grand design" or unifying theme about the transformation of markets during the course of history. Different phases of this trajectory were thought to result in successive economic states of society, or "stages" based on a linear or unidirectional causal process (Rostow 1960; 1990). In this interpretation, the causal relationship runs almost exclusively from economics to other fields, with structural and institutional change emerging from growth and spread of the market economy and essentially serving its purpose. All economies in the contemporary world are viewed as members of the same analytical and interpretive category, which involves historical generalization and abstraction across the globe and its many distinct epochs.

Not only is humanity as a whole treated as homogeneous, but the modern phase of development is thought to constitute an undifferentiated mass of peoples in LDCs (what Hicks, reminiscent of Karl

Marx, called the "proletariat" of world history) who are similar in culture and conduct to their counterparts in industrialized nations. The only difference is that the latter cadres are wealthier. This blatant lack of differentiation suggests that diverse groups such as super-rich Arab sheiks, African dictators, Indian farmers, sharecroppers and untouchables, Latin American industrialists, Amerindians, and aboriginal peoples, as the case may be, are cast in the same conceptual net or perceived to be at the same stage of development as Europeans during the 18th and 19th centuries (Bauer 1981). Hence, the differential impacts of norms, value systems, and specific institutions count for nothing.

Nevertheless, the deterministic perspective underlying Western cosmological beliefs still remains a paradigm case of influential and tenacious research programs that attempt to ground the development discourse in general theories of global history and economic transformation. These are exemplified by a constant search for an Archimedean point or universal compass of reference. It is driven by a widespread proclivity to uncover immutable laws about human progress, which is usually defined in terms of material prosperity or economic growth (measured by average income profiles of countries and other qualitative referents of the modernization ethic). Hence, Nobel Laureate Sir Arthur Lewis has remarked that LDCs "can grow simply by modeling themselves on the more dynamic features of the more advanced" (1955, 8).

More generally, this orientation lies at the heart of the historically dominant paradigm in which development is interpreted as a uniform and linear process of evolutionary change designed to enhance some specific and inanimate objects of convenience. These include, inter alia, gross national product (GNP) per person, average household incomes, Industrialization, technological change, as well as social and political modernization. As we argue, these are indeed laudable yardsticks, especially of a country's economic performance. However, very little, if any, moral energy powers them. They are essentially proximate aims or instrumental means of authentic development, which is an intrinsic or constitutive human end.

Given the preoccupation with economic dimensions of change, the noted development economist Henry Bruton (1997) has raised what is called the *Great Question*: "Why has sustained economic growth – the continuous rise in real incomes and living standards in modern times – been confined until very recently to a relatively small number of countries in Western Europe, their overseas extensions in North

America, Australia, and Japan?" Bruton's answer to the Great Question is that only the former group of countries experienced the Renaissance, Reformation, Enlightenment, and associated Idea of Progress derived from these accomplishments. As emphasized by Morishima (1982), Japan was a very innovative outsider that managed to foster a Confucian equivalent which somewhat bypassed its parent Chinese civilization. Bruton's interpretation forms an integral part of a much more embracing Eurocentric vision that focuses almost exclusively on the Anglo-Saxon or Protestant Ethic provenance for the modern world economy.

Contextually, the West is thought to have emerged as the locus of modern economic growth and progress because of a unique set of historical and cultural determinants, economic and social structures, and political organization. These advantages, it is claimed, provided Western Europe and its overseas extensions with an edge over other civilizations that were initially more advanced and dynamic. Such "environmental factors" are also stressed by Diamond (1999). He points out that by the year 1000 A.D., Eurasia had already possessed at least four great civilizations: Chinese, Indian, Islamic, and Christian. All were more sophisticated – in intellectual, technological, and socio-cultural senses – than any other to be found elsewhere. They not only boasted larger numbers of domesticated plants than other continents, but also a far greater opportunity for the growth and spread of agricultural technology. Yet, and for reasons mentioned above, modern economic growth did not start there, but rather in what was then the least impressive continent.

Another variation on this theme is provided by David Landes (1998). He posits that, with the rise of the mercantile economy, imperial powers such as the English and the Dutch not only sought trade but also aimed at a managed civilization that went beyond what nature had provided. Overseas expansion was a story of botanical enterprise, or the concerted movement of crops to soils and climes of opportunity: *sugar*, starting in the Indian ocean and working its way around the globe to the Caribbean islands and South America; *tea*, transplanted from China to India and Ceylon (Sri Lanka); *cinchona* (a source of quinine) from South America to St. Helena and Java; *rubber seeds* smuggled from Brazil and introduced into Malaysia; and *oleaginous plants* (oil-producing) from the New World to West Africa. The Royal Botanic Gardens at Kew on the banks of the river Thames started off as the hobby of a princess, but later became a global model of science and profits combined.

In the post-Cold War era, a new triumphalism has surfaced about the validity of the universalist thesis and historical generalizations concerning a Western-oriented mode of growth and development. The dominant thesis is that capitalism has delivered the good life in Western industrial nations, which have emerged as centers of global power and influence. The free market is thought to have won the argument so comprehensively in the West that the global future belongs to it. The demise of communism in the erstwhile Soviet Union and Eastern Europe has been interpreted as signaling the "end of history" and the historically entrenched dichotomy between capitalism and socialism. As Fukuyama (1991) argues, liberal democracy is so superior to totalitarianism, communism, and fascism that any competition among such political systems is all but over. This ideological stance suggests that the future reflects an extension of past and present trends.

Dissent From Eurocentrism

The utopian dream of modernization, or the optimistic historical promise of equality, happiness, and generalization of material prosperity, is now in shambles. The postulates of liberal economic theory and deterministic global history had projected universal convergence, or a process of international diffusion in which economic opportunities available to a relatively small portion of humanity would become available to all. The evidence suggests that convergence has occurred for only a small group of industrial nations, but even in that case, the record has been a very mixed one. The global financial debacles of the late 20th century have cast considerable doubt on expectations that the new millennium will belong to newly industrializing countries (NICs) in Asia and Latin America. New fears of global recession and other potential spin-offs of international terrorism also suggest a very gloomy future for the less developed sector of the world.

Dissent remains rife over attempts to establish general principles about human progress. As Landes emphasizes, the alternative is a multicultural and egalitarian global history that tells us something good about all peoples. This perspective suggests that the historical trajectory of development could have been different from the "accidental" or "contingent" path of high modernism trammeled by the industrial North. An extension of this argument is that the significance of history should be recognized as a source of knowledge about the *plurality of cultures*, each with its own center of gravity, unpredictable outlooks, and conflicting attitudes. The idea that cultural diversity is endogenous to history entails that it does not move in straight lines, and that there may be no single master key to unlocking the past or future.

In a world defined by varying degrees of moral equality, cultural heterogeneity, and relativistic values, the very notion of a uniform global history based almost exclusively on Western cosmological beliefs is viewed in some circles as arrogant and oppressive. The deliberate intent, it is claimed, has been to justify Western domination over other spheres by extolling Western values as the only worthwhile ones. Once again, this puts into bold relief the perennial debate about the relative merits of historical determinism or predictability vis-à-vis pluralism. In the former case, the claim is that the course of history or economic development is predictable, that is, based on recognizable patterns. By contrast, pluralists deny the importance of determinism. Their contention is that the course of history is influenced by crucial moments, turning points, chance events, individual acts, and cultural dynamics. The common analogy is to a "highway of history" with many twists, turns, deviations, and ditches.

One normative implication is that history should be restored to its proper place in the interpretation and understanding of human relationships. In this regard, it is believed that serious mistakes are sometimes made by those analysts who merely record how things happen, thereby suggesting that no alternatives existed or that events had to occur the way they did. In his book, *The Ultimate History of Humanity*, the Oxford historian Theodore Zeldin argues that there are other possibilities but they have been glossed over. As he states,

> history with all its endless procession of passers-by, most of whose encounters have been missed opportunities, has so far been a chronicle of ability gone waste. But the next time two people meet, the result could be different. This is the origin of anxiety, but also hope, and hope is the origin of humanity (1997, 8).

Hence, people are encouraged to look beyond their own cultures and societies for other options, and as a means of liberating themselves from self-imposed blinkers and tunnel-visions. They can then form a fresh view of their own personal histories and humanity's entire record of cruelty, misunderstandings, and even joyous episodes.

Beyond the limitations of immanent global history, supporting historical generalizations, and the need for a more humanistic reinterpretation of past events, there are visible failures of development that contradict the modernization ethic. The negative implications for human development potentials and prospects for authentic development in LDCs have been described under a variety of rubrics: for example, "anti-development," "mal-development," "mis-development," "lopsided or uneven development," "growth without development," and "arrested development." While the list goes on, the collective import of such labels is at least twofold. First, they transcend the "diplomacy of terminology" or semantic debate associated with the traditional distinction between, say, "underdeveloped" and "developing." Second, they highlight the need for renewed attention to be paid to the deep-seated structural and institutional characteristics of LDCs that continuously militate against the quest for human betterment.

Contextually, anti-development connotes "negative freedom," that is, the pervasive lack of freedom from want, fear, oppression, exploitation, and government coercion. It also signifies an absence of the "positive freedom" to choose viable alternative human futures. Maldevelopment depicts a condition in which the search for material prosperity is accompanied by a ruthless destructive capacity and the most glaring forms of inequality. These elements are part and parcel of a "race to the bottom" or fundamental disequilibrium in society. This is so because wealth creation involves not only pauperization of some groups, but also wasteful consumption, diseconomies of production, and environmental degradation. The growth of income or output has been accompanied by destructive forces that continue to threaten the habitat in which humans live and have their being. The attendant mismanagement of resources is sometimes described as mis-development.

The modern story of development is replete with gory details of how the process of modernization and economic transformation has generated corrosive structural and institutional weaknesses, culminating in lopsided, uneven, or disarticulated forms of developmental change. In most LDCs, the picture of development reality is still exemplified by many islands, enclaves, or oases of material progress surrounded by veritable oceans, seas, or desert-like wastelands of endemic deprivation. In the typical case, meaningful development has virtually bypassed those sectors of the economy in which the majority of people live – notably traditional agriculture and the urban informal sector, which are known for spreading income-earning opportunities and generating less inequality.

On an overall basis, what seems to have emerged is a glaring lack of synergistic development. This is evidenced by serious incongruities among the economic growth process, people's life chances, and their perpetual struggle for survival and relevance. The landscape mirrors "growth without development," or an extremely faulty orientation in which the very processes responsible for generating growth and prosperity have turned out to be highly rootless (a-historical, a-cultural), ruthless (inequitable, oppressive), jobless (insecure, inhumane), and voiceless (undemocratic). Such outcomes reflect the cumulative interplay of external and internal causal forces.

The concept of "arrested development" puts an embracing historical spin on the argument, by linking development and underdevelopment to the growth and spread of the modern world system. A general thesis is that neither the development nor underdevelopment of any specific territorial unit can be properly interpreted or understood without fitting it into the cyclical rhythm or trends of the world economy as a whole. Its structure and functioning has formed the basis of heterodox research programs variously stressing "structural dependency," (Furtado 1965; 1983), "global capitalist economy" (Wallerstein 1974; 1979); and "development of the underdevelopment" (Frank 1967; 1981).

A unifying theme is that the emergence and maturation of national societies in the less developed sector of the world should be interpreted from the more organic perspective of economic, socio-cultural, and political linkages that are now endemic features of the world order. Its historical evolution is thought to reflect an intentional forging of reciprocal relations that now constitute an integrated but contradictory whole. From the perspective of humanitarian development, these cannot be simply construed in rational evolutionary terms, but rather reflect the result of human, primarily European, forms of intervention into world affairs.

During the pre-modern era, people tended to live in compact but separate communities and were only aware of their immediate neighbors. Each of the great empires existing in ancient times was restricted only to a limited portion of the globe. None of them was totally successful in fully integrating the separate communities under their control into a single or unified social and economic system. In the eyes of radical heterodox theorists, it was the ever-expanding system of capitalism that provided Europeans with an unprecedented urge to capture the entire globe and unify it into an overarching world system. Correlatively, the historical significance of Western capitalism is traced to its ability to establish reciprocal chains that have successively linked raw materials, industrial processes, incomes, consumption, transport, communications, and distribution throughout the globe.

In structuralist research programs, the underlying processes are seen as generating an inherent conflict between rich and poor. The attendant inequality in wealth and power is the result of a system that is based on the exploitation of subordinate classes by a dominant one. The argument is that a capitalist system driven by private ownership of the means of production is a breeding ground for a vicious system that is replete with class conflict and contradiction. As a result, the individual freedom of a powerful few to accumulate wealth has consistently blocked or interfered with the freedom of the majority to survive and fulfill their basic human needs.

A basic premise is that the economic systems of LDCs are socially and technologically heterogeneous. Non-economic factors such as the landowning system, control of firms, and composition of the labor force form the "structural" parameters of the economist's model – hence, those stressing the study of such parameters are called "structuralists." Accordingly, the structuralist approach has been viewed as

> attempts to identify specific rigidities, lags and other characteristics of the structure of developing economies that affect economic adjustments and the choice of development policy. A common theme in most of this work is the failure of the equilibrating mechanism of the price system [market exchange] to produce steady growth or a desirable distribution of income (Chenery 1975, 310).

Many structuralists have returned to the Marxian tradition by emphasizing the analysis of social structures as a means of understanding the behavior of economic agents. Dependency theories grew out of an extension of this conceptual framework to include external and internal factors conditioning the decision-making process. They rely on a broad interpretation of capitalism as a system constituting heterogeneous social forms and expanding both horizontally and vertically. Such theories allow us to consider the diversity of the accumulation process in space and time and, as alluded to earlier, links between external relations and internal forms of social dominance – reflected in complex center/periphery, development/underdevelopment, and dominance/dependence polarities.

From the very inception, it is argued, capitalist relations have stood at the apex of a world economy driven by capital accumulation. Such accumulation on a global scale has resulted in a division of the world into two broad sectors or "spaces" – super-ordinate and subordinate. In the relatively developed "center" or "core," development and structural change are endogenous, that is, based on internal dynamism. By contrast, the same processes are exogenous, or externally propelled, in the lagging or dependent "periphery." Moreover, specific dimensions of center-periphery relations, including those of a constantly emerging "semi-periphery," are defined not only by the structure of economic activities, but also by a number of significant non-economic variables. These constitute values, beliefs, the respective roles of individuals and groups within the networks of institutions embodying and expounding such values and beliefs, and phenomena in the sphere of action. The center is supposed to represent values, beliefs, and institutions that give order to society and the world system, while the periphery is a passive recipient.

The visible consequences for the periphery are considered to be a cumulation of the forces of underdevelopment: low levels of capital accumulation, little or no technological progress, low employment and productivity levels, rising inequality and poverty, and a pervasive lack of structural and institutional change. What seems to be a highly deterministic result is that while the world system develops apace, the unequal relation remains an essential and structured feature of the interactive processes. Hence, "arrested development" is thought to be continuously reproduced by various interdependent and mutually supportive mechanisms that are endemic to the global spread of the capitalist mode of production. If this is true, poor countries might have been left with very little freedom of maneuver, and especially in the eyes of heterodox determinists, have inevitably become structurally crippled and debilitated.

Such purportedly negative effects of peripheral capitalism have resulted in a very jaundiced view about development. The entire idea is sometimes repudiated on the grounds that it is utilized as an effective weapon by center nations to enforce certain forms of compliance by dependent peripheral states. The overall intent, it is claimed, is to keep in check or otherwise destroy cultures and related institutional, social, political, and economic referents in sovereign peripheral states. However, the evidence suggests that global forces have tended to influence national outcomes in different ways and that the underlying processes of interaction have never been equally beneficial or harmful to all groups or players.

A related counter-argument is that the evolutionary interaction between the two poles has been a potent force for opening up hidden transformation possibilities, and will therefore be ultimately beneficial to poor countries in Africa, Asia, Latin America and the Caribbean. One contention is that there were never any great prospects for rapid, easy, or sustained economic development in many LDCs. The reason is that the scope for progress was limited by the relatively small size of some domestic markets, technological backwardness, and not the least by political and social forces which inhibited successful adaptation of the capitalist mode of production. Under the circumstances, these countries have demonstrated a continuous need to be linked to wider markets and sources of technological innovation.

In other words, and from the very inception, their development prospects have been historically contingent upon incorporation into a more dynamic global political economy. Nevertheless, the findings of revisionist historical research have shown that even before such international integration, some peripheral countries, especially in Africa, boasted relatively sophisticated industrial and commercial structures that belie older stereotypes such as "backward" or "pre-capitalist" (Fieldhouse 1986; Hopkins 1986). Hence, some scholars are wont to ponder the counterfactual question about historical possibilities for authentic development in many LDCs if they were freed of the exogenous constraints imposed by colonialism and neo-colonialism.

In the final analysis, however, countries and peoples in the respective spheres do not necessarily constitute homogeneous or monolithic groupings that can be uniquely categorized as belonging exclusively to the center or periphery. At one level, the unbounding of the globe in many ways might have led to a significant intensification and reconfiguration of the duality in polarization based on material inequalities. There is now a periphery within the center and a center within the periphery. Furthermore, many new alliances and creative forms of organization are being constantly forged as a means of reinforcing or enhancing bargaining processes among countries with similar interests. New "rules of the game," elements of *realpolitik*, and ruthless conditions of sheer political survival seem to have dictated a global ideological convergence or *rapprochement* among countries that would otherwise be viewed as "strange bedfellows."

A pivotal role is played by the G-7 democracies in spreading the virtues of open markets, privatization, deregulation, trade and financial liberalization. The new order is sometimes interpreted as an extended model of "hegemonic stability" which, under the aegis of the United States, has perhaps become the centerpiece of global life, as well as the most powerful institutional order since the Second World War (see Kindleberger 1988; Gilpin 1987). Whatever the merits or demerits of hegemonic stability, the new rules of the game have emerged without any formal treaties, declarations, protocols, or parliamentary approval by the main players, not to mention ordinary people whose life chances are directly affected. In the overall scheme of things, dominant economic powers now perceive free trade, investment, and closer ties with "emerging markets," post-communist regimes, and even authoritarian governments in LDCs as a sine qua non for sustained growth in their domestic economies, industrial profits, and employment creation.

Countries such as Brazil, Mexico, Indonesia, South Africa, Russia, and other transitional economies in Eastern Europe now willingly permit G-7 industrial centers to channel investments into those economic centers that transnational corporations (TNCs) and other powerhouses deem profitable or of strategic interest. What seems to be a new institutional order is being tested in several unexpected ways. Its intended and unintended consequences have not been mutually beneficial to all parties. Furthermore, it is replete with conflicts and double standards that are not always synergistic with the ideals of humanitarian development. An apparently unwritten rule is that certain policies of new partners, for example, abridgment of human rights, crony capitalism, corruption, and poor enforcement of labor standards should play second fiddle to the new economic logic of global capitalism.

Chapter 2

Economism and Humanism

> The ideas of economists and political philosophers, both when they are right and when they are wrong, are more powerful than is commonly understood. Indeed the world is ruled by little else. Practical men, who believe themselves to be quite exempt from any intellectual influence, are usually the slaves of some defunct economist. Madmen in authority, who hear voices in the air, are distilling their frenzy from some academic scribbler of a few years back.
>
> John Maynard Keynes (1936).

Historically, the growth and spread of powerful Western-oriented cosmologies have formed the bedrock of a far more complex system of controlling ideas, images, metaphors, and institutional orders that inexorably configure human development potentials and people's life course patterns throughout the globe. As noted in the previous chapter, the ideational substructure has been associated with a tendency for dominant paradigms, clusters of interconnected theories, or schools of thought to maintain their tenacity even in the face of serious challenges demanding or asking for "problem" or "paradigm" shifts. The denouement of this process has been marked by intellectual hubris or an entrenched proclivity for leading communities of scholars to conduct intimate discourses among themselves as "insiders" while maintaining intellectual, social, and institutional distance from others who are viewed as "outsiders" (Merton 1973).

Members of the former group constantly coalesce with other consanguinial cadres in advancing universal precepts about development, or what is essentially an orthodox paradigm based on global convergence of values, beliefs, analytical constructs, and policy prescriptions. A pertinent question arises about whose images of development shall prevail, how the benefits are shared out, and the respective roles and responsibilities of diverse sectors of interest. The focus of this chapter is on the close-knit academic community of scholars and researchers, predominantly neo-classical economists, and related policy analysts who share a common belief in the evolutionary possibilities of societies based on the inculcation of standard economic principles. The search is for universally applicable theories and models based on sophisticated mathematical and empirical reasoning. In the eyes of economists, such procedures help to guarantee conceptual rigor and analytical tractability, thereby enhancing academic achievement and reputation through publication in refereed journals.

Imperialism of Economics

The economy has become the engine of society and continues to provide the values and modes of rationality for the entire human and social order – a process originally called the *Great Transformation* by Karl Polanyi (1944). From this perspective, the march of modernization in both rich and poor countries has resulted in the subordination of society to the economy instead of the economy being in service to society. The economic sphere has become a morally neutral zone in which only legal restraints can temper the pursuit of pecuniary gain.

A defining characteristic of individual, group, societal, and transnational relations is reflected in the absolute domination of money, with all human values being increasingly defined in terms of "dollars and cents." The new fundamentals about the provenance, value, and control of money are ultimately linked to what Robert Kuttner (1997) calls "turbo-charged capitalism." In his view, this projects a human condition in which "everything is for sale," as well as an amoral vision of human goals and what the larger society should achieve. The ascendancy of material values, deification of money, or the perception that "Croesus shall rule" have moved in tandem with the maturation of a dominant economics paradigm in which intrinsic human ends and vital relationships count for little or nothing.

Human-centered goals have come to play second fiddle to the gamut of economic instrumentalities, such as efficient resource allocation, production efficiency, market-based consumption, profit maximization, deregulation, free trade, and financial liberalization. These, in turn, have become enshrined in the immanent authority of formal economics and its imperialistic orientation. Beyond the problem-solving role of basic economic principles, dominant perspectives of economic development have been firmly entrenched in this imperialistic economic ideology. The pervasive "economistic" stance rests on a hidden and often unexpressed assumption that there is only one acceptable and proven method for studying rich and poor countries alike.

In this regard, Nobel Laureate Gary Becker (1976) has reminded us that, whether we are conscious of it or not, the *economic approach to human behavior* boasts unlimited explanatory scope and power. In his eyes, it suffuses the entire gamut of individual decisions and choices: in areas such as human capital formation, family relations, crime, suicide, divorce, discrimination by race and gender, fertility, and political decision-making. A guiding preconception is that all human beings in modern society consciously or unconsciously utilize the economic calculus to balance benefits and costs at the margin, and in order to satisfy diverse personal desires and interests – or example, whether to pursue another year of education, whether or when to marry or divorce, how many children to have and when, and whether or not to commit a crime or suicide.

The apparent ubiquity of the economics calculus has also been championed by another noted economist (Hirschleifer 1985, 53):

> [I]t is ultimately impossible to carve out a distinct territory for economics, bordering on, but separated from all other disciplines. Economics penetrates them all and is reciprocally penetrated by them. *There is only one social science.* What gives economics its

> imperialist invasive power is that our analytical categories – scarcity, cost, preferences, opportunity, etc. – are truly universal in application. Even more important is our structured organization of optimization on the decision level and equilibrium on the social level. Thus economics does constitute a universal grammar of a social science.

Hence, economic decision-making is viewed as a multidimensional process, or something that can be rationalized in terms of an "optimizable objective function" or "structured organization of optimization" measured in monetary terms. The guiding premise is that an "optimal" situation is always attainable, in the sense that it is always possible to make everyone better off without making anyone worse off. In this zero-sum world of what economists call "Pareto optimality," the optimization process is interpreted as an elaborate economic or societal game in which individuals who already have command over resources continuously exchange them until it is no longer possible to set up an exchange arrangement in which each economic agent still believes that he or she can gain from the results.

Such an outcome is predicated on the rational, consistent, and "efficient" behavior of self-interested economic agents. This economic logic lies at the heart of the standard social cost-benefit analysis commonly used by economists to determine the viability of investments and social policies. The assumption is that one can measure relevant "benefits" and "costs" to society based on the subjective preferences of individuals as revealed in the marketplace. Hence, the "social optimum" has no meaning outside the parameters of individual consumer choice. The anticipated social benefits of a policy or investment are conceived as the "sum" of individual preferences. The implicit monetary standard then becomes the "willingness to pay" or "consumer sovereignty," which is a surrogate for market demand.

A now notorious example of the economistic view of the world is provided by the controversial memo written in 1991 by Lawrence Summers, now President of Harvard University, while he was Chief Economist at the World Bank. In it he explained why the Bank should encourage relocation of more environmentally hazardous projects to LDCs. The full text is reproduced here, since it provides one of the best examples of the economic logic used by powerful economists and policymakers in advancing their policy prescriptions. As it states (reported in Vallette 1992):

1. The measurement of the cost of health impairing pollution depends on the foregone earnings from increased morbidity and mortality. From this point of view a given amount of health impairing pollution should be done in the country with the lowest cost, which will be the country with the lowest wages. I think the economic logic behind dumping a load of toxic waste in the lowest wage country is impeccable and we should face up to that.

2. The costs of pollution are likely to be non-linear as the initial increments of pollution probably have very low cost. I've always thought that under-populated countries in Africa are vastly UNDER-polluted, their air quality is probably vastly inefficiently low compared to Los Angeles or Mexico City. Only the lamentable facts that so much pollution is generated by non-tradable industries (transport, electrical generation) and that the unit transport costs of solid waste are so high prevent world welfare enhancing trade in air pollution and waste.

3. The demand for a clean environment for aesthetic and health reasons is likely to have very high income elasticity. The concern over an agent that causes a one in a million change in the odds of prostate cancer is obviously going to be much higher in a country where people survive to get prostate cancer than in a country where under 5 mortality is 200 per thousand. Also, much of the concern over industrial atmosphere discharge is about visibility impairing particulates. These discharges may have very little direct health impact. Clearly trade in goods that embody aesthetic pollution concerns would be welfare enhancing. While production is mobile the consumption of pretty air is a non-tradable.

    The problem with the argument against all of these proposals for more pollution in LDCs (intrinsic rights to certain goods, moral reasons, social concerns, lack of markets, etc.) could be turned around and used more or less effectively against every Bank proposal for liberalization.

Returning to the theoretical underpinnings of optimization, the rules constitute a paradigm case of what is known as "situation analysis," which forms the lynchpin of, and the most powerful method used, in modern economics (Latsis 1976; Caldwell 1991). A few ramifications may be mentioned. First, the situation facing the individual economic agent (consumer, household, business firm, worker, capitalist) is described in terms of given preferences, tastes, technology, and the relevant constraints they face, for example, incomes and relative prices.

Second, the situation is thought to reflect certain motivational considerations: the desire of consumers to maximize their utility or satisfaction, the propensity of business firms to maximize profits, and the quest of workers and other owners of factors of production such as land and capital to earn the highest possible levels of income. In a third step in the analysis, formal deductions are made, usually in mathematical terms, of the tenets or "optimal" rules governing appropriate behavior of individual economic agents in the particular situations they face.

Fourth, such behavior is usually explained by recourse to the rationality principle, which links the analysis of the situation and the behavior or action to be explained. At the heart of this analysis is an idea of "comprehensive" or "substantive" rationality. Behavior that is comprehensively or substantively rational occurs when the individual economic agent attempts to achieve given goals within the limits imposed by the environment. The bases of such action are decisions that yield accurate predictions about the individual agent's choices among a given set of alternatives or options. A contrast is sometimes drawn with "bounded" or "procedural" rationality, which refers to behavior resulting from a process of deliberation (Simon 1978). In this case, the rational purposes of economic agents are combined with their cognitive limits as human beings. In actuality, all forms of human behavior are highly variable, since they reflect the differential effects produced by human motivations, organizational structures, and institutions.

Nevertheless, the (comprehensive) rationality principle still forms the bedrock of the standard textbook elucidation of microeconomic theory. The core consists of axiomatic and mathematically formulated propositions, with the abstract deductive model as the paradigm case. Concepts are presented as axiomatic "givens" or immutable categories that form the "essence" of an economy, which is conceptualized as a static system with fixed parameters. The "givens" are supposed to represent certain "facts" about human behavior, such as universal psychological motivations – innate selfishness, individualism, and a constant search for maximum private gains or satisfactions. The parametric system relies on an assumption about certainty. This follows because uncertainty can be introduced into the analysis only when we are dealing with a dynamic system operating over long periods of time.

Nobel Laureate Paul Samuelson is considered the modern pioneer of the formalized or abstract approach to economic modeling. As he states, most economic treatises are concerned with either the description of some part of the world of reality or with the elaboration of particular elements abstracted from reality. Implicit in such analyses are certain recognizable formal uniformities, which are indeed characteristic of all scientific method (1983, 7).

In its extreme form, the strict formalized approach and axiomatization of economic theory are considered necessary steps for imbuing the analysis of human behavior with "standards of rigor of the contemporary formal school of mathematics" (Debreu 1959). Members of this school (including Johann Von Neumann, David Hilbert, Haskell Curry, and G.H. Hardy) view mathematics as being independent from empirical evidence. This entails that it is possible to conduct economic inquiry without meaningful assumptions about, or reference to, any kind of actually existing entity, for example, particular households, firms, or workers.

Thus, in making statements about the vector of relative prices governing economic transactions, the theorist is saying nothing about real economic phenomena but merely expressing axioms that have a formal mathematical structure and timeless truth values similar to the axioms of geometry. Under the circumstances, he or she is under no obligation to provide any justification for the empirical plausibility of a given set of axioms. The only requirement is that the rules of deductive procedure should be explicitly stated as a means of ensuring that the axioms are consistent. The mathematical model is presumed to provide the economist with a language or heuristic device for studying highly complex economic systems with a large number of goods and services. However, execution of this task "ceaselessly asks for weaker assumptions, for stronger conclusions, for greater generality" (Debreu 1991, 4).

In this regard, mathematics has been a potent tool in the formulation of equilibrium theory, which is the standard fare of modern neoclassical economics. Correlatively, the state of an economic system at any point in time can be depicted in terms of solving a system of simultaneous equations. These refer to consumers' demand for goods and services, their supply by producers, and the equilibrium condition that supply must equal demand in all markets. Individual economic agents can select the most beneficial courses of action because it is assumed that prevailing markets are open and perfect. Such behavior is facilitated by the existence of a set of market prices that give appropriate signals to individual consumers and producers who, in turn, respond in varying degrees to such signals. A fundamental premise, therefore, is that there is a complete set of smoothly functioning markets for final goods and factors of production, and that their operation provides the most efficient and effective mechanism for organizing domestic and international relations.

The overall conceptual result is a highly flexible economy in which changes in relative prices in commodity and factor markets tend to elicit corresponding responses in consumption, production, and economic institutions. Lack of information or sheer ignorance on the part of economic agents may temporarily prevent them from achieving their goals. However, the assumption is that they will continuously strive to reach their objectives until costs of such goal-attainment are just equal to the benefits to be derived therefrom. The latter principle underscores the economist's idea of competitive market equilibrium. This means that the multiple markets in an economy have a tendency to clear, which is defined in terms of the equalization of demand, supply, and price. The clearance mechanism is supposed to operate in individual markets (partial equilibrium) or reflect a simultaneous clearing of all markets (general equilibrium), that is, the case where there is a set of relative prices for all goods and services.

Hence, equilibrium analysis does not confine itself to the study of narrow types of functional relationships, but attempts to achieve a generality in its theoretical formulations. As noted above, the concept of equilibrium is presumed to apply to both single and multiple sets of variables. In a logical sense, determination of the output of a perfectly competitive firm is precisely the same as the simultaneous determination of an endless number of prices and quantities, or the solution of a similar number of simultaneous equations. In either case, the equilibrium conditions refer only to the values of variables as determined by a set of conditions, and therefore do not carry any moral connotations. Related to this is the economist's proclivity to view certain things as external data (parameters) that are outside his or her range of vision, for example, ethical beliefs of human agents and the institutional environment.

Critiques and Limitations: Humanizing the Emperor

The humanitarian perspective rests on the imperative of shifting the center of gravity of the economics discourse from ruling preconceptions about people's place in the order of things based on economic calculation of their worth in the marketplace. It can be argued that such criteria are neither rules of the universe, adequate measures of the efforts people expend, nor of their contributions to the needs of others and the larger society or community. The universalist epistemology, scientism, and impersonal mode of interpretation that form the lynchpin of modern neo-classical economics have apparently undermined the human conceptual system in which people's normative self-concept, moral worth, and motivations are embedded.

The tension between economic logic and human values was already implicit in Aristotle's original distinction between *oikonomia* and *chrematistics*. In terms of intellectual history, oikonomia (the root of "economics") connoted household management and its capacity to increase "use-values" (human well-being) over time. But the scope of the household can be broadened to encompass the larger community, resources, and institutions. Aristotle did project a "moral economy" in which the basic unit of the family or household should be replicated in the larger economy or society. By contrast, chrematistics referred to the ownership of wealth, monetary aspects of business activity, or the manipulation of wealth and property to maximize "exchange-values" or private gains in the short run – what Aristotle termed the "art of acquisition."

In modern economic terms, there are at least three basic differences between the two concepts. First, oikonomia projects historical consciousness, that is, more emphasis is placed on long-term dynamics rather than the short-run. Second, benefits to the community as a whole take precedence over private economic transactions based on rational self-interests and markets. The latter derive their significance only within the larger purview of the human and social goals inherent in the "public household economy." Third, the focus of oikonomia is more on concrete use-values rather than on the more abstract exchange-values (Daly and Cobb 1989). The tension between oikonomia and chrematistics not only persists in the modern world order, but increasingly defines the life chances of people throughout the globe. The chrematistic economy is exemplified by provenance of money, speculative financial flows, computer-driven currency trades, and related forms of "paper entrepreneurship" that now define the global financial architecture.

Adam Smith, the "father" of modern economics, also highlighted the tension between economism and humanism. On the one hand, his *Wealth of Nations* (1776) projected a dynamic economy in which people produce goods and services based on their self-interests, whether or not they are sympathetic to the strivings of others. On the other hand, he provided a moral vision of human goals or what society should achieve, as distinct from what economic theory tells us about the limits of material prosperity or economic growth. While recognizing that wealth creation based on self-interest may generate inequality, he deplored its social effects. Hence, he recommended that something should be done about it by individuals as *citizens* rather than as simply *economic agents*. As forcefully stated in the following excerpts from his *Theory of Moral Sentiments* (1759):

> He certainly is not a good citizen who does not wish to promote by every means in his power the welfare of the whole society – the whole society – of his fellow citizens.... It does not follow that a regard to the welfare of society should be the sole virtuous motive of action, but only that in any competition it ought to cast the balance against other motives.... [The] disposition to admire, and almost worship, the rich and the powerful, and to despise, or, at least to neglect persons of poor and mean condition, though necessary both to establish and to maintain the distinction of ranks and the order of society, is, at the same time, the great and most universal cause of the corruption of our moral sentiments.

Given the class structure of his day, Smith argued that workers should be paid well because, when they are, they tend to be more "active, diligent, and expeditious." While the supply of and demand for labor in the marketplace may determine what wages *are*, such factors do not constitute sufficient conditions of what they *ought* to be. In more general terms, while economic theory plays a vital role in speculations about how an economy functions, knowing what parameters to alter in order to make an economy more dynamic or efficient is not on the same footing as achieving a life that people would want to live, or the need to establish a just, pleasant, and cooperative society, that is, one fit for human beings to inhabit.

The apparent paradox or contradiction posed by the "two faces" of Adam Smith is also apposite to Immanuel Kant's distinction

between "regulated" or "constructed" vis-à-vis "constitutive" phenomena or behavior. The former are socially or ideologically delimited,
that is, they draw their substance or significance from mere conventions. They are exemplified by prominent analytical concepts such as
"economy," "competition," "market," and "equilibrium." Mainstream
or orthodox economists generally behave "as if" such regulated or constructed categories are primarily constitutive of human and social reality. In the case of formal economic theory, the objective is to discern
what life would be if human agents behaved in accordance with the domain assumptions of the pure economic model, the ideal metaphysical
standard against which actual behavior can be appraised and measured.
The hidden assumption is that pure economic interests always take precedence over human or moral values. It is evident that people may not
behave in ways that coincide with the tenets of the economic ideal. The
precise outcomes usually depend on the extent to which they are socialized into such behavior, or whether the systemic order sufficiently
rewards them for acting in one way or another.

Constitutive phenomena have an intrinsic quality, even though
this may not be readily discernible to the naked eye. Humanity is constitutive because it encapsulates several attributes of the *centrality of
human being*. These "human universals" are further discussed in Chapter 3. They accord with the *Categorical Imperative* of Immanuel Kant:
"So act as to treat humanity, whether in thine own person or that of any
other, in every case as an end, and never as means only." The implication is that no person's ends should be systematically subordinated to
those of others. People should be treated as beings of intrinsic worth,
or as ends in themselves.

This moral vision transcends the rigid and aprioristic judgments
that lie at the heart of the neo-classical paradigm. The latter makes no
value judgments about the actual constitution of economic behavior.
This value-neutrality is defended on the grounds that there is no objective or extra-economic criteria by which society can guide its policies, or for deciding between right and wrong, good and bad. The only
desirable standard, it is believed, lies in the necessity of increasing the
total quantity of physical commodities and making these available to
persons with adequate purchasing power. The overall implication is
that, when markets prevail, one can buy almost anything – "from
Nobel prizes to murders, slavery, sexual favors, and even love" (Goode
1985, 55). The inexorable economic stance is that the "prices" of these
"commodities" could be set in accordance with the pre-ordained logic

inherent in the equilibrating forces of supply, demand, and price. Given their "preferences" and "tastes," those boasting adequate incomes would be able to exercise their free choices in the "market," and without any moral compunction whatsoever.

This hallowed procedure is highly self-serving and even suspect. The evidence suggests that economists and other social scientists usually betray strong value preferences for some courses of action rather than others. Such discrimination is not always based on outcomes of rational or logical analyses. For example, economists subscribing to different value systems may arrive at diametrically opposed conclusions – for example, about the effects of a tax cut, budget deficit, or development strategy. In fact, many constitute a lobby for some types of policy and against others. The very idea of value-neutrality implicitly expresses a value preference and tends to detract economic and social inquiry away from human concerns. In many cases, the insistence on value-neutrality functions more to suppress dissent about basic human values than to support actual neutrality. Every economist or social scientist is a prisoner of his or her own value standards (Streeten 1958; Daly and Cobb 1989).

Hermeneutic philosophers, sociologists of knowledge, and other relativists argue that value-neutrality, and hence the time-worn distinction between "fact" and "value" or an "is" and an "ought," is untenable. The general claim is that statements about human affairs are relative to our values in such a manner that they cannot be meaningfully characterized as true or false. The noted sociologist Max Weber (1949) has emphasized that there can be no absolutely objective or scientific analysis of society. The reason is that value standards tend to intrude into the most austere attempts at objectivity in at least two points in our investigations. They tend to determine the subject matter that is selected for study, and influence our judgments about the causes of specific events. In turn, these evaluative choices enable us to attach "significance" to certain situations and events. How we attach significance depends on our interests, and therefore involves value judgments.

Nobel Laureate Gunnar Myrdal has also championed the idea that our knowledge is always "opportunistically" conditioned and therefore tends to deviate from so-called objective truth. Echoing Max Weber, he states:

Every study of a social problem, however limited in scope, is and must be determined by valuations. A "disinterested" social science has never existed and will never exist. For logical reasons, it is impossible. A view presupposes a viewpoint. Research, like any other rationally pursued activity, must have a direction. The viewpoint and the direction are determined by our interest in the matter. Valuations enter into the choice of approach, the selection of problems, the definition of concepts, the gathering of data, and are by no means confined to the practical or political inferences drawn from their theoretical findings (1968, 32).

In economic orthodoxy, a discrete reality is abstracted away from the totality of human relationships, or at least those features not readily accessible to the hypothetico-deductive method, mathematical symbolism, and quantification. A dogma or giant epistemological error is perpetuated as long as the legitimacy of research is inherently linked to the analyst's ability to construct abstract mathematical or quantitative models. "It is often easier to mathematize a false theory than to confront reality" (Morgenstern 1972, 1169). More often than not, formal economic reasoning tends to commit the error or "fallacy of misplaced concreteness," which is defined as "identifying abstract conceptions with reality," or "neglecting the degree of abstraction involved when an actual entity is considered merely as far as it exemplifies certain categories of thought" (Whitehead 1929, 11). In other words, the fallacy occurs when the formal economic model is made coterminous with reality itself and human behavior is deemed relevant only insofar as it corresponds to the postulates of the pure model.

The fallacy is particularly apposite to the study of LDCs, since formal economic reasoning has come to shape the rational determinism and economistic orientation of the dominant development paradigm. Once again, this has proved to be highly self-serving, and has enabled prominent economists and development experts to construct reality from a distance. The atmosphere of hubris has enabled universal types of concepts, models, theories, and language to be confused with development reality itself. As a corollary, domain concepts such as "economic growth," "poverty," and "unemployment" are accorded significance because they can be mathematized or measured, that is, quantified in terms of relative income levels for purposes of comparison and contrast. As alluded to earlier, the overall result has been a particularly narrow view of reality. It has been superseded by sophisticated development models and a technical vocabulary designed to add "scientific" status to the discourse.

But, the preoccupation with universalism, scientism, and analytical tractability has produced the following lingering results. First, increased technicalization of both the general economics and derivative development discourses has led to a decentering of the subject matter, removal of human agency from any serious analysis or interpretation, and an erasure of the human person as an active agent of change. Second, the technical language and vocabulary have generated considerable confusion, misunderstanding, and distorted communication not only among technical specialists themselves, but even more importantly, between them and the public at large. Third, the dominance of certain academic and institutional substructures has enabled the technical vocabulary to be used as an instrument of control and/or for the exercise of power and influence from Europe and North America.

Finally, and perhaps most important, the technical edifice is oftentimes far removed from what matters most for the majority of people living in LDCs - the traditional "objects" of the development discourse. Even if it is accepted that human nature is more or less the same everywhere, knowledge and understanding garnered from observation and experience *in situ* consistently show that people's concerns and priorities are usually at variance with the axioms of scientific economic methodology as well as the agendas, logical rigor, and iron-clad postulates of economists and development experts (Geertz 1973). It is no longer acceptable to design human futures according to the tenets of a rationalist-scientific program that is divorced from the practical intelligence or social praxis of society's members.

In the study of rich and poor countries alike, the precision of formal economic models often falls victim to the vagaries of institutions and, as mentioned earlier, the psychological motivations of human beings. A primary reason is that institutions are typically treated as "parameters" rather than as "variables" in such models. When the fixed parameters are lifted out of the overarching institutional contexts in which they are embedded, very little room is left for independent or critical interpretation of a given societal or development reality and potential for change. There is a corresponding failure to divine the results of dynamic changes among patterns of consumer, producer, and institutional behavior. Such considerations mirror the "social efficiency" of economic systems or the myriad non-economic – normative, psychological, and political – forces influencing their structure and functioning.

Institutions Matter: Institutional Economics

In the march of intellectual history, the study of the factors mentioned above has formed the subject matter of research programs in the following broad areas: economic history, neo-classical revisionism in the form of a "New Institutional Economics;" an Old Institutional Economics or "neo-institutionalism" proper; and comparative institutionalism, which combines economics and political economy. The widespread tendency among orthodox economists, other mainstream analysts, and policymakers has been to ignore institutionalist approaches. This is perhaps linked to a perception, right or wrong, of too close an association between institutionalism and the more radical programs of structuralists and Marxists. Schools of thought based on economic history and neo-classical revisionism now rule the roost.

Institutions can be defined in various ways – for example, abstract or concrete, formal or informal. In a theoretical or quasi-metaphysical sense, they have been conceptualized by Nobel Laureate Douglass North (1981, 1991) as a set of rules, compliance procedures, and moral or ethical norms that structure or condition behavioral patterns. As fundamental "rules of the game," institutions reflect the norms that have evolved in different societies about appropriate and inappropriate forms of behavior among individuals and groups. As such, they help to define the rights of members of a community, mold their expectations, and lend predictability to such expectations.

Formal institutions are exemplified by constitutions, laws, and rules governing property rights, while informal ones are typified by customs, traditions, codes of conduct, and a variety of behavioral expectations that form the basis of a cultural milieu. In the latter case, the principles of group dynamics are reflected in the common practice encountered in many LDCs where people join together in "middle rung" ROSCAS (rotating credit associations) that provide jointly produced goods, such as credit, that are not available in the formal marketplace. Examples are *esusu* and *tontines* (West Africa), *susu* (Trinidad and Tobago), and *partner* (Jamaica). Such informal credit systems are not only based on trust, but are also well-entrenched local institutions linking savings and investment. The general objective is to provide collective financial resources and support for diverse functional needs of individuals, groups, and the larger community.

What are known as "cellular organizations" also represent an important form of local group dynamics. They include social and political movements and are primarily concerned with championing special sectors of interest such as human rights, the biophysical environment, peace, and the liberation of women, ethnic minorities, and indigenous peoples. In general, such movements facilitate opposition to formal economic, social, and political systems that are intolerant of dissent. They enable specific constituencies to pursue goals that are not easily achieved on an individual basis, and essentially challenge the legitimacy of the status quo. Since such activist groups typically set themselves up against the existing power structure, they may be instrumental in shaping alternative goal-oriented human futures by enabling participants to better distinguish between "what is" and "what might be" (Coleman 1990). In a pragmatic sense, institutions are sometimes viewed as "organizations," that is, those tangible structures through which everyday life is ordered. These consist of political parties, parliaments, government ministries, business firms, trade unions, banks, and the like. This definition is typically used by aid donors and national government authorities. From the this perspective, the process of institutional "building," "design," or "development" becomes coterminous with studying how such organizations work, analyzing their capabilities and deficiencies, and proposing corrective measures. However, a clear distinction is not always drawn between the internal rules of efficiency determining organizational effectiveness and goals vis-à-vis their contribution to the larger society.

The influential variant of the new institutionalism developed by Douglass North and others has been particularly concerned with explaining factors underlying institutional evolution and adaptation. In their schema, the historical process of institutional ordering usually follows an incremental path linking past, present, and future. The historical trajectory demonstrates certain *path dependencies* that reflect how power is distributed among interest groups in society. Thus, the histories of different countries and regions are likely to vary because each pursues a path that evolves from institutional adjustment and adaptation. As North states,

> [a]lthough formal rules may change over-night as a result of political and judicial decisions, informal constraints embodied in customs, traditions, and cultural constraints not only connect the past

with the present and future, but provide us with a key to explaining
the path of historical change (North 1990, 6).

The historical approach also posits that the traditional exchange
institutions in many LDCs have not evolved into the more complex,
open, and impersonal rules associated with modernization in Europe.
These are exemplified by the merchant guilds in Italian city-states, the
Hanseatic League in Germany, and the communal system of responsibility in Mediterranean and European trade during the 11th and 14th
centuries (Greif 1992). Extrapolation of this experience leads to a generalization that a society's capacity to develop is indicated by the institutions it creates for commerce, trade, credit and markets, so that formal contracts and property rights can be effectively enforced.

However, this judgment must be tempered by the fact that the
process of institutional evolution is neither linear nor uniform. Many
LDCs boast a long history of indigenous and mercantile institutions of
trust and commitment based on informal conduct and reputation.
Examples are the variety of structures governing long-distance trade in
Africa and India, Chinese traders in Southeast Asia, and the Arab trading diasporas in West Africa. As comparative institutionalists argue,
we have to look at particular historical contexts and try to dissect the
specific institutional arrangements that can enable or disable the development quest. Such an exercise may help to throw further light on why
certain institutions may work in some normative settings and not in
others.

A second but related variant of the New Institutional Economics
is embedded in a basic preconception about the need to develop impersonal markets based on contractual obligations and the rule of law.
Given the standard constraints encountered in mainstream or neo-
classical economics, institutions are thought to define production and
transaction costs, and therefore the feasibility or profitability of engag-
ing in any type of economic activity. Contextually, transaction costs
are defined as

> a spectrum of institutional costs including those of information, of
> negotiation, of drawing up and enforcing contracts, of delineating
> and policing property rights, or monitoring performance, and of
> changing institutional arrangements. In short, they comprise all
> those costs not directly involved in the physical process of produc-
> tion (Cheung 1989, 77).

Its major protagonists contend that the transaction-cost approach is not only superior to the traditional interpretation of efficient resource allocation, but that it is also applicable to a wide range of institutional arrangements – for example, in political life where exchanges occur between politicians and voters, among politicians themselves, and between politicians and interest groups; and the behavior of "international regimes" where certain norms, rules, and procedures govern the behavior of powerful actors such as the World Bank, IMF, and WTO.

In the above context, *transactions* in an economy or society connote transfers of *property rights* on goods, services, and assets. They permit the exploitation of potential gains from voluntary exchanges, specialization, and trade, which constitute essential prerequisites of economic progress. In a market economy, institutions are supposed to specify who owns what (property rights) and how property can be exchanged through transactions. These are regulated through formal or informal *contracts* that determine the conditions under which property rights are transferred, including relative prices, conditions and methods of payment, and the like. Contracts are rules establishing conditions parties must satisfy in order to reap the benefits of exchange. In turn, they are regulated by a number of higher institutions – both formal rules (bureaucratic procedures, the legal system, and regulation) and informal ones (trust and acceptable business practices).

One prominent variation on this theme is provided by Oliver Williamson (1975, 1995) who interprets the New Institutional Economics from the perspective of the institutional environment, including political and legal rules of the game as well as modes of contract. The alternative modes of organization encompass markets, hierarchies, public agencies, and hybrids. Markets are institutions (rules and enforcement mechanisms) that define the environment for conducting discrete and impersonal transactions, but without a continuous contractual relationship. Hierarchies are rules governing transactions based on vertical lines of decision-making authority. They set up contractual obligations, for example, between employers and employees in private and public organizations to produce goods and services at lower transaction costs than would be required under pure market arrangements.

Hence, given the objective of economizing on transaction costs, institutions are established to govern contracts and investments. Each relies on different incentives and controls that lead to varying degrees of cooperation and competition, credible investment conditions and contracts. Contextually, Douglass North's approach shows that institutions are not simply the results of efforts designed to lower transaction costs of market exchanges, but are also a function of divergent political and social interests. In this regard, institutions

> are not necessarily or even usually created to be socially efficient; rather, they, or at least the formal rules, are created to serve the interests of those with the bargaining power to devise the rules. In a zero-transaction-cost world, bargaining strength does not affect the efficiency of outcomes, but in a world of positive transaction cost it does (North 1990: 16).

Variations in institutional arrangements are also sometimes explained under the game-theoretic approach, which identifies the properties of cooperative and non-cooperative games. At one end of the spectrum lies the simple exchange economy based on a relatively high degree of cooperation. Institutions permit low-cost transactions in this case. Individuals seeking to maximize their own welfare find it beneficial to cooperate because the following conditions are presumed to hold: plays in the game are repetitive; the number of plays is small; and complete information exists about the past performance of other players. Cooperation is difficult to sustain in the obverse situation where plays in the game are not repeated, the number of players is relatively large, and information about other players is lacking. In a complex and specialized world with multiple players and divergent interests, institutions have to solve difficult problems of coordination, cooperation, and conflict. The guiding premise is that effective institutions tend to enhance the benefits of cooperation and raise the transacttion costs of non-cooperation.

In a third variant of the new institutionalism, emergence of institutions is viewed as a corrective to or substitute for elements of "market failure," such as imperfect information and missing or incomplete markets. This is perhaps one of the most significant "problem shifts" within the neo-classical paradigm. Nobel Laureate Joseph Stiglitz (1988; 1989) has explained the rationale for institutional arrangements in terms of asymmetric information among different parties involved. Such asymmetry arises when one or more parties have information about aspects of their economic transactions that are not readily available to others, or where it is too costly for them to obtain and evaluate such information. Imperfect information affects all economic transactions when the relevant information about particular transactions changes over time.

It should be mentioned that the theory of imperfect information was originally used to model key agrarian and related institutions in poor countries. Such institutions are considered substitutes for missing credit, insurance, and futures markets in environments replete with pervasive risks, information asymmetry, and moral hazard. This aspect of modern institutionalism started with the study of sharecropping and went on to examine interlocking transactions in labor, credit, and commodity markets (Bardhan 1989; Hoff, Braverman, and Stiglitz 1993). It is a truism that rural development invariably depends on the receipt and utilization of appropriate information. Both formal and informal institutions can help avert market failure stemming from inadequate and inaccurate information.

Within the revisionist perspective of Stiglitz, information asymmetry results in what is termed the "principal-agent" problem. This arises when an interested party (the principal) motivates another (his or her agent) to act in the principal's interest. In essence, this type of problem arises when there is imperfect information about actions the agent has undertaken or likely to take. It is exemplified by several kinds of relationships: politicians do not always represent the interest of voters; policymakers and bureaucrats do not always carry out the mandates of politicians and voters; and teachers may not act in the interest of students and/or parents. The implication is that the negative effects associated with such problems can be prevented or reduced by institutions that promise to make performance and actions more transparent.

A more general implication of the research program on information asymmetry is that factors giving rise to market failure tend to cast doubts on standard neo-classical assumptions about efficient resource allocation. One reason is that the decision-making environment is usually fraught with risk, uncertainty, and moral hazard. Another is that the terms and conditions of contracts associated with transactions critically depend on the ownership structure of assets and their distribution. Under the circumstances, the perennial attempt by neo-classical economists to separate efficiency and equity of resource use cannot be maintained. But, the revisionist literature focuses predominantly on efficiency-improving institutions. It can be argued that issues of redistribution are much more important than efficiency ones in the process of institutional change. While institutions evidently improve efficiency, pressures to bring them about often turn on redistributive effects.

Related to this is the difficulty of mobilizing relevant interest groups and building coalitions to effect meaningful tradeoffs between potential gainers and losers. The issue is addressed in research programs dealing with what is called the "logic of collective action." In this regard, institutions are supposed to play a key mediating role by providing individuals and organizations with incentives to honor their collective or public commitments. In other words, institutions can become critical instruments in reducing transaction costs by eliminating opportunistic behavior on the part of individuals and groups.

The implications for promoting collective human welfare are stressed by Mancur Olson (1965; 1982), Russell Hardin (1982) and others who have challenged the thesis that individuals and groups sharing common interests will normally organize themselves in pursuit of common goals. For example, it is well known that consumers, taxpayers, and poor people do not typically join organizations pursuing their common interests. Contextually, Olson cites two conditions that can make collective action possible: (i) the size of the group, that is, the number of individuals or group members acting collectively should be sufficiently small; and (ii) groups should have access to what are called "selective incentives." These refer to a class of benefits that can be restricted solely to those who have joined the group, and therefore denied to non-members.

While some groups never act collectively in pursuit of their common interests, it remains true that individual participate in organizations because, among other things, they feel that they are likely to gain more or lose less than if they did not become involved. Small groups tend to make collective action possible because individuals in a group sharing common interests can be assumed to pursue more or less identical aims. By contrast, it is particularly difficult to organize collective action in large groups in which all members are likely to receive equal benefits. Large groups make it easier for individuals to "free ride" without being noticed or otherwise subjected to sanctions. This occurs when some members of an organization feel that they will eventually derive benefits without incurring any of the costs of membership, for example, the time, money, and energy expended.

The voluntary provision of public or collective goods, such as education, health, and clean air, is plagued by the free rider problem. Such goods play a critical role in guaranteeing the rights of citizenship, and their provisioning is predicated on the imperative of achieving national solidarity by satisfying collective human wants or needs. The process is supposed to benefit all citizens, irrespective of whether they have contributed to the costs of achieving this humanitarian end. In economic terms, public goods display two related properties: (i) "non-excludability," that is, once they are provided to one individual or group, they cannot be denied to others; and (ii) "non-rivalry" in consumption, that is, enjoyment of a public good by anyone person does not preclude, or detract from, its availability to others in society.

As alluded to earlier, the basic problem surrounds the difficulty of reaching the kinds of consensual or cooperative agreements that would promote common interests. The assumption is that each partner in a transaction would try to maximize his or her share of the benefits while minimizing the corresponding share of the joint costs of providing public or collective goods. Free riding occurs when there is zero contribution to such costs. Persons with unconditional access to such goods have little reason to pay their appropriate share of the costs. The overall result is a tendency for public bads to be oversupplied and public goods undersupplied. As Streeten states, "everyone's attempt to free ride has led to disappearance of the horse" (1989, 1171). If every rational person were to reason in an opportunistic manner, free riding would become universal, no groups or organizations would be formed, and collective action would become a virtual impossibility.

Needless to say, governments, interest groups, lobbies, and other vehicles of group solidarity are a reality in public life. But, collective action defining such institutions is typically based on "selective incentives" that often display very strong pro-establishment and anti-egalitarian biases. The reason is that selective incentives are more often available to well-established and prestigious groups and less to potential entrants or those at the lower rungs of the socio-economic ladder. Highly trained cadres and professionals boasting superior levels of education and skill tend to have unequal access to selective incentives compared to low-income and other powerless groups.

Germane to this trend is the role played by "distributional coalitions" in collective action. Such coalitions emerge and grow primarily because of struggles over the distribution of income and wealth in society. Most interest groups at the national level take the form of special distributional coalitions. Such collectivities are prone to spend their resources on efforts designed to redistribute society's output in favor of their selected members. If the same resources were to be spent on, say, expanding the growth rate of the economy as a whole or providing basic social services, all members of society would stand to benefit. Where distributional coalitions proliferate, their self-serving activities may cause a slowdown in the pace of economic growth, unemployment, and a worsening of poverty, further pushing the distribution of income and wealth in society in directions more favorable to privileged groups.

This brings us back to the contention, usually encountered in older forms of institutionalism, that the separability between efficiency and distributive equity is impracticable and untenable. From this perspective, institutional theory is mainly concerned with the process of change rather than its economic or other disparate elements considered separately. What is valued by people tends to change over time and as conditions, especially technology, undergo change. Implicit in processual change and its historicity is a need for a holistic interpretation of institutional dynamics. The guiding preconception is that the performance of anyone institution depends on the entire structure of institutions.

In similar vein, comparative institutionalists argue that the economistic and strategic approach to problem-solving underlying neo-classical orthodoxy cannot adequately explain away deep conflicts over societal goals and the allocation of power. Their contention is that conflicts and differential power relations among human agents usually result in rules being negotiated or otherwise imposed in order to benefit dominant interests. In this context, interest groups can be construed as associations of like-minded persons who band together to champion specific issues, especially those promising to enhance their material well-being. Asymmetric power relations always generate concrete benefits for "winning" vis-à-vis "losing" groups. Therefore, a reasonable judgment is that new rules or institutions often emerge as outcomes of historically embedded conflicts over the distribution of power, and should be interpreted as either negotiated or imposed settlements and/or overt or covert contestations among different sectors of interest (Evans 1995; Grindle 2001).

Chapter 3

The Humanitarian Perspective

> We are discovering the essential truth that people must be at the center of development. The purpose of development is to offer people options. One of these options is access to income – not as an end in itself but as a means of acquiring human well-being. But there are other options, including long life, knowledge, political freedom, personal security, community participation and guaranteed human rights. People cannot be reduced to a single dimension as [mere] economic creatures.
>
> United Nations Development Programme (1994).

The dominant paradigm rests on a preconception that the hard core of development is primarily "economic," with political, social, cultural, ecological and related forms of integration viewed as its inevitable consequences. While the fundamental importance of economic categories of interpretation and understanding cannot be denied, these cannot be meaningfully divorced from the lives people succeed in living, including the basic opportunities and freedoms they are able to enjoy. This entails an imperative of reorienting the conventional development discourse toward a more emancipatory, people-centered, but culture-sensitive conversation about alternative goal-oriented human futures. The focus is on enhancing human development potentials through a dialogue that is anchored in core human values, basic human rights, global justice, and cosmopolitan standards.

Such a perspective of liberation calls for nothing short of a "humanistic renaissance," or revisionism based on explicit or overt norms emanating from within rather than implicit or overt ones imposed from outside or above. Also entailed is a more or less endogenous development trajectory that starts with the basic right of people everywhere to set their own agendas based on their own self-interpretations, equal moral worth, and the primordial need for recognition, identity, security, autonomy, and participation. Hence, the humanitarian vision is predicated on a reversal of the traditional chain of development logic, epistemology, ontology and axiology, starting with people's own self-consciousness and self-awareness, and a transcultural order that projects the fullest expansion of human capabilities and choices. Achievement of this end requires deliberate actions or concerted processes of change designed to enlarge freedoms and opportunities of human beings so that they can lead valuable and valued lives (Sen 1999).

Contextually, economics and other social sciences can be viewed as moral-practical or humanistic practices that were originally designed to generate reflexive knowledge about the human condition based on a judicious intermeshing of theoretical claims and practical discourses about the daily lives of ordinary people. In this regard, it should be remembered that all of the well-established and self-contained fields of social inquiry (for example, history, jurisprudence, economics, psychology, sociology, anthropology, and political science) were originally conceived as integral parts of an ongoing human project designed to interpret and enhance human well-being. Needless to say, increased specialization has meant that some, like economics, have lost their intellectual moorings in moral and political philosophy, and arguably the ability to generate precepts and normative rules that can serve as a basis for establishing a good, pleasant, cooperative, and decent society, both nationally and internationally.

Humanitarian versus Human Resource Development

The need for a paradigm shift in the dominant discourse toward hu-man-centered or authentic development is grounded in a mode of inter-pretation that relies on the primordial philosophy of "humanitarian-nism." The *Shorter Oxford Dictionary on Historical Principles* defines humanitarianism as "chiefly or wholly advancement of the human race" or "having regard to humanity or mankind at large." However, skeptics are wont to argue that the very term "human" or "humanita-rian" development is a tautology, the reason being that development is inherently concerned with human beings. The implication is that no rational person is likely to openly disagree with this form of upliftment or progress without wanting to be accused of absurdity or boorishness.

But, even if some credence is given to such a putative claim, it does not tell the entire story. In the contemporary world order, most academic treatises and policy studies tend to link human or humanita-rian development to specific empirical or policy-based concerns about economic growth rates, poverty redressal, and basic human needs fulfillment. While this is a step in the right direction, the interpretation of such policy aims is usually devoid of any critical interpretation of the relationships they bear to intrinsic values pertaining to human secu-rity, freedom, empowerment, community, sociability, sustainability, and related aspects of human well-being. Furthermore, and as previ-ously emphasized, it would be foolhardy to expect a policy discourse essentially driven by imperialistic economic postulates to generate the wherewithal of a liberating conversation about the fundamentals of authentic development.

Even more disturbing, perhaps, are the implications of rapid tech-nological change. Technology, or the interaction between machines and human organisms, is supposed to overcome human frailties and li-mitations by making us stronger, healthier, smarter, happier, and so on. But this raises some intractable questions about the real contribution of all technology to human well-being: are human lives better because of the existence of automobiles, television, nuclear power, and bioengi-neering? While most people are well adapted to technology, there have always been questions whether humanity thrives best in what is some-times perceived as an oppressive technological world that its more for-tunate members have created. Nowadays, human beings must inevita-bly confront a new phase in the powers of technology, as evidenced by the discovery and implementation of an alternative to the evolution of the species – direct intervention into the genetic process itself.

Skepticism about the hegemony of economic and technological worldviews can be further explained in terms of the apparent lack of consensus between so-called *humanitarians* (HUMS) and *human resource developers* (HURDS). In general, HUMS regard the enhancement of human potentials as the ultimate end of authentic development, or its entire purpose. This *intrinsic* perspective is buttressed by a portrayal of people as self-interpreting, self-motivating, and self-regulating human agents. Accordingly, humanitarian development becomes coterminous with enlargement of people's choices, capabilities, opportunities, and options. By contrast, HURDS tend to pay more attention to *instrumental* objectives or proximate ends of development, such as material prosperity, economic growth, wealth creation, and increased productivity. They are wont to portray people as productive means only, human "resources," or as specific forms of human "capital" engaged in generating material output.

This perspective, which also forms the essence of the orthodox paradigm of economic development, rests on a preconception that people are primarily *means* to an *end*, malleable, and therefore have to be directed, monitored, and controlled. Other points of divergence between HUMS and HURDS are summarized in Table 3.1. These include disagreements about the "target groups" to which policies should be directed, time horizons, sectoral priorities, the content of economic and social programs, and the respective political constituencies. The *instrumental-intrinsic* or *means-ends* dichotomy that purportedly separates the two perspectives helps to explain the self-referential nature of paradigms. Theorists, policymakers, and practitioners subscribing to one or the other are wont to behave in ways that contribute to outcomes they expect. In other words, they typically interpret events or situations as reinforcing their own beliefs and expectations.

However, the intrinsic (HUMS) and instrumental (HURDS) life-and-world visions are not necessarily mutually exclusive. Both elements are relevant and necessary, but we may have to go beyond one or the other as a means of achieving the higher-order synthesis needed for comprehensive interpretation and understanding of human development potentials. In any event, the debate between the two realms may well be rendered moot by the exponential growth in the speed and intensity of information, and by the practical demands of people, governments, and other institutions. Humanitarians and human resource developers need to embrace each other and strive to promote a common goal of sustainable human development. As Streeten reminds us: "[s]uch common ground would be reinforced by the faith that all good things go together, and by the fact that the means are means towards the same ends of those who stress the ends" (1995: 20).

Table 3.1: Humanitarians versus Human Resource Developers

Humanitarians	Human Resource Developers
Goals	
Well-being in terms of empowerment, human security, freedom, community and overall quality of life.	Material goals, economic growth, efficiency, and trickle down.
Orientation	
People regarded as active human agents or participants with purposes and aspirations.	People treated as individuals, resources, means, or passive presumptive "targets."
Target Groups	
The disadvantaged, including women, youth, children, unemployables, old, infirm, and disabled.	Concern directed at just those who can contribute to economic activity (productive adults).
Sectoral Priorities	
Social sectors – emphasis on general and vocational education, primary health care, preventive medicine.	Economic sectors – emphasis on human capital (specialized training and skills), and curative medicine.
Political Constituencies	
Appeal to idealists, utopians, action groups, grassroots organizations.	Appeal to economists, bankers, Wall Street, technocrats, business firms.

Source: Author

Correlatively, he advances six reasons why human development should be accorded primacy: (i) it is desirable as an end in itself (intrinsic); (ii) it is an instrument for promoting higher productivity, thereby enhancing people's command over goods and services; (iii) by reducing human reproduction, human development can produce desirable demographic and economic outcomes; (iv) since poor people are not so much victims of environmental degradation but more often its cause, the inclusiveness inherent in human development can be a potent force for achieving environmental sustainability; (v) in similar vein, human development lays the foundations for promoting democracy and healthy civil society by improving the lot of the poorest groups and giving them more "voice" in decisions governing their lives; and (vi) it promotes political stability and social peace. The guiding normative principle is *equity*, that is, the choices of no one individual or group should be enlarged at the expense of those of others.

More generally, the humanitarian development trajectory is coterminous with development *of* the people (employment and incomes), *for* the people (basic social services), and *by* the people (participation, democracy, empowerment). But such a synergistic outcome would be realized only if rigid linkages are established between economic production (livelihoods) and fuller lives. GNP per capita (as an indicator of economic performance) is not always strongly correlated with human development yardsticks such as education (literacy), and health (life expectancy and infant mortality). This is partly explained by the unequal distribution of incomes and wealth (David 1997a; Ranis, Stewart, and Ramirez 2000). Moreover, the ability to convert income into a good, pleasant, and decent life tends to vary according to the quantity and quality of education, health status, and other factors associated with working conditions and the public provision of basic social services.

Our Common Humanity

It is a truism that every person is human by nature, as distinct from mere convention. A given person's economic, political, socio-cultural, and ecological environment is usually determined by sheer accident of birth or force of historical circumstances. One is accidentally an American, Nigerian, rich or poor, but no one is accidentally human. Our common humanity can be interpreted as a "transcultural universal," that is, the ultimate point at which particularistic differences among people tend to vanish. In epistemological terms, the proposition that "all people are human" is an "analytic" one. This means that it cannot be falsified by empirical data or contingent facts of human experience.

The concern for humanity, or the community of humankind, has long been a subject of philosophical speculation. For example, this was implicit in the *Aristotelian principle*, which interprets human life as a sequence of things people do or states of being they are able to achieve. Contextually, Aristotle conceived the human good in terms of goals people are seeking; these, in turn, were thought to be intrinsic to human nature. What people seek, or the ultimate end of human life, was given the formal name *eudaimonia*. This is usually translated as "happiness," but the precise meaning is subject to interpretation (Nussbaum 1986). It is not a matter of deliberation or choice but rather, as noted above, something endogenous or intrinsic to human nature. As such, *eudaimonia* connotes "the shape of one's entire life" (Williams 1985, 43; Griffin 1986, 322), or the basic capability "to live, to live well, and to live better" (Whitehead 1929).

It is not a mere utopian goal, but also involves an active subscription to rules, conventions, and social norms that determine the desirability and feasibility of our actions. This "creative utopian" vision is forcefully articulated in Book VI of his *Ethics*, where Aristotle links human well-being to two dimensions of intellectual virtue – *sophia* ("theoretical wisdom") or the human capability to contemplate universal or immutable truths, and *phronesis* ("ethical consciousness" or "practical wisdom"). *Phronesis* bears the primary responsibility for discovering what is right in human action, and therefore makes it possible for our desires to conform to reason. Such a synergy is achieved by projecting desirable human ends (goals) and balancing them against appropriate *means*.

While the Greeks and Romans made appeals to some notion of humanity, it was not until the modern emergence of natural law that humanity became a definitive moral, legal, and political concept. Its centrality was undoubtedly influenced by so-called European "discovery" of the New World and subsequent moral contestations over the status of perceptible "barbaric" or "exotic" peoples encountered in other lands. Thus, the idea of "humanity" became the subject of contentious debates as moral, legal, and political thinkers grappled with the status to be accorded these non-European, pagan, and non-Christian peoples. By the 18th century, such misgivings were linked to strong concerns about the treatment of indigenous peoples and the institution of slavery. As a result, humanity became one of the central preoccupations of the European Enlightenment and the corresponding quest for emancipation. Based on a notion about the "perfectibility of man," the objective was to liberate the whole of humankind and to bring equality and justice to all human beings irrespective of their class, color, race, sex, or creed.

One of the central sentiments of the Enlightenment was exemplified by Rousseau's eloquent statement that while all human beings were born free, they were everywhere in chains. Mention was also made earlier about Immanuel Kant's *Categorical Imperative* and his idea about the "constitutive" nature of humanity. In his essay "What is Enlightenment?" [*Political Writings* 1970, 59], Kant considers enlightenment and freedom to be intimately connected, with the raising of consciousness being intrinsic to overcoming constraints to freedom. Hence, enlightenment involves the development of humanity's capacities to think and act freely. Only then, he opines, will humanity emerge from the cold and dark shadows of "self-incurred immaturity" into the warm light of freedom and self-regulation.

For Kant, the imperative of giving political expression to humanity is a moral requirement. The argument is that we have a duty to associate with all other humans as co-legislators in an imagined "kingdom of ends." The belief is that all citizens should enter into a legal relationship with all humanity, thereby concretizing cosmopolitan law and affirming the moral dimensions of politics. This follows from the hypothesis that humanity has a moral disposition or character, which is itself a testament to the proclivity within humanity of continual moral improvement.

In passing, it should be added that the prospects for reconstructing normative principles in the contemporary world order are inherently related to the issue whether authentic development may be construed as a sign of humanity's perpetual process of "enlightenment." The rise of humanitarian discourse and corresponding search for "emancipatory ideals," seem to have provided various constituencies – individuals, communities, nation-states, international institutions, and non-governmental organizations (NGOs) – with a growing set of rules, norms, and expectations with which to assess economic, social, political, and legal relations within and between peoples and states.

However, we hasten to add that the emphasis placed on the enlightenment ethic is not meant to convey a message of parochialism or ethnocentrism. Rather, it can be argued that the particular philosophy of life is inherent in the "overlapping consensus" encountered in all major religions or systems of thought – ranging from the Graeco-Roman and Judeo-Christian ethic undergirding Western civilization to

African humanism, Hinduism, Islam, and Confucianism. The universal *Weltanschuung* is grounded in the humanitarian life-and-world vision that no person is inherently a solitary or independent entity. A person is human in the fundamental sense that he or she is enveloped in the community of other human beings, that is, inevitably caught up in the totality of life. The governing dynamic is not independence, but caring, sharing, and interdependence. Each person achieves full humanity by reaching out to others in constructive relationships.

For example, the ancient African non-discursive philosophy of human well-being, known as *Ubuntu*, emphasizes simultaneous legitimacy, that is, wholeness and relatedness of humanity and creation. *To be is to participate.* In the Hindu philosophy of *Dharma*, people's duties are supposed to evolve from the simultaneous interaction of the cosmic order, the nature of things, moral righteousness, and the shared rules of right conduct. In the Islamic tradition of thought, humanity is grounded in the principle that

> as a small thorn in any part, a thorn in the human body pricks one spot but pains the whole to restlessness. Similarly the needy pricked and pinched by the thorn hunger destroy the peace of the whole of humanity (Siggi 1970, 24).

While there are now repeated calls for concerted action toward emancipation of the entire human race by rethinking obligations owed beyond "our" own particularistic identities, what may be termed a "counter-discourse" or "theoretical anti-humanism" has surfaced in some circles. It casts doubts on the suitability of humanity, especially as a political concept. The critique is that appeals to humanity and liberation more often than not presuppose a universal human essence, that is, something which not only exists everywhere, but homogeneous, and irrespective of time, place, and circumstances. The effect of this presupposition, it is argued, is to erase all particularities of class, ethnicity, race, and gender, which ought to be recognized. But, as noted earlier, humanity operates like an overarching regulative idea, which allows for appeals from diverse overlapping and even competing moral communities.

This interpretation accords with the philosophy of life encountered in hermeneutic traditions of thought, which suggest that human existence is not merely a biological condition that is shared with other animals. Rather, it exhibits a distinct complexity and subtlety. A guiding preconception, therefore, is that any philosophy of life must by necessity be comprehensive. Since such life is not made up of an array of unconnected or discrete facts, any serious attempt to comprehend it must be based on the broadest possible grasp of the diverse ways in which it manifests itself. Hence, belief in the *centrality of human being* implies a necessity of moving away from depersonalized and mechanical models emphasizing the malleability of human beings toward a more syncretic life-and-world vision based on self-other attributes and vector-space relations.

The organic perspective of human being is sometimes explained by reference to the hermeneutic properties of "facticity," "existentiality," and "forfeiture" (Grene 1967). Facticity connotes "being-in-the-world," or the idea that human beings are already in a world defined by common spheres of activity and interests. These inhere in a mental universe through which a given person's historical, physical, and social environments become his or her very own. Another significant implication is that for most of our lives we are caught up in a world of practical living that is defined by functional relationships. Our participation in this world is ontologically antecedent or prior to theorizing about or knowing it, and also transcends the more constricted horizons of intellectualism, rationalism, and positivism.

Inherent in *facticity* is also the general hermeneutic claim that commonsense beliefs are fully constitutive of human and social reality. As Schutz (1962, 69) states:

> The world of nature, as explained by the natural scientist, does not 'mean' anything to molecules, atoms, or electrons. But the observational field of the social scientist – social reality – has a specific meaning and relevance structure for human beings living, acting, and thinking within it. By a series of *common-sense constructs* they have pre-selected and pre-interpreted this world which they experience as the reality of their daily lives (emphasis added).

The idea of *existentiality* refers to the act of making the world our own. It is grounded in the principle of "transcendence," that is, human being exists in anticipation of its own possibilities. While it is forever reaching beyond itself, human being can never outrun the world it is given. It is a projection *of*, *in*, and *with* the world. *Forfeiture* connotes the constant tension between freedom and necessity. Human beings are free, yet determined or enslaved. While we are essentially "in the world" and tend to shape our world, the drive for creativity is also forfeited by the same world. This creative drive for "being" or individual freedom is continuously frustrated because attention has to be paid to the cares of others and the larger community.

Beyond hermeneutics, what is at stake is not merely economic survival, but the capabilities and freedom of ordinary citizens, as active agents of change, to become architects or arbiters of their own destinies. A basic premise is that all human beings are endowed with a self-defining value that makes us who we are and allows to seek alternative goal-oriented futures. Moreover, each person achieves full humanity by reaching out to others in cooperative relationships. To reiterate, when human development potentials are allowed to freely emerge and flourish, the development discourse will be driven by the ends of its primary stakeholders, people themselves, rather than by the authoritative perorations of dominant communities of scholars, especially mainstream economists, who are wont to interpret development reality from a distance.

All human beings have "mental self," reflecting the fact that mature individuals typically display certain patterns of thought, feeling, and action based on self-other attributes. We have inner lives, memories, and purposes that enable us to formulate plans, make decisions, and choose among alternatives. This human capability is reflected in a person's "normative self-concept," which is usually the motive force or organizing principle behind his or her life. As described by Adams,

> one's self-concept defines the parameters of one's life, charts one's course, and drives, pulls, and steers one along life's way... Indeed, one's core self-concept, one's concept of oneself as human being, shapes one's moral feelings and appraisals not only of oneself but of other *human beings* as well (1997, 25).

The normative self-concept plays a pivotal role in generating worldviews, that is, our conceptions and understanding of the world and our place within it. A successful life requires a worldview, which hinges on a positive attitude to life or an operating faith in the possibilities of living a life that is meaningful and worthwhile. Hence, humans should not be conceived as passively reacting to the world around them, but as being continuously motivated by positive qualities such as self-consciousness and self-awareness. The latter connotes a tendency to summon up a vision of past experiences and project what the world would be ("becoming"), as distinct from what it is at present ("being"). Also implied is an uncanny instinct of survivability, that is, humans have preferred outcomes, are able to choose, exercise options, and not repeat past mistakes.

At another level, the human self, morality, and society are inextricably intertwined, especially in terms of the tendency for human beings to habitually subscribe to rules and norms that define their membership of perpetual social units. The saliency of person-to-person and person-to-society interactions inheres in the fact that human being involves a "dialogical self," or intrinsic "self-other" attributes. Dialogical acts involve the optimal sharing of human agency. Related to this is a recognition of rights, responsibilities, and obligations that are attached to individuals themselves, others, and society at large.

The Quality Of Life Circle

Achievement of authentic development depends on enhancement of *total human welfare,* or the overall quality of life, and not just preferred parts of it. As indicated earlier, this implies a need and willingness to accept a greater degree of pluralism in the development discourse, its multifaceted constitution, the way benefits are shared out, and the models of policy formulation and social organization on which it relies. Accordingly, the development trajectory is predicated on the imperative of drawing on the entire gamut of human values − from the moral, spiritual, and aesthetic at one end, through the economic, sociocultural, political, and ecological, to the scientific and technological at the other end, as yardsticks of success.

The ramifications are schematically pictured in Figure 3.1 − the Quality of Life Circle, which illustrates major components of the quest for human well-being. If the figure were to be viewed three-dimensionally, the components would actually reveal a number of complementary and constantly changing positions similar to overlapping spheres of a spinning gyroscope. At the core of the Circle stands the individual, and collectively the society or community, all striving to fulfill their human development potentials. The goal of human interaction is to generate mechanisms that allow each of the components to function harmoniously and productively in the face of constantly changing circumstances. The supporting processes of change are supposed to promote moral and spiritual growth, personal fulfillment, or "perfectibility of the individual" by ensuring that his or her potentials are developed to the fullest extent possible.

Figure 3.1: Quality of Life Circle

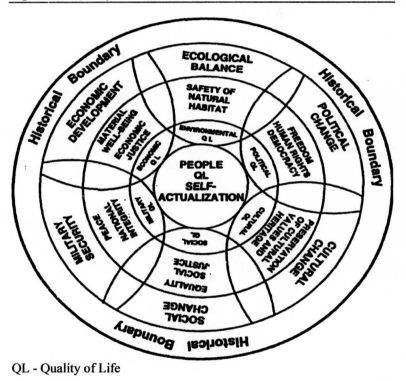

QL - Quality of Life

Source: Author.

The Circle demonstrates that development reality, and its changing potentials, as a mirror of human life itself, represents multiple layers or components of a totality comprising different patterns of action, interaction, and interdependence. It depicts a world in which no single component can be conceived as an unambiguous antecedent or explanatory variable. While economic phenomena, social forces, culture, politics, and ecology may be separate disciplinary or analytical domains, in reality they mirror elements of human life that deeply interpenetrate one another, generating what may be termed a "palimpsest of holistic meanings" or reflecting a "diachronic landscape" of human and societal development (Shackle 1972). Each component tends to display varying characteristics at different times and places. The interactions and feedbacks also differ from society to society and at stages of development in a particular society.

The idea is not to project an image of human society as a seamless web in which fundamental changes in any one part can be expected to generate equally significant changes in others. Rather, the focal point is that each systemic order should be studied in all its intricate aspects. As one noted development economist remarks,

> we must find out how each social system works, which improvements will bring about other improvements, which will bring what kinds of retrogression, which will leave the system unchanged. Plans must operate on all strategic variables in order to achieve all of the objectives of development (Higgins 1977, 122).

These objectives inhere in the necessity of moving away form conditions of life widely perceived to be undesirable to other alternatives that are much better in human terms, that is, more synergistic with people's continuous strivings the world over for freedom, security, material prosperity, equality, equity, and social relevance. As shown in Table 3.2, attainment of the requisite human or humanitarian ends entails a retreat from the forces of ill-being, anti-development, or underdevelopment that tend to perpetuate deep-rooted conflicts, social strain, anomie, and alienation. The latter reflect the structure and functioning of systematic orders that perennially ignore or suppress essential development needs. As a result, billions of people the world over have been forced or otherwise mandated to make dysfunctional adjustments to their behaviors and expectations, a situation that is anathema to human tolerance and security.

The transition to authentic development is predicated upon far-reaching changes in the interconnected systemic orders – supra-national, regional, national, and local systems – governing people's lives. At one level, reference is to the overarching global system or "sociosphere." The diversity existing within and amongst its distinct, but ultimately related layers, must bear a prime responsibility for enabling or disabling the quest for human betterment. It goes without saying that the future welfare of humankind cannot be secured without a here-tofore unprecedented degree of global cooperation based on initia-tives by a variety of institutions, including rich and poor nations and peoples. These constitute an international system of relations linking persons living under groups of interacting behavioral units – variously called "societies," "countries," and "nation-states." There are activities

Table 3.2: Human Ends and the Forces of Anti-Development

Components	Human Ends	Forces of Anti-Development
Human, Moral Homo Sapiens Humanis	Human freedom Self-realization	Moral Decay; decline in personal responsi-bility
Economic Homo Oeconomicus	Material welfare Economic growth	Poverty and Economic stagnation
Social Homo Socialis	Social cooperation Social equality	Social Decay Alienation
Cultural Homo Culturalis	Value-Consensus Cultural identity	Hierarchism Cultural domination
Political Homo Politicus	Human rights Empowerment	Authoritarianism Insecurity
Ecological Homo Oecologicus	Nature-Nurture balance Environmental rights	Habitat destruction Resource management

Source: Author

and features of nation-states that are concerned with purely domestic matters which have no bearing on the international system. However, the distinction between "domestic" and "foreign" policy becomes blur-red all the time, simply because of the great interrelatedness of all aspects of the sociosphere or global social system.

Of particular relevance to the development quest is the role of certain intermediate but powerful institutions. One group is what we term the "global public sector" (GPS), including the United Nations and its agencies; the Bretton Woods institutions (BWIs) – IMF, World Bank, and WTO; and other forms of bilateral and multilateral contact, including the Organization for Economic Cooperation and Develop-ment (OECD), European Union (EU), and North American Free Trade Area (NAFTA). Another group includes transnational corporations

(TNCs), which at times negotiate with national governments almost as if the former were sovereign states. In terms of their economic power and financial resources, TNCs operate on a scale that is larger than many countries. Third, there is the large and growing group of non-governmental organizations (NGOs), which have been instrumental in forging a global compact among the diverse institutional orders based on justice, fairness, and new rules of the game.

Hence, the Quality of Life Circle projects a comprehensive understanding of human well-being based on (i) the realities and potentials inherent in *wholes*; (ii) the relative influences of *parts*, that is, the extent to which each part is autonomous or controlled; and (iii) a determination of which has priority, if any, and making informed judgments about what the multiple interrelationships among the interacting parts are and/or ought to be.

Outcomes of the vertical and horizontal processes of interaction are constrained by the "historical boundary" of shared memory, which determines the extent to which individuals in a social system can identify as a group. Ideally, the shared experience of the historical boundary should facilitate the ability of human beings and the institutions they create to interact synergistically in pursuit of common goals. But, each society or collectivity with its own shared memory is not an island unto itself. Not only must it be concerned with its own indigenous perspective of synergistic harmony, but it must also continuously create effective mechanisms of interaction with other collectivities whose experiences might have been different or which, in one way or another, might have inflicted harm on other groups. In other words, the historical boundary is not an impenetrable wall of steel, but rather a porous curtain that is being constantly pierced by a number of exogenous forces.

The heterogeneous groups of countries and other collectivities throughout the world suggest that there is no single historical recipe, at least for sustained economic development. In this context, influential analysts such as Alexander Gerschenkron (1962) and Barrington Moore (1966) have stressed the importance of "historical variations" in their "late industrialization theory." The basic hypothesis is that developmental outcomes within and across countries and regions are a product of the nature of the global economy, technological change (timing), international competition, and the character of state-society interactions at the time countries enter their industrialization paths. These motive forces (centrifugal and centripetal) also undergo change over time such that LDCs are often confronted with different sets of circumstances compared to now advanced nations or early industrializers.

Beyond the historical boundary, it is also a truism that humans also live and have their being in socio-cultural space, which is occupied by a panoply of other social entities and institutions. The organic socio-cultural whole reflects multiple facets of a layered development "cake" or integral parts of what may be called an "ontology of social life." It is being constantly reconfigured by a moving synthesis or dialectical interface among people's life course patterns, national and subnational structures, and the global political economy. The patterns of interaction reflect the fact that the human quest for liberation is embedded in (i) common reciprocating attitudes and conventional behavioral patterns underlying processes of group interaction – for example, love and other forms of affection, cooperation, loyalty, and systems of subordination and super-ordination; (ii) cultural objects or behavioral traits that either carry symbolic value or become the means of satisfying wants and needs; and (iii) patterns of communication that describe or prescribe acceptable interrelationships and beliefs.

Socio-cultural Space and Social Capital

As Adams remarks,

> human beings have their more specific identity as individuals, largely in terms of their relationships to other persons and the offices they hold and the roles they play in social structures. Thus, persons are not only in society and occupy offices, play roles, and stand in relationships to it, but the social structure is internalized in them. We are who we are largely in terms of our relationships, offices, and roles (Adams 1997, 27).

To reiterate, the collective socio-cultural order can be interpreted as a background or context in which all individual and group actions take place, and from which they derive their meaning and significance. It reflects the fact that there are certain self-reproducing and recursive elements of human and social life. Human agents simultaneously "structure" or create social systems while being "structured" or created by them. Giddens (1984) explains this phenomenon in terms of a "duality of structure" or double hermeneutic undergirding human consciousness and action.

The upshot of the argument is that society or community is an "emergent" entity which is partially planned, designed, or controlled by human beings. It is often driven or conditioned by natural and psychological factors that are anchored in beliefs, perceptions, attitudes, motives, expectations, and aspirations of its human participants. The reality of any human or social system is a product of what actually exists in the world as well as what human agents project unto it. At the same time, systems of social stratification constantly constrain human action. In more general terms, the myriad structural properties tend to generate intended and unintended consequences that may be harmonious or conflictual, emancipatory or oppressive.

At the most basic level, a person's behavioral expectations can be identified with socio-cultural resources that are usually connected with family ties and communal relations. In the original formulation of this idea, Loury (1977) saw these as constituting assets or "social capital" on which people can potentially draw in order to achieve certain outcomes. All economic activities, including decisions about consumption, production, distribution, occupational systems and rates of pay are systematically structured elements of an institutional and larger socio-cultural logic that people come to live with, in varying degrees. Economic actions and processes are "embedded" in social networks and other types of social structure (Polanyi 1944; Granovetter 1985; Ben-Porath 1990). As Loury remarks, "[o]pportunity travels along the synapses of social networks. An individual's inherited social situation plays a major role in determining ultimate economic success" (1998, 119).

This goes against the grain of the dominant economic paradigm, which is grounded in a belief that behavior of the free market and price system provides the best answer to the three basic questions confronting any economy: what to produce?, how to do it?, and for whom? Markets are not mere mechanisms for production, exchange, and distribution, but more importantly, institutions having diverse legal, political, and normative connotations. At both national and international levels, they have come to represent places where powerful economic actors cooperate with one another and form alliances or networks of contacts.

This is particularly true of labor markets. In the eyes of Nobel Laureate Robert Solow (1990), they are essentially social institutions. To a large extent, labor productivity depends on how workers get along with their peers, managers, and customers. In turn, this process has led to discrimination against ethnic minorities and other disadvantaged groups such as women. The reason is that their presence in the open market tends to upset prevailing employment practices, established forms of organization, and social networks. Even when minorities or women are hired, coworkers sometimes shun, harass, or refuse to work with them, and sometimes even sabotage their work. As a result, the productivity of such groups is usually lower, but this does not stem from a lack of conscientiousness, training, skills, or merit. Rather, the outcome results from a complex set of entrenched behaviors and attitudes that are difficult to counteract under normal circumstances.

In general, the unequal relationships inherent in factor and commodity markets enable some human agents to influence the course of interaction with other groups, and ultimately the nature of developmental outcomes, through abuse of social networks and manipulation of resources and other bases of power to which they have access. There are at least three broad categories of resources that are interwoven with concrete economic and social practices. At the economic level, they typically constitute "allocative resources" such as raw materials, means of production, finished goods, and money. Control of these strategic resources tends to be rooted in ownership rights and entitlement systems that enable or disable human capabilities. They are intertwined with noticeable differentials in power and command over the material conditions of life.

In the arena of politics and public management, there are "authoritative resources" that generate human capabilities to exercise power and control over the socially constituted world in terms of people's life chances, spatio-temporal positioning, and relations with other human beings. At a third level, mention can be made of "stored information," which now constitutes the most influential resource that powerbrokers continually utilize as a means of exercising economic, social, and political power in space and time. It is intertwined with the "culture of secrecy," or the highly restricted sharing of knowledge that has come to be associated with modern bureaucratic forms of administration and policy formulation.

On the more positive side, the social capital of a community encompasses relationships that are grounded in reciprocity and cooperation, attitudes of social trust and respect, and structures of voluntary association. As such, it plays a pivotal role in the cumulative causal processes explaining communal identity and the symbiotic forces enhancing human development potentials. Social capital differs from conventional forms of private or physical capital in at least two ways. First, while physical capital is alienable, social capital is practically inalienable. It involves "value-in-use," or immanent value, and it is not easily exchanged, in the sense of generating "exchange-values." Since it is an attribute of the larger socio-cultural order in which it is embedded, social capital cannot be construed as the private property of any person who benefits from it. Second, while physical capital is a private good, social capital is more like a public good, that is, the primary purpose is to satisfy collective wants or needs (Coleman 1990).

High levels of social capital formation are associated with cooperative approaches to problem-solving, effective forms of governance, and sustained economic development (Putnam 1993). One variation on this theme is that economic success depends only partly on factors customarily emphasized in endogenous economic models, such as open markets, competition, technology, and skills. Equally important is a supportive culture of trust or "spontaneous sociability," which Fukuyama (1995) defines as a readiness to get along with one's fellows in ways that are economically useful and productive. This is borne out by the experience of countries in which civil society flourishes or where diverse social institutions, operating in the space between the family and centralized state, play significant roles in people's lives.

In general, the economic and social welfare of individuals and groups are significantly enhanced when the structure of human relations is based on these socio-cultural resources. The motive force emanates from two interdependent sources – the normative structure of society and what Putnam calls "networks of civic engagement." The normative structure of society is usually associated with disparate sets of economic, socio-cultural, and political interchange. Some are horizontal, or based on a coalescence of persons sharing equal status and power. Others are vertical, linking persons of unequal status in hierarchical and asymmetrical relations. Vertical relations are much less efficient than horizontal ones in promoting civic virtues and social cooperation. Across societies and cultures, observed levels of socio-economic development are positively correlated with strong civic traditions and citizen participation in social life. This arises because members of a civic community are imbued with equal rights and obligations. Citizens interact as equals and not as patrons and clients, or on the basis of hierarchical relations of power, authority, and dependency.

People in general are likely to achieve more than individuals when their actions are motivated by group solidarity and a strong sense of community. The process is usually accompanied by relatively high levels of inter-personal and inter-organizational relations and effectiveness (Uphoff 1992; Tendler and Freedheim 1994). When people from different social and ethnic backgrounds begin to cooperate, the probability of overcoming traditional problems of suspicion, disruption, and instability can become as strong or even greater that when relatively homogeneous groups initiate a program or project (Hirschman 1984a). The dynamic provided by "social energy" or synergy is likely to cumulate in future rounds. The argument is that once collective action has proven to be successful in one area of endeavor, the practice is likely to spread, organizational skills will become more widely diffused, and the fundamentals of civic engagement – social trust, tolerance, cooperation, and solidarity – are likely to grow exponentially.

Systemic Conflicts

The component parts of the Quality of Life Circle may interact in a number of unpredictable ways (mutually supportive or substitutive) which cannot be generalized. The intercausal linkages are not necessarily linear or unidirectional, but typically reflect heterogeneous processes that are riven with tensions and contradictions. Examples abound at the global, national, and local levels of the undesirable consequences for individual and collective human welfare that are inherent in systemic conflicts. While the business of society is social reproduction, the nature and degree of each individual's participation in the organized core of reciprocal relations are a product of historical circumstances, psychological factors, group interests, and power relations. Such influences variously result in forms of conflict, coercion, and control that have constantly undermined people's potential bargaining power.

In most LDCs, for example, the utopian dream of authentic development is continuously stymied by societal polarization or entrenched patterns of social differentiation based on class, caste, ethnicity, and gender. Some writers have characterized this situation as an absence of a "middle class consensus." The latter refers to a national situation in which there are no strong class, ethnic, gender and related differences among people (Sidanius and Pratto 1999; Easterly 2000). The absence of a middle class society implies that forces of dominance and hierarchy tend to perpetuate the unequal access of certain groups to resources.

A longstanding debate has centered around the extent to which dominant indigenous classes are able to block the quest for human betterment or authentic development. We do not enter into the controversial debate whether such classes are autonomous, that is, whether they are essentially extensions or "clients" of what is perceived to be a subversive foreign class. Even if some foreign control is presumed to exist, it cannot be denied that dominant local groups in LDCs tend to frustrate the popular will and corresponding calls for appropriate structural and institutional change. Through their self-awareness and creativity, ordinary citizens constantly try to satisfy their needs and socially change themselves. But their human development potentials are forever diminished or squelched by a social structure designed to preserve the status quo.

The institutional structure is linked to the nature of class interests, especially in societies where powerful cadres control the production process and dominate the organization of social relations in pursuit of private gains. Industrial and commercial classes have become notorious for resisting reforms designed to promote fair labor standards, such as increases in the minimum wage and rates of pay, improvements in environmental and safety conditions, and the subscription to elemental principles of collective bargaining. Landowners are usually more interested in maintaining control over dependent classes who have no alternative but to seek employment as tenants, sharecroppers, and wage laborers. As a general rule, the historically entrenched mode of interaction among landlords, land, and ordinary people tends to die hard (Domar 1970; Lal 1999).

Landowners have been known to express the most vocal opposition to egalitarian programs such as land reform, which are likely to reduce the political and economic value of their assets. In any event, the benefits and costs of such redistributive reforms have to be carefully evaluated. Without complementary measures to assist the poorest economic classes, such policies may produce a number of unintended consequences. Many potential beneficiaries of such reforms are often bypassed. For example, the bold state-sponsored land reforms in Latin America during the 1960s and 1970s provided estate workers with land, but seldom rewarded landless workers. Since the programs granted land titles to heads of households, who were presumed to be men, they tended to produce a strong male bias, generally overlooking women.

Land redistribution programs in Africa have resulted in major land grabs by powerful bureaucratic and other organized interests who have been able to extract significant monopoly rents from substantial land purchases. The land frontier has been pushed back in some countries, but ownership rights of disadvantaged groups remain un-enforced. In Africa as elsewhere, the period since the 1990s has witnessed a shift from state-led land reforms toward privatization of land and other natural resource assets, that is, an upsurge in private property regimes at the expense of more traditional land tenure systems. In general, by conferring and solidifying formal land ownership rights, privatization has strengthened the control of extant powerful groups to the detriment of traditional rural producers, including women (Lastarria-Cornheil 1997). What seems to have been glossed over is that while, in principle, land markets may be open to everyone, in reality poor cadres in rural areas – both men and women – are unable to take advantage of the market system because they lack three basic prerequisites for entry: money to buy land, access to credit, as well as sufficient knowledge and information about new laws and programs.

In the case of caste-based society, Nobel Laureate Amartya Sen has alluded to the labor bondage system persisting in many parts of India where "the upper-caste landowners in one of the most backward parts of India (viz., Bihar) are terrorizing - through collective murder and rape -the families of laborers "tied" to their land" (1999, 113). More generally, the Hindu system of social organization is based on numerous endogamous and hierarchically ranked occupations. Contextually, Deepak Lal notes that the "division of labor by caste and its enforcement by social ostracism was central to the schema" (1999, 29). He further indicates that the system of occupational specialization or segregation resulted from an Aryan response to the problem of securing a stable labor supply for the relatively labor-intensive agriculture practiced in the Indo-Gangetic plain. It continues to be ope-rationalized through a decentralized system of control that does not re-quire peremptory orders or authoritative instructions from an over-arching political system.

In many parts of Africa, ethnic polarization has been a major cause of pervasive inequalities, poor economic growth, and low levels of public goods provisioning. There, as elsewhere, ethnic groups con-tinue to act selfishly in promoting their own vested interests. Nigeria is usually cited as a country where parasitic elites "place their Nigerian identity below that of their local community, nation, or ethnic group" (Ake 1996, 67). The dominant ethnic divide has been between the Muslim North and Christian South, with Northern interest groups manipulating successive governments during the postcolonial era. This has resulted in what is called the "Nigerian factor" – the widespread tendency to sustain patron-client relationships by using every conceivable means to circumvent government rules and regulations for personal benefit. However, the problem is not uniquely Nigerian but pervades Africa, Asia, Latin America and the Caribbean where a crisis of social order and governance underlies the litany of development challenges.

Finally, the above-mentioned examples of social disorder show that the ability of a system to promote goal-oriented human futures and enhance the overall quality of life depends on a judicious intermeshing of values, behaviors, and structures. The social system and its constituent parts are not only influenced by values, but invariably promote particular ideas or ideologies about the good life. Values and institutions tend to move in tandem, and there is an inherent inseparability between human behavior and structures. This preconception can be further elucidated by briefly considering certain qualitative dimensions of developmental change, or differences in structures that typically accompany the transformation process.

As indicated earlier, such "structural change" transcends the mere economic sphere, since it involves concomitant alterations in the sociocultural, political, and ecological environments. The underlying processes of interaction can either enable or disable behavioral change, which connotes changes in people's value-orientations. These are typically reflected in people's psychological, social, and cultural constitution. The view persists in some development circles that the value systems prevailing in many LDCs remain "barriers to change." This means that they are difficult to uproot, at least in the short run. But, this view must be tempered by the reality that in many instances specific value systems have traditionally played a critical functional role in ensuring the stability of certain socio-economic arrangements. Changing structural and environmental conditions have given rise to adaptive modes of production and uses of labor that are primarily responsible for the survival of many communities.

The nature of the interaction between values and structures helps to explain the persistence or otherwise of certain configurations of development and underdevelopment. The ideal case is where changes in values, behaviors, and structures are complementary in nature. Such a symbiotic relationship helps to promote human security and guarantee stability, order, and social peace. In actuality, however, the interactive processes typically display significant lags, tensions, and ambiguities. Values and behaviors may change while the prevailing set of structural conditions remains intact. This occurs, for example, when human motivations about felt needs or people's aspirations for a better quality of life run ahead of the ability or willingness of the entrenched system of power relations in society and its institutions to deliver the goods.

The experience suggests that this "structural lag" usually results in value conflict, which may be expressed in diverse ways: anomie, alienation, civil disobedience, riots, military coups, or revolutions, as the case may be. Alternatively, the frustration may generate a search for new values through other adaptive mechanisms such as emigration abroad. The obverse case of "value-behavioral" lag may occur when structural conditions change without corresponding shifts in value orientations and behavioral patterns. For example, conservative attitudes embedded in customs and traditions may militate against the adaptability to new production systems, technologies, and institutions. Under the circumstances, steps may have to be taken to change the prevailing value system.

This is likely to be a formidable task even in situations where the requisite changes promise to substantially improve the overall quality of life and enhance human development potentials. Not only do values and behavioral patterns boast their own inertial force, but different societies are wont to doggedly defend their prevailing value standards and preferred methods of adjustment. This is particularly true of theocratic states. As a general rule, liberal democracies tend to favor a gradual or evolutionary process of value or behavioral change. By contrast, socialist-oriented countries and authoritarian regimes have been known to rely on more dirigiste options – for example, compulsory schemes and other institutionalized arrangements such as early childhood education and "re-education" of adults. The ideological intent has been to shape, raise, or change people's consciousness in preferred directions. Needless to say, state control or manipulation of the socialization process may run counter to the pluralistic and synergistic outcomes required for promotion of human well-being.

Chapter 4

The Epistemological Transition

> To put it formally, we live in a material world which is an ontological unity, but which we approach with an epistemological diversity.
>
> S. Rose (1997)

As previously emphasized, the evolution of economic and social thought has been based on "multiple paradigms," each with its own strengths and weaknesses. Hence, the search for the truth about development or any other form of human reality must inevitably rely on a mode of interpretation and understanding based on open-mindedness, flexibility, and eclecticism. This calls for a skilful melding of theoretical and practical wisdom and a multiplicity of creative dialogues in intellectual discourse, or across academic disciplines, as well as between them and the social praxis (practical consciousness) of ordinary citizens. However, reciprocity between intellectual and other dialogues can be achieved only if the epistemological foundations of dominant paradigms are challenged and changed.

A guiding premise lies in the hermeneutic claim that all forms of knowledge are situation-bound or from a given background or context. The degree of understanding is inherently linked to the analyst's purposes, intentions, and what he or she is able to project onto the object of interpretation. This entails that understanding is not passively neutral, but actively structures what it encounters. Our investigations cannot escape the fact that "all understanding is interpretation" (Gadamer 1979, 350), which, in turn, is perspectival and indeterminate. It takes place in plurivocal and open-ended ways, none of which is capable of generating propositions that are absolutely or objectively true. Under the circumstances, the epistemological transition is predicated on an imperative of "interpretive pluralism." No single interpretation should be singled out as being uniquely correct, no kind of cognitive activity can be accorded privileged status, and there can be no univocal understanding of anything or phenomenon.

Logico-Epistemic Types

There are many partial ways of viewing the disparate patterns of human experience and development reality. Actual patterns of interpretive pluralism reflect the differential influences of cultural heterogeneity, corresponding differences in individual behavior, and interactions among persons subscribing to different logical beliefs and perspectives of knowledge. Just as social, biological, and ecological processes display varying degrees of diversity and difference, there is also a multiplicity of "logico-epistemic types." They tend to vary from individual to individual, as well as within and across social groups and cultural contexts. The evidence suggests that cultural differences typically manifest themselves in the same manner that most dominant logico-epistemic types are able to exercise control over others. The epistemologist Marogoth Maruyama (1996) provides a useful demarcation of pertinent mindsets.

The number of logico-epistemic types is arguably infinite. Hence, there may some danger in attempting to fit them into neat interpretive categories. However, four broad types are identified in Table 4.1. These H, I, S, and G-types depict orientations of the majority of individuals in most societies. H-type persons are presumed to subscribe rigidly to absolutist principles, regardless of circumstances. They purportedly believe in "one truth," universally generalizable laws, and are prone to arrange things into neat ontological categories. Hence, they constantly search for polar contrasts and tend to compartmentalize things into opposing conceptual boxes.

Homogeneity is anathema to I-type individuals, since they are more oriented toward seeking freedom from interference and usually exhibit a strong belief in their own uniqueness and subjectivity. In the case of S-type persons, individual differences are presumed to make some measure of cooperation possible while homogeneity is thought to breed competition and conflict. This stems from a belief that heterogeneous and other mutually reinforcing characteristics of society or culture may actually coalesce into well-defined patterns. G-types usually display a similar mindset, except for a belief that interactive processes may generate novel patterns.

Table 4.1: Logico-epistemic Types

H-Type	I-Type	S-Type	G-Type
Homogenist	Heterogenist	Heterogenist	Heterogenist
Hierarchical	Isolationist	Interactive	Interactive
Classifying	Randomizing	Stabilizing	Change-generating
Opposition	Independence	Absorption	Exploration
One Truth	Subjective	Poly-objective	Poly-objective
Competitive	Uniquing	Co-operative	Co-generative

Source: Maruyama (1996, 13)

Such divergent typologies help to explain why patterns of reasoning, epistemological presuppositions, and corresponding modes of interpretation tend to vary across major academic disciplines, interpretive communities, and professional groups. For example, it is commonly thought that mainstream economists, accountants, physicists, and some experimental scientists are predominantly of the H-type. As indicated earlier, most orthodox economists are linked by an idealistic vision of markets and mathematical abstractionism.

Hence, heavy reliance is placed on the discovery of abstract knowledge or immutable laws via axioms or theorems forming a connected theoretical system. The "universal grammar" of analytical economics also suffuses pure mathematics and theoretical physics.

It is also believed that I, S, and G-type individuals are primarily found among linguists, artists, anthropologists, sociologists of knowledge, institutional economists, political economists, ecologists, and similar cadres. They are sometimes demarcated from H-type individuals in terms of perceptions about the relative "softness" vis-à-vis "hardness" of the subject matter or discipline. The former interpretive groups are joined by hermeneutic philosophers and paradigm theorists who emphasize the relativistic nature of all knowledge and that only partial models or theories can be generated in an uncertain societal or global environment.

As a consequence, very rigid barriers of communication are often erected between those using H-type logics and epistemics and their I, S, and G-type counterparts. But, the differences do not preclude the divergent groups from reaching consensus about the desirability of alternative courses of action or development paths. This is possible even when the point of convergence is based on different beliefs, interests, and values. For example, the possibility of "cooperative conflict" may be illustrated by the kind of pluralistic outcome or agreement that may emerge about the appropriateness of a particular policy prescription or development program, such as increased community participation or devolution of state power to local districts.

H-type analysts or policymakers may support such an initiative based on the assumption that the entire country is more or less homogeneous. Hence, nothing significant is perceived to be lost from decentralization. Their I-type fellows may agree because of their basic preconception that people living in different parts of the country form an integral part of an interdependent whole. While S and G-types may share a strong belief in heterogeneity, the basis of their agreement may hinge on a consensual belief that divergent groups can still put aside their differences and cooperate for the common good. The point of emphasis is that the different bases of consensus need not imply that a uniform logico-epistemic stance is taken in each case. Nevertheless, such "democratic" outcomes may not be sufficient to overcome the intractable problems surrounding the transition from a unitary to a more pluralistic epistemology.

Transdisciplinarity

This pluralism entails a refusal to generalize from the domain assumptions and images that belong almost exclusively to one category of thought. As we have shown, the interactive processes inherent in the multiple layers of society and the world order tend to differ from the picture conventionally painted in uncomplicated discipline-based models of development economics and social science theory. Not only are their boundaries too constricting, but the interpretation and understanding of development reality and its complexity must necessarily transcend disciplinary boundaries. "We have to look at the parts trying at the same time to keep sight of the whole in the mind's eye" (Herrick and Kindleberger 1983, 17). While there is still richness in the wide variety of disciplinary perspectives, grasping the dynamics of human development requires a *trans-disciplinary* mode of analysis and interpretation.

This attempts to organize and synthesize information drawn from disparate areas of human experience, even though there may be no master key to integrating discipline-based inquiries into the human condition. Nevertheless, interpretation of development processes at each level of aggregation and disaggregation is a paradigm case of how the disciplines can meet and coalesce. It entails "interface," "inter-mingling," "decoupling" of individual parts and simultaneous "embedding" of micro-processes into the overarching system of supranational, national, and local interactions. While human and social problems might have changed drastically over the centuries, the transdisciplinary mode of interpretation, or interdisciplinary interface, was already in the tradition of political economy pioneered by classical luminaries such as Adam Smith, John Stuart Mill, and Karl Marx.

While they were known primarily as economists, they were also historians, moral philosophers, political theorists, and social activists. They were able to achieve some measure of integration in the social sciences by locating the inherent dynamics of the economic system in the much larger contextual framework provided by the structure and functioning of society as a whole. Despite his contributions to economics. Smith essentially viewed human progress as a moral problem. As noted earlier, his *Theory of Moral Sentiments* articulates the pivotal role played by rules of conduct in our lives and in guiding perceptions about the right things to do. John Stuart Mill compared the human development potential to the model of a tree, which grows from the inside or on all sides, and not just by accretion, as a crystal does. Marx pioneered the notion that people's identity is socially determined and intrinsically bound up with our memberships of particular groups and classes.

The transdisciplinary perspective inheres in a necessity to move away from what we term "idealist-essentialist" to "realist-existentialist" categories of thought and epistemology. The idealist-essentialist orientation of social science theory and derivative fields such as the study of development and underdevelopment is traceable to a long list of consensual philosophical traditions: the absolutism of Pythagoras and Plato; Aristotle's two-valued or syllogistic logic; the rationalism of René Descartes; and the "scientific" or hypothetico-deductive method of modern positivists and empiricists. They are consonant with the dominant rationalist theory of knowledge, or what is known as the "foundationalist epistemology." It posits that the full grasp of social consciousness, and hence human development potentials, emerges from an analytical procedure in which our minds become passive and disinterested conduits of "objective" or scientific truths.

The perspective is grounded in an immutable "either/or" dichotomy, that is, a claim that there must either be one unique category of understanding or absolute truth or else the result will be total skepticism, subjectivity, or mere opinion (Bernstein 1988). A sharp distinction is usually drawn between *res cogitans* (mental constructs) and *res extensa* (material things as extended substance). The duality is exemplified by contrasting pairs of opposites – for example, modern and traditional, mind and body, subject and object, intellect and emotion, objectivity and subjectivity, observer and observed, and developed and underdeveloped. Moreover, the dominant intellectual discourse usually accords greater power and control to the first part of the dichotomy (Toulmin 1990; Rorty 1991; Gudeman 1996).

As alluded to earlier, the dualistic method relies on an "antogonism of opposites" that lies at the heart of logical reasoning from the days of Aristotle to foundations of modern formal logic. The latter provides an ideal language or set of syntactical rules for deciding the truth or falsity of propositions. There are two broad classes of such propositions – tautologies and contradictions. The statement 'p v –p' (p *or* not p) is a tautology, that is, it is logically true whatever the empirical content of p. By contrast, the statement 'p & –p' (p *and* not

p) is a contradiction. It is logically false irrespective of whether p is empirically true or false. The implication is that some statements are necessarily true (tautologies) and others necessarily false (contradictions) solely by virtue of the meanings attached to the logical connectives (in this case "v" and "&") involved, that is, their truth or falsity does not depend on anything taking place in the real world.

More generally, knowledge and certainty are assumed to be synonymous, with the rules of formal logic and mathematical axioms providing an ideal language or inferential properties for demarcating truth from falsehood. For example, Descartes tried to discover one universal and indubitable truth on which to build the permanent foundations of science. Mathematics was placed at the center of his rationalist program, since its postulates could be deduced from a few axiomatic propositions. In his *Discourse on Method*, Descartes linked the rational mastery of nature and society to a search for universally valid laws that could be discovered through pure reason and mathematics. He was convinced that human reason could give knowledge the same certainty with the support of innate ideas and self-evident truths. The relevant concepts about reality are supposed to be self-evident because they follow necessarily from the laws of thinking, as exemplified by the oft- quoted dictum: *cogito, ergo sum* ("I think, therefore I am [exist]").

Descartes is mentioned because much of what followed in the subsequent history of scientific thought and epistemology can be construed as attempts to criticize or improve upon Cartesian tenets. According to what is known as the Cartesian "anxiety" or "angst," the world of science necessitates that we always seek an objective "Archimedean point" in all academic disciplines if we are ever to arrive at scientific truth. Whether the objects of investigation are natural or social phenomena, physical or chemical reactions, works of art, or processes of development and underdevelopment, we must be able to refer to an objective (non-humanistic, a-moral, a-historical, a-cultural) standard by which members of a given scientific community can be compared to others.

This perspective entertains no middle ground or compromise. By contrast, the "realist-existentialist" alternative rests on the more realistic or pragmatic claim that some practices are based on both rational and non-rational (subjective, normative, ideological) referents. Given the ceaseless changeability and flux of human affairs, our hallowed epistemological and logical categories can no longer be taken as given, that is, simply interpreted as permanencies whose meanings are walled up behind ontological boundaries that are categorically frozen in space and time. As one scholar notes, we are dealing with a world where

> interactions, interdependencies, and relations are in a relentless state of becoming – never motionless or at complete rest, but relentlessly reconstituted and reconfigured.... Like it or not, whatever the boundary-drawing ontological categories we choose to deploy in forming our questions and performing our inquiries, we are dealing with phenomena that at some fundamental level involve boundaryless interactions of power relations, meanings, and embodied-situated practices (Pred 1995, 1068).

Hence, the transdisciplinary enterprise emphasizes the need for a logical and epistemological transition from knowledge or truth claims based on an immutable "either/or" dichotomy to blurred zones involving "both/and." Table 4.2 juxtaposes some broad elements of the paradigm shift from a unitary to a more pluralistic methodological stance. A focal point is on the imperative of moving away from uniformity and homogeneity toward heterogeneity and pluralism. The latter perspective shuns aprioristic goals, attempts to build on those generated by people themselves, accommodates diversities and differences, and continuously interprets and reinterprets the ramifications of what may be termed an "intercultural ecology." A guiding preconception is that patterns of understanding undergirding the conventional wisdom – for example, rules based on generalizability and universality – are neither organizational principles of the universe nor do they necessarily connote desirable societal goals or emancipatory human futures.

What will ultimately survive the fitness test of authentic development is not likely to be the dominant and homogeneous, but rather the pluralistic and symbiotic, or rules based on the heterogenization of processes (Maruyama 1972). A differentiated organic whole will always be preferable to one exclusively based on a linear or undifferentiated trajectory. But interpretation and understanding of this totality entail that analysts must be prepared to go beyond the mere appearances inherent in the appurtenances of conventional life and constantly delve "below the surface" as a means of unearthing the real operative mechanisms that lie behind the veil of perceived reality and theoretical constructs.

Table 4.2: The Epistemological Transition

Conventional Wisdom	Alternative Vision
Disciplinarity	Transdisciplinarity
Idealist-Essencialist	Realist- Existentialist
Universal Truth	Cultural Interpretation
Either/Or	Both/And
Antagonism of Opposites	Dialectical Contradiction
Absolute Separation	Multiple Interconnections
Unproblematic Facts	Problematic Understanding
Homogenization	Heterogenization
Statis	Process Transformation
Closure	Permeability
Logical Time	Historical Time
Linear Evolution	Differentiated Growth
Individual Self	Dialogical Self
Value-neutrality	Value-endogeneity

Source: Author.

Phenomena that are apparently diametrically opposed to each other or mutually exclusive ("either/or," "idealist/essentialist") may turn out to be functionally interrelated or mutually reinforcing ("both/and," "realist/existentialist"). This is sometimes explained by the difference between "analytical" and "dialectical" concepts. The former are "arithmorphic," that is, they are like numbers and do not overlap, while the latter partially overlap (Georgescu-Roegen 1971). The epistemological and logical principle underlying dialectical relationships is that everything is inherently linked to its opposite by virtue of the very negativity that defines its own nature (Marcuse 1964; 1968). This principle of *self*-contradiction is apposite to the way in which concepts such as "development" and "underdevelopment" are interpreted.

As noted in Chapter 1, they are viewed in the conventional development discourse as distinct analytical categories that are in direct opposition to each other. In other words, they are typically located in divergent poles along a differentiated continuum of economic modernization and related institutional development. By contrast, dialectical contradiction interprets the same phenomena in terms of a simultaneous unity and conflict of opposites. Accordingly, the state of underdevelopment can be construed as a product of history, and latterly globalization, or as an integral part of the same process producing its putative opposite – development. While it goes against the grain of the conventional wisdom, this life-and-world vision helps to explain why (a) no teleology can be attributed to the development trajectory; and (b) the underlying patterns of change are not necessarily harmonious, linear, or unidirectional, but fraught with ambiguities, non-linearities, conflicts, and contradictions.

Hence, the transdisciplinary mode of interpretation is grounded in a recognition that non-equilibrium states are a rule rather than the exception. Interpretation and understanding of what we term the "diachronic kaleidoscope" of humanitarian development entails coming to grips with holistic processes or dimensions of human management that transcend the conventional preoccupation with the explanatory power of mechanical forces. Recognizing the inadequacy of modern equilibrium theory, several economists have used a biological analogy in order to project a comprehensive vision of processual change (see Kornai 1971; Shackle 1972; Elster 1989). In general, they show that discrete or individual events constitute only one element of the general map of human development, and that interpretation requires historical intuition, empathy, and social per- spective. In other words, and as previously emphasized, the world is made up of myriad complex processes rather than readymade, dis- crete, phenomena or quantitative measurements that can categori- cally freeze reality in space and time.

Others have tried to garner historical insight by drawing on the principles of Hegelian dialectics. Hegelian conflict is resolved through a moving synthesis or form of social organization in which the appearance of contradictions prevents society from remaining in a changeless state. These, in turn, induce societal changes, readjust- ments, fresh contradictions, further changes, and so on. The overall picture is one of an ongoing socio-economic evolution that is oriented toward maintaining human persons as full members of a species and improving their life chances. The dialectical underpinnings of this process imply that there is no necessary or uniform developmental sequence, but rather a continuous evolution or "emergence" that is capable of maintaining and stabilizing symbiotic regimes.

Critical Theory

A useful variation on this theme is provided by critical theory, which locates structural organization within the historical context of change. Each society is conceived as an exemplar of the way in which human agents interface with nature and are able to maintain their cultural practices. Like other research programs, such as modern structuralism and Marxism, critical theory purportedly provides an inspiration to those who have an interest in inducing changes in cultural patterns and the structure of social values. Pertinent to the focus on transdisciplinarity and the realist-existentialist perspective is the fact that critical theorists reject the epistemological underpinnings of positivism and stress the determining influence of the accepted cultural background.

Beginning in the 1920s, members of the Frankfurt School of critical theory had argued that the issue of understanding in the human and social sciences cannot be divorced from the larger problem of living in an age of technology in which traditional forms of understanding become problematic. They elaborated a contextual framework of reasoning that was designed to recover people's political and cultural energies which were thought to be suppressed by various forms of exploitation and domination. In the eyes of critical theorists, various forms positivism, scientism, and the context-free method on which they rely tend to distort both reality and our knowledge about it. Accordingly, they advocate a dialectical criticism of society based on a comprehensive interpretation of contemporary conditions.

According to Horkheimer (1982), critical theory begins with the theorist's awareness of his or her own partiality or subjectivity. Thus, theory is neither neutral nor objective. Its partisanship is traceable to its own goals: the attempt to reconstruct society on the basis of non-exploitative relations among people and the restoration of human beings to their central place in the evolution of human society as a self-conscious and self-managing subject of social reality. From this perspective, the world of perception is construed as a "product of human activity" and the object of cognition therefore becomes humanized nature. Thus, there can be no radical separation of subject from object, nor can the object be subsumed under the contemplative subject, as suggested by positivistic modes of analysis. Recognition of this enables us to look behind the alleged "facts" and distinguish the superficial from the essential without minimizing the significance of either.

Critical theory emphasizes the pivotal role of cultural values and ideology in giving meaning to, or *legitimating*, the social order. As such, it interprets social and economic struggles in terms of a contest between competing ideas and values, or between rival interpretations (paradigms) of social and economic reality. It does not deny that people interact with the physical world and that factors such as power and material interests at times determine the nature and direction of this interactive process. However, greater emphasis is placed on people's intentional activity and consciousness as central to the con- stitution of society and its potential for transformation. In the overall scheme of things, social life is interpreted as a process of historical transformation in which critical thinking plays a strategic role in enabling people to recognize and seize opportunities for liberation that may not directly reveal themselves in any given form of society.

In this context, a central theme of critical theory revolves around what is perceived to be pervasive forms of domination in modern life and how these are integrally connected with the manner in which the social system reproduces itself. Domination is thought to be reinforced by at least three interactive factors or processes: (i) the emergence and prevalence of "instrumental reason;" (ii) the increasing paramountcy of a "one-dimensional" culture in which people have been successively integrated into the system; and (iii) the development of a personality structure that is highly receptive to, and actually seeks, domination.

The motive force behind instrumental reason is thought to be provided by our perceptions of the world and the related theoretical framework of knowledge. Contextually, the instrumental worldview suggests that we tend to see the structures of society, including other people, as mere tools or instruments in the attainment of our ends. For example, critical theorists argue that in the evolution of modern capitalist society, human interactions have increasingly become rela- tions among things, in the sense that people have come to view them- selves and others as mere objects. This process has witnessed the "eclipse" of critical reason due to the growth of technological rationality, the idolatry of science, and the tendency to view nature as an instrument to be exploited rather than as a basic life-supporting system (Horkheimer 1974 [1947]; Adorno and Horkheimer 1972).

In modern society, it is argued, instrumental reason has become far removed from the choice of the ends of life, and fails to provide, as critical reason did in the past, a sound justification for the role of knowledge in freedom and human progress, for example, as happened during the European Enlightenment. The feeling is that such reason has been assigned to a level of "subjective consciousness" and has come to be defined by the "demand by an industrially advanced society that it look after its survival on an escalating scale of continually expanded technical control over nature and a continually refined administration of human beings" (Habermas 1973, 24). The point of emphasis is that when knowledge is equated with the successful control of human beings and nature, it can no longer remain neutral, objective, or disinterested with respect to its goals, but actually presupposes a particular kind of interest, that is, manipulation and control.

Critical theory in the hands of Jurgen Habermas interprets social processes in terms of wholes emerging from the modes of production encountered in different societies. His *Theory of Communicative Action* presents a comprehensive picture of the linkages between macro- and micro-processes based on several levels of structural interaction: the social system, cultural and institutional ordering of action, and the interpretive beliefs and practices of human agents. A central thesis is that the modern systemic order of markets and bureaucracies has "invaded" and "colonized" the "lifeworld," thereby blocking its ability to perform the essential role of reproducing society and socializing its members. The lifeworld represents a form of social order constituted by linguistic interaction, shared cultural knowledge, and a normative consensus.

The increasing independence of systems from the lifeworld is exemplified by the growing and widespread capacity of institutions of exchange, governance, and law to define the character of social relationships. Thus, it is argued, the historical evolution of modern social systems has resulted in a variety of dysfunctional structural effects and unintended consequences that are pathological in terms of the visible conditions of human reason, biological existence, and sociality. At the normative level, Habermas (1993) calls for a *discourse ethics*, or model of a deliberative, consent-oriented, dialogical approach, that can be used for resolving attendant political, social, and economic issues within a moral framework. Such discourse ethics can be viewed as a procedure for moral-practical reasoning which aims at establishing principles, norms, and institutional arrangements that can command the assent of all relevant parties.

Finally, we briefly address the emphasis placed by critical theory on the emergence of a "one-dimensional" culture, how it has been allegedly used for integration of people into the social system, and therefore guarantees the latter's perpetuation, or "social reproduction." A basic thesis is that the "culture industry" that has become pervasive in modern society has tended to "deform" the creative and collectively rational powers of human beings by successfully manipulating and controlling the most powerful artifacts and vehicles of cultural transmission – notably art, music, film, literature, the mass media and the information system in general. Considerations about so-called "high-brow" vis-à-vis "low-brow" culture aside, the pertinent claim is that the domination effect has been achieved by a "popular culture," which has produced an artificial or false need and security in people through a standardization of cultural products – television, soap operas, pop records, horoscopes, and even the kinds of literature audiences are encouraged to read. At a more fundamental level, one powerful explanation is provided by the fact that modern life is lived in an essentially mass-oriented society in which a symbiosis has been effected among lifestyles, ways of viewing the world, and mass media technologies that have become pervasive channels for informing, educating, and socializing large segments of the population.

One contention is that in their evolution, the powerful tools of the modern mass media have enjoyed a free and complementary relationship between their unique qualities and the Western cultures in which they have flourished, that is, the cultural demands of the mass media have helped to form the conceptual vocabulary of media practitioners while simultaneously determining the design of the tools. In turn, such tools in the hands of media practitioners have contributed toward shaping of the culture. At one level, therefore, it can be commented that development of the mass media – newspapers, magazines, books, journals, films, radio, and television – has marched in tandem with Western social evolution and, in a sense, has never been truly traumatic to the societies in question.

At another level, however, studies on mass media management and derivative consumption habits constantly point to the capacity of the mass communications system to manipulate the ideas, opinions, and emotions of its vast audiences. As a general proposition, the majority of people in society depend on what they read in the daily newspapers, or what radio and television commentators say, for their opinions. To the extent that this is true, people tend to function passively, by and large, and form their ideas, opinions, and even prejudices in a readymade fashion from the mass media. As a result, they are generally less prone to examine a number of alternative choices and make up their minds on an independent basis. In such a setting, and through the lens of critical theory, the conscious or unconscious misapplication of powerful media tools translate into the creation and nurturing of a society geared toward the renunciation of critical thinking and independent thought.

The manipulation of behavior, emotions, and ideas through the mass media has also been noticeable in several late-developing countries, especially those with authoritarian structures of government. When confronted with the reality of statehood as prescribed by the former colonial powers, many governments, especially in Africa, increasingly took on an authoritarian stance in their efforts to hold together arbitrarily drawn boundaries under which diverse peoples were compelled to live. Upon departure, the colonial powers succeeded in leaving behind an entire array of institutional structures, including mass media systems. These institutions, with some surface modifications, were to provide the major internal cohesive force during the post-colonial period. In authoritarian settings, mass media systems have been manipulated by dominant elites who use them as instruments for ideological propaganda and maintenance of the status quo.

A liberating role is usually played by journalists and throngs of media workers. Ideally, they should act as mediators between other groups by telling an objective and unbiased story about development reality to the public. Since they purportedly "have their eyes and ears on the ground," journalists and other reporters tend to be more perceptive and capable of identifying "missing variables" in development thinking and practice compared to academics, technical experts, central government officials, and technocrats of lending agencies. As such, they have been known to close the information gap or reduce the "coefficient of ignorance" by bringing to light some of the flagrant abuses of development – for example, mismanagement of resources, corruption, and environmental degradation.

In many instances, however, their expertise, observations, and insights are ignored or questioned, especially by academicians. The obvious reason is that journalistic accounts are not normally grounded in rigorous theoretical models. Politicians and policymakers often listen to journalists in order to grasp the ebb and flow of public opinion, but they are notorious for not tolerating dissenting voices or unfavorable reportage. Journalists and other media workers are sometimes perceived as *agents provocateurs* whose "biased" accounts and "meddling" could cause harm to the status quo and/or potentially derail the smooth, preferred, or mandated development trajectory. While foreign media personnel have been moving targets of political anger, the polity-media dissensus in most LDCs is largely traceable to the lack of a free press and other basic liberties.

Toward Conversation

A plea was made earlier for a more open-ended or inclusive "conversation" or multiplicity of creative dialogues between academic discourse and people's practical consciousness. The process involves a reversal of the distantiated mode of interpretation and understanding underlying the conventional development discourse. It has been driven by the iron-clad theoretical postulates emanating from the banks of the Thames (London), Cam (Cambridge), Cherwell (Oxford), Charles (MIT and Harvard), and Lake Laguna (Stanford). However, some of the development discourses that really matter continue to take place on the banks of the great rivers of the Tropics – the Nile, Zaire, Zambeze, Ganges, Demerara, and Amazon, to name a few, as well as under baobab, mango, and coconut trees. This suggests that authentic conversations start with people's self-interpretations, value systems, social organization, patterned arrangements governing their lives and livelihoods, or simply *metis* – the practical wisdom in Greek mythology that is supposed to have guided Odysseus on his journeys.

This entails an optimal sharing of human agency based on "dialogue" rather than "monologue," talking *with* people rather than *at* them, and a reduced predisposition to "put them 'off' or 'down'." Dialogical acts reflect people's ability and willingness to consort with one another through openness, trust, and shared understandings. They involve the capability of listening to other people's viewpoints and learning from the discourses of others. This is particularly true of the human "objects" or "outsiders" who have been traditionally denied effective *voice* in matters affecting their own well-being. In more general terms, the idea of a conversation stresses the pivotal role of discursive acts in knowledge, understanding, and human affairs.

Contextually, in his *Pragmatism*, William James posed a fundamental question about how we arrive at the "true" or "real," as well as the processes of thinking and naming that are involved. His answer was that "all human thinking gets discursified; we exchange ideas; we lend and borrow verifications, get them from one another and by means of social intercourse." Thus, a conversation enables us to merge different outlooks on the basis of communication and interpretation, and to work toward mutual understanding through continuous interaction. This is related to the fact, previously emphasized, that authentic development is plurivocal, that is, speaks with many voices.

Any enlightened conversation about authentic development should be grounded in a familiarity with and empathetic interpretation of the concrete insecurities and well-known aspirations for human betterment and liberation of disadvantaged groups living in all corners of the globe. In other words, it should reflect the strivings and hopes defining the lot of the jobless, homeless, poor farmers, those who are too old without adequate social security, and others such as women, children, adolescents, ethnic minorities, and aboriginal peoples who constantly face various forms of vulnerability. Yet, such cadres remain silent listeners to a well-scripted monologue that they are unable to decipher or fully comprehend.

A conversation may be portrayed through the metaphor of a play, drama, or dance. One implication is that we are all participants in a development story that can be interpreted through insights drawn from our acting out disparate roles in the drama of human or social life. The same is true for actors or players on a stage. An early insight was provided in Shakespeare's play *As You Like It* (Act 2, Scene VII), as follows:

All the world's a stage,
And all the men and women merely players;
They have their exits and their entrances,
And one man in his time plays many parts....

Plays are most successful when individual actors work in unison, and perceive themselves as cooperative members of an organic collectivity. The same is more or less true for dances, since each partner or participant is expected to move in step with others and execute his or her assigned role or part to the best of his or her ability. Such solidaristic action is the obverse of a situation in which each player is in conflict with, and/or constantly struggles against, his or her fellows in pursuit of personal ends or self-aggrandizement.

Plays, dramas, dances, and conversations are different from "games," and represent a more emancipatory genre. Here, reference may be made to the competitive ethos that lies at the heart of development orthodoxy, which is sometimes interpreted as an "international chess game." The ruling paradigm reflects an ideologically-charged archetype based on an implicit metaphor of a "race," or eventually a "rat race" – poor countries of the world must constantly try to "catch up" with the rich. Based on materialistic values, outcomes are typically evaluated in terms of a dire "win or perish" imagery, or a dualistic world that optimizes private lives and satisfactions. What is forgotten is that many would-be competitors are "non-competing" actors who are not afforded adequate incentives or the full equality of opportunity necessary for them to even show up at the starting line of the race. The moral of the story is that such races should be abolished altogether and replaced by more dances.

Anomalies, Tensions, And New Vistas

The call for more conversation and dances may seem to be too utopian and unrealistic, especially when juxtaposed against the plethora of national and international conferences, summits, symposia, and other meetings ostensibly designed to debate critical issues of international development. However, the experience suggests that the majority of these gatherings are veritable "talk-fests" that accomplish very little and cost too much. A widespread perception is that the main protagonists - academics, policymakers, government officials, think tanks, business leaders, donor agencies, NGOs, media interests, etc. - are wont to engage in endless talk: they talk, look for consensus or compromise, and then hold follow-up meetings to talk and talk again. But, are these genuine conversations or dances?

While we advocate the need for more dialogical acts, the multi-perspectives and divergent worldviews informing the various discourses continue to corroborate what is perceived as the self-referential nature of paradigms. In essence, the representatives of different sectors of interest seem to talk to themselves in a Global Game (what we have called an "international chess game") that is played through a house of mirrors. In other words, they typically project their own images and tend to see only their own reflections in the behaviors of others. A visible consequence is a one-way flow of attendant images and messages from the core cultural settings of North America and Europe to the more passive environments in LDCs. Furthermore, the transmission process and cascading effects have been facilitated in an age of Internet and information technology in which approximately 2 billion email messages cross national borders every day.

Through the lens of genuine conversation, the foreging image of development futures is not only flawed, but an emancipatory discourse calls for new perspectives, research agendas, and options. One important reason is that the ongoing debates or discourses are trapped in ideological polarities and corresponding assumptions, explicit and implicit, about appropriate development paths or styles. In a world where the "either/or" epistemological duality still rules the roost, the "conservative," "right wing," "libertarian," or "orthodox" automatically take precedence over their putative ideological opposites, and presumably inferior categories or options - the "liberal," "left-wing," and "heterodox" alternatives, as the case may be. The relatively closed mindsets and their absolutist orientations show little concern for the properties of synergistic development.

The development trajectories of a given country should be allowed to tilt in several alternative directions over time - for example, individualistic and communitarian, market-oriented and statist, export-oriented and inward-looking. Rather than being mandated to follow one uniform or linear path, it should be afforded the optimal freedom to move in one preferred direction, then another. A beneficial process of social learning will take place as it experiences successes and there is an emergence of problems that successive developmental orientations cannot solve. The paradigm shift toward authentic development is predicated on a learning process which shows how a country can best manage alternative development orientations, paths, or styles. Hence, the metaphor of conversation is guided by a "both/and" epistemological stance, which emphasizes the necessity of a retreat from ideological segmentation, and a concomitant need to embrace integrative development based on judicious melding of apparently competing ideologies.

A related consideration is that we live in a complex world of reality that is constituted by different memetic codes (value-orientations) or what are sometimes described as "cultural DNA codes." As alluded to above, this carries both descriptive and normative or evaluative significance, that is, the perpetual threat to compartmentalize the world into alternative ("superior" and "inferior") ideological and conceptual systems or boxes. What remains true, however, is that given its heterogeneity, different individuals and collectivities in the world find themselves at varying levels of psycho-biological growth or liberation. This is traceable to the differential influences of historical circumstances, unique conditions of life, socialization, and human capabilities.

As emphasized throughout this book, the sociosphere is not an undifferentiated locus of equal opportunities for all, or people hankering after one lifestyle. Rather, it represents variegated spheres in which inhabitants have developed priority memetic and cultural codes that can purportedly help them shape their worlds and adapt to changing conditions. The self-evident missive, or truism, is that no immanent or uniform model of change should be imposed on all humanity irrespective of the potency of different memetic and cultural codes. Correlatively, the idea of conversation or dialogue underscores the imperative of designing systems of thought and action based on cohesive principles and processes - the "intercultural ecology" mentioned earlier. The overriding implication for promoting alternative humanitarian development futures lies in the possibility of enabling all segments of humanity to coexist and participate, to the fullest extent possible, in the dynamics of their collective experience. This cannot be meaningfully achieved without creative and genuine attempts to meld the theoretical and practical discources enherent in diverse cultural settings.

In contention are the basic policy and methodological research agendas that should guide the study of development and change in the contemporary world order. One projects the imperative of devising interpretations and strategies that are simultaneously transformative, cohesive, integrative, and project a moral vision. The guiding premise inheres in a necessity to foster a conversation that effects creative balance among worldviews, that is, based on a search for a synthesis that is comprehensive enough to embrace human life in all its mani-

festations. Among other things, this new "dialogue among civilizations" would attempt to establish the variable parameters of
authentic development through the following alterations, among
others, in the received paradigm.

One relates to the necessity of establishing a symbiotic
relationship between the principles of scientific rationality (objective
reality) and the forces of internal psychological development (subjective reality) based not only on individualism but also shared
feelings, bonding mechanisms, and mutual resonances. Second, and
on a related basis, the logjam needs to be broken or fissures effectively closed between dominant perspectives of Western scientific
materialism and deep human values. This is exemplified by an emancipatory cosmopolitan ethic that is capable of providing solutions to
modern problems such as technological change, cloning of human
beings, and weapons of mass destruction. Third, evolutionary
possibilities underlying the complex world order require a melding of
"Individual," "collective" and "community" consciousness. This
entails merging prerequisites of individualism and autonomy with the
whole self-actualized human collective ranging from the family to
community, nation, globe, and cosmos.

The methodological, epistemological, and policy challenges are
further complicated by the fact that the pathways to change are highly
unpredictable. While the pace of change is much faster than in the
past, it normally reflects a dialectical unity of dynamic dislocation,
endemic patterns, and inertial forces. The processes of change depict
a variety of apparently contradictory or conflicting but unifying
events that occur simultaneously and are causally related. These have
been described under a variety of rubrics or heteronyms: *chaord* - a
fusion of "chaos" and "order" that purportedly defines the
contradictory tensions simultaneously pulling systems toward both
coherence and collapse; *fragmegration* - the processes of both
"fragmentation" and "integration" or disintegrative and integrative
forces occurring within and among institutions, communities,
countries, and other collectivities; and *glocalization* - the simultaneity
of globalization and local dynamics.

As analyzed elsewhere in the book, such polarities reflect the
endless series of tensions and ambiguities at several levels of human
interaction: between self and others, cultures and sub-cultures, universals and particulars, states and markets, national and transnational
systems, center and periphery, and so on. Moreover, each tension has

several configurations and takes different forms in different places, spaces, and institutions. They reflect the diverse ways in which people experience and attempt to overcome the tensions governing their lives. The causal factors are multifaceted, mutually reinforcing, and inhere in complex dynamics or non-linear processes. Hence, they cannot be explained, interpreted, or understood in terms of grand theories. The inter-causal links tend to cumulate over time, in the sense that some elements on one side of the polarity (orderly, integrative, local) typically produce others on the other side (chaotic, disintegrative, global), and vice-versa.

Part Two

Global Asymmetries
and
Human Deprivation

Chapter 5

The Global Development Antinomy

What emerges is an arresting picture of unprecedented human progress and unspeakable human misery, of humanity's advance on several fronts mixed with humanity's retreat on several others, of a breathtaking globalization of prosperity side by side with a depressing globalization of poverty. As is so common in human affairs, nothing is simple and nothing is fixed forever.

United Nations Development Programme (1994)

We are all willing or unwilling participants in a materially wealthy world system that is prone to generate varying degrees of inequality and human deprivation. Despite highly laudable improvements in people's life chances throughout the globe, several centrifugal forces have apparently gathered momentum at the expense of sustainable human development. These have cumulated into what may be interpreted as a fundamental *antinomy* of giant proportions. The *Shorter Oxford Dictionary* defines an "antinomy" as a "paradox, a contradiction in a law, ... or between conclusions that seem equally logical, reasonable and necessary." The paradoxical results tend to mirror the undesirable consequences for individual and collective human welfare that are inherent in systemic conflicts at the global, national, and local levels.

As emphasized in the previous chapter, the situation reflects a multiplicity of inter-causal linkages and heterogeneous processes that are riven with tensions, ambiguities, and contradictions. They are intimately bound up with visible profiles of vertical and horizontal inequality, or the polarization that has been structuring what is ostensibly a dualistic global society and its underlying power structure. Its contours are being continuously shaped and reconfigured to reflect a classic picture of unequal exchange and uneven development: rich nations, what are known as "emerging markets," upper classes and ruling elites constituting a relatively prosperous global market sector at one end of the spectrum; but with millions of people in the less developed sector of the world remaining largely untouched by the globalization of prosperity, at the other end.

Global Hierarchies and Power Structure

Society at both national and international levels is by and large hierarchically structured and vertically integrated. The imbalances have been associated with an increasing concentration of resources, wealth, and opportunities among a relatively few countries, people, and corporations. At the top of the hierarchy stand the Group of Seven (G-7) nations, which have only 12 percent of the world's population but account for about 64 percent of its gross domestic product (GDP). The larger group of high-income countries of the Organization of Economic Cooperation and Development (OECD) account for only 19 percent of the world's population, but are responsible for 71 percent of global trade in goods and services, 58 percent of direct foreign investment, and about 91 percent of all Internet users. In 1998, the United States was instrumental in creating the G-22 group – consisting of the G-7 and 15 other countries drawn from the largest "emerging markets" – to review the global financial system following the Asian financial crisis. This enlarged group has about 65 percent of the world's population and accounts for about 82 percent of global GDP.

Approximately 35 percent of the world's population lives in the G-24 group of major LDCs, but its members account for only 9 percent of world income. The remaining 134 "G-77" nations remain at the bottom of the pyramid. They contain 76 percent of the world's population, but control only about 17 percent of its aggregate income. Hence, despite rapidly changing patterns of institutional differentiation at the global level, the picture remains one of a "core" majority of late or less developing countries with relatively little power, status, and prestige in the increasingly stratified sociosphere.

The overarching institutional order is suffused by a "power structure," which ultimately determines the life chances of people throughout the globe. Needless to say, power is a multidimensional concept, with different components and origins. The underlying structural relations may be described at several levels of specificity, depending on how they actually manifest themselves. Three broad but overlapping categorizations are utilized below. First, one broad classification reflects the fact that, over the centuries, factors such as geopolitics, military strength, commodity production, international trade, and resource transfers have become mutually supportive activities that tend to produce and reproduce one another.

From this perspective, the traditional viewpoint identifies the following basic components: (i) forms of *physical violence*, such as utilized by armies, police forces, informal groups, and even individual political extremists and so-called "terrorists;" (ii) *economic power* derived from the possession of relatively scarce resources. This may take the form of (a) a capability of marshalling and strategically utilizing technological, financial, and human resources (education, skills, etc.), as exemplified by advanced OECD nations; and/or (b) scarce natural resources such as oil, the most prominent example being the "commodity power" wielded by the oil-rich sheikdoms of the Middle East; (iii) another form of *economic power*, such as that wielded by financial institutions and TNCs; (iv) the power of *custom* or *law*, sometimes recognized as a legitimate basis for certain types of behavior: and (v) the power of ideas which, as indicated earlier, helps to explain the tenacity of certain dominant ideologies and paradigms (Timbergen 1976).

A second way of looking at the matter is in terms of the unequal distribution of status, power, prestige, and access to opportunity in the asymmetric world order. In this context, a country's *economic status* in the sociosphere can be said to depend on the cumulative interplay of strategic factors such as national income attainment, level of technological development, as well as extensiveness and depth of its industrialization process. Economic status bears a strong positive relationship to *economic power* which, as alluded to above, is also a very complex phenomenon. It connotes an ability to exploit a wide range of economic and technological opportunities, as well as a given country's capacity to penetrate and maintain control over world resources and markets. Both economic status and power are inextricably linked to international financial prowess, which is defined by the depth of a country's system of financial intermediation and its corresponding control over global monetary and financial flows.

A close and positive correlation also exists between economic strength and the polity. In this context, *political status* refers to a country's level of constitutional development. In essence, this reflects its national autonomy and corresponding ability to exercise control over its own political destiny. This entails freedom to formulate policies and exercise discretionary power over the national decision-making process. It also connotes a capacity to respond effectively to unforeseen economic, social, and political crises. These conditions, combined with military might, tend to determine the nature of a country's *political power*. The latter is reflected by its bargaining prowess in the world, and its ability to influence the decision-making environment and development outcomes in other countries.

The dynamic processes of interaction among the economic, financial, political, and military spheres tend to determine a country's international *prestige*, which is a broad measure of its "social status" in the global hierarchy. In general, this reflects the extent to which people in the less developed sector of the world have been willing to embrace others in geographically distant lands in North America and Europe as their "reference group" countries. High status or reference group countries purportedly boast value systems, social norms, lifestyles, and consumption patterns that have come to determine individual and collective behavior patterns in relatively low status ones. Historically, the diffusion process has been fuelled by diverse mechanisms such as imperialism and colonialism, international trade, cultural penetration, and dimensions of imitative behavior.

An important variation on the theme of power differentials is provided in Professor Joseph Nye's recent tour-de-force: *The Paradox of American Power* (2002). He identifies three forms of power – "hard," "soft," and "dispersed." The differentiation is one of degree, and relies on behavior and the deployment of power resources. Both facets mirror the ability of one country or international actor to achieve its own goals by influencing or manipulating the behavior of others. This results in what Nye calls "command power" or "the ability to change what others do through coercion or inducement;" and "co-optive power" or "the ability to shape what others want." The latter depends on the "attractiveness of one's culture or ideology," or the ability to manipulate the "agenda of political choices" of others.

Forms of behavior and resources associated with command and co-optive power range along a continuum: command power, coercion, inducement, agenda setting, attraction, co-optive power. Military and economic power exemplify hard command power that can be used as inducements or threats to others to change their positions or agendas. By contrast, the deployment of soft power is usually more indirect. It co-opts people rather than coerce them. As indicated earlier, a country may obtain the outcomes it desires in the global political economy because it functions as a "reference group" country, that is, others admire its values and wish to imitate them. These go beyond mere cultural penetration or transmission, and may encapsulate an array of values used to influence the preferences of others – for example, democracy at home, "listening to others" in international institutions, and promoting peace and human rights in foreign policy.

The distribution of hard and soft power indicates an enormous disparity between the United States of America and the rest of the world. Besides its lead in military expenditure, America's gross domestic product (GDP) of $10.2 trillion in 2001 accounted for about 33 percent of global GDP ($31.2 trillion). This share was more than the GDP attainment of the next four major countries combined – Japan ($4.2 trillion), Germany ($1.9 trillion), the United Kingdom ($1.4 trillion), and France ($1.3 trillion) [see World Bank 2003]. America's colossal economic power is also manifested in the corporate sector. Of the largest 100 corporations in the world, 59 are American, 31 are European, and 7 are Japanese. This reality reflects the fact that private business has undoubtedly emerged as the most powerful form of organization on a global scale. In particular, transnational corporations (TNCs) dominate the global system, and their awesome economic power has become an essential symbol of the inexorable logic that guides the free enterprise system. We return to this subject below.

At another level, America's soft power remains a predominant force because of the global reach of its culture. A main example is the intense consumerism that has apparently become an indispensable cultural trait of modern mass society and especially the more "moneyed" regions of the world. In this regard, the successive transnationalization of American consumer culture continues to produce a growing and irreversible influence on tastes, preferences, and lifestyles throughout the planet. Global advertising through subliminal images is an integral part of a silent revolution designed to create a "global village" whose inhabitants tend to internalize not only American-style consumerism, but also related moral and political ideals. What seems to be sold is not so much a variety of consumer goods, but more a way of life predicated on consumerism.

Even more significant for the escalation of soft power has been the apparent rise of culture as a profitable commodity. The "commodification of culture" has intensified people's proclivity to identify it with goods that can be bought and sold in the marketplace – for example, crafts, tourism, literature, music, and films. The past two decades or so have witnessed a manifold increase of world trade in commodities with a cultural content – printed matter, music, visual arts, cinema and photographic, radio and television equipment. In the case of the United States, the single largest export industry nowadays is entertainment, mainly in the form of Hollywood films, music, and television, rather than aircraft, computers, or automobiles, as is commonly believed. The U.S.–led global spread of new technologies has provided a major catalyst for the growth of trade in cultural products. The corresponding rise in satellite communications technology has been a powerful vehicle for the global reach of transnational media networks such as CNN. Development of the Internet over an expanded telecommunications infrastructure has also been an important mechanism for transmitting American culture around the world.

Needless to say, considerable controversy has surrounded the global influence of Hollywood, CNN, and the Internet. In general, while the spread of ideas, images, and information enriches the world, there is a risk of reducing cultural concerns to protecting what can be bought and sold, neglecting community, custom, and tradition. A related concern is that while American television and films purportedly promote the virtues of capitalism, freedom, and change, they are morally suspect when it comes to the portrayal of explicit sex and violence. American values such as liberty and freedom may be attractive to some people but repulsive to others, especially fundamentalists. Our brands of feminism, open sexuality, and individual choice are profoundly subversive of the value-orientations encountered in traditional and patriarchal societies.

Even more crucial is that disparities in the distribution of hard and soft power have implications for our worldviews and related preferences for particular foreign policy options. The collapse of the erstwhile Soviet Union and America's subsequent rise as the only "superpower" have led some analysts to view the world in "uni-polar" rather than "bi-polar" terms. However, in Nye's eyes, this view should be tempered by the fact that power is distributed among countries in a pattern that resembles a "complex three-dimensional chessboard." The top echelon is uni-polar due to the military power of the United States. The middle rung constitutes what is termed a "hybrid multi-polar" world. This claim is justified on at least three grounds.

First, China, as the world's most populous country, is likely to emerge as a major challenger to American hegemony. While the American twentieth of the world's population now represents more than half of Internet users, Chinese will probably become the dominant language on the Internet in a decade or so. The prognosis is that while English may not be dethroned as the lingua franca, the Asian cyber-network may loom larger than its American counterpart in the not too distant future. Some scholars envision a Russia-China-India coalition as a potential threat. Second, economic power is thought to be multi-polar because the United States, Japan, and Europe collectively generate about two-thirds of gross world product or income. Third, continued growth of the European Union (EU) tends to suggest that the United States must increasingly bargain on equal terms with its European partners. At the bottom of the three-dimensional chessboard stands "a realm of transnational relations" that is outside the control of nation states or governments. It encapsulates a panoply of non-state actors – ranging from bankers electronically transferring sums larger than most national budgets at one end of the spectrum to terrorist attacks, at the other end.

In this context, transnational corporations (TNCs) have been playing a predominant role in the rapidly globalizing world economy. Some of the largest TNCs command more economic power than several nations do. Their total corporate sales and financial assets exceed by far the national income or output of the majority of poor countries. Estimates by the UNCTAD (2002) provide the following picture. The 65,000 TNCs existing in 2001 had about 850,000 foreign affiliates across the globe, with the latter accounting for about 54 million employees. Their total sales of almost \$19 trillion were more than twice as high as world exports, with foreign affiliates accounting for about one-tenth of global GDP and one-third of world exports. The evidence also suggests that TNCs have been growing in size at rates exceeding those of many economies. While global GDP at current prices increased 1.5 times between 1990 and 2001, the sales of the largest 500 firms in the world nearly tripled during this period. Moreover, TNCs would account for even larger shares of global aggregates if the value of their worldwide activities associated with non-equity relationships (such as, international subcontracting and licensing) were to be taken into account.

The Bretton Woods Policy Paradigm and Global Justice

By the end of the Second World War, the consolidated efforts of the major powers to promote national economic progress and global economic productivity took place within an institutional framework known as the Liberal International Economic Order (LIEO). The concept, while based on a recognition of the central importance of national sovereignty and political autonomy, was also predicated on the fact that international economic policies and inter-governmental organizations exist in the sociosphere to advance the cooperative and mutual interests of states on a fair and reciprocal basis. The struggle for international distributive justice during the early post-war years and after was largely waged within the institutional context of the LIEO. The subsequent experience has given rise to the contention that it was created not so much as a mechanism to promote global justice and fairness but more as a tool, or set of agreements, to protect the stability of international economic relations.

In particular, many LDCs have accused its members of mainly serving the interests of advanced nations or, at the very least, preserving an unfair game or race in which the cards are stacked in favor of the rich. Proper assessment of this ongoing claim ultimately depends on how one views its institutional pillars. As mentioned earlier, these include: (i) the three organizations emanating from the Bretton Woods Agreement of 1944 – the International Monetary Fund (IMF), the International Bank for Reconstruction and Development (IBRD or World Bank), and the General Agreement on Tariffs and Trade (GATT), which came into existence in 1947 and took on many of the functions intended for the International Trade Organization (ITO). The

World Trade Organization (WTO) became a successor to GATT in 1995; and (ii) the United Nations (UN) system, which was established as a separate institution in 1945.

Our primary focus is on the "Bretton Woods trio," which have functioned as a "global public sector" (GPS). This entails that they have been granted or otherwise abrogated powers to decide the nature and direction of global economic governance. In this context, they typically set the rules of the game and settle disputes within and among nations on a whole host of economic and financial matters. For this reason, both the LIEO and its Bretton Woods infrastructure have been viewed as an international regime. In general, regimes are defined as formal and informal principles, rules, and norms within specific issue areas (Krasner 1984). Since compliance is usually voluntary, the principles, rules, and norms are not strictly enforced. Nevertheless, regimes typically provide enough beneficial inducements to elicit conformity. As institutions based on fixed rules and consensual behavioral guidelines and procedures, regimes, at least in the eyes of their creators, boast the advantage of coordinating numerous state and non-state activities. As such, they purportedly reduce uncertainty and obviate the need for costly and time-consuming negotiations among international actors.

The significance of regimes, as filters of international behavior, has generated a significant body of literature on their creation and maintenance. A central theme has centered around the thesis of hegemonic stability (Krasner 1984, 38). The idea is that a powerful state or "hegemon" is required to provide effective leadership. Regimes of free trade and the gold standard developed more or less unconsciously under British hegemony. The Bretton Woods system has represented a much more purposeful approach to institutional creation and maintenance, which was inaugurated under the subsequent American hegemony. It was established after long negotiations between the older and newer hegemons and basically reflected their vision of what was good for the world, that is, what could help transform the post-war environment especially in the interests of the United States.

The Fund, Bank, and Washington Consensus

The purposes of the Fund (IMF), as set out in Article 1 of its Articles of Agreement, were six-fold: international monetary cooperation; expansion and balanced growth of international trade; promotion of exchange rate stability; promotion of a multilateral system of payments; mitigation of disequilibria in balance of payments; and provision of resources and liquidity when needed for these purposes. In the same Article, a fundamental objective of the Fund was defined as "the promotion and maintenance of high levels of employment and real income and the development of productive resources of all members."

A dire economic atmosphere was created during the 1920s and 1930s when conditions of mass unemployment, deflation, competitive currency devaluations, collapse of commodity prices, crashes of stock exchanges, and protectionist beggar-thy-neighbor policies ruled the roost. In the eyes of influential policymakers, the cures revolved around the following radical policy options: full employment in place of mass unemployment; fixed but adjustable exchange rates to avert currency chaos; rule-governed trade expansion as a substitute for nationalistic protectionism; and commodity stabilization in the face of collapsing commodity prices. In particular, the objective of full employment was in line with the Keynesian vision of full employment. The Great Depression of the 1930s gave rise to Keynesian analysis, which contradicted its orthodox or conservative counterpart. The most influential script became *The General Theory of Employment, Interest and Money* (1936) by John Maynard Keynes, the British economist who was also an architect of the Bretton Woods system.

The original intent was that the Fund would exercise supervision symmetrically over all member countries, but inevitably concentrate its attention on the financially powerful ones. The premise was that their actions mattered more than those of small or poor countries. But, as further discussed below, things turned out differently. A combination of debt crises, successive oil shocks, deteriorating terms of trade, and slower growth in the world economy has driven poorer member countries to increasingly depend on the Fund. The economies of most LDCs are now or have been under Fund conditionality, which reflects a neo-liberal agenda. At the same time, its supervisory powers over the rich and powerful members have more or less decreased.

The primary purpose of the World Bank was to cover the expected demand for credit during the post-war period for the "reconstruction" of war-damaged Europe, Japan, and East Asia, as well as "development" of both Latin America and colonies in Africa, Asia, and the Caribbean that were on the verge of political independence. The lion's share of the daunting task of reconstruction was taken over by the United States under the Marshall Plan and other generous aid programs. This enabled the Bank to concentrate on development, which became its exclusive task. To some extent, history has repeated itself, since the Bank is now involved with reconstruction of the Gaza strip and may be called upon to undertake similar activities in war-torn countries such as the Congo, Angola, and Mozambique.

In the case of development, a major objective of the United States (as hegemon) was to ensure that loans channeled to poor countries were used productively and repaid on a timely basis. This was to ensure that the bankruptcies and financial debacles of the 1930s were not repeated. Hence, the Bank's Articles of Agreement mandated that the proper use and repayment of loans should be guaranteed by governments of recipient countries. Furthermore, the Bank was only allowed to provide development loans for "productive" projects, such as roads and dams, and not for hospitals, schools, or housing; and then, only if private creditors, such as foreign corporations and commercial banks, were not willing to finance such projects on favorable terms. Hence, Bank credit was expected to complement private foreign investment. This lending approach was synergistic with the ruling development paradigm of the day, which emphasized a necessary connection between investment and economic growth.

This approach to development lending partly explains why the erstwhile Soviet Union, one of the participants in the Bretton Woods Conference, refused to ratify the Bank's Articles of Agreement. In its eyes, the institution had degenerated into an instrument of U.S. superpower interests, that is, "it was no more than a branch office of Wall Street" (Mason and Asher 1973, 29). The controversial issue remains whether the Bank can still be perceived as purely an instrument of power, ensuring the consolidation of U.S. interests in the less developed sector of the world. Whatever the stance one takes on this issue, it remains true that decisions about the allocation or refusal of loans to potential borrowers are usually influenced by the highly skewed voting power of the main shareholders of the Bank's constitutive capital – the United States and other rich industrial nations.

In this regard, one should be reminded that the national governments and private investors that lend money to the Bank are not usually motivated by humanitarianism. Related to this is the fact that borrowers' notes from the Bank represent one of the most secure capital investments in the world and carry a fairly good rate of interest. While it remains an inter-governmental (public) institution, the Bank has to borrow on private capital markets and make loans with an amortization period of 10 to 15 years, and at an interest rate of approximately 8 percent.

By the late 1950s, it was realized that on account of the massive growth in development lending many cash-strapped LDCs could no longer meet the conditions of the Bank's normal loans unless it could provide additional funds on "softer" terms. The International Development Association (IDA) was founded in 1960 for this purpose. In essence, it is a special fund of the Bank to provide loans to the least developed countries on favorable terms – the loans are essentially interest free (only an administrative fee of 0.75 percent is levied) and do not have to be repaid for 50 years. Considering what poor borrowers would have to pay in order to receive loans on the same scale under normal business conditions, IDA loans have a considerable "gift" or grant element.

A special feature of IDA, in contrast to the Bank itself, is that it receives its capital exclusively in the form of general tax funds from the wealthy industrial powers and a few OPEC (Organization of Petroleum Exporting Countries) nations. Hence, it is always dependent on the goodwill of governments, which must provide several billion dollars every three years for IDA replenishment. The U.S. Congress was instrumental in funding IDA with a great commitment in 1960. America provides more than one-third of the funds for IDA which by law is not allowed to make any loans whatsoever without American participation. But the experience suggests that the main contributor poses a serious threat to IDA's existence by opposing further funding at times of replenishment. The main domestic economic reasons typically given by members of Congress have included: the budget deficit, worsening of U.S. balance of payments, a feeling that the United States would profit less from IDA projects, and a disenchantment with development policy in general.

The Bank has always been plagued by the dilemma of how it could convince Congress, which authorizes funds for IDA, about its pivotal role in development without jeopardizing the Bank's inter-governmental function of promoting the overall interests of all its members, and especially the rich nations. This is part of a much larger problem of legitimacy and reaching consensus among its members. Right up to the early 1970s, it was perceived as a rather conservative institution that behaved more like a private "bank" providing investment for development. As indicated earlier, its policies were based on the ruling paradigm of the 1940s and 1950s which viewed "development" as being coterminous with export-oriented growth based on high levels of capital formation or investment.

Moreover, the Bank drew criticism for its policy of not giving loans to those LDCs that deviated from the straight and narrow path of private enterprise, but rather relied on building up state-owned Industries. Its bad image was depicted in the following terms (Mason and Asher 1973, 478-79):

> As one reviews the history of the Bank, taking into account the predominant ideology of the directors representing countries having a majority of votes (and for much of the twenty-five years, the ideology of management itself), one must in all fairness concede a measure of validity to the left-wing criticism. The way in which the ideology has been shaped confirms in significant degree to the interests and conventional wisdom of its principal stockholders. International competitive bidding, reluctance to accord preferences to local suppliers, emphasis on financing foreign exchange costs, insistence on a predominant use of foreign consultants, attitudes toward public sector industries, assertions of the right to approve project managers – all proclaim the Bank to be a Western capitalist institution.

While this perception lingers on, the climate of opinion shifted at the margin when Robert McNamara, a former United States Secretary of Defense, became President of the Bank. For example, his two early books: *The Security of the West: Threat and Defense* (1967) and *One Hundred Countries, Two Billion People* (1971) suggest that he underwent a measure of change. He came to believe that *security* of the West, as a guiding principle, could no longer be guaranteed in the Third World by military means, but rather through employment of capital to promote economic growth and social development. Contextually, the widespread social misery of the masses was viewed as a primary cause of revolutions and internecine conflicts. Under the circumstances, there was a *political rationale* for the rich to do something about poverty in LDCs – for example, through a more just distribution of land and other assets, as well as greater participation of medium-sized and small farmers in the growth process.

McNamara is said to have "discovered" poverty at the now historic meeting of the governors of the World Bank (finance ministers of member countries) held at Nairobi, Kenya, in September 1973. There he proclaimed that the future strategy would be based on improving the lot of the 700 million people living in poverty in LDCs. He noted that, hitherto, economic growth had by and large bypassed the "lower 40 percent of the population." Details of the new strategy for "growth with redistribution" and "investment in the poor" were outlined in a series of policy papers dealing with pertinent topics such as rural development, agricultural credit, land reform, rural enterprise, and non-farm employment. However, projects designed to promote small-scale agriculture, rural development, and redistribution had mixed results for a number of reasons highlighted in Chapter 7 below.

By the early 1980s, the global economy was in disarray and the external environment facing poor countries had worsened significantly compared to previous years. Escalating oil prices, burgeoning balance of payments deficits, the crushing burden of external debt, and abrupt cuts in foreign aid brought several of them to the brink of economic collapse. To avoid total collapse, many countries came to depend on new loans from the Bank and Fund as the primary, and sometimes sole, avenue of new capital. In order to meet the critical demand for such capital injection into poor countries, the Bank and Fund shifted the focus of their operations to what now goes under the general rubric of growth-oriented "structural adjustment" or "policy-based" lending. The new emphasis on structural adjustment programs (SAPs) rested on the untested preconception that borrowing countries could "grow" out of their stagnation by using concessional finance from the GPS.

The adjustment loans were based on specific sets of monitorable and stringent conditionalities, reflecting a mandated array of economic objectives, measurable targets, and policy instruments to be satisfied during periods of loan negotiation and/or disbursement. A summary is provided in Table 5.1 for ease of reference. As indicated, the policy measures form the bedrock of what is known as the "Washington consensus" (Williamson 1990). It reflects a global convergence of orthodox economic theory and practice into a standard Bretton Woods policy paradigm, or a framework of policy reform based on injunctions to borrowers to "marketize, liberalize, and tighten their belts."

Table 5.1: The Washington Consensus

Policy Objectives	Policy Instruments
INTERNAL BALANCE	Demand restraint through monetary, fiscal and pricing policies
Macroeconomic Balance	Expenditure reduction by aligning domestic absorption with national income/output
Budget Balance	Greater fiscal discipline through tax and expenditure reforms
Credit Restraint	Ceilings on government borrowing from the banking system and external sources
Financial Reform	Liberalization based on market-determined interest rates and expanded financial intermediation
Pricing Reform	Price liberalization by raising domestic prices to international levels
EXTERNAL BALANCE	Balance-of-payment equilibrium through expenditure switching – changes in relative prices
Exchange Rate Reform	Devaluation of domestic currency and introduction of competitive exchange rates to induce export-led growth
Trade Reform	Liberalization through elimination of quantitative restrictions and introduction of a uniform tariff structure
Investment Reform	Liberalization of private foreign investment by eliminating barriers to entry facing foreign firms and enabling them to compete with their local counterparts
Marketization of Economy	Reform of incentive structure through deregulation, privatization of state-owned enterprises, and reducing the role of the activist state

Source: Author

While the typical adjustment program is conceived in a single country context, the uniform policy paradigm has been imposed on all capitals of borrowing countries on pain of international ostracism or penury. The Bretton Woods twins have been doggedly applying the standard remedy or blueprint for problems facing all borrowers. The process of homogenization has been marketed under the powerful rubric "There Is No Alternative" (TINA), which is more or less accepted by governments of borrowing countries desperate for external finance. In general, interactions between the Bank, Fund, and borrowers have frequently conjured up images of multilateral lending agencies that produce professionally written reports based on an impeccable economic logic, but not widely shared with the local people.

The first generation of SAPs focused almost exclusively on attainment of standard economic objectives such as efficient growth, macroeconomic balance, price stability, and balance of payments equilibrium. Very little systematic thinking was given to human development goals such as employment creation, poverty redressal, and distributive equity.

Neither was sufficient attention paid to the possibilities of countering the adverse effects and minimizing the human, social, and political costs of SAPs. From the very inception, however, the following types of key unanswered questioned were evident: (i) how could the mandated belt-tightening, economic austerity, and cutbacks in spending be effectively introduced? (ii) how could any detrimental effects on long-term growth be minimized or avoided? and (iii) whose living standards would be reduced?

The basic problem revolved around the possibility of broadening the focus of SAPs so that a stable macroeconomic environment could be established while protecting the minimum needs of the population. This perspective formed the focal point of the UNICEF-sponsored basic needs approach to development, or "adjustment with a human face" (Cornia, Jolly, and Stewart 1987). Among other things, the approach stresses the importance of reallocating resources based on priority human needs. Such "restructuring" was deemed to be clearly essential if resources channeled to vulnerable groups were to be protected or even augmented in a situation of general resource scarcity. Other members of the United Nations family urged the BWIs to incorporate long-term development concerns, such as adequate funding for social sectors, human resource development, and the biophysical environment in the design of SAPs (UNECA 1989).

In its response to the claim by UNICEF and other critics that SAPs had led to cuts in social sector spending, especially in health and education, the World Bank pointed out that several intensely adjusting countries, notably Ghana and Kenya, had actually increased total per capita spending in the social sector. However, its *Third Report on Adjustment Lending* (World Bank 1992a) concedes that total social sector spending was often maintained at the expense of "excessive cuts" in related operations and maintenance, resulting in "schools without teaching materials, health clinics without drugs and supplies." The effects of reduced expenditure on operations and maintenance included dilapidated infrastructure, "leading to serious deterioration in the efficiency of personnel and the quality of basic social services." The World Bank also admits that adjustment lending has seldom placed a high priority on improved delivery of such services.

A related issue concerns the impact of SAPs on poverty groups. Besides the perennial issue of statistical measurement (see Chapter 7), one difficulty relates the counterfactual question: would adjustment programs have resulted in a specific profile of poverty that would not have come about without them? Here it may be useful to note that the philosophy of adjustment rested on a presupposition that income losses, unemployment, and poverty could have become much more severe at a later date if the prevailing pre-adjustment economic conditions were allowed to continue. While the nature of impacts have varied across regions and countries, adjustment policies and specific policy instruments do not have unambiguous or uniform consequences for all poverty groups (UNCTAD 1994; Stewart 1995). This subject is further discussed in Chapter 6.

What remains true, however, is that SAPs seem to have put the poor at risk. Their living standards have been eroded by measures that raise the prices of basic consumer goods – for example, the effect of devaluation on the prices of "wage goods" such as basic food items. In some instances, however, devaluation and other export promotion measures have been responsible for creating a variety of employment opportunities and, depending on the distribution of ownership rights, have raised incomes of certain smallholder farmers. The removal of price controls has raised living costs, but in many instances consumers already paid decontrolled or market-related prices in the parallel market. Measures such as the reduction or elimination of government subsidies for food and increased user costs for transportation, electricity, and other basic services have also produced negative impacts on the cost of living via increased prices and reduction in the quality of services. Moreover, indirect taxes designed to reduce budget deficits are usually passed on in the form of higher prices for many products traditionally purchased by poverty groups.

Many second generation adjustment programs have included measures for reducing the negative impacts on poverty and income distribution that may result from mandated changes in public expenditure patterns. The "new" emphasis has been on carefully targeting programs toward intended beneficiaries by providing "social safety nets" through compensatory schemes designed to offset adjustment losses and protect vulnerable groups. But, such programs highlight the potential conflict that might arise between easing the adverse impact of adjustment on the one hand, as distinct from counteracting the effects of desired reforms, on the other. If a positive contribution is to be made to human welfare, the expected benefits (for example, in terms of income maintenance, infrastructural development, and improved social services) must in some sense outweigh the negative effects of countering adjustment reforms.

Since different groups and perspectives are involved, no single criterion can be used to evaluate the success or failure of measures designed to mitigate the social costs of adjustment. Some commentators believe that such initiatives are no more than incremental schemes of piece-meal social and economic engineering. While development objectives such as social equity and poverty eradication now have the official backing of the BWIs, the argument is that the standard economic objectives, policy instruments, and supporting technical criteria seem to have changed only at the margin. However, an emerging difference between the IMF and World Bank may be mentioned. On a qualitative basis, the hard core of programs backed by the IMF has not changed in any significant manner. In this case, fiscal and monetary restraint, combined with exchange rate devaluation, remain central to conditionality. By contrast, the World Bank now avidly champions the pivotal role of human and social policy based on robust social safety nets.

This may be interpreted as a forerunner to a newly emerging outlook, or what is nowadays called the "post-Washington consensus." For example, Joseph Stiglitz, the former Chief Economist of the World Bank, has challenged the "Washington consensus" in the following terms:

> The Washington consensus advocated use of a small set of instruments ... to achieve a relatively narrow goal (economic growth). The post-Washington consensus recognizes both that a broader set of instruments are necessary and that our goals are also much broader (Stiglitz 1998b, 31).

More generally, the World Bank now emphasizes the imperative of widening development goals beyond the traditional economic ones mentioned earlier. In many public speeches, its President – James Wolfensohn – has paid lip service to "comprehensive development," "societal development," or a concept of well-being encompassing basic human rights, literacy, good health, environmental integrity, and adequate incomes. As further elaborated in the Bank's Conference report on the *Frontiers of Development Economics* (Meier and Stiglitz 2001), a number of heretofore neglected items must be incorporated into a person's quest for well-being.

Many, such as reasonably clean air, feelings of participation and community, and an atmosphere of security and trust within and among nations, are indivisible, difficult to measure, and have the quality of "global public goods." The more comprehensive goals of development are a challenge to development economists to broaden their horizons and craft a new body of theory, or at least modify existing theory, and integrate it with those workable dimensions of neo-classical development economics in order to make it more compatible with human capabilities and development potentials. Apposite to a basic preconception underlying our humanitarian development paradigm, such a reinterpretation requires a transdisciplinary mode of analysis. It entails that greater attention should be paid to the contributions of other social scientists and humanistic theorists, such as historians, neo-institutional economists, anthropologists, sociologists, political scientists, ethicists, and political philosophers.

The GATT-WTO System and North-South Relations

Historically, how countries treat each other in international trade has always reflected the pressing need of sovereign nations to develop some inter-state mechanism for allocation of control and authority in order to maintain a system of order. A recurrent theme has been that trade liberalization has to be deliberately pursued and enhanced. The main reason, confirmed by experience, is that free trade is not a natural state of affairs and trade warfare has to be averted by some form of multilateral surveillance. As previously mentioned, it was in this context that the WTO was created as a successor to GATT, which itself was given many of the functions that were to have been the responsibility of the ITO.

Ever since the early days of decolonization, and especially since the mid-1970s, LDCs (the South) have been making constant demands to improve the terms and conditions of trade with rich industrial countries (the North). The fundamental issue has always centered around the possibilities for authentic development in a liberalized global economy. Misgivings and public unease were visibly expressed at the WTO meetings held at Seattle in 1999 and later in other international gatherings. Implicit in such warning signals is the search for a new model through coordination around a guidance system of global justice and populism. If it is true that such a model is the only one congenial to sustainable human development, then a question arises about efforts to reform the global trading system.

Pressures stemming from inexorable global megatrends and the new rules of the game have signaled the necessity for all LDCs to climb on to the mandated bandwagon of trade liberalization and export-oriented growth, successively dismantling tariff and other protective barriers erected around domestic producers. In theory, they are expected to reap gains in efficiency by aligning production in accordance with their comparative advantage and world market prices. In practice, the rationale behind creation of the GATT-WTO institutional order is grounded in the expectation that trade liberalization would actually produce far-reaching and sustained benefits in terms of structural change, employment, and consumption. The general framework of rules and standards guiding the behavior of trading partners were based on three fundamental principles of GATT: (i) non-discrimination in trade, with all contracting parties bound by the most-favored-nation clause; (ii) protection of domestic industries only through customs tariffs and not through other commercial measures such as quotas; and (iii) the use of consultation as the only means of resolving trade disputes.

Non-discrimination means that a country is not allowed to extend better treatment to one trading partner in favor of others. If a country cuts tariffs on trade with one other, it must do so for all. The principle, grounded in the liberal theory of international trade, posits that if a country reduces tariffs on a non-discriminating basis it is likely to benefit more than if the reduction is just for a favored few. Moreover, the theory rests on the preconception that when tariffs are cut in the markets of developed countries, and even more crucially in those of LDCs, domestic industries are exposed to more international competition. This, in turn, is expected to shift resources to more efficient uses, thereby boosting productivity and living standards.

In practical terms, non-discrimination hinges on the principle of reciprocity whereby tariffs are reduced by negotiation – a concession for a benefit. Concessions – promises to lower a duty on a commodity and keep it at or below that level - are negotiated with the principal supplier and then generalized to all suppliers. Historically, such concessions have been bargained for at periodic conferences or "Rounds" of the GATT: the Dillon Round (1960-61), Kennedy Round (1964-67), Tokyo Round (1973-79), and Uruguay Round (1986-94). It is commonly believed that the Uruguay Round, which established the WTO, resulted in the most fundamental reform of the skewed global trading system since the GATT was originally founded. It included LDCs in the multilateral trading system, introduced some new aspects of trade, and extended coverage to more countries and products.

Under the second principle – tariff protection – countries were allowed to protect their domestic industries only with customs duties. These operate through the price mechanism and not by quantitative restrictions, which rely on volume. Accordingly, quotas are considered to be detrimental because they tend to impede the total volume of trade, shelter domestic production and prices against a changing world economy, stifle private enterprise, induce over-regulation of domestic business, and encourage bilateral and discriminatory flows of trade. Voluntary export restraints (VERs) are similar, but they are usually supplied by the exporter, for example, Japanese exports of cars to the United States. Such bilateral arrangements tend to evade the principle of transparency whereby any departure from GATT commitments would be open to international scrutiny. The third major principle – consultation – allows aggrieved members to get together and discuss their disputes.

The framers of GATT had envisioned a world of independent and equally treated trading partners interacting in competitive markets in a non-discriminatory fashion. As LDCs began to escalate their participation in the trading system, a controversy arose about allowing different trade rules for countries at different stages of development. In its initial provisions, GATT did relieve LDCs of some obligations. The Agreement made specific reference to the type of country "the economy of which can only support low standards of living and is in the early stages of development." Such a country was offered privileges of withdrawing a tariff concession, increasing tariff rates to protect infant industries, and invoking quota restrictions on imports.

Contextually, a widely expressed fear is that globalization of the liberal trading model will not only heighten asymmetries between North and South, but also balkanize poor countries that are not strong enough to enter the global trading and payments system on an equal footing with powerful transnational firms from North America, Europe, and Japan. From this perspective, the battle over the WTO, which is not part of the UN system, is essentially about who controls the globalized economy. While it apportions rights and sanctions to traders and business firms, encouraging them to enter markets, it does not equally dole out citizens' rights to democratic decisions, full employment, or a sustainable society. While this may not be the role of the WTO, the gravamen of the argument is based on a perception that it pits unequal societies and economic actors against each other.

Under the circumstances, trade liberalization should be interpreted as more than a mechanism for freeing markets because of a belief that it concentrates economic power and choices in the hands of private business. The increased competition and aggressive search for markets and profits puts a pressure on social rights and deemphasizes people's basic needs. To the extent that this is true, GATT-WTO practices have deviated substantially from the original intent behind the creation of the ITO (International Trade Organization) after the Second World War. While it was conceived as an integral part of the Bretton Woods system, it never saw the light of day. However, it was designed to link societal problems to the trading system via emphasis on competition policy, commodity prices, labor rights, technology transfers, and so on.

Be that as it may, an intractable question still centers around the extent to which countries at different levels of development will gain or lose from free trade and related WTO initiatives. The answer is by no means unambiguous because the large and growing number of empirical studies on potential costs and benefits have reached divergent conclusions about the differential impacts on countries or regions of the world. One primary reason is that they rely in varying degrees on different sources of data, contestable theoretical assumptions, and ideological biases about trade liberalization.

For example, an early salvo was fired in a study by the GATT Secretariat (1993), which attempted to estimate whether countries benefiting from privileged exports under the GSP (Generalized System of Preferences) and the Lomé Convention – the ACP (African, Caribbean, and Pacific) group of nations) – stood to lose from the Uruguay Round. It predicted gains in every sector, the explanation being that the scope for preferences is almost always more limited than it seems on the surface. In addition, all countries would benefit from the new rules for customs and shipment, more transparency in trade, and better mechanisms for settling disputes. Only time will tell whether such expectations will be corroborated or falsified.

In general, protagonists in the North contend that trade liberalization and open markets have been engines of growth for decades and will continue to do so. In its study *Open Markets Matter* (1998), the OECD emphasized that "liberalization brings clear benefits to our countries." It cited as evidence the fact that world merchandise trade had grown 16 times since 1950, and direct foreign investment increased by a staggering 25-fold during the last quarter of the 20th century, growing from \$14 billion to over \$350 billion per annum. Furthermore, a plethora of econometric studies by influential economists have confirmed that trade does promote economic growth and development. Not all economists, however, are convinced about the regression evidence. For one thing, some of the precise economic linkages underlying the correlations are sometimes difficult to uncover.

Beyond problems of statistical measurement, even some of its staunchest supporters view orthodox trade liberalization with a skeptical eye. Historically, this has been associated with a longstanding argument about "export pessimism," which has taken a variety of forms. In the first place, the absence of industrialization in the majority of LDCs cannot be attributed to any lack of trading possibilities. Many countries have experienced impressive bubbles of impressive growth based on agricultural exports. The widely recognized problem is that over the years changing structural conditions in international trade have increasingly inhibited this approach to economic development.

Among the contributory factors, a most commonly cited one has been the adverse terms of trade against primary commodities. Not only have producers of these commodities faced persistently falling export prices, but demand for them has failed to keep pace with the phenomenal growth in global incomes. The situation continues to be exacerbated by international fluctuations and the relatively high levels of protection afforded the domestic agricultural sectors of industrial nations.

Related to this is a fear that world food prices may rise if the major subsidizers of agricultural exports (primarily the European Union, Japan, and the United States) reduce the surpluses they usually dump on world markets. If this happens, food importers, including some of the world's poorest countries, will face inordinate import bills.

Trade liberalizers sometimes use the East Asian "miracle" as an exemplar, thereby urging LDCs to move on to an industrial path based on switching from primary commodities to exports of manufactured goods. While the scope for meaningful structural change is much wider, pursuit of this option is complicated by at least two factors. One rests on the idea, implicit in modern variants of the export pessimism argument, that liberalizing trade will be self-defeating if too many LDCs try to jump on the bandwagon simultaneously. Considerable uncertainty exists about the global demand for imports from LDCs. This remains true even if it is admitted that a concerted export drive by the less developed sector of the world may not necessarily put a great strain on the global trading system. Another factor relates to the negative fall-out from technological progress in the industrial world.

This puts into bold relief the issue of fairness underlying the standards set by the WTO for intellectual property rights through measures such as TRIPS. This agreement guarantees royalties to holders of patents and copyrights (primarily the "rich country club"), but it is unclear what LDCs will gain by honoring such payments. The standard response is that the intellectual property rights system will enhance the transfer of knowledge and technology from rich to poor countries, but this answer is questionable. First, commitments under TRIPS and other multilateral agreements to transfer technology to LDCs are "paper promises" that are often neglected in implementation. Second, instead of giving LDCs the flexibility needed for their own national development, the system is likely to pave the way for more control of their domestic markets by foreign firms. If this is true, then private foreign gains will be guaranteed at the expense of the general welfare.

Germane to this is the belief that laws governing patents and copyrights pay insufficient attention to indigenous knowledge and traditional ownership rights. In this regard, the WTO standards tend to downplay a number of areas of critical importance to LDCs: the implications of patenting life forms; the contribution of indigenous and rural communities in terms of genetic resources and biodiversity; the indiscriminate patenting by foreigners of medicines, plants, and other products well known to local people; and the consequences of genetically engineered and patented seeds. The underlying issues were also missed by protesters at the WTO meetings at Seattle. While a predominant concern was with protecting endangered species, such as turtles, the health of poor people was accorded less significance.

As signatories of the 1994 TRIPS agreement, some LDCs are implementing national systems of intellectual property rights based on a universal set of minimum standards, such as 20 years of patent protection. While a uniform set of minimum rules may seem to level the playing field, in actuality the game is not fair because the players have unequal institutional, economic, and bargaining strengths. Since LDCs own less than 1 percent of the patents granted worldwide, the system portrays one of the most unjust and unequal relationships between rich and poor nations (Patel 1996). Enforcement of the rules tends to put inordinate strain on the scarce resources, administrative, and legal skills of LDCs. Moreover, the high costs of settling disputes with OECD powerhouses tend to discourage LDCs from asserting their rights. The dilemma is that technology is both a tool of development and a weapon used by rich nations to gain competitive advantage in the global economy. As the experience with patenting pharmaceuticals shows, the two separate goals or interests are not always compatible (UNDP 2001).

The Scourge of Global Inequality

The forces highlighted earlier help to explain why the global distribution of income and wealth has become more unequal during the past three decades or more. On the one hand, average per capita incomes have registered a more than threefold increase as the world's aggregate income escalated on a ninefold basis – from $3 trillion to more than $30 trillion over the past 50 years or so. On the other hand, the lion's share is increasingly concentrated in the more affluent or developed sector of the world. More than 78 percent of global GDP accrues to rich nations, with the remainder having to be shared by LDCs, which account for nearly 80 percent of the planet's people. The gap in average per capita incomes between rich and poor sectors of the world has nearly tripled – from $5,700 in 1960 to $15,400 by the late 1990s.

The subject of inequality remains paradoxical. Governments and multilateral lending agencies are often more interested in poverty rather than inequality. In the eyes of the World Bank, for example, inequality should not be viewed in negative terms if the incidence in poverty is reduced and incomes of those at the bottom do not fall. The downplaying of inequality also stems from the orthodox view that economic growth will ultimately lead to a reduction of both poverty and inequality. This perspective is shared by ruling elites and policymakers in both rich and poor nations. They continue to believe that either inequality is falling or that it has positive effects related to the incentives provided for savings and economic growth. As in the case of the World Bank, no clear linkage is seen between income distribution and poverty, and more attention is paid to the latter. In essence, the dominant mindset is that the problem of poverty can be solved by providing people with more state-sponsored opportunities and welfare without effecting requisite institutional and structural changes determining profiles of income and asset distribution.

Not only are poverty and inequality inextricably linked, but it can also be argued that inequality per se matters over and above what it implies for poverty. In terms of measurement, three related concepts of inequality may be mentioned. One concerns *intra-country* inequality, which refers to widening income disparities in specific countries. A second is *inter-country* inequality, which connotes international differences among countries with respect to relative growth ratios or performance measured by the behavior of average per capita incomes. Third, *global* inequality encapsulates both intra-country and international inequality. As such, it captures average income differentials among all groups of people in the world.

But, interpretation of the global yardstick is not always unambiguous. One reason is that global inequality may increase even when average incomes are rising, thereby obscuring the widening disparities within countries. For example, if an agrarian economy experiences economic growth through integration into the global market, the aggregate statistics may indicate rising per capita incomes even though poor fanners are no better able to sell their products, lose their markets to powerful transnational competitors, or are otherwise dispossessed of their land by large landowners. Over the past two decades, millions of Asian workers have moved up the global income scale, but inequality has increased because governments have lost or given up their ability to protect vulnerable groups.

One useful way of comparing patterns of global income distribution is by looking at the increasing distance between the richest and poorest countries, and/or the richest and poorest 20 percent in each sector or country grouping. In the former case, Maddison (1995) has marshaled evidence to show that global inequality has been rising steadily for nearly two centuries. The income gap between the top and bottom countries increased from 3:1 in 1820 to 11:1 in 1913, 35:1 in 1950 and 72:1 in 1992. According to the UNDP (1996, 1999), the top 20 percent of people living in the world's richest countries received average incomes 30 times greater than the poorest 20 percent in 1960, but by the late 1990s they were receiving about 74 times more. Even more striking is that the top 20 percent of people living in high-income countries increased their share of global GDP from 70 to 86 percent over the same period, while the poorest 20 percent living in LDCs saw their already miniscule share decline from 2.3 to 1.1 percent of world income.

Two influential studies by World Bank analysts also confirm that global inequality rose markedly between the 1980s and 1990s. A study by Milanovic (1998) computed the Gini coefficient for global income distribution by combining trends in inter-country and intra-country inequality. The Gini coefficient is commonly used by economists to measure inequality. A coefficient of zero represents perfect equality while a score of 100 means perfect (most extreme) inequality, that is, one group appropriates all the income. While it covers only a relatively short time period, the study shows that global inequality increased from a Gini coefficient of 62.5 in 1988 to 66 in 1993. A similar study by Dikhanovic and Ward corroborates this trend, showing that the Gini coefficient increased by about 6 percent over the same period. It also reveals that the share of global income accruing to the richest 10 percent of the world's population rose by 8 percent whereas the share received by the poorest 10 percent declined by 25 percent.

Robert Wade (2001) interprets such income divergence in terms of a polarization between two distinct zones of the world system – termed a "zone of peace" and a "zone of turmoil." The former pole constitutes regions of wealth based on a combination of strong economic growth, "liberal tolerance (except towards immigrants)," and technological dynamism. The latter comprises lower- and middle-income countries where the tenets of good governance are either non-existent or disappearing. They can be found mainly in Africa, the Middle East, the new Soviet Republics, Central Asia, and parts of East Asia. A very large proportion of people living In the zone of turmoil lack access to basic necessities while a privileged few are able to flaunt their material gains through conspicuous consumption of imported goods.

In Wade's eyes, rising inequality may be an indicator of a dire political strain confronting the global political economy. Short of "wars of redistribution," if the poor majority in the world continue to perceive that the gap between themselves and their richer fellows is widening, they are likely to respond in unpredictable and unpleasant ways.

> The result is a lot of unemployed and angry young people to whom new information technologies have given the means to threaten the stability of the societies they live in and even to threaten social stability in the countries of the wealthy zone (Wade 2001, 74).

The situation is further complicated by the apparently unwritten rules governing certain policies of new partners in the emerging inter-national investment order. The dogged pursuit of industrial profits sometimes leads to the undesirable result that oppressive policies and corruption in LDCs are not of primary interest to foreign investors. But, universal standards such as good governance do sometimes creep in through the backdoor. While industrial powers and TNCs are wont to protest human rights violations and the like, the hidden assumption is that they must do so quietly. This stance results from fear that open criticism of client countries may foment internal unrest and militate against promotion of democracy.

In conclusion, polarization at the global level is highly correlated with intensification of inter-country and intra-country inequalities. Income and wealth concentration remain a ubiquitous feature of all major world regions. In the more opulent sector of the world, for example, the staggering concentration of wealth among the super-rich was accompanied by rising inequalities during the 1980s and 1990s. The deterioration has been apparently worst in the United States, Canada, Sweden, Britain, and Australia. Contextually, the net worth of the world's 200 richest people doubled during 1994-1998 to over $1 trillion. The assets of the top three billionaires exceed the combined gross national product (GNP) of the 600 million people living in all the least developed countries of the world (UNDP 1999).

In LDCs as a whole, prospects for enhancing human development potentials are being continuously hampered by political and social strife caused by vast gaps between the rich and poor. The data in Table 5.2 provide income distribution profiles of selected African and Latin American countries. While there are significant variations across countries, a uniform feature of inequality in both regions is the enormous gap between the richest and poorest segments of the population.

Table 5.2: Income Distribution in Selected African and Latin American Countries (Percentage share of income during 1980s and 1990s)

Country	Richest 20%	Poorest 20%
Africa		
Egypt	41.1	8.7
Ghana	42.2	7.9
Cote d'Ivoire	44.1	6.8
Tanzania	45.4	6.9
Morocco	46.3	6.6
Nigeria	49.3	4.0
Zambia	50.4	3.9
Senegal	58.6	3.5
Botswana	58.9	3.6
Kenya	62.1	3.4
Zimbabwe	62.3	3.0
South Africa	63.3	3.0
Sierra Leone	63.4	1.1
Latin America		
Uruguay	48.7	5.0
Costa Rica	50.6	4.3
Peru	51.3	4.4
Ecuador	59.6	2.3
Brazil	63.4	2.5

Source: World Bank, *African Development Indicators*, 1998/99; Inter-American Development Bank (1998)

The East Asian region experienced a secular decline in poverty right up to the late 1990s when the financial crisis struck. At the turn of this century, average per capita incomes in this dynamic region were more than 7 times the levels attained in 1960, and about 3 times what they were in 1980. However, income inequality has grown markedly in some East and Southeast Asian countries – for example, China, Indonesia, Malaysia, the Philippines, South Korea, and Thailand. In earlier decades, such countries registered relatively high economic growth rates while reducing poverty and inequality. Among other things, the financial crisis resulted in bankruptcies, falling incomes, escalating unemployment, dropouts from education, reduced food consumption, restrictions in access to credit, declines in the use of social services, as well as increased social stress and domestic polarization. It must remain an open question whether such dislocations will become part of a long-term trend.

The Inter-Governmental Modus Vivendi

The various forms of inequality by and large reflect the fact that, despite constant shifts in the dispersion of power, the conduct of international development is essentially influenced by what is termed an *inter-state or inter-governmental modus vivendi* (Pogge 1989). It connotes a global institutional order that is continuously shaped and reshaped by both tacit and explicit agreements or "rules of the game" purporting to regulate human interactions. The historical experience suggests that the system of rules can be arranged along a continuum – from the implicit norms and procedures underlying international regimes and/or bilateral understandings at one end to the most comprehensive and enduring accords and treaties at the other. Examples of the latter are the Universal Declaration of Human Rights and the Millennium Development Goals.

The rules of the game help to explain why the conduct of global political economy is marked by a constant disregard for the poorest and strategically insignificant actors - nations, societies, regions, and peoples. Germane to this is the fact that participation in the modus vivendi is usually motivated by competing interests and disparate values. In the overall scheme of things, each international actor has good reasons to cooperate with others on the basis of the shared institutional rules. However, governments tend to fear and distrust one another and their behavior is typically governed by rivalry, competition, and conflictual struggles.

The bargaining strength of a government within the modus vivendi is a function of its hard power, military and economic, with the latter playing a partly subsidiary and independent role. Given the exigencies of competition and parameters of *realpolitik*, most governments are usually more concerned with their own bargaining power and that of their allies and less so with cosmopolitan issues such as human rights, fulfillment of basic needs, and eradication of poverty. Hence, they are not known for making sacrifices designed to enhance the overall quality of life. Furthermore, increase in bargaining power depends to a significant degree on a government's strength and popularity at home. As a result, many governments are wont to utilize and support a variety of measures that fly in the face of humanitarian development. The long list includes modes of repression, such as secrecy, surveillance, and intimidation that stifle dissent and maximize domestic control.

The structure and functioning of the inter-state modus vivendi also help to explain the significance of geopolitics in the global stratification system - for example, why great powers have historically maintained special claims to countries and regions that are perceived as economically and strategically important to their national interests. Hence, they have effectively utilized their power, status, and dominant positions in the global hierarchy to "persuade" dependent and weaker states to pursue externally mandated policies and options. These include, inter alia, changes in their political and economic systems; opening their doors to imports, credits, and production facilities; and pressures to internalize complementary policies of privatization, deregulation, free trade, and financial liberalization.

Despite the inexorable march of globalization, a basic preconception underlying the inter-state modus vivendi is that sovereign nation-states and their political organs remain as the essential pivots of collective decision-making in the world. This life-and-world vision is consonant with a variety of theories and perspectives about "statecentrism", the causes of war and preservation of peace, the "morality of states," and their potential for promoting human betterment. The unifying theme is that nation-states are rational actors, seriously concerned with their own national power and capacity (military, economic, etc.) to influence others, and are always guided by their own interests.

From this perspective, the fundamentalist view of international affairs has hardly changed since Thucydides wrote his classic treatise: *History of the Peloponnesian War*. In the eyes of some scholars, the original perspective of Thucydides has not been transcended in modern times because international development is still marked by struggles of states for power, prestige and wealth in a condition of global anarchy (Gilpin 1981). Central to our understanding of the global development antinomy is the fact that states tend to fear one another, and the more power they wield (in terms of military and economic clout, wealth, and population), the more others are likely to fear them. In this context,

Mearsheimer (2001) reminds us that in looking after its own interests, there is no higher authority on which a state can call upon for help, and no emergency 911 number it can dial in order to seek assistance from an imaginary "global police" force.

Despite the persuasiveness of this argument, it can be countered that states are not necessarily alike in their will to act offensively, seek hegemony, or otherwise pursue cosmopolitan or humanitarian goals. This depends on the nature of their political and economic systems. Furthermore, it can be argued that states are not homogeneous or indistinguishable entities that are solely motivated by self-interest. In some instances, their policies are shaped by what their citizens feel about other peoples. For example, interactions among Americans, Canadians, and Europeans are sometimes guided by sentiments such as common ancestry, cultural similarity, and a shared corpus of political and economic ideals. In similar vein, it is not by chance that many Europeans have supported America in the fight against international terrorism. Even if such considerations provide grounds for realist optimism rather than pessimism, misgivings atill abound about the consequences of the inter-state modus vivendi and its potential for promoting the human good.

In conclusion, a burning issue centers around establishment of a superior institutional order that transcends the extant modus vivendi. This entails concerted efforts to change what is morally objectionable about the latter through synergistic improvements in the overall quality of life. The material presented in this and the next two chapters amply demonstrates that global inequality, economic maladjustments, and poverty have culminated in widespread fear by people for their security and values. Besides having to devote their energies to the everyday struggles for survival, the majority of people worldwide are disempowered, that is, disabled from participation in key decisions governing their lives.

Such exclusion is a primary cause of conflict. It is now known that civil wars often result not so much from ethnic rivalries, as is commonly believed, but from a combination of factors of which inequality and poverty are central ingredients. At the same time, more than $1 trillion are spent annually on "defense" worldwide as a means of preserving or shifting the existing distribution of power. Conflict-ridden societies have often become safe havens for terrorists. Persistence of such societies would entail a modus vivendi pervaded by violence, or threats of it, and the strategic marginalization of entire populations. Such a gloomy scenario also implies destroyed lives and livelihoods, since millions of people will remain trapped in internecine conflicts, competing predations among war lords, and campaigns of repression and insurrection.

Since the early days of the Cold War, prospects for creating a more just and fair modus vivendi have been associated with certain broad movements in global political economy – the decolonization process of the 1950s and 1960s; the call for a new international economic order (NIEO) during the 1970s and 1980s; and the current preoccupation with "democratic" capitalism based on the idea that the "West is the best." As previously indicated, this has been driven by the "end of history" thesis or what is essentially an "Americocentric" worldview.

The decolonization process ushered in the idea that LDCs (South) were nominally equal to their more developed counterparts (North). However, *de jure* political equality in the same global society or modus vivendi was not necessarily on the same footing as *de facto* economic inequality or colonialism. Correlatively, the North was thought to have an obligation to assist in the economic development of the South, and that the requisite transfers should be justified on the basis of global justice rather than charity. Such moral considerations were taken one stage further in the NIEO debates of the 1970s. But these were not successful in changing international practice, even though most sovereign states paid lip-service to the to the goals of global restructuring underlying the NIEO. However, the revisionist onslaught of Reaganomics, Thatcherism, and the neo-liberal paradigm of the 1980s undermined the ideological and moral foundations of the NIEO, ultimately shifting the agenda of North-South relations toward structural adjustment and crisis management.

At the present juncture in world affairs and international development, a burning issue is whether democratic capitalism, which Fukuyama describes as the "final form of human government" and "triumph of the Western idea," can stand the test of ushering in a regenerated world order. While the debate continues, an interesting perspective has seen provided by Zbigniew Brzezinski (once National Security Adviser in the Carter administration). In his book *Out of Control* (1993), he saw around him a spiritual desolation of unrestrained hedonism and a new "permissive connucopia" mirroring the self-indulgence of advanced Western nations whose psyches are fixated on the instant gratification of material, sensual, and sexual desires. Greed, Brezezinski argues, has blinded the eyes of rich, pleasure-seeking, minority to the plight of the poor majority. Furthermore, while America stands unrivalled at the pinnacle of the modus vivendi, it is thought to lack the binding moral imperatives required for its fitness to lead the rest of the world. It must remain an open question whether the latter will inexorably or inevitably approximate to the American paradigm.

Chapter 6

Globalism of Displacement

> Development is necessarily an indigenous process. This approach
> is in contrast to that which emphasizes the replacement of these
> characteristics of the indigenous community by those from the
> North. The latter process is not ... development. It is simply
> displacement.
>
> Henry Bruton (1997)

The march of globalization has put the development conversation on
the horns of a dilemma. This entails that it must be pushed into two directions simultaneously: *upward*, beyond the nation state and *downward*, into several "indigenous" layers beneath it. What is evident is
that critical problems of development, such as the debt overhang, fair
trading relationships, and external finance, can only be solved at the
supranational or global level. Nevertheless, it is by no means sufficient
for citizens of poor countries to be merely equipped with the

knowledge and skills required for competition in the global marketplace. They must also be imbued with a very strong confidence and self-assurance that their efforts will not be squandered, dominated, or otherwise squelched by distant, overarching, and soulless forces and institutions whose immanent logic they cannot understand.

The critical task inheres in discovering creative ways of contending with inexorable global megatrends, while at the same time establishing an enabling environment that gives full expression to the distinctiveness of people's identities and felt needs at the local or community level. This underscores the idea of authentic development being propounded in this book. It connotes enhancement of human well-being through a process that involves internalizing values and norms emanating from within rather than uncritically subscribing to explicit ones imposed or emanating from outside. A related imperative is the optimal utilization of the technology and institutions of society. The idea of endogenous development oftentimes runs counter to the prerequisites of global integration based on the mobility of capital, free trade, and rapid international diffusion of products, technologies, and information.

Contextually, Bruton's notion of "displacement" mirrors concerted attempts, be they deliberate or unintended, to transform the South in the image of the North based on complete openness of the former to the latter. As emphasized earlier, it involves pursuit of a development style that extols the virtues of foreign investment and capital flows, imported technology to make economies internationally competitive, minimal government, and market fundamentalism. Such pillars of the new economic globalism have deeply encroached into, and essentially guide, national policymaking throughout the globe. The preferred policy mixes are usually credited with reducing "rent seeking," improving competition, and offering opportunities for financial viability, export growth, and sustained economic development in poor countries. However, misgivings have surfaced over the exact nature of benefits and costs. One claim is that the potential benefits are dwarfed by the actual harm, insecurities, and risks imposed on LDCs.

The global structures providing the distinct character to the contemporary world order not only regulate the parameters of cooperation and conflict, but also define relations of risk, uncertainty, and trust that lie at the heart of human well-being. Economic restructuring aimed at promoting flexible production, cost competitiveness, and adaptability to changing market conditions in the world economy has involved severe adjustment costs. These include, inter alia, an inordinate increase in the turnover rate of labor and workers in transition, reduced social protection of the vulnerable, an unequal spread of adjustment costs among different groups in society, and transformation of the public policy environment. Furthermore, while the "global" and "local" are now inextricably interlinked, the increasing burden of adjustment might have heightened the proclivity of people to migrate in search of a better quality of life.

Resource Flows: Who Pays? Who Benefits?

We begin by highlighting critical elements of the global financial architecture. While internationalization of capital now straddles the globe like a colossus, greater integration into the global economy involves both benefits and costs for capital-importing nations. The period since the early 1980s has been one of inordinate financial stringency for heavily indebted countries, and demonstrates their vulnerability to external shocks. The march of events also suggests that there are great differences in the survival prospects between the relatively few countries enjoying access to private capital markets and those that do not. The former face the problem of managing capital flows efficiently, that is, ensuring that they are channeled into productive investments. The latter group must continue to rely on official transfers from the BWIs and bilateral donors. But, official aid has been shrinking, and its traditional role in long-term development has been superseded by funding for peace-keeping, emergency relief, and to support reform in the transitional economies in Eastern Europe and the Soviet Republics.

Historically, the opening up of financial systems on a global scale was associated with a process of capital substitution based on cross-investments among industrial nations, and flows from them to less developed regions. The United States used foreign capital extensively during the 19th century, as did Canada, Australia, New Zealand, and Argentina during the late 19th and early 20th centuries. Modern forms of global economic integration have witnessed an expansion and deepening of capital transfers among the G-7 nations. Foreign capital substitution has also played a critical role in the dynamic development of the four small East Asian countries – Hong Kong, Singapore, South Korea, and Taiwan – and a few other select developing countries.

Global trends in capital movements have been increasingly facilitated by a supranational system that continuously devises mechanisms to safeguard the process of capital accumulation on a world scale. Prima facie, the integrated global financial system provides an efficient mechanism for matching investors to savers (Bryant 1987). Hence, the inconvenience of not generating adequate national savings to finance current investment needs tends to be minimized because the overall system of financial intermediation has been effectively globalized. As a result, the domestic management of money must now compete with an array of global monetary and financial practices. These include, inter alia, the intractable flow of "hot" money in search of lucrative and safe havens throughout the globe; hedging by major TNCs against threatened currencies as a means of protecting their vast reserves of accumulated investment funds from loss in value due to inflation and/or devaluation; and the placing of trillions of dollars of convertible currency in short-term "spot" markets at relatively high interest rates in order to earn maximum returns.

The human development potential is constantly debased by the controlling activities of private financial speculators and money launderers such as arms dealers and traders in narcotics. It is estimated that more than $1.2 trillion crosses national borders every day in the unregulated market for speculative currency trading. This amount represents about 50 times the value of global trade in goods and services. Speculative decisions are guided primarily by the appetite for private profit, and very little attention is paid to the health of economies. The sheer financial wizardry and technological sophistication of speculators and other global financiers enable them to conduct transactions of a considerable size, but without scrutiny from any external authority. Organized crime syndicates are estimated to gross over $1.5 trillion a year. The value of the illegal drug trade reached approximately $400 billion in 1995, an amount equivalent to total direct foreign investment flows in 1997 (UNDP 1999).

At the same time, the following major trends have emerged with respect to net resource transfers from capital-rich to capital-poor countries over the past two decades or so. Until the early 1980s, official development assistance (ODA) accounted for the lion's share of international capital flows. The latter was comprised mainly of official aid, grants, and commercial bank loans to governments of LDCs. The debt crisis in the early part of that decade was concerned primarily with sovereign debt, that is, borrowings by governments. However, the value of private capital injection has now overtaken official flows by a wide margin. Africa remains the only region where official transfers are larger than private capital flows, but the amounts have been declining in real terms.

The largest form of net capital transfers to LDCs has been foreign direct investment (FDI), but short-term flows in the form of portfolio equity have been growing at a much faster pace. As alluded to earlier, an increasing proportion of short-term flows takes the form of "hot" money searching for speculative earnings in currency and financial markets. Some of the major trends are illustrated in Figure 6.1. What it does not show is that the financial flows have been highly concentrated and uneven.

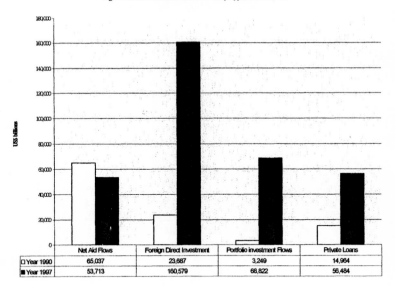

Figure 6.1: Net Resource Flows to LDCs by Type, 1990 and 1997

	Net Aid Flows	Foreign Direct Investment	Portfolio Investment Flows	Private Loans
☐ Year 1990	65,037	23,687	3,249	14,964
■ Year 1997	53,713	160,579	68,822	56,484

Source: World Bank (1999)
Note: The Net Aid Flows depicted for 1990 are actually for 1992

The newly-found abundance of foreign capital benefits only a relatively small number of countries that are able to tap private international markets. This remains true even though the largest countries in the developing world are included in the select group that financial analysts characterize as "emerging markets." Over 75 percent of FDI and portfolio investment has gone to only ten such countries (Argentina, Brazil, China, Hungary, Indonesia, Malaysia, Mexico, Thailand, Turkey, and Venezuela). Moreover, the bulk of such resource transfers has been channeled into services rather than to economic sectors deemed more conducive to broad-based development.

One primary reason is that many capital-importing countries are now lucrative markets for service providers, and most TNCs need a presence in the market to compete effectively. Since such firms increasingly integrate production across national borders, factors such as geographical location and home market size are becoming less important in their investment decisions. The latter now depend more on access to technology and capacities for innovation that recipient countries are able to offer. This trend has put greater pressure on them to pursue more sophisticated and flexible policies to attract TNCs, enabling such enterprises to create a diverse range of resources that would enhance their global competitiveness and profits.

Under the new rules of the game, countries are generally expected to adopt a uniform mix of global monetarist policies in order to attract financial capital inflows. These include, inter alia, tax increases and curbs on public expenditure to keep budget deficits under control; high interest rates to provide attractive rates of return on investment; low inflation to ensure that the real value of financial investment does not erode over time; and trade-related currency fluctuations or floating exchange rates (the weak currency mantra) to reduce balance of payments deficits. Identical to the conditionalities undergirding the "Washington Consensus" or Bretton Woods policy paradigm, these measures tend to have a deflationary bias by keeping output and employment growth below their potential. Many governments may or may not be aware of the costs that offset the benefits of foreign capital, but the changed global environment nevertheless propels them to adopt such policies. Hence, the overriding necessity to garner more financial resources from abroad may actually induce governments to adopt macroeconomic policies that conflict with their domestic development goals.

Foreign investors typically expect governments to embrace contractionary fiscal policies because budget deficits are believed to be inflationary, and as incurring the displeasure of financial markets. In turn, tight monetary policies are expected to dampen inflationary tendencies in an economy, keeping prices down and protecting the real value of investments. High interest rates are expected to establish "credibility" with financial markets and stabilize capital flows. However, the combination of fiscal restraint and tight monetary policies necessary to attract global capital tends to produce effects that are contradictory to those caused by capital flows. While the latter may stimulate growth, the deflationary fiscal-monetary policy mix tends to dampen aggregate demand and slow down the growth process.

The advice given to Asian countries during the 1997-99 financial crisis was apparently based on the theoretical presupposition that a mix of slower macroeconomic growth rates, weaker currencies, and higher taxes would guarantee a smooth process of economic adjustment and encourage more foreign investments. Contrary to expectations, the mandated weak currency mantra led to their decapitalization. People and their families have paid a high price for the failure of national governments and the international financial regime to discern, prevent, and deal effectively with the attendant instability. Not only did millions lose their jobs in countries such as Indonesia, Malaysia, South Korea, and Thailand, but social disorder and food riots have resulted from the rise in prices of basic goods such as rice, cooking oil, and fuel. Furthermore, the job losses and falling incomes greatly increased the risk of political and social unrest.

A widespread perception is that global capital markets and external influences now have an independent capacity to destabilize poor countries and increase their vulnerability to financial crises. As foreign capital injection proceeds apace and global financial integration deepens, each episode of crisis comes with greater force and inflicts irreversible damage on the real economy. It has been argued that international financial instability now constitutes the single most important impediment to rapid growth and sustained economic development in LDCs (UNCTAD 1997, 1998). Under the right conditions, capital flows can provide the needed stimulus to growth, employment, and incomes. But, such potential benefits require the presence of supporting institutions. The positive impacts are reduced because capital flows under extant institutional arrangements tend to be extremely volatile.

Since the global environment is characterized by unregulated financial flows, it tends to increase economic instability and reduce the ability of countries to deploy counter-cyclical policies to fight recessions. Financial liberalization tends to amplify the upswings and downswings of business cycles in nations receiving foreign capital. The tendency is for capital to flow in when an economy is performing satisfactorily, but to quickly leave when the economic fundamentals indicate any sign of deterioration, thereby exacerbating the economic downturn. As indicated earlier, governments are also expected to control budget deficits by curtailing public spending, and maintain high interest rates in order to gain the confidence of financial markets and minimize the risk of abrupt reversals of capital flows. But the actual results may be counterproductive. High interest rates purportedly attract foreign capital and increase the incentive to borrow abroad, but this may actually weaken the domestic currency and escalate the exposure of capital-importing countries to currency risk.

As the East Asian experience amply demonstrated, increased interest rates under conditions of monetary stringency and financial panic can actually lead to declining creditworthiness, greater default risk, a squeeze on sales of domestic currency, and economic depression rather than increased fluidity in foreign capital flows. More generally, contemporary capital markets are organized not so much to create employment and wealth, but more to extract rent by trading in second-hand assets. The objective is to impose "discipline" on policymakers as a means of reinforcing the advantageous positions of owners of capital. At the same time, when global markets fail, swift measures are taken to bail out international creditors at the expense of the stability and development of debtor nations, not to mention the living standards of ordinary citizens. As the record amply shows, the proliferation of bank failures, corporate insolvencies, and the sinking of currencies of borrowing countries are accepted as inevitable while funds are being used to protect powerful international financiers.

One perception is that the lion's share of the impetus behind increased private capital flows to select LDCs is related to a hidden crisis of commercial banking in some industrial nations. The argument is that financial deregulation has intensified competition, forcing major banks to find alternative sources of lending in order to maintain or increase profits. The result has been excessive lending for certain types of assets such as real estate and bonds. Combined with speculative bubbles, there has been an increased tendency for transnational banks to move into such forms of lending for the first time, even in the face of weak financial regulation and supervision in recipient nations. In the eyes of some influential commentators, this practice has resulted in "moral hazard:" major banks, knowing that they have access to funds and will be rescued no matter what happens, overlend or lend imprudently, encouraging investments that would not otherwise be made (Soros 1998).

As a consequence, international credit is now a major source of instability. It remains unregulated because there is no international central bank or regulatory authority comparable to those existing at the national level. This reflects a much larger issue of global justice that is inherent in the visible asymmetry between lenders and borrowers. In the overall scheme of things, the former group always fares better than the latter and can create severe disruptions in economies through changes in the ability and willingness to lend. The unequal relationship is further corroborated by critical factors underlying the ongoing debt crisis.

The total external debt of LDCs reached over $2.2 trillion during the late 1990s, but the hardest hit are 41 heavily indebted poor countries (HIPCs), 33 of them in Africa. Since 1980, their debt has tripled to over $245 billion, with about two-thirds resulting from unpaid arrears or earlier debt. Today's debt crisis is primarily about official debt – the amount owed to multilateral lending agencies such as the IMF and World Bank. A description was previously provided (Chapter 5) of how this debt was accumulated. After the first debt crisis of 1982, the international financial community responded by establishing processes for rescheduling debt servicing (payment of interest and amortization). The Paris Club was set up to deal with bilateral (government-to-government) debt, the London club for commercial debt, and "Brady bonds" were issued to reduce the principal of debt outstanding.

These initiatives eased the short-term burden by reducing outstanding debt, spreading out repayment, and providing soft loans to support debt servicing. Until October 1996, it was an article of faith that countries could not default on debts owed to the IMF and World Bank. Under popular pressure, they announced that multilateral debt owed by the HIPCs would be remitted, but within very restricted limits related to what is defined as "sustainable" debt. Under the HIPC initiative, it takes at least six years for a country to become eligible for debt relief. The debt sustainability ratio - the amount of debt deemed manageable by an indebted country – was set at 200-250 percent of its annual exports, and debt payments were thought to be bearable at 20-25 percent of such exports. Since the debt owed by these countries is excessive and unpayable, there is now general agreement that the proposed relief is miniscule, especially when humanitarian development needs are taken into account.

During the late 1990s, debt service payments exceeded annual expenditure on health and education in 8 HIPC countries, and for health in 29, including 23 in Sub-Saharan Africa (World Bank 1998a). In this regard, a poor country like Tanzania has been commonly cited as a case where debt service payments were nine times the expenditure on primary health care and four times that on education. While HIPC-type measures do provide for debt relief, the processes are entirely controlled by the IMF, World Bank, and OECD countries that finance them. This raises a more general issue surrounding the need to recognize the benefits derived by the global financial community from the crisis of credit oversupply during the 1970s through 1990s, and to apportion the costs among principal actors – creditors, debtors, and the BWIs. As a general rule, lenders never abandon their claims and always recover a part of bad debts.

> Although the debtor countries may not be able to pay off their obligations in full, they will be obliged to pay to the limits of their ability. The burden of doing so will usually weigh them down for many years to come (Soros 1998, 12).

Over the past few years, there have been vocal calls and formidable pressure by debt campaigners, such as Jubilee 2000 and Oxfam, for generous debt relief including cancellation of unpayable debts by HIPCs. This resulted in the Cologne Debt Initiative in which the G-7 nations agreed, among other things, to take a new look at the stock of debt; lower target ratios of debt to exports and fiscal revenue; forgive what is owed on bilateral development assistance; sell up to 10 million ounces of gold in IMF coffers; and a need for increased contributions to the HIPC Trust Fund by rich countries. Responses to these initiatives have been mixed, and in some cases, highly controversial.

In general, a question has arisen whether generous debt relief or cancellation will help the poorest people in the world, especially if it is linked to the high conditionality of the IMF and World Bank. One argument is that debt forgiveness would not release additional funds for heavily indebted countries since such debts would be continuously rolled over anyway. But even if debt forgiveness does not release new resources, it may not help the development effort if the recipients' priorities are inappropriate, for example, if the proceeds continue to be misallocated for military purposes and more perks for the ruling elite rather than applied to education, health, and other basic social services. This concern reflects a longstanding claim that foreign aid does not help poor people but rather their rulers. Over the past four decades or so, more than $1 trillion was channeled into such aid, but this transfer has failed to produce desired results in terms of intended beneficiaries reached, the effectiveness of programs, and ultimately the contribution to sustained human development.

In the final analysis, debt relief cannot be feasible or viable unless solutions are structured and delivered in the context of self-help efforts on the part of debtors themselves. This will end the perception of mendicancy and dependency. At the same time, there is a glaring need for more fairness in burden sharing in addressing the issue surrounding financial contributions of major creditors as well as between creditors and debtors. The enduring solution must be based on a full understanding of the structural causes of debt and their implications for the promotion of authentic development.

The New International Division of Labor

A critical issue underlying the march of economic globalism is that internationalization of production and its correlates might have ushered in an era of "jobless growth" or a so-called "end of work" as most people have come to know it (Rifkin 1995). The phenomenon of jobless growth (when a country's gross domestic product [GDP] increases with no substantial improvement in job or employment growth) is sometimes rationalized on the grounds that it is the best that can be hoped for in an increasingly flexible and competitive world economy, or that currently high rates of unemployment somehow constitute a natural and inevitable outcome of market forces. By contrast, the humanitarian perspective rests on a preconception that nothing short of a renewed international commitment to full employment is required to reverse persistent trends of unemployment, underemployment, and poverty throughout the globe. Accordingly, it challenges the implicit belief that no effective or feasible remedy exists for unemployment.

In particular, the problem of providing productive and remunerative jobs remains a critical one for the majority of LDCs. On a worldwide basis, it has long been recognized that it is not sufficient just to provide a few high-wage jobs for a relatively small group of workers, but rather gainful employment for the large and growing numbers emanating from the rapidly increasing labor forces. In rich and poor countries alike, new dislocations generated by trade liberalization, acquisitions, mergers, and dismantled social protection have heightened job and income insecurity due to layoffs and worsening employment conditions. The structural weaknesses that continue to produce negative consequences include: (i) the progressive eviction of the long-term unemployed from the world of work, combined with an increasing casualization of millions of workers in both formal and informal sector activities; (ii) the fact that the majority of workers in LDCs remain trapped in low-productivity jobs that are oftentimes physically onerous, but yet yield only the most meager earnings; and (iii) prevalence of what may be termed the "post-Washington consensus blues." This refers to the burden of adjustment costs, reflecting the fact that most poor countries have not yet recovered from the economic crisis of the 1980s.

These problems are compounded by the emergence of a "new international division of labor," a corresponding transformation of work, and the "flexibilization" of labor. Since the 1970s and 1980s, TNCs have been shifting certain stages or types of their production activities to free-standing units in other locations. The new international division of labor is one in which the industrial nations would specialize in the production of high-skilled and capital-intensive products, with low-skilled and labor-intensive processes relocated in low-wage LDCs. This trend began in the U.S. where many firms using labor-intensive methods to produce garments, footwear, and electronics were relocated to lower-wage sites in East Asia and Latin America. Along similar lines, a number of Japanese firms were relocated to parts of Southeast Asia. The process has gathered momentum worldwide on the heels of market liberalization, reductions in trade barriers, and the escalation of FDI to LDCs.

TNCs in the industrial nations now routinely export goods produced in low-wage locations back to their home countries and around the globe with fewer restrictions. As mentioned above, labor-intensive jobs were first exported to LDCs. However, with the better organization of production globally and increased ease of transferring technology, capital-intensive manufacturing began to move to foreign locations. Nevertheless, the industrial nations have retained skilled jobs in research and development, product innovations, engineering, advertising, and more generally, those knowledge-based jobs that create international property rights.

> Writing computer programs and revealing genetic codes have
> replaced the search for gold, the conquest of land and the
> command of machinery as a path to economic power. Knowledge
> is the new asset (UNDP 1999, 57).

Attempts to make global production more flexible in response to
competition, market volatility, and demands of the new technological
age have induced nations and employers to adopt more "flexible" labor
market policies. According to the World Bank, "increasing labor
market flexibility – despite the bad name it has acquired as a euphe-
mism for pushing wages down and workers out – is essential in all
regions of the world undergoing major reforms" (1995a: 109-110).
Contextually, labor relations in all parts of the globe are now governed
by a ubiquitous *cost-cutting* assumption. In theory, it is grounded in the
"distortionist" perspective of collective bargaining and related neo-
classical theorems about wage determination and flexibility in an ideal
competitive market economy. A basic preconception is that the free
play of market forces governing the supply of and demand for labor
essentially guarantees market adaptability, and that a decentralized
wage bargaining process would restrain wage demands and increases.

In practice, operationalization of this philosophy has produced
several negative consequences for the long-term interests of workers.
At one level, it has become the dominant motive force behind PDI
flows to LDCs. This implies that employers are prone to seek "cheap
labor" solutions, and have become preoccupied with reducing production costs via lower wages and benefits, reduction of the permanent
full-time workforce, and increased employment of part-time, temporary, and contingent labor. At another level, work arrangements with
no long-term commitment between employers and employees have
proliferated. In most countries, standard labor legislation now covers
fewer workers, as governments increasingly abolish labor regulations
or fail to enforce them. For example, worker dismissal laws have been
weakened in Belgium, France, and Germany. Systems of decentralized
wage bargaining have been introduced in Britain, the Netherlands, and
Spain. Most LDCs have also been reforming their labor laws and
crafting more flexible labor contracts.

These pervasive trends toward the "flexibilization of
employment" have shifted many of the costs of market uncertainty to
workers, making them more vulnerable to economic recessions, and

threatening their job and income security. In the context of globalized production and trade liberalization, such proclivities increasingly define a world that has been described as a huge bazaar in which nations peddle their labor forces in competition with each other, and offer the lowest prices for doing business (Donahue 1994, 47). The displacement effects have varied across countries at different levels of development, and with specific socio-economic structures and forms of integration into the global economy. Within individual countries, there have also been disparate polarization effects on different age groups, classes, ethnic groups, and between men and women.

As previously mentioned, trade liberalization has resulted in increased unemployment in some LDCs. For example, the increased competition from low-cost Asian producers has led to the displacement of workers in labor-intensive industries in some African countries (Biggs and Srivasta 1996). The direct impact of import expansion has also been negative. Local producers tend to lose market shares to cheaper imports, resulting in a reduction of available jobs. In most cases, smaller entrepreneurs, notably women, are ill-equipped to upgrade their productive activities in the face of increased competition.

More generally, cheap labor may no longer be one of the main determinants of comparative advantage for poor countries. Using the East Asian "miracle" as an exemplar, the international development community has been goading LDCs to move on to a modern development path by switching from primary products to export of manufactures. While the scope for structural change is evidently much wider, pursuit of this option is complicated by the negative fallout from technological progress in the industrial world. Besides the general tendency toward reduced use of raw materials per unit of output, technological advances in computer-assisted designs, machines numerically controlled by computers, and electronics tend to drive a wedge between the traditional distinctions based on capital-intensive products from the North vis-à-vis labor-intensive ones from the South.

Hence, countries that have historically specialized in labor-intensive products for export markets may find themselves at an increasing disadvantage. The quality of the labor force as reflected in skills and training may be more important than raw labor power in determining competitive advantage. The only exception is perhaps China where the supply of cheap labor has been a primary catalyst in the country's rise as a major exporter. By contrast, the "East Asian tigers" have discovered that they can no longer rely exclusively on low-cost labor as an engine of growth. While they are usually credited for their achievements in adult literacy, sufficient attention has not been paid to vocational and higher levels of training that promise to enhance technical skills of the labor force.

Given the labor-displacing effects of certain types of techno-logical change, globalization may have foreclosed any hope for full employment in many rich and poor countries. The latter still lack the industrial base needed for successful competition in the new growth sectors of the globalizing economy. This partly explains the increasing "informalization" of work, or what is apparently a resurgence of em-ployment in the informal sector. During the 1960s and 1970s, it was discovered that many LDCs had an unregulated but thriving sector that was creating jobs where there were none before. The ILO had charac-terized this sector in terms of ease of entry, family ownership of enterprises, reliance on indigenous resources, small scale of operation, labor-intensive methods of production and adapted technology, skills acquired outside the formal schooling system, and unregulated markets. Conventional development theory posits that the "productive" formal and "unproductive" informal economies not only exist as separate entities, but that the latter would eventually wither away in the same manner that "tradition" will inevitably give way to "modernity."

Contrary to expectations, the informal sector became a locus of employment growth since the 1980s in the less developed sector of the world. With the global spread of structural adjustment, many govern-ments simply abandoned full employment as a feasible goal of au-thentic development. At the same time, only a relatively small and de-clining proportion of the urban population belongs to the fortunate few earning salaries or wages on a regular basis. An increasingly hostile international environment defined by a new ethic of "downsizing" government programs has also led to a shrinkage of the modern wage-paying sector. In a global milieu in which austerity policies are man-dated by a neo-liberal ideology, changing production profiles and in-creased competition have been accompanied by a failure of the formal sector to generate sufficient employment for the burgeoning labor force. As mentioned earlier, growth in the size of the formal sector tends to make it increasingly difficult to associate the dichotomy between "formal" and "informal" with that between "modern" and "traditional."

It is a very heterogeneous sector, reflecting distinct types of activity in terms of productivity and linkages to the formal economy.

The top echelon is constituted by many independent professionals, a minority of successful businessmen, and similar operatives who provide high-priced, customized products and services to satisfy the demands of high-income customers. Members of this informal sector "elite" usually reinvest their capital in various formal and informal sector enterprises and skillfully utilize their contacts with influential persons in the formal sector to ensure safe operation, that is, without penalty or threat of harm. Such cadres generally find it advantageous to invest in unregulated activities because of the relatively low costs of conducting business.

The middle rungs are constituted by diverse groups: relatively productive workers engaged in wage-labor in a quasi-capitalistic setting, and therefore with a close link to the formal sector; private entrepreneurs, crafts-persons, as well as middle-level bureaucrats and other government employees who have suffered from employment retrenchment, or who otherwise are able to use state resources for private purposes and generate untaxed income from "moonlighting." The very bottom of the ladder is reflected by the "own-account" activities of self-employed urban and rural poor people. Their productivity levels are very low and links to the formal economy are tenuous. Women comprise the majority of informal sector workers in most countries, especially among the last two groups. Since they typically lack marketable skills, they tend to flock into informal activities to generate whatever income or livelihood they possibly can. The overall environment is marked by ease of entry and exit, high rates of turnover, and relatively short life cycles of economic activity.

In the above context, the transformational potential of the informal sector hinges on the fact that it displays a distinct pattern of socio-economic stratification based on access to and control of resources. At one level, its resurgence has become an integral part of economic restructuring, providing both flexibility and an opportunity for formal sector establishments to lower costs. There are typically no government regulations, taxes, minimum wages, and/or age restrictions constraining the behavior of informal enterprises. Overhead costs are virtually non-existent because they do not require permanent locations or sites to conduct business. Moreover, since such activities are labor-intensive, there is no need to upgrade technology and machinery on a constant basis. Such incentives have proven to be highly attractive to the class of "elite" entrepreneurs who have access to financial resources and are seeking avenues to generate profits (Castells and Portes 1989; Castells 1993).

At another level, the informal sector works as a giant "labor sponge" that mops up excess labor from the formal economy. Many of its establishments cater to specific local needs and what may be described as a "subsistence ethic," as distinct from a search for private profitability based on entrepreneurial spirit. They are predominantly owned and operated by self-employed producers with little capital, skills, technology, access to markets, public services, and other amenities. Under the circumstances, they are able to provide very low and irregular employment and incomes. This basic problematique is that the informal sector has been forced to bear a disproportionate share of the employment costs associated with economic globalism and adjustment, but without any concerted attempts to provide the targeted assistance needed for this people-oriented sector to realize its full potential.

The Movement of People

Finally, the unequalizing trends generated by the globalization process in terms of systemic transnational flows in money, goods and services, information, values, and culture should be linked to the continuous movement of people from South to North in search for a better quality of life. In this regard, it is perhaps useful to restate the truism that as long as the species *homo sapiens* has been living on the planet, its members have been migrants. We have never been sedentary animals, but highly peripatetic. It is probably true that humans must constantly move in order to progress. As Whitehead (1925, 297-98) has emphasized, "animals that wander must adapt or die. When man ceases to wander, he will cease to ascend in the scale of being." Patterns of migration in the contemporary world are not so much the result of natural propensities, but more a reflection of endemic and deepening structural inequalities between rich and poor nations or regions.

Historically, the movements have been grouped into three broad categories: group movements, free-individual, and restricted migration (Thomlinson 1965). Three types of group movements have also been identified: invasion and settlement, characterizing population movement up to the 17th century; forced migration, for example, slavery and the millions of displaced persons or refugees during the 20th century; and colonization-settlement of the Americas by Europeans. Free-individual migration is the voluntary movement of people from one area to another with the intention of permanent settlement. However, most migration in the modern world is restricted. Industrial and other wealthy nations admit migrants selectively, utilizing a variety of instruments: visa restrictions, border controls, and legal conditions for admission such as age, education, wealth, national origin, and family ties. Even though restricted migration has increased, this must be linked to a more general pattern whereby lower transportation costs and related modernizing influences continue to generate a considerable upsurge in international labor mobility. The free movement of labor and the march of free trade are perhaps inseparable.

It is estimated that more than 150 million people are living outside their own countries. While many do so voluntarily, large numbers do not. At least 14 million have fled over a border, but this figure does not include the more than 3.5 million Palestinian refugees. At the same time, the reasons for the increased numbers of refugees and displaced persons have changed over the years. Initial causes such as political repression based on ethnic and national origin have been overwhelmed by new factors such as tribal conflict, drought, famine, and the nature of political regimes which are common in LDCs, especially Africa.

The figures above do not include large numbers who do not cross borders but remain displaced in their own countries. There are about 25 million such displaced persons in about 40 countries. About one half of them are in Africa, with the remainder living mostly in the Balkans, Central Asia, Sri Lanka, and Latin America. Hence, there are many more people adrift in their own countries than there are refugees. While they are not normally recognized as refugees, they are just as vulnerable.

More than one half of global migratory flows take place among countries and regions in the less developed sector of the world. Notable examples include people from Southeast Asia moving to oil-rich countries in the Middle East and the prosperous small East Asian economies; migration of Egyptians, Jordanians, and Sudanese to the Gulf states; and the movement of people from the relatively poor countries in Sub-Saharan Africa to others where economic and employment prospects look better, for example, Cote d'Ivoire, Nigeria, and South Africa. Of late, however, some critical concerns have surfaced about historically accepted forms of migration from South to North, that is, from LDCs to Europe, North America, and to a lesser extent, Australia. Such human flows did not pose a problem in the past, especially during the boom years of the 1960s. Nowadays, rising unemployment in some European countries, a flood of both legal and illegal entrants into the United States, and fears about international terrorism have exacerbated political and social tensions, including what is sometimes perceived as xenophobia.

But, European hostility to immigrants is by no means new. For example, riots erupted in the poor overcrowded London borough of Fulham as far back as 1916 when the local population thought that Belgian refugees were receiving higher welfare payments than British soldiers. The Notting Hill riots of 1958 and attendant episodes of racial prejudice against "West Indian immigrants" have been well documented. In more recent times, the situation seems to have hardened in the face of growing numbers of asylum seekers. In August 7, 2002, the influential *London Times* published an editorial article entitled "Britain is losing Britain." It claimed that immigration from LDCs was transforming Britain into "a foreign land," against the wishes of the majority of the population, damaging the quality of life and social cohesion, exacerbating the housing crisis and congestion, and burdening the health service to a breaking point.

As the article further stated,

> you can wander around for hours without seeing a white face, one monoculture having replaced another ... In the past five years, while the white population grew by 1 percent, the Bangladeshi community grew by 30 percent, the black African population by 37 percent and the Pakistani community by 13 percent ... Whole villages in Bangladesh have been transplanted to northern English towns.

Across Europe, such sentiments have resulted in a rise of populist anti-immigration parties such as France's National Front, the Freedom Party of Austria, the Pim Fortuyn in the Netherlands, the Northern League in Italy, and the Danish People's Party.

While Europe seems to be engulfed in spasms of xenophobia, the United States still accepts immigrants of all kinds and at a faster rate than at any other time since 1850s. According to the results of the 2000 Census, the 31.1 million foreign-born residents represent 11.1 percent of the U.S. population, or one in nine residents. The foreign-born population grew from 7.9 percent of the total in 1990 to 11.1 percent in 2000 – the fastest in 150 years. There has been a big shift in the birthplaces of immigrants. Right up to 1970, Europeans constituted the majority. But, they now trail persons of Latin American origin who now make up 51.7 of immigrants and those born in Asia who are now responsible for 26.4 percent of the total.

In the above context, the perennial but highly intractable question has always centered around who migrates and their reasons for doing so. In a fundamental sense, all human history can be interpreted as a history of migrations. As Pagden (2001) reminds us, some of the most conspicuous mass migrations of the past 500 years can be traced to Western imperialism. Among other things, it resulted in the exportation of elites, re-shuffling of labor forces, transportation of slaves and coolies, and triggering of "counter-colonizations" during the last half-century or so as the former "victim" peoples planted roots in the "mother-countries" of their erstwhile masters. In general, migrants have been vectors of change in their host-communities, bringing fresh ideas, new skills, and cultural change. From this perspective, it can be said that opposition to immigration is historically ignorant, irrational, and even immoral (Dummett 2001; Hayter 2001)

In his *Seventh Law of Migration*, the British geographer Edward Ravenstein concluded in 1899 that

> bad oppressive laws, luxury taxation, and unattractive climate, uncongenial social surroundings, and even compulsion ... all produced and are still producing currents of migration, but none of these can compete in volume with that which arises from the desire inherent in most men to 'better' themselves in material prospects.

Hence, it may be hypothesized that no amount of political rhetoric, or even military force, will ever stem the flow of people from poorer lands looking for economic survival and a better quality of life in richer ones.

The motive force behind such movements essentially lies in the centrifugal forces underlying the dialectics of global stratification. Given the widening gap between the "haves" and "have-nots," it is not surprising that free labor mobility constantly results in burgeoning immigrations to the industrial world, ostensibly producing enormous social, ethnic, economic, and political dislocations in the latter. The argument, therefore, is that international migration will persist as long as endemic inequality, poverty, and related forms of ill-being continue to define people's life chances the world over.

The simpliest economic interpretation of migration is based on a *gravity model*, which is concerned with human flows between markets in response to expected differentials in earnings. In this analytical framework, migratory movements tend to occur at the margin. This implies that people leaving low wage markets are the least employable, with the least attractive positions in relatively high wage markets filled by immigrants. The idea is that, by raising the capital/output ratio, migration tends to increase labor productivity in the country or region of emigration while raising output, employment, and capital productivity in the receiving country or region. The prediction is that increased interaction between different labor markets will generate substantial aggregate benefits. However, such an optimal result may not be realized if unskilled workers in the high-wage receiving country are disadvantaged and/or capital in its low-wage counterpart is misallocated.

Moving beyond market fundamentalism, inequality – technological, economic – and resource imbalances between the two sectors of the world help to explain the potency of "push" and "pull" factors inducing migrant flows. They suggest that migration is by and large due to socio-economic imbalances between countries, with certain factors "pushing" people away from the countries of emigration and others "pulling" them to the receiving countries. Both push and pull factors tend to operate simultaneously. Extrapolating from Ravenstein's hypothesis, most people tend to move either because conditions are perceived as intolerant at home and/or the opportunity to enjoy a superior standard of living is thought to exist elsewhere. Bouvier, Shyrock, and Henderson (1977) explain the differential impact of push and pull factors in terms of "positive" and "negative" selection. Migrants responding to pull factors in countries of destination are positively selected, while those responding to push factors in their home countries tend to be negatively selected.

The movement of people across national frontiers is not costless, but involves myriad challenges associated with travel, resettlement, uncertainties about employment, and overcoming language and cultural barriers. Hence, those who migrate tend to boast higher education, skills, ambition, and savings than their relatively poorer compatriots. The loss of such cadres is likely to impose a greater opportunity cost on the sending country than if less productive workers were to migrate. This brings us to the widely discussed *brain drain* perspective of migration, which stresses that a significant component of human and sometimes financial capital is transferred with the migration of highly qualified persons such as teachers, university professors, physicians, engineers, and managers. The perceptible effect is to lower labor productivity in the sending country, while raising it in the receiving one. Thus, the result is the opposite to that predicted by the gravity model.

It is undoubtedly true that most developing countries are in desperate need of the skills of such high-caliber persons for their sustained development. For some countries, however, emigration essentially represents a stopgap or safety valve that enables them to postpone internal institutional and structural reforms that would make such exodus unnecessary. Yet, it must be admitted that the brain drain does not always affect poor countries adversely. The market for skills, like that for capital and commodities, has been globalized. The implication is that people should be allowed to work in those environments where they can be most productive. In countries such as India, Pakistan, and the Philippines, the supply of skills is no longer constrained by the paucity of highly educated nationals. There are cases where the "brain drain" contains significant elements of a "brain overflow." Many developing countries have expanded their tertiary education beyond the point where the skills of graduates can be effectively utilized locally. In the wake of stagnant modern sectors and maldeveloped economies, generous subsidies for higher education have produced more graduates than the economy can absorb, imposing large budgetary costs and creating pressures to migrate.

In the case of receiving countries, virtually all labor flows, especially to the industrial world, have been encouraged as a matter of deliberate policy. Skilled migrants bring substantial benefits to economic and intellectual life because of economies of agglomeration. Inflows of unskilled workers benefit owners of capital and the more skilled segment of the labor force. They often fill unskilled manual jobs which native workers typically avoid, and sometimes take jobs that would otherwise disappear. For example, unskilled migrants from North Africa and Turkey now make up 60 to 80 percent of total migratory flows to France and Germany, respectively. Nevertheless, the fear persists in receiving countries that migrants may hurt the job prospects of unskilled native workers by depressing wages. This can occur if migrants bring characteristics that are substitutive of rather than complementary to the existing mix of national skills.

Thus, the picture of immigrants stealing jobs from indigenous workers, or becoming a burden to the state, can be overdrawn. In a systematic study of the economic and fiscal effects of immigration, the National Research Council (1997) has reported that it provides substantial economic benefits for the United States as a whole, but only slightly reduces the wages and employment opportunities of low-skilled American workers, especially high school dropouts. A significant conclusion of the study is that immigration contributes about $10 billion a year to national economic output. Buyers of goods and services produced by immigrant labor also tend to benefit because prices are lower than they would otherwise be. Employment prospects of low-skilled native-born workers are sometimes hurt by competition with immigrants, resulting in a fall in their incomes. But the effects are relatively small and not concentrated in areas where immigrants live. Rather, the effects are dispersed across the United States, in part because low-skilled native-born workers typically move to other areas of the country in search of jobs.

The developmental consequences of migration continue to generate considerable controversy. As the foregoing discussion indicates, these are not clear-cut and involve a complex interaction of economic, social, political, and demographic factors. Some are positive while others are negative for both the countries of emigration and immigration. In economic terms, and as the gravity model suggests, international migration produces efficiency gains when workers move to countries where they are more productive. Such potentially beneficial effects may be distributed in diverse ways, for example, in terms of higher earnings and better living conditions for migrants, more remittances to countries of origin, and lower production costs in receiving countries. Needless to say, everyone does not necessarily gain. Unskilled immigrants may displace workers with similar skills in host countries. As indicated above, the ultimate effects will depend on whether the skills of immigrants complement or are a substitute for those of indigenous workers or others left behind in sending countries.

In the latter case, remittances of migrant workers usually constitute the most important benefit. Such remittances typically account for between 10-50 percent of the GNP of countries such as Lesotho, Jordan, and the Yemen. The corresponding ratio of remittances to export earnings is also about 25-50 percent in Bangladesh, Burkina Faso, Egypt, Greece, Jamaica, Malawi, Morocco, Pakistan, Portugal, Sri Lanka, the Sudan, and Turkey (World Bank 1995a). Moreover, since international wage differentials are extremely large, remittances (both monetary and non-monetary transfers) often constitute a multiple of the value of what migrants would have earned at home, but such flows tend to decline as migrants become more integrated into the host country. The overall development impact on home countries depends on how the remittances are utilized, that is, whether they are channeled into productive investment, thereby augmenting local demand, or otherwise utilized to finance conspicuous consumption, luxury imports, and even forms of speculation. In cases where migrants are from higher income households, remittances can actually lead to increased inequality, but there may be certain offsetting spread effects. In any event, potential gains have to be balanced against reduced economic growth opportunities stemming from the continuous loss of skilled labor.

The international labor market is controlled by the more affluent nations. The barriers to entry associated with immigration control were estimated to cost LDCs about $250 billion a year during the early 1990s (UNDP 1992). Moreover, policies to restrict immigration continue to encourage illegal entry and various forms of exploitation. It is estimated that Western Europe has more than 5 million illegal immigrants, mostly from Africa. The United States boasts the largest number, about 6-7 million, due in part to its long border with Mexico. In this case, immigration serves as a safety valve that partially alleviates Mexico's rapid population growth and poverty. Accordingly, fears are constantly expressed about the chaos that would ensue from much stricter controls and drastic reductions in emigration. Besides the further overburdening of Mexico City and other urban places, confrontations among peasants, government authorities, and landowning classes are likely to escalate.

Counterintuitively, the realization that such a dire outcome is a real possibility may actually produce more salutary outcomes over the longer run. But this result depends on the extent to which national authorities are sensitized to the fact that immigration, as a Janus-faced creature, cannot provide a lasting answer or effective solution to the structural problems that are its main causes: global inequality, unemployment, poverty, and human insecurity. The impasse takes on added significance when the rich (receiving) and poor (sending) countries happen to be close neighbors. The main challenge over the short and medium terms is to discover desirable ways of managing normal flows of legal immigrants without creating hidden incentives for illegal ones. In the final analysis, the issue boils down to a potential conflict between societal interests and individual freedom. While free international migration may no longer be feasible at the societal level, in the eyes of would-be migrants it still remains one of the best avenues for enhancing the overall quality of their lives.

Chapter 7

Persistent Poverty

> Poverty we think is not a disgrace to acknowledge but a real degradation to make no effort to overcome.
>
> Thucydides

Poverty remains one of the most intractable conditions of human deprivation to be resolved on a global scale. Needless to say, its eradication has long constituted the professed objective of multifarious development policies and strategies. The situation has been exacerbated because the widespread increase in inequality over the past two decades or more has proven detrimental to the achievement of poverty alleviation targets adopted by the international community since the late 1980s. In its *World Development Report 1990*, the World Bank envisioned that the total number of people living in poverty would have decreased from 1.125 billion in 1986 to 825 million in 2000. Yet, more recent assessments indicate that such a target was highly optimistic.

Depending on how poverty is measured, it is now estimated that the number of poor people worldwide has reached between 1.3 and 1.6 billion. However, there is still a lack of consensus about how poverty should be conceived, measured, and eliminated.

Interpretations and Concepts

Historically, the development discourse has focused primarily on the "economics of the poor" or the "poverty of nations," with the lion's share of international assistance directed toward promotion of national economic growth. Hence, the technocratic solution has been viewed as an outcome of the overall growth process. As such, very little attention was paid to the development potentials of people themselves. In other words, the so-called "development problem" was principally conceived in terms of something that happened to "the poor" on a trickle-down basis. Poor people were largely portrayed as peripheral to modern production systems, or as not being fully integrated into economic processes. From this "externalist" perspective, they are viewed as beneficiaries of material progress in the larger exogenous systems. Once poverty groups are viewed from afar, myths are likely to persist about their actual condition, in the sense of doing something "about" or "for" them rather than involving them in their own destiny.

The humanitarian perspective looks askance at the now falsified prediction that it is still possible for the majority of poor people to benefit substantially from national economic growth without full account taken of their self-interpretations, choices, capabilities, and aspirations. It posits that poor individuals and groups are not necessarily hangers-on or idle folk, but are normally engaged in useful work. No human being is simply "poor." In this regard, the term "poor" is more accurately used as an adjective rather than as a noun. People may be poor farmers, workers, women, or fishermen, as the case may be. Except for the extremely destitute, they are in one sense or another either (a) producers lacking resources, or whose inadequate incomes are derived from the fruits of their own labor; or (b) individuals who suffer the consequences of social exclusion or neglect. As a general proposition, it can be said that no human being wishes or desires to be poor, and few who are trapped in a marginalized or deprived state are willing to accept passivity, or are devoid of initiative and will.

Poverty is less a failure of the poor, than a failure of policymakers to grasp their potential. Far from being a tradeoff between poverty and growth, the persistence of poverty represents a limit to growth (IFAD [International Fund for Agricultural Development] 1992, 15).

Since poverty has many mutually reinforcing facets, it is usually defined in several alternative ways which do not always identify the same individuals or groups as poor. Hence, the process of measuring poverty tends to throw up many hurdles which must be overcome if we are to get nearer to the truth about the human reality we are trying to understand. As Streeten (1995, 42) states:

> In trying to measure poverty we may envisage the process as a removal of six veils. The removal of each veil gets us nearer to the facts that we want to measure, but the outer veils are not therefore unnecessary.

Over and above technical economic or statistical details, the favored criterion typically depends on a particular perspective and supporting preconceptions about human welfare. For our purposes, three broad perspectives and measurement criteria may be identified: income, basic needs, and capabilities.

Historically, poverty has been defined as a more or less discrete characteristic, that is, a person is either poor or not. On this basis, a certain standard or line (the "poverty line") is drawn and an individual or household is presumed to fall on one side or the other. Accordingly, the standard economic definition or conventional measure of poverty locates persons or households into two basic groups – poor and non-poor. It seeks to aggregate the "amount" of deprivation into a single statistic – the income, consumption, or expenditure level that is capable of potentially sustaining a minimum standard of living or level of food consumption. This minimum is usually determined by two alternative methods: (i) the food energy profile whereby dietary energy intake per adult equivalent has a statistical value just enough to meet require-ments; and/or (ii) the purchasing-power-parity (PPP) method, that is, where the value of the poverty line, expressed in terms of standardized dollars and prices, is just sufficient to buy a set amount (say, US$1 per day) of the consumption-bundle of an average citizen (see Lipton 1997).

Hence, the poverty line separates the population believed to have an adequate level of welfare. A person is deemed to be poor if his or her income or consumption falls below the minimum. The "incidence" of poverty is measured by the "headcount index" or ratio, which indicates the proportion of a given population whose level of income or consumption falls below the poverty line. An indication of the intensity or depth of poverty is usually provided by the "poverty gap," which measures the extent of the shortfall or the average distance of the poor from the poverty line. Given these measures, most LDCs have established national poverty lines indicating insufficiency of economic resources to meet basic minimum needs for food, i.e., they typically rely on a "food poverty" method. The World Bank relies on a poverty line of $1 a day per person (based on consumption) for purposes of international comparison. The UNDP employs a standard of $2 a day for Latin America and the Caribbean, and $4 a day for Eastern Europe and the CIS (Commonwealth of Independent States) countries. A minimum income corresponding to the U.S. poverty line of $14.40 a day per person is used for comparisons among industrial nations,

On the above basis, the following balance sheet has emerged for income poverty at the end of the 20th century. First, about 1.3 billion people subsist on incomes of less than $1 a day. Second, South Asia has the largest number of people (about 515 million) who are income poor. Third, more than 950 million of the 1.3 billion people who are income poor live in South Asia, East and Southeast Asia and the Pacific. Fourth, some 220 million people in Sub-Saharan Africa suffer from income poverty. Fifth, such poverty affects the lives of about 110 million people in Latin America and the Caribbean, and continues to grow. Sixth, in Eastern Europe and the CIS countries, income poverty has spread from a relatively small proportion of the population to about one-third, with some 120 million people now living below the poverty line of $4 a day. Seventh, in the rich industrial countries, more than 100 million people live below the poverty line. Britain; Ireland, and the U.S. have higher levels of human poverty than other industrial nations; and nearly 20 percent of the American people have incomes below the poverty line (UNDP 1997, 1999).

These figures are startling in themselves, but the income or consumption measure does not tell the entire story. One reason is that it rests on an implicit assumption that poverty is homogeneous, that is, the uniformity of poor people exists simply by virtue of the fact that they lack income/consumption power. Money income tells us nothing about changes in the prices of goods and services that are purchased. Real income, or money income adjusted for such changes, does not usually capture non-priced subsistence income, such as food crops consumed within the household, or the services of housewives. Further, a variety of economic and non-economic factors tends to influence human welfare across socio-economic environments, cultures, and climates.

The major income-oriented measures such as poverty lines and the headcount index not only vary across locations, but also raise an issue about the significance of absolute vis-à-vis relative poverty. On the one hand, it can be argued that one component of poverty will always be absolute or inevitable, in the sense that some people will always fall below the average or mean defining a minimum decent standard of living in society. On the other hand, all poverty can sometimes be viewed as relative. However, such an interpretation confuses one type of deprivation (inequality) with another (poverty). Where it exists, relative poverty typically results when comparisons are made between one's own level of living with that of reference groups boasting higher incomes. It is explained by a number of factors, such as changes in societal conventions and laws; other deep psychological causes – for example, shame stemming from the inability to afford goods and services perceived to be socially necessary; and, on a related basis, where certain goods and services are no longer available and/or their prices rise more than money incomes.

Beyond this issue, money or real income attainment only provides an indication of the *means* available to purchase bundles of goods and services. The income measure does not necessarily reflect human *achievements* within and across societies and regions. These reflect the quality of life people succeed in living, as has been achieved in terms of adequate levels of nutrition, education, health, and other attributes of human well-being. The significance of such basic needs indicators lies in their ability to capture what are termed people's "functionings" and "capabilities" (Sen 1985, 1989). From this perspective, poverty represents the absence of some basic capabilities to function, for example, where a person lacks the opportunity to achieve some minimally acceptable levels of these functionings. The relevant functionings may vary from physical ones such as being well nourished, adequately clothed and sheltered, and avoiding preventable morbidity to more complex achievements such as community participation.

Yardsticks such as the *Human Development Index* (HDI) and the *Human Poverty Index* (HPI) are meant to juxtapose the essential elements of human life against backlogs of such deprivations (Haq 1995; Sen 1999). They are of the same genre as the "capability poverty measure" (CPM), which is intended to determine "hidden" or "potential" poverty and society's inability or ability to lift itself out of this condition. The CPM relies on three yardsticks reflecting the lack of basic capabilities: (i) the proportion of children under five who are underweight – an indication of the capability to be well-nourished or healthy; (ii) the proportion of births unattended by trained health personnel – defining the capability for health reproduction; and (iii) the female illiteracy rate – mirroring the capability to be informed, educated, and knowledgeable. Computations of the CPM by analysts at the UNDP and UNICEF show that while about 1.3 billion people are "income poor," over 1.6 billion are "capability-poor." This suggests that approximately 37 percent of the population in LDCs face hidden or potential poverty.

Finally, the World Bank (1992b) has identified three broad poverty groups who might have suffered from the negative impacts of structural adjustment programs. First, there are the "borderline" poor, comprising vulnerable low income cadres who might have been affected most severely by belt-tightening and austerity programs – reductions in the availability and increases in the prices of major consumption items, especially food, and cutbacks in social programs. This group constitutes a substantial proportion of the general public. It includes low-wage government employees, casual workers, poor farmers, pregnant and lactating mothers, senior citizens, and children. While some of its members move in and out of poverty, others never cross the poverty threshold. A very thin line separates the borderline poor from a second group – the "new" poor.

They consist predominantly of urban personnel who are direct victims of structural adjustment, for example, those who have experienced deep cuts in wages and salaries, retrenched civil servants, and private sector employees who have lost their livelihood because of a shift in production priorities. Most of them, while by no means rich, enjoyed a stable and reasonable standard of living before the introduction of structural adjustment programs. The majority in their midst have definitely become "poorer," even though it is difficult to speculate whether their initial pauperization has become more extreme with the passage of time. A third group – the "structural" or "hard-core" poor – can be located in the bottom 20 percent of the income distribution profile. As alluded to earlier, they continue to struggle under a "seamless web" of poverty, defined by the cumulative interplay of low incomes, a lack of productive assets, low productivity, illiteracy, and short life expectancy.

To reiterate, such cadres have been traditionally left out of the development process. Great physical, social, and cognitive distances separate them from ministers of finance, high status government officials, and development technicians. Perceptions of the latter are typically guided by the "Washington outlook" or "view from the road" that consciously or unconsciously excludes those at the bottom: inaccessible households; "invisible" children who never attend school; the sick who never show their faces at health clinics; and diffident women who must bear the responsibility for maintaining their families.

Poverty Gaps: Cumulative Causal Processes

While income attainment (means) or consumption levels provide an indication of the symptoms of poverty, they do not come to grips with the relational factors generating or perpetuating this evil. As alluded to earlier, poverty is neither a state of being nor traceable to people's genetic makeup, but is more fundamentally the outcome of structural, institutional, and dynamic processes. While it is important to have information about the "amount" of deprivation, it is even more crucial to discern why it exists. Individually and collectively, most forces creating poverty reflect the nature of the larger physical and socio-economic environment, or systems of resource allocation established by societies. Thus, the real problematique is not so much that poor people cannot handle resources, but more because they do not have sufficient access to them.

Such a worldview leads us away from a consideration of the attributes of poor people as individuals, and brings us closer to an understanding of the multifaceted causal factors and processes. They include: (i) socio-economic status; (ii) class, ethnic, and gender biases; (iii) population growth, and family characteristics; (iv) place of residence; (v) economic dualism and other structural imbalances; (vi) political conflicts and civil strife; (vii) domestic policy biases; and (viii) the effects of international processes and policy mandates.

In elaboration, social and economic status are a function of ownerships rights (what people are allowed to own) and their exchange entitlements, that is, what they can receive in exchange for what they own (Sen 1981a). Inadequate incomes and unequal access to resources lie at the heart of poverty. The unequal distribution of income and wealth typically reflects inadequate means of production, with poor people either lacking access to physical assets or having income-earning assets of very low value. Such constraints are often closely correlated with inadequate access to education and other basic social services, leaving them with few skills and undeveloped human capital. As a result, the assets available to the poor are very low in productivity, partly reflecting a lack of synergy with modern technological development. Poor people are continually bedeviled by inadequate market power, which ultimately translates into weak political and social power.

Their membership usually includes the laboring class, casual workers, landless laborers, and small farmers who must eke out subsistence on tiny unirrigated plots. Not to be excluded are also members of the so-called "underclass" who are not usually mentioned in official statistics, or even the development discourse itself. As previously noted, they include persons defined by a pariah or caste-like status, such as aboriginal peoples, certain ethnic minorities, and the untouchables in India; inaccessible households; homeless or "street" children; and migratory workers who cannot take advantage of new technological and organizational developments. The unifying force defining the lot of such cadres is their economic, social, and political powerlessness.

With rapid population growth, unemployment and underemployment are concentrated in poor households. At the beginning of the 1990s, there were more than 500 million people in poor countries who were either unemployed or underemployed – a number equal to the entire labor force of the industrial nations (UNFPA 1991). This trend has continued and, as shown in the previous chapter, the situation might have worsened. The stark implication is that in order to accommodate their growing labor forces, LDCs must create more than 30 million new jobs every year just to maintain their current levels of employment. This inimitable task is further complicated by low educational and skill levels.

In its *State of the World's Children 1999*, UNICEF painted the following grim picture: nearly one-sixth of humanity – 855 million people – were illiterate at the end of the 20th century; women and girls constitute nearly two-thirds of those who cannot read, write, or count;

130 million, or 21 percent of children aged 6-11 in LDCs are not in school; about 13 million of these, or nearly two-thirds, are girls; and, 150 million children do not complete the fifth grade. The lack of educational opportunities is blamed on the fact that many governments in LDCs are yet to provide the leadership and financial resources needed to turn the situation around. With ever-changing technology, people are in constant need of skills. But many lack the basics even in rich countries. Despite universal primary and secondary education in OECD countries, one person in six is functionally illiterate – unable to fill out a simple job application and hence excluded from a world of work that demands new skills.

Population growth is associated with relatively large family sizes and high dependency ratios. LDCs caught in this situation tend to save less than others, resulting in low incomes and wealth creation. In this case, the age profile of the population becomes the critical demographic variable. Contextually, the dependency ratio is defined as the number of dependents – young and older people – as a proportion of the active labor force. This implies relatively higher levels of private household and aggregate spending for schooling, social security, and related forms of "consumption." Since poverty and high population growth rates are highly correlated, deprivation, low levels of savings, and subsistence incomes become endogenous to the development process itself. The situation can be likened to an Alice in Wonderland world in which poor people "have to run in order to remain in the same place."

Human poverty is concentrated in a variety of locations in LDCs: urban, rural, and in places far from capital cities. Its incidence is relatively high in urban areas, especially in what is known as the "urban informal sector" or "survival economy." But, it primarily affects rural dwellers: smallholders, landless or near-landless farmers; agricultural workers, sharecroppers, and tenants; pastoralists – nomadic and agro-based; small-scale fishermen; unemployed school leavers and graduates; and war refugees and other settlement groups. The differential fates of these diverse groups provide an explanation of the interacting typologies of rural poverty shown in Table 7.1.

In the face of rapid population growth, the rural poor have been forced to exploit their limited resources in an unsustainable manner through practices such as overgrazing, denuding forests for fuel, and in some countries, farming on steep slopes. As a result, they have been drawn into the downward spiral of poverty-population-environment.

Table 7.1: Typologies of Rural Poverty

Interstitial	Pockets of poverty surrounded by affluence, ownership of assets, and power. Primary causes are material deprivation, alienation, and distributional inequity.
Peripheral	Mainly found in marginal areas where material deprivation is combined with isolation and alienation.
Overcrowding	Alienation caused by material deprivation due to population pressure and limits on resources.
Traumatic or Sporadic	Deprivation caused by vulnerability to natural disasters, physical accidents, and labor displacements
Endemic	Permanent or less transitory insecurity signaled by a cumulation of alienation, dependence, technological deprivation, and lack of assets

Source: Adapted from IFAD (1992)

This type of syndrome suggests that poverty forces growing numbers of rural folk into environmentally vulnerable areas, with the resultant environmental stress becoming yet another causal factor in their continued deprivation. The dénouement of this process has witnessed a heightening of cumulative causation, which occurs when the number of people has grown extremely large in relation to the available stock of mal-distributed resources. In some countries and regions, the latter are so inequitably distributed that it is often impossible to determine their capacity to sustain a given population.

In many parts of the world, resource scarcities are already a significant source of violent internecine conflict, refugee movements, and other insurgencies. It comes as no surprise, therefore, that many analysts now fear that poverty, population growth, and environmental degradation will continue to ignite political conflicts and civil unrest. For example, Kaplan (1994) has sketched a frightening picture of "the coming anarchy" – in which nations collapse under the tidal flow of refugees stemming from environmental and social disasters and wars fought over depleted resources. A widely reported case is Rwanda where the most brutal massacres have occurred against a backdrop of rising population growth, environmental degradation, and an unequal distribution of resources. The country's fertility rate is one of the highest in the world – over 8 children per woman. About one half of the nation's agricultural land is severely eroded, and the depleted soils have failed to support its burgeoning population. Food shortages may have helped to spark long-simmering tribal and class conflicts.

In Chiapas, Mexico, similar problems constantly threaten to destabilize the nation. Unequal distribution of land and rapid population growth have forced indigenous peoples and poor peasants to eke out a meager living by farming uplands that are environmentally fragile. The irony is that such lands are quickly degraded, thereby plunging the peasants more deeply into poverty. Dwindling resources are also a key factor in the economic and social collapse of Haiti, forcing continuous waves of refugees and asylum seekers on to the perilous high seas. The island's population of more than 7 million is expected to double over the next 18 years. The land is almost completely deforested, and the poor croplands are divided into smaller and less productive parcels with each new generation. Historically, the deepening development cachexy has been exacerbated by predatory rulers who have drained the nation's resources and failed to invest in its people.

This situation mirrors a more generalized problem encountered in the less developed sector of the world. Poor people are usually surrounded by dense networks of highly exploitative intermediaries who constantly drain the few resources they have, prevent them from acquiring more, and restrict their freedom of action. Members of such private and public networks typically include: (i) traders and moneylenders who capitalize on the economic weaknesses of the deprived, and engage in blatant forms of unequal exchange; (ii) government agencies which either show indifference to the needs of those who are powerless and unorganized, or otherwise actively engage in extracting socio-economic "surplus" for the private use of more influential groups; and (iii) a host of organizations, such as political parties, interest groups, and private voluntary organizations (PVOs) which are ostensibly "for" the poor, but in fact serve the status quo of containment and control.

One of the ironies of global development is that national development policies and strategies have tended to worsen the vortex of poverty and underdevelopment. While no government explicitly desires poverty, public powerbrokers have by and large failed to compensate for fundamental inequities between rich and poor. Oftentimes, what one hand gives in the name of "anti-poverty" programs is taken away by the other through dysfunctional policies. Poverty groups do not always come out ahead in the overall scheme of things, and they are often net "donors" to the rest of society. Historically, they have had to pay an inordinate price for unsustainable development policies – urban sprawl, rural neglect, low producer prices and subsidized food imports to urban voters, industrialization based on inappropriate subsidies, taxation of agricultural exports, and unnecessary public sector engagement. The structural imbalances have not only proved a recipe for increasing external indebtedness, but also a primary factor in the deepening of rural stagnation and penury.

The Green Revolution is sometimes cited as a case of national development policy gone awry. While it has produced tremendous increases in per capita food production, the bounty has not been evenly distributed. Global food markets have registered substantial surpluses, yet more than one billion of the world's people remain malnourished. In major clients of the Green Revolution, such as India, Indonesia, and the Philippines, more than half of the rural population still lives in absolute poverty. Some analysts have placed the blame on the emphasis accorded cash crops and capital-intensive inputs such as tractors, pesticides, and fertilizers. Capital-intensive agriculture entails that the wealthier fanners are in a much better position to benefit from the new technologies, thereby widening the gap between rich and poor persons. Furthermore, since Green Revolution techniques of production tend to make farming more profitable, rich farmers and corporations buy up the best land, while smallholders and poor peasants are forced to till environmentally fragile plots, marginal areas, and rocky hillsides.

Gender Inequality and Feminization of Poverty

Gender disparities persist in all regions of the world, and do not necessarily depend on per capita income attainment or stages of development. While there are variations across cultures, they remain most acute in certain societal settings where females play complex roles not only as child-bearers and housekeepers, but in crop production, fetching water and wood, and more generally as traders and breadwinners. Not only are they not adequately compensated for the beastly burden of their work, but it remains undervalued because of a lack of understanding of the inimitable contribution women make to the economic, social, and cultural lives of their communities and societies at large. The situation has culminated in a "feminization of poverty," which is traceable to both historical and contemporary forms of disempowerment, including; (i) structural inequality, reflected in historically sedimented gender relations; (ii) the overrepresentation of women among poverty groups; (iii) the fact that the incidence of poverty has been rising faster for women compared to men; and (iv) the growing number of female-headed households, with an increased tendency for the poorest ones to be headed by women.

Historically, a major bone of contention surrounding the status of women has centered around the simple fact that both "reproduction" (the private sphere) and "production" (the public sphere) are fundamental to human life and its continuity. In his essay *The Subjection of Women* (1869), John Stuart Mill argued that the real question was whether women must be forced to follow what is perceived as their "natural vocation," that is, taking care of the home and family, or whether in both private and public life they are viewed as equal to men. While separation of the spheres, traditionally based on sex or patriarchy, may have been justified as a necessary division of labor during the earlier evolution of the human species, it has outlived its basic functionality. In Mill's eyes, marriage should not be thought of as a partnership of equals analogous to a business partnership: the family is not a "school of despotism," but the "real school of the virtues of freedom."

The distinction between production and reproduction was also articulated by Friedrich Engels ([1884] 1972, 71-72) as follows:

> The determining factor in history is, in the final instance, the production and reproduction of immediate life. This, again, is of a twofold character: on the one side, the production of the means of subsistence, of food, clothing, and shelter and the tools necessary for that production; on the other side, the reproduction of human beings themselves, the propagation of the species. The social organization under which people of a particular historical epoch and a particular country live is determined by both kinds of production; by the stage of the development of labor on the one hand and of the family on the other.

While production usually connotes participation in the labor market, reproduction encompasses household management, procreation, and the care of children and other dependents. Many forms of such nurture and care are not organized through the market process or cash nexus. They typically constitute unpaid labor, or what is termed "reproductive work" or "domestic labor" in the feminist literature. But the allocation of such work tends to be based on a sexual division of labor that is reinforced by gender-ascriptive characteristics. While it does not carry independent income, such work can be construed as an important aspect of "production." The "either/or" dichotomy underlying women's historical roles has been a major stumbling block to their full integration into the development paradigm, since it must encapsulate an emancipatory discourse on engenderment.

Many theories of social organization posit that while women's decision-making rights have varied widely in the past due to the differrential influences of institutional arrangements and socio-cultural norms, females wielded effective authority in at least one segment of society. In those agricultural systems characterized by substantial female subsistence work, women had considerable leverage in the allocation of land and labor resources to satisfy the essential needs of the family. In many African countries, for example, women were not totally dependent on men for their economic and social sustenance. They boasted their own leaders, age-grade associations, and wielded power in many spheres regarded as exclusively feminine. Under the circumstances, they were guaranteed some measure of voice, which entitled them to negotiate successful bargains with men.

Over time, however, the primordial and consensual relationship of complementarity and interdependence between the sexes was transformed into one of dependency of women on men. In the evolution of the sexual division of labor, women's power and spheres of influence were largely eroded by the combined impact of colonialism, and the spread of individual liberalism and market competition. In African and other dependent states, the "customary" laws of marriage were created in response to men's anxieties about women's independence. As a result, the previously negotiable and fluid sexual relations were transformed into very rigid duties and obligations for women as wives and mothers. Enhanced property and inheritance rights for men also sedimented the dependency status of women, especially in Africa.

Most regions of the world still suffer from tremendous gender gaps due to the historical rise of *hegemonic masculinity*. Some major

areas of concern are identified in Table 7.2. These have been successively addressed in several international conferences attempting to put
gender at the center of the development debate, including: the *First
World Conference on Women* in Mexico City in 1975, similar forums
in Copenhagen in 1980 and Nairobi in 1985, and the *Fourth World
Conference on Women* in Beijing in 1995.

Table 7.2: Structuring Gender Equality and Well-Being

Quality of Life	Areas of Concern
Gender Identity	• Rigidity of sexual division of labor
Autonomy of the Body	• Control over sexuality • Control over reproduction • Access to sleep and leisure • Protection against violence
Family and Household	• Decision-making power • Access to household assets
Employment and Income	• Distribution of paid and unpaid labor • Gendered wage differentials
Material Resources	• Access to land • Access to credit
Social Resources	• Access to food and nutrition • Access to education • Access to health
Political Power	• Decision-making in supra-house-hold levels (e.g., government) • Women in managerial positions

Source: Author.

A voluminous literature also exists on critical aspects of the
problem (see, for example, World Bank 1995c, ILO 1998b, and United
Nations [UN] 1999). Hence, our commentary is highly selective.

It is now a stylized fact that most households in LDCs have traditionally allocated a disproportionately high share of expenditure for
education, health, food and nutrition for boys in comparison to girls.
Such inequalities have become critical because education, health, and
nutrition are highly correlated with economic efficiency, growth, and
human well-being. Low levels of educational attainment and inadequate access to basic social services have consistently aggravated the
poor living conditions of women and reduced their capacity to work
productively. Through the lens of modern economic theory, education
is a strategic factor in raising output because it improves a country's
stock of human capital, that is, a better educated labor force spurs economic growth and employment. However, there is an additional bonus
for girls and women. From the very inception, educating females tends
to reduce high fertility levels. For any given level of investment, lower
fertility implies more capital accumulation per worker, and therefore
faster per capita growth rates. Studies of individual countries suggest
that even one year of female schooling could reduce the fertility rate by
5-10 percent. Better education reduces fertility in several important
ways that are crucial to women's advancement and the overall
development process. First, it increases the potential wages women can
command in the market, thereby raising the value of their time and
escalating the effective cost of bearing additional children. Second,
women who are better-educated tend to marry later, and know more
about reproductive rights and family planning. Third, besides having
fewer children, educated women are more likely to have better-fed,
better-educated, and healthier children. Educated mothers are more
prone to send their off-springs to school. Hence, improvements in
women's education, income, and ultimately their control over
household expenditure tend to have a direct and positive impact on
children's education, nutrition, and health. The obverse is a downward
vortex defined by poor living conditions, blighted lives, and
dysfunctional families.

This brings to what is known as a "puzzle of the sexes." In
theory, if improvements in opportunities for women are so beneficial
why do sexual inequalities persist? One answer lies in differences in
perceptions about how economic decisions are made within the
household. The standard economic explanation is based on a view of
the household as a single decision-making unit, which makes certain
choices that do not maximize its own welfare. But the unitary model is
incomplete, because the household is a collective entity involving

elements of both cooperation and conflict. In the typical case, each member of the family has his or own motivations, preferences, and objectives. These result in decisions that reflect not just market efficiency, but more importantly, the relative bargaining power of different household members. Hence, the welfare of individual members does not necessarily move in tandem with that of the household as a whole. Women are usually in a weaker bargaining position compared to men due to the factors mentioned earlier.

When people collaborate in a family, workplace, or other kind of environment, differential gains can be expected from their alternative positions, with some parties benefiting more than others. This is implicit in a factory, for example, where the wage bargaining process usually results in conflict between employers and employees. But elements of cooperation are also present in the profitability of the firm and the employment it generates. This cooperation-conflict nexus tends to be much more hidden in the case of the family or household. Its survival is predicated on mutual self-help, but elements of conflict are always embedded in such cooperative relations. As previously mentioned, males always win out in the distribution of food, education, and other scarce resources. Where the division of benefits is jointly produced within the household, with some members working inside and others inside, males normally appropriate a larger share of the joint product. This is the case even in Sub-Saharan Africa where women are involved in extra-household activities, and in contrast to, say, North Africa and South Asia where they are presumed to do better in terms of distribution within the family.

When conflicts are hidden, there is an implicit perception about how they should be resolved. This usually takes the form of some notion of "legitimacy," which all family members come to accept. In other words, such "subjective" perceptions play an "objective" role in the actual division of benefits and disbenefits within the family. Hence, interpretation and understanding of women's deprived status should take account not only of the objective reality inherent in people's subjective perceptions, but requires a more inclusive notion of rights, that is, who deserves how much of what, and under what circumstances (Sen 1983, 1987).

The precept that all human beings should receive their just rewards as a matter of right puts into bold relief the perennial undervaluation of women's contribution. In economic terms, only production for the market is valued, and significance is attached only to the exchange-value of women's work rather than its intrinsic or human value. It goes without saying that human activity does not always have to be assigned a market value for it to carry instrumental, intrinsic, and ultimately moral worth. Most activities carried out by women within the family and community have a value that transcends the narrow economic calculus. Even in a market environment, women, on average, earn 30-40 percent less than men. It comes as no surprise, therefore, that fewer women than men participate in the labor force. The under-valuation of their work, earnings disparity, and other discriminatory aspects of society combine to decrease women's influence on decisions within the household and in society.

The problematique surrounding the lack of training, work experience, and influence is a reflection of the more embracing fact that women still have little or no ability to influence the policymaking process, or to make decisions about their own self-development. They hold only about 12 percent of parliamentary seats worldwide, 19 percent in industrial nations, and 10 percent in developing countries. The female/male ratio for managerial and administrative positions still remains at a miniscule 13 percent for Africa as a whole, and 11 percent for Sub-Saharan Africa. Even more crucial, the intractable problem remains whether there is sufficient political will and sustained commitment on the part of male-dominated bureaucracies and local authorities to meeting women's strategic and practical gender needs. While most LDCs have ratified relevant United Nations treaties and agreements such as the Convention or the Elimination of Discrimination against Women, the visible gap between record and rhetoric persists. The universal rules have not necessarily informed progressive policymaking, nor have they been translated into sustainable livelihoods for the majority of women.

Children and Youth at Risk

An increasingly large proportion of the planet's human resources is under the age of 21, and many are not only uneducated but left uncared for, socially isolated, and without any durable skills for living. Since children and adolescents hold the gateway and hope for the future, the paradox becomes even more telling when the expected surge in their absolute numbers is pondered. It is estimated that there are about 1.06 billion young people in the world, with nearly 900 million in LDCs. By 2010, more than 700 million youth will enter the labor force in LDCs (more than the entire labor force of the industrial nations in 1990). Many LDCs will reap a "demographic bonus" if the new entrants are equipped with the knowledge and freedom that would allow them to make a meaningful contribution to development (UNFPA 1998, 1999).

It is expected that the demographic bonus will become a reality over the next 15-20 years, as the "bulge" of young people enter the labor force and fewer children are born (due to projected lower birth rates in today's LDCs). The optimistic belief is that if requisite employment is created, the "workforce bulge" can be a basis for more investment, greater productivity, and rapid economic development. This will generate more revenues for social investments, such as health, education, and social security, to meet the needs of both young and old and secure the foundations for sustainable human development. But, if past and present trends continue, reaching adulthood will continue to pose an inordinate burden for the majority of young people. A growing number must now work as child laborers.

While this phenomenon exists in all regions of the world, its incidence is highest in poor countries. The ILO (1998a) has estimated that over 200 million children worldwide are at work, with the largest concentration in Asia. The major causal factors are rapid population growth, decline in living standards, family disintegration, and inadequate schooling. The gender factor is also of some significance. In many LDCs, girls are fed less, receive less medical care, withdrawn from school earlier, and forced into hard labor sooner than boys. The evidence suggests that Africa has the highest labor force participation rate for girls. Approximately 37 percent of girls work in Africa compared 20 percent in Asia and 11 percent in Latin America. Although boys account for three out of every five child laborers in the reported statistics, the proportion of girls may actually be higher because of the under-reporting of their activities carried out in and around the household. A distinction needs to be drawn between normal family obligations on the one hand, and activities which give rise to exploitation and abuse, on the other.

While work subjecting children to exploitation and abuse is prohibited under international labor standards, such practices are still rampant on a worldwide basis. For example, child laborers are frequently employed in domestic service, which is rich in potential for exploitation. Due to the clandestine nature of this activity, little comprehensive information is available about the living and working conditions of domestics. But there is disquieting evidence of widespread physical, mental, and sexual abuse of young females working in house-holds other than their own. In the eyes of the ILO, the consequences of long hours, emotional deprivation, and servitude on young female workers include "withdrawal and regression, premature aging, depression, and low self-esteem."

Virtually all foreign aid channeled into the youth sector has been concentrated on the under-six age group, and the financing of university education for a few lucky 18-year olds. As a result, the relatively huge but highly vulnerable group aged 15-20 has been left out of the equation. In general, uneducated children and unemployed youth will continue to pose the most severe domestic and international policy challenge. Besides the problems of young females who work as domestics, young alienated males are also a critical group at risk, since they are most likely to commit petty crimes and engage in acts of political violence. To compound the problem of marginalized youth, estimates suggest that more than 100 million children live on the streets. The "street children" phenomenon is a most extreme and visible expression of persistent poverty, social injustice, and erosion of social norms. It is a painful reminder of the failure of governments and society at large to address the worst forms of mass deprivation and inequality; in fact, many government authorities deny the existence of street children, while others are engaged in open confrontations with them. The result is that street children, who are adept at mastering survival skills, are constantly involved in "games of despair."

The majority of them can be encountered in major urban centers such as Rio de Janeiro, Nairobi, Addis Ababa, and Johannesburg where city life has become extremely expensive. In many cases, children working on the streets may be a response on the part of desperate and needy families to generate funds in whatever ways they conceivably can. Working children of needy families, as well as homeless children, are sometimes drawn into more affluent urban areas to supplement family income. The children's survival, and in many cases that of their entire family, is made possible by dogged efforts to skim off a very miniscule share of the personal wealth concentrated in richer locations. Girls are sometimes sent on the streets to earn money by prostitution, while other children may be working on the streets because their parents cannot afford the cost of books, uniforms, and other expenses of schooling. Thus, the disheartening phenomenon of street children can be interpreted as a part of the family's striving to survive under conditions of endemic poverty.

Despite the unique cultures and societal values of different countries, street children typically share some common behaviors, risk factors, and characteristics. Across LDCs, the problem starts with the economy, as evidenced by macroeconomic crises, rapid urbanization, inappropriate forms of industrialization, and the inequitable distribution of income and wealth. In many areas, overall economic insecurity, armed conflicts, and natural disasters such as droughts have taken millions of lives, leaving behind broken homes, families, and orphanized or runaway children in extremely hostile environments. In Rio de Janeiro, for example, many street children are inhabitants of shanty towns or slums in which government provides very little or no public support or services. The socio-economic circumstances of Brazil have produced a fundamental rip in the social fabric of society, enormous pressures on low-income families, and in many cases propelling their disintegration. In many Asian and African countries, the breakdown of the extended family which was once a pillar of social life has resulted in an abandonment of children who are forced to live on the streets by their wits.

In conclusion, it is evident that the plight of street children in particular and youth in general cannot be divorced from the more embracing failure to achieve sustainable human development in the face of widespread deterioration in social and economic welfare. As explored more fully in later chapters of this book, one credible long-term solution centers around the imperative of crafting a global human rights strategy that puts an end to child labor and related abuses. Another points to the duty, responsibility, and obligation of national governments and friendly aid donors to design and implement structural policies for humanitarian development, full employment, social protection, and the eradication of poverty. At a third level, the emphasis should shift toward concrete and sustainable community-based programs. Inherent in the communitarian focus is a response to the problems facing youth in constructive ways by providing them schooling, shelter, and protection, especially in those situations where they must work. What is envisaged is a comprehensive strategy based on a continuum of services – from family support programs and public housing for destitute families to rehabilitation and alternative forms of schooling and training of youth at risk.

Part Three

Goal-Oriented Human Futures

Chapter 8

Quest for Human Well-Being

> When one day our human kind becomes fully grown it will not
> define itself as the sum total of the whole world's inhabitants, but
> as the infinite unity of their mutual needs.
>
> Jean-Paul Sartre (1961)

The development anomalies inherent in the cumulation of global inequality, the new international division of labor, as well as persistent poverty and related correlates of human ill-being clearly suggest an imperative of reorienting development thought and policy toward a more
emancipatory conversation about the enhancement of well-being and
prospects for alternative goal-oriented human futures. At the heart of
this quest lies the humanitarian end of human security in all its multifaceted but ultimately inseparable dimensions. This entails a concerted
shift from the narrow military definition to a more holistic conception
encompassing the totality of human well-being.

From this perspective, all human beings are entitled to enjoy at least a minimum level of security as a basic condition of life. This is predicated on four potential achievements guiding goal-oriented human futures: provision of opportunities to fulfill the basic need of earning an adequate livelihood; security from life-threatening forms of ill-being such as chronic disease and oppression, as well as protection from sudden and harmful disruptions in people's daily lives; removal of threats to human life by domestic violence against women, child neglect and abuse, crime, and acts of terrorism; and guaranteeing the survival of indigenous and aboriginal peoples.

Human security also signifies empowerment, or the imperative of human beings emerging to fulfill their best nature through full realization of their capabilities and enhancement of their choices. It entails freedom from the constraining forces of anti-development and its correlates, as well as the positive freedom of people, as active agents of change, to choose in their own right. Contextually, the basic freedoms can be said to encapsulate freedom from fear, want, hunger, and oppression; freedom to choose based on increased incomes and corresponding improvements in the overall quality of life; freedom to receive unbiased information and to move about; and the freedom of people to participate fully in decisions governing their lives and livelihoods (Sen 1999).

Hence, security as a general sense of human well-being implies being in control of one's development, that is, taking charge of one's behavior, who we are, and what we are seeking to achieve – what Standing (2002) calls "sustainable self-respect." Correlatively, it can be construed as a necessary condition for real freedom and autonomy. The significance of this is also related to the historical fact that much of the evolution of human society can be defined by attempts by some individuals or groups to control others through a variety of mechanisms and in varying degrees. In this regard, there is also a necessity to distinguish between individual and collective forms of security.

The former refers a person's search for self-fulfillment while the latter is more concerned with group-oriented identity based on societal, class, ethnic, occupational, and similar referents. In other words, it reflects the primordial human proclivity or need for belongingness and identification with a social group. As emphasized in Chapter 3, while the norms, social capital, and institutional rules inherent in group behavior are essential prerequisites for human well-being, group member-ship is often used as a means of controlling others. Furthermore, the history of political economy can be interpreted as attempts to determine the extent to which forms of security are desirable or feasible. This enduring issue remains central to human life in the 21st century where a major challenge still centers around the need to establish the Good Society.

Psycho-Biological Security

A person's normative self-concept or the "mental self" is linked to a big and complex mind, or the very intricate combination of specialized mechanisms depicted by the human brain. Studies by neurobiologists have consistently shown the presence of active mental characteristics based on a close association among neurological complexity, its con-tinuous growth, and human Intelligence. It is now known that evolution of the species *homo sapiens* has been accompanied by a remarkable growth in brain size and the cortical area associated with thinking. Distinct patterns of human intelligence that are closely correlated with brain size and cortical sophistication include: (i) an A-factor, or the capacity of human beings to abstract, generalize, and contrast events and situations; (ii) a C-factor of memory storage that enables us to store information over long periods of time; (iii) a D-factor, or the human proclivity to execute patterned responses based on motor-sensory mechanisms; and (iv) a P-factor, defining the human ability to automatically pause before responding to a situation (Stenhouse 1974).

While the *brain* interacts with the *mind* in complex ways, the cul-tural context of teaching and learning has been primarily responsible for evolution of the latter, which transcends the former – a physiolo-gical entity. Many animals have brains, but minds are of a higher order, facilitating sophisticated forms of intelligence. Having a "mind" connotes the ability to formulate "goals" to be achieved. Since human beings possess minds, they are presumably in control of, and can make informed decisions about, alternative developmental futures. This means that human consciousness is an emergent or intermediate non-material characteristic of life.

In some comparisons of humans with other animal species, it is claimed that human beings are simply at one end of the mental or psy-chological continuum. In other words, we are presumed to differ from other animals and plants only to a certain degree. The belief in human uniqueness rests on the assumption that while many lower animals share our psychological powers, humans are the only beings on the planet whose lives are defined by rational knowledge, critical judgment, a normative self-concept, a worldview, and a moral constitution. However, a new chapter is being written in ethology (the study of animal behavior), suggesting that these behavioral traits may have evolved from lower animals to humans. In this context, de Waal (1989, 1996) has provided many exemplars of "social animals" which behave in ways that humans might call "ethical": whales and dolphins that risk their lives to save injured companions; chimpanzees that come to the aid of victims of aggression; and elephants that attempt to revive slain comrades and refuse to leave them. The general claim is that other animals may have many of the psychological mechanisms or emotions governing human behavior and morality, but that "they don't piece it together as we do."

Moral behavior would be impossible without both sympathy and empathy. Sympathetic behavior is observed in a variety of higher animals: dogs that stay protectively close to crying children; monkeys that help handicapped individuals; and killer whales that follow their sick companions into shallow water and beach with them. By contrast, empathy – the ability to comprehend the thoughts and feelings of others – is usually reserved for species boasting relatively high levels of cognition. Empathy and reciprocity are key elements in human morality. Humans can be said to have a moral conscience, which is typically reflected in the ability to distinguish right from wrong and to recognize intentionality and responsibility.

Nevertheless, numerous unanswered questions still remain about the human brain and mind – for example, how memory is stored and the nature of human consciousness (Hazen and Singer 1997). In the field of development biology, there is still a lack of clear understanding about the enormously complicated processes that maintain the life of a biological cell. While substantial progress has been made toward unraveling the genetic code and in the amazing project of mapping the human genome, significant lacunae still exist in knowledge about how information stored in a single cell can generate an extraordinarily complex organism such as the human person. Despite such knowledge gaps, the known attributes of human cognitive complexity do project a personality that constantly displays well-defined and specific traits that are peculiar to human beings.

These characteristics transcend the historically dominant psycho-biological "model of man," or the generic "mind-machine" metaphor. It posits a mechanistic mind that is passive, empty, and receptive. But, humans are unique as "knower-agents," in contrast to "behavioral agents" who act purely in response to external stimuli. This is not to deny that humans sometimes act as behavioral agents. The point of emphasis is that they do not characteristically accept instinct, impulse, or external stimuli at face value. As indicated earlier, humans operate with a normative self-concept that not only imposes internal constraints on them, but also one that is more positively motivated by goals, plans, principles, critical judgment, and knowledge.

Evidence derived from modern development psychology suggests an extraordinary cognitive complexity and capacity for interpersonal relations among human beings. These are thought to constitute motivational factors that are crucial to the interpretation and understanding of the organic human world and how it impinges on the quest for well-being. Certain attributes of the human personality, such as self-consciousness and freedom, are deemed critical to "ego development," or the character of human development that has occurred during various stages of evolution (Loevinger 1976). The guiding analogy is to the human person as a "psychobiological organism," implying that humans select their environment and actively interpret what they select.

The organismic analogy is anathema to mechanistic models, or the perception of a human personality that is infinitely malleable in a biological sense. Of course, a human person may be malleable in the limited sense that he or she is responsive to opportunities for improvement in the quality of life. However, such malleability stops when his or her ontological needs are being constantly ignored or suppressed. "Needs" represent the principal elements of the human cognitive structure, that is, things constantly motivating human behavior. Some needs are basic while others are transitory, depending on how human cognitions change over time. With a few minor exceptions, however, basic survival needs are much the same everywhere. This remains true even though common survival needs can be met in a variety of ways, for example, through variations in farming, health care and educational systems, specialization, and trade.

Useful insights into the psychodynamics of needs have been provided by social psychologists who link their fulfillment to processes of social and organizational learning through which humans are socialized to make certain demands on the larger society. The resultant "patterns of human concerns" are summarized in Table 8.1.

Table 8.1: Patterns of Human Concerns

Life	The perennial quest by humans to enlarge and enrich the quality of their lives and satisfactions.
Needs	The satisfaction of survival needs
Choices	Humans have the capacity to make choices and always desire to exercise this capacity
Freedom	Freedom is required to exercise the choices humans are capable of making
Security	The need for a sense of both physical and psychological security
Order	A constant craving for sufficient order and certainty so that accurate judgments can be made about what will or will not occur
Hope	As creatures of hope, humans are not genetically designed to resign themselves
Personality	Humans have a need for personal dignity and want to experience their own dignity, integrity, and self-worth
Values	Humans constantly seek some value or system of beliefs to which they can commit themselves
Expectations	Humans want a sense of confidence and surety that the society to which they belong holds out a fair degree of hope that their aspirations will be fulfilled

Source: Author

Motivational psychologists interpret the same mechanisms in terms of recursive linkages among personality formation, self-actualization, and human cognitive development. The general thesis is that cognitive structures provide the governing dynamic behind social and psychological development as a whole, and in terms of acquisition of specific personality traits.

The original formulation was provided by Abraham Maslow (1954, 1962) who viewed self-awareness and a concern for autonomy as essential attributes of the human personality. This idea formed the starting point for a long tradition in psychology, which interprets personality formation in terms of the acquisition of successive freedoms – from impulses derived through assimilation of cultural norms and social expectations to the continuous struggle to secure liberation from social conventions and pressures. However, Maslow was primarily concerned with human motivation. In his view, all human beings are motivated by a desire to satisfy a complex array of instinctual needs – for example, biological existence and reproduction, life-sustenance, security, identity, belongingness, love, self-esteem, and self-respect. These represent "deficiency needs," which are crowned by one of a different order – self-actualization and human growth. While the needs are present in everyone, most people tend to function at a lower level than that required for self-actualization, or what is dubbed the "psychopathology of normalization." The following properties of deficiency motivation are identified (Maslow 1962: 20):

> 1. its absence breeds illness, 2. its presence prevents illness, 3. its restoration cures illness, 4. under certain (very complex) free choice situations, it is preferred by the deprived person over other satisfactions, 5. it is found to be inactive, at a low ebb, or functionally absent in a healthy person. Two additional characteristics are subjective ones, namely conscious and unconscious yearning and desire, and feeling of lack or deficiency, as of something missing on the one hand, and, on the other palatability.... The original criterion of motivation and the one that is still used by all human beings except behavioral psychologists is the subjective one.

The typology based on Maslow's hierarchy of needs is now well entrenched in motivational psychology and development thought. The preconception that all human behavior is motivated is also widely accepted. Nevertheless, skepticism remains about the distinction between deficiency motivation (seeking only relief) and growth motivation (seeking fulfillment). The perspective of a self-actualizing person – thought to be synonymous with someone over fifty years of age – as an exemplar of mental health and maturity is also problematic. Young people, including many children, constantly try to develop before concepts such as self-esteem and identity can be given any meaningful application. Thus, Maslow's schema should be modified to account for the possibility that self-actualization or growth motivation may not come into play only after deficiency motives have been satisfied.

While there may be disagreements about the ordering of need achievements, Maslow's pluralistic conception of motivations still provides the paradigm case for the interpretation of human needs fulfillment. Two broad implications for the human development quest may be emphasized. One follows from the hypothesis that, beyond the obvious deficiency needs, there are basic social and psychological ones pertaining to human growth and development. Even if the need for, say, food and shelter are satisfied, human development capabilities would still remain wanting unless other core human values are incorporated into the equation. Goulet (1978) and Sen (1999) have identified these as self-esteem and freedom. The former refers to feelings of independence, identity, integrity, self-respect, and a general sense of people's own worthiness and personal dignity. To these should be added other universal human "goods" such as hope and the capacity to love.

Love is not only a subject of longstanding philosophical speculation, but still remains one of the most powerful human impulses. Within the overall context provided by people's concrete social praxis and the universality of life's claims, the concept may be used to connote human capabilities such as public spiritedness, civic belongingness, and a willingness to observe elementary cosmopolitan norms. In this sense, love can be construed as a global public good that carries both immanent and instrumental value. At one level, it is valued for its own sake, since those who experience it know that it carries its own rewards. At another level, it is valued more because it can facilitate the production of other collective goods such as peace and authentic development through social tolerance, benevolence, altruism, and cooperation.

A question then arises about how it can be utilized as an input or ingredient in decision-making in order to achieve desired ends of human welfare. The dominant perspectives of social and economic theory – from classical liberalism and scientisrn to modern neo-classicism – are rooted in a basic preconception that human society is much more salutary and secure when built on self-interest rather than on love and benevolence. This has resulted in a pervasive economistic interpretation of love and its correlates as relatively "scarce resources."

The implicit assumption is that the proper functioning of society requires an institutional structure and patterns of human motivation in which as small a burden as possible is placed on love and benevolence.

Once love is conceptualized as a scarce resource, the standard private cost-benefit calculus and maximizing ontology typically encountered in economics would require an "economizing" of its use. This follows from the fundamental neo-classical rule about deployment of scarce resources among alternative uses: the scarcer is a resource, the higher is its price and a lesser amount will be used in combination with other inputs by the economizing agent. From the humanitarian development perspective, the supply of love and benevolence cannot be equated with factors of production such as land and capital because it is not fixed or limited. The analogy is faulty because of at least two reasons. First, the supply of moral or humanitarian resources may well increase rather than decrease over time. Second, they may well lose their potency or potential for doing good if they are unused, underutilized, or abused for long periods of time (Hirschman 1984b). As our troubled human condition amply demonstrates, constitutive resources such as love, social tolerance, and public spiritedness are skills and capabilities which improve through constant use but atrophy if neglected.

In conclusion, the primacy of place accorded human motivation, needs, and expectations suggests a necessity of moving away from mechanistic models of explanation that stress the malleability of individuals and groups toward a life-and-world vision based on transcultural human universals. Contextually, it cannot be overemphasized that inequality, poverty, underdevelopment, and other manifestations of ill-being are direct causes of frequent dislocations such as internecine conflicts, wars, military insurgencies, and related forms of instability. Their primary loci can be attributed to institutions and policies promoted by systemic orders that continuously ignore or suppress elemental development needs. In the overall scheme of things, individuals and groups are mandated to make a variety of dysfunctional behavioral adjustments that are anathema to human tolerance, capabilities, and freedom. If it is believed that deep value-laden human motivations and needs cannot be compromised, then extensive restructuring of values, institutions, and policies may be required in order to make the development transition more synergistic with humanitarian goals.

Consumption Standards

Consumption can be interpreted as a proximate end of development, or as an essential means of ensuring people's participation in the community and for enhancing the overall quality of life. Its linkage to humanitarian development inheres in the universalism of life claims.

> At the foundation of human development is the principle of the universalism of life claims, acknowledging the life claims of everyone – men, women, and children – without discrimination. It demands a world in which consumption is such that all have enough to eat, no child goes without education, no human being is denied health care, and all people can develop their potential capabilities to the fullest extent (UNDP 1998, 38).

From this perspective, the consumption-development nexus can be construed in terms of disparate activities that are geared toward providing public and private wants or needs.

As such, consumption transcends the mere ability to provide material commodities based on personal income. It also includes collective and non-material goods and services supplied through public provisioning, such as social security, education, health and transportation, as well as those produced outside the monetized or market economy. Examples of the latter are goods and services generated through unpaid work, especially by women, and the stock of natural resources constituting the biophysical environment. The humanitarian goal of sustainable development is predicated on intra-generational and inter-generational equity, or a universal claim that the present level of development and consumption patterns should not be allowed to perpetuate today's inequities.

The human-centered approach to consumption must necessarily rely on a transdisciplinary mode of interpretation, even though perspectives differ within and across disciplines. The focus of mainstream economics is on individual utility maximization or satisfaction at the micro level, and the generation and use of national income at the macro level, with the alternative to consumption viewed as savings, that is, deferred consumption. In this regard, Keynes's *General Theory* was mainly responsible for ushering in the macroeconomic perspective of consumption. He not only regarded aggregate consumption as an important component of national income, but the effective demand of the consumer as the principal vehicle of national economic growth. Furthermore, this has implications for production and employment.

Declines in consumption are usually accompanied by downward movements in economic growth, incomes, production, and job creation. The cumulative impact on human development ultimately depends on the production process, which dictates who is employed or earns income, and the nature of their involvement in the economy. At the most basic level, labor or work plays a critical role in the production of goods and services necessary for people to achieve employability or a status of human beings capable of making decisions about their life plans and purposes. At the same time, the availability and distribution of goods and services necessary for human needs fulfillment requires full employment, that is, jobs for all those willing to work and at wages adequate enough to purchase those goods and services. At another level, production of certain goods can generate fair employment, for example, crops grown by small-scale producers rather than by large plantations, or activities that empower women through wage employment. By contrast, consumption of goods whose production exploits producers or laborers tends to militate against human development. Included in this category are garment industries employing the sweated labor power of women, or forms of child labor that deprive children their childhood and education.

Among economists, Sen (1985) has emphasized the fact that the uses to which commodities are put may enrich human lives and enhance people's capabilities, but their effectiveness depends on personal characteristics and social circumstances, variations in which can contribute to inequalities in society. This brings us to the sociological perspective which places consumption in the larger context of social relations and institutions. People's consumption decisions are thought to be influenced by social commitments, such as social class, social norms, and other means of communication or interaction. In this regard, Max Weber (1968) utilized the concept of a "status group" sharing a common lifestyle to demonstrate how consumption patterns based on class and social differentiation can be used for group identity, inclusion or exclusion. Other social commentators, philosophers, and theologians usually express concern about the potential conflict between the materialism inherent in modern forms of consumption and the wider set of human values, including the need for simpler lifestyles.

It is estimated that global consumption expenditure, private and public, more than doubled over the past generation, reaching $25 trillion in the late 1990s. On the surface, this expansion can be interpreted as an unprecedented improvement of humanity. But a deeper look shows the promise for human advancement to be highly problematic. Not only are consumption growth and patterns unevenly distributed but, in the eyes of many, they have been environmentally damaging and produced social impacts that deepen social exclusion and inequalities. The grim picture of unequal and unbalanced consumption has been interpreted as a tale of gluttony, or as private opulence in the midst of public squalor.

The richest 20 percent of the world's population consume 86 percent of its goods and services, over half of its energy, and nearly half of its meat and fish. Meanwhile, consumption in the poorest countries is too low to meet even the most basic needs of 1 billion people. For example, average protein consumption per person is 115 grams a day in France, but only 32 grams in Mozambique. It is reckoned that Americans spend about $8 billion a year on cosmetics and Europeans $50 billion on cigarettes, but it remains a difficult, and virtually impossible, task to find the $9 billion the UN estimates is needed to provide all human beings on the planet with access to clean drinking water and sanitation.

Such glaring imbalances persist even though consumption has been growing faster in LDCs than in the industrial world. This brings us back to the question about the relationship between want creation and human needs, and the extent to which the culture of "overconsumption" contributes to the human good or social well-being. From this perspective, the unequal nature of consumption reflects a dysfunctional pattern of behavior in a modern world system in which people in the more developed sector continue to enjoy an abundant supply of material prerequisites, whereas the majority in the less developed sector desperately struggle for access to the elementary necessities of life. In addition, the worsening of global income distribution might have further disturbed the entire production-consumption-distribution cycle of goods and services. The ensuing pattern of global development has indulged groups of people in all segments of the world to consume beyond the natural limits of their material wants.

A general concern is with the potentially negative consequences of a value system that increasingly serves as a hallowed model for the entire globe. The charting of an authentic or humanitarian development path is inherently linked to the imperative of closing the escalating gap between what is commonly perceived as massive consumerism or "waste" in some parts of the world in the face of glaring unmet needs in others. The materialistic ethic and corresponding trends in consumerism can be linked to social and psychological pressures that have historically conditioned economic behavior in modern society. The *Croesus factor*, or what is perceived as a veritable worship of money, has apparently become embedded in the very fabric of human relations and takes precedence over other valued things.

This tendency is explained by the psychology of satisfaction, which is primarily derived from "having money." However, it is not simply a matter of "having enough" money, but "having more" than other people, or more today than yesterday. The presence of this proclivity (rational or irrational) is confirmed by the results of various cross-cultural studies. For example, Argyle (1987) has marshaled evidence demonstrating that while the opulent in any one societal setting may be more satisfied with their standard of living than their less fortunate peers, they are typically no more satisfied than rich people in other societies. In other words, the unending quest continues for "having more" than other rich people everywhere, since this is equated with "being more." Germane to this is the relationship between economic growth and affluence, people's access to different kinds of commodities, and the relative degrees of satisfaction expected to be derived therefrom.

In the latter context, Hirsch (1976) has advanced the thesis that, as people become better off, there is a heightened tendency to purchase more "positional goods" such as luxury homes, cars, and expensive art. The "charm" of owning such artifacts lies in their absolute or relative scarcity. As such, they are valued more for their "extrinsic" rather than "intrinsic" worth and will remain outside the reach of the majority of the population, no matter how much their incomes increase. Since positional goods usually play an instrumental role of satisfying luxury consumption wants, their acquisition tends to be motivated exclusively by the status or prestige that ownership confers. By contrast, basic necessities are valued more for their intrinsic properties. For example, food items are valued because of their inherent nutritive and survival characteristics.

In general, it can be hypothesized that material prosperity and o-pulence may not necessarily bring further satisfaction once the average person has reached a certain threshold of wealth and acquired goods and services betraying that status. Once this stage is reached, a second or third expensive automobile or vacation home may be bought, but certainly not a fourth or fifth. This is not meant to deny that people with adequate means are free to choose and purchase whatever they wish. If the above assumption is correct, however, it belies the econocentric belief that more happiness results from higher and higher levels of compulsive consumption, or the satisfaction of insatiable economic wants. It is now a truism that income and consumption attainment are not necessarily the main determinants of human welfare. Some crucial factors in the search for goal-oriented futures include: satisfaction with family life, job satisfaction, friendship, and the ability or opportunity to enjoy leisure (see Wachtel 1989; Scitovsky 1976; and Durning 1992). The rankings may vary according to country and individual circumstances.

The increased expenditure on positional goods associated with opulence and imitative behavior may be perfectly rational from the standpoint of those who can afford them. This raises the issue whether such expenditures or corresponding behavioral patterns are wasteful and constitute a misallocation of resources that could otherwise be redirected toward enhancing the overall standard and quality of living. As Veblen ([1899] 1965) noted a long time ago, such outlays are not wasteful in the strict economic sense, since people boasting adequate incomes are free to purchase luxury consumption goods in the market-place. However, such behavior becomes immoral or irrational when interpreted through the human-centered lens of basic needs fulfillment, or in a situation where unmet human needs and endemic poverty continue to coexist with plenty and conspicuous consumption in all parts of the globe.

The argument is not that a materially wealthy society cannot take care of the basic needs of those who have been left behind. Rather, its capacity for doing so on a sustained basis depends on the inculcation of a value system that transcends the pure economic calculus and is predisposed toward building a more humane, pleasant, and cooperative society. In situations where opulence, conspicuous consumption, and related social influences constantly induce or socialize people to place an inordinately high premium on luxury or positional goods, their acquisition may become an end in itself and societal norms will be defined in purely materialistic terms. Under the circumstances, those cadres lacking the income or wealth to purchase such goods may develop an inferiority complex and related negative feelings or attributes such as low self-esteem and a lack of moral worth or social respectability.

As a general rule, human betterment is less dependent on the ability to purchase positional goods and more on people's access to basic goods and services necessary for them to lead a decent, pleasant, and fulfilling life. However, we hasten to add that advocacy of this standard is not meant to deny people's basic freedom to choose whatever it is they feel that they want. The point of emphasis is that such "freedom" has been increasingly compromised through the influence of exogenous forces associated with social conditioning and cultural penetration. The march of globalization has culminated into a fully integrated space of economic and information flows, cultural homogenization of disparate geographical places, and a successive de-linking of development processes and consumption profiles from their national and local settings. In the final analysis, the freedom of choice guiding appropriate consumption potentials is intrinsic to human well-being itself, and should be located in ethical space and the domain of basic human rights. Thus, pertinent outcomes cannot be solely arbitrated in the court of economics.

Empowerment Through Participation

In the original sense, participation was coterminous with the empowerment of people. This connoted concerted efforts designed to increase human control over resources and institutions, thereby enhancing the power of those previously excluded from involvement in the decision-making process. It also suggests a political and structural role for participation that is not simply linked to the efficiency of development programs. Hence, participation as empowerment should be understood as a multidimensional process reflecting structural relationships among people, institutions, and the community at large. The overall implication is that development initiatives should always be construed as means or instrumental mechanisms facilitating this process, as well as giving meaning and significance to the higher order matrix of shared values and local norms.

However, the original meaning of participation has undergone some substantial changes in recent times. For example, it is dressed up in new clothes by the World Bank, which views it as a process whereby *stakeholders* influence and share control over development initiatives as well as the decisions and resources affecting them. It is predicated on the establishment of a planning process in which project designers first identify those stakeholders whose interests are affected by Bank-financed projects. While such interests and relative degrees of power and influence tend to vary from project to project, the major stakeholders are thought to include: poor people, since one of the Bank's professed objectives remains poverty reduction; those directly affected, positively or negatively, by a project; governments and governmental organizations responsible for devising and implementing public policies and programs; entities that are indirectly affected, for example, NGOs and private sector agencies with an interest in outcomes; and World Bank staff, management, and shareholders who have their own objectives, policies, and institutional responsibilities.

The problem with this interpretation is that it is too broad and diffuse, and fails to address the very problem that participation was supposed to solve in the first place. The grouping of stakeholders under one uniform umbrella seems to beg the question, since the expectations of poor people and grassroots participants are normally in conflict with those of Bank officials, central government authorities, and private sector agencies. But, the stakeholder approach is consistent with an emerging consensus, especially among aid donors, that participation represents a *partnership* based on negotiation and compromise among diverse sectors of interest. It is envisaged that people would increasingly become active agents rather than mere passive beneficiaries of development programs and projects. The optimistic view is that agendas would no longer be imposed from the top or outside, but mutually set, with deliberate efforts made to seek and incorporate local views and indigenous knowledge.

In particular, the idea of partnership underscores the role played by NGOs as important catalysts in spreading the message about the lasting benefits of participation. They constantly demonstrate the value of participatory and related forms of appraisal in empowering rural communities. Such appraisals consist of coordinated approaches and methods that enable people to express and interpret their own development reality, draw up relevant plans, as well as monitor and evaluate results. The process has been facilitated by geographic information systems showing where people live and specific locations of farmlands, forests, water, schools, health facilities, and so on; flow diagrams that help in problem-solving; and seasonal calendars and matrices that can aid agricultural planning.

Participatory appraisals were originally introduced by NGOs working in East Africa and South Asia, but grew significantly during the 1990s and are now being used worldwide by aid donors, governments, universities, and training institutes. The data and information garnered from such pragmatic tools have increased the awareness of people and involvement in their self-development, thereby making an invaluable contribution to the design and execution of policies that can better serve their interests. Policymakers and analysts are now in a better position to build a more comprehensive picture of the complexity and diversity inherent in local realities. They are also afforded a greater opportunity to meet people face to face, and make relatively quick and accurate assessments of the potential impacts and implications of alternative policy mixes.

The diverse perspectives of participation may be interpreted as a continuum ranging from the *nominal* in which there is very little involvement in development to the *transformative* which results in people's empowerment. Alternatively, they can be viewed in terms of levels or degrees of participation – running the gamut from the minimalist case where it is contrived as an opportunity to indoctrinate, or essentially an act of manipulation, to the opposite end of the spectrum in which people at the grassroots become full partners in development, and begin to assume responsibility for its management. The alternative perspectives essentially boil down to two broad life-and-world visions and supporting styles of developmental management.

One views *participation as a means* (instrumental), or a process whereby local people cooperate or collaborate in externally designed and controlled development activities. In this case, it is perceived as a technique to gauge the progress of projects and ensure successful technocratic outcomes. This planner-centered approach is consonant with the conventional "top down" model of decision-making, as well as the neo-classical proclivity to separate means from ends. While the instrumental view seeks to provide more immediate panaceas or short-term access to the benefits of development, it fails to address the ramifications of people's full human development potentials that are inherent in a longer term vision or trajectory.

By contrast, the intrinsic perspective views *participation as an end* in itself. This entails changing the balance of power between elites and the community so that central governments and leading policymakers at the center can increasingly serve the interests of the many rather than those of a select few. The underlying philosophy is synergistic with the "bottom up" or communal approach to transformation. It rests on two related preconceptions. One is that genuine or authentic development is not so much about "successful" programs or projects, but rather issues from the socio-structural and institutional processes that enable or enhance people's capabilities to develop themselves. The other is that change is a *process*, with a primary end of authentic development interpreted as the process itself. This processual change is not a discrete linear policy sequence designed to attain specific quantified targets, as in the case of most externally funded programs or projects, but a cumulative causal trajectory of communal interaction that is defined by inseparability between means (processes) and ends (goals).

The contrasting development orientations underlying the two perspectives of participation may be described as "project orientation" vis-à-vis "humanitarian development orientation." While the two approaches may not be mutually exclusive, they help to explain divergences in lending policies of major aid donors and their potential impacts on local development efforts. By defining everyone as a stakeholder, the World Bank does not seem to have committed itself to a specific position, or set any identifiable goals. In practice, however, its approach to project lending typically associates participation with the provision of local inputs, since this is viewed as a means of lowering the maintenance costs of projects, potentially improving their economic efficiency, and ultimately maximizing rates of return on its investments.

For most bilateral lending agencies, participation is viewed as both a means and an end, that is, commitment to participation is linked to the wider set of humanitarian goals – democracy, good governance, equity, and human rights. At least in their objectives, some are primarily interested in influencing the political empowerment of the poor, since this is deemed critical to endeavors aimed at building democracy, as well as a mechanism enabling poverty groups to sustain the benefits of participatory development after external assistance ends. For example, a guiding principle underlying the approach of the United States Agency for International Development (USAID) to participation states:

> *We will ensure that projects we support strengthen the capacity of the poor to take the next steps in their own and in their community's development.* That is, in all our efforts – not just those aimed explicitly to promote our 'democracy' objective – we will seek to empower the poor to sustain the development process (USAID 1993; emphasis in original).

In similar vein, SIDA (Swedish International Development Agency) has not only emphasized the need for participation in all stages of project development, but also the imperative of long-term commitment, dialogue, and cooperation with client countries. One of the clearest construals of participation in the empowerment sense as a primary objective of development aid can be found in the following statement by the German Agency for Technical Cooperation (GTZ 1998):

> Participation can no longer be seen merely as a means of making projects more successful in reaching their objectives. If participation is to make a difference and contribute to sustainable development, a shift in perspective is required. Participation has to be understood as a social and political process which has a general bearing on the relationship between people and institutions in society. Projects and programs can still make important contributions in support of these processes, as well as to the structures, norms and attitudes in which they are embedded. However, in order to do this, we must learn to accept that their new role is primarily an accompanying, enabling, and facilitating one.

An important advantage that bilateral aid agencies, such as the GTZ, Canadian International Development Agency (CIDA), Swedish International Development Agency (SIDA), and perhaps the United States Agency for International Development (USAID), boast over the World Bank is their extensive presence at the grassroots in host countries. Their experiential knowledge has been a major catalyst in fostering an enabling environment for participatory, and ultimately authentic or humanitarian, development.

Sustainability: The Human-Ecology Dialectic

The full realization of human development potentials is ultimately dependent on the nature-nurture dynamic or interface between "human" (socio-economic) and "natural" (physico-ecological) systems – what we term the "human-ecology" dialectic. Pictures of the planet coming back from space consistently demonstrate that we live in a remarkable global home. They show that terrestrial socio-economic systems are only one part of a much more intricate suprasystem that displays a complex, orderly, and skillfully interwoven pattern. This includes *biotic* systems of living organisms (human and non-human) and the fragile balances they maintain with *abiotic* systems consisting of air, energy, water, and soil. Contextually, the science of ecology has emerged out of an urge to increase knowledgeability about interactions between human strivings and natural systems. It is defined as the "study of the structure and function of nature, it being understood that mankind is a part of nature" (Odum 1971, 7).

The overall pattern of interaction has increasingly come to reflect a "man-world" dominated by human cognition and material wants, with every element of the system displaying evidence of man's artifice, intervention, and even recklessness or what is sometimes perceived as destructive tendencies. For more than three centuries, human activity has become the dominant force for change on the planet. With the advance of civilization, people have learned to use various mechanisms to modify and better control the biophysical environment. This has enabled human populations to appropriate large portions of the earth's total life supporting capacity for their own use. As a result, long-term changes have been accelerated and a considerable number of life-threatening hazards introduced. The quest for mastery of nature has been fraught with countless "existential self-contradictions," in the sense that these very efforts have tended to undermine the conditions necessary to maintain an appropriate human-ecology dialectic and equilibrium.

In the contemporary world order, the imbalances stemming from dysfunctional patterns of human-ecological interactions are manifest at the global, regional, and national levels. Some of the resultant disequilibria are summarized in Table 8.2. It is now widely recognized that global warming and pollution can have far-reaching effects on the entire planet, even though there may be significant variations across countries and regions. Some problems have emerged slowly, and their long-term consequences are still not fully understood. Regional problems such as desertification usually affect groups of countries (for example, those in the Sahelian zone, Senegal, and the Gambia in Africa), or may extend considerably beyond a specific region or country. Country-specific or local interactions such as soil erosion, inappropriate irrigation practices, and misuse of fertilizers and "biocides" usually have an impact primarily within national boundaries.

However, it is evident that changes taking place at the global, regional, and local levels are interdependent. Many regional and local changes have significant global effects, and vice-versa. Poor natural resource management in some countries not only destroys local ecosystems, but also the fragile biophysical environment of the entire planet. Destruction of the Amazon rainforest, for example, not only threatens the life chances of indigenous peoples but also raises the global atmospheric carbon dioxide level and the earth's surface temperature.

Table 8.2: Environmental Degradation

Global
- Global warming: induced changes in global climatic patterns due to increased atmospheric carbon dioxide levels stemming from burning of fossil fuels, use of chlorofluorocarbons (CFCs), deforestation, and the like.
- Pollution of oceans from land resources, e.g., run-off waste, oil spillage, and dumping from ships; transmission of chemical pollutants far beyond points of origin through wind, water, and human agents.

Regional
- Spread of desertification across national boundaries, e.g., the Sahelian and West African regions.
- Upstream or downstream effects of river basin developments in one country on others.
- Transnational forms of air pollution, e.g., acid rain.

Local
- Negative effects on farming systems produced by soil erosion, irrigation practices, salinization, and population displacement.
- Endangerment of public health caused by water pollution and residues from herbicides, pesticides, poisonous fertilizers, and biocides ("killers of life").
- Loss of natural resource base, e.g., eutrophication of lakes, and loss of valuable fishing grounds due to contamination by industrial wastes.
- Air and environmental pollution resulting from economic activity, e.g., hazardous waste and car emissions of surphur dioxide.
- Loss of animal and plant species.

Source: Author.

Extinction of animal and plant species and the attendant loss of bio-diversity not only affects specific countries such as Brazil, Madagascar, and Malaysia, but also has significant global consequences related to the deprivation of other countries and humankind of present and future medicinal benefits.

Moreover, there is still a considerable lack of knowledge about the human use and potential benefits of multi-species ecosystems and the more complex biological and economic discontinuities that large-scale habitat alteration and species extinction may entail. This underscores the ongoing necessity of coming to grips with the imperatives of biodiversity, aesthetics, and cultural preservation. The standard economic approach to resource management is incapable of assigning relevant monetary values to the risks and uncertainties associated with *irreversibility*. Outcomes of many economic decisions cannot be reversed, for example, destruction of ancient monuments and wilderness areas, or the loss of tropical rainforests. The many complex habitats connected with rainforests, animal and plant species, and the ecological services they render are non-renewable, at least within the lifespan of human civilization as we have come to know it on the planet earth.

The potency of such concerns has fuelled a renewed interest in the idea of sustainable development. This connotes the multifaceted processes whereby available ecological resources are marshaled to meet the needs of the present generation without unduly compromising the ability of generations yet unborn to meet their own needs. As such, the interpretation of sustainability transcends specific goals of environmental protection. It involves organic processes of change in which resource exploitation, the orientation of investments, and corresponding forms of socio-economic organization become synergistic with human lives and livelihoods through space and time. Hence, sustainability does not represent a fixed state of harmony but rather a coherent and dynamic process of systems interaction and adjustment at the global, regional, and local levels. In an ideal sense, advancement of no one system or subsystem should take place at the detriment of others, or progress today at the expense of tomorrow.

Decisions on how the balance or moving synthesis between human and natural systems should be maintained or orchestrated involve painful policy and moral choices about intergenerational equity and efficiency. These have generated some fundamental questions about environmental integrity and sustainability. First, do poor people deserve an equal opportunity to share in the benefits derivable from the use of resources in all spheres, or should pertinent decisions be governed by the ability or willingness to pay? Second, should future generations have an equal right to the current stock of resources, or is the present generation entitled to their full use by virtue of the prevailing system of property rights? Third, and as a corollary, should the objective of resource utilization be primarily geared toward maximizing present consumption benefits and private monetary gains vis-à-vis protecting or conserving the birthright of natural resource assets? It is evident that any attempt to provide meaningful answers to such questions must rely on both economic and extra-economic judgments, and therefore on a holistic vision of development.

Competing Voices and Conflicting Goals

The task of identifying an appropriate conception of sustainability cannot be divorced from particular images or philosophical perspectives about the role of nature in the human-ecology dialectic. The latter are value-laden, ideologically-charged, and mirror human-engendered cultural facts that may or may not fit the realities of nature. In turn, alternative valuations of nature also point to the seemingly irreconcilable agendas that demarcate the issues of environment and development between rich and poor nations. The impasse was recognized long ago at the 1972 *Stockholm Conference on the Environment*, and is thought to have precipitated the failure of the *World Conference on Environment and Development* (the "Earth Summit") held at Rio de Janeiro in June 1992. It also purportedly contributed to the undistinguished results of the "Earth Summit + 5" meetings held in New York in 1997 and the *World Summit for Sustainable Development* held at Johannesburg in 2002.

The historically dominant perspective of sustainability is rooted in classical and modern forms of scientific materialism, which conceive nature as merely material and mechanical forces with no particular intrinsic value other than its practical utility to humans and other species. This suggests that we can use the biophysical environment exclusively for our own purposes. Correlatively, the development path trammeled by the majority of rich nations has rested on an implicit view of nature as "valueless," or as resource assets available for the pragmatic use of humans. Hence, the environmental services and wealth provided by nature have been conceived as things to be fully exploited rather than frugally used, contemplated, and enjoyed. In the extreme case, the concerted reliance on an economic strategy of heavy industrialization by the former Soviet Union sacrificed human values and systematically ignored ecological concerns, resulting in a devastated economy, a toxically polluted environment, and severe public health crises.

In classical political economy, the supply of natural resources was perceived to be infinite and indestructible, or as playing a more of less passive role in production, economic growth and development. Modern economic orthodoxy implicitly assumes resource expansibility because technological progress has made it possible for previously inaccessible resources such as coal, oil, and nuclear power to become more readily available. In general, mainstream economists and corporations view sustainability as "sustainable *growth*," that is, in terms of the exploittation of nature to generate maximum gains in consumption, private profitability, and relatively high macroeconomic growth rates in the short run. The services rendered by natural resource assets such as land, water, climate, and biological resources are evaluated in terms of the creation of "exchange values," or the production of marketable goods and services. As detailed elsewhere, the standard cost-benefit calculus and techniques of "discounting" are then used to measure gains and losses associated with alternative investment mixes (see David 1988b, 101-129).

The underlying preconception or value standard is based on a "willingness to pay." This represents the monetary value that can be placed on the environmental services provided by a given mix of natural and other resources. Hard-nosed economists consider what people are willing to buy and sell in the marketplace as the ultimate measure of sustainability, since it purportedly reflects what is termed "consumer sovereignty." As a surrogate for market demand, willingness to pay depends on factors such as individual and collective income, wealth, cultural tastes and preferences, and knowledge. It implies that monetary choices guiding sustainability tend to vary among different individuals, groups, national societies, and other collectivities (Freeman, Haveman, and Kneese 1973).

The economic perspective also rests on an assumption that people are prone to attach more weight to present consumption benefits compared to future ones. This proclivity is normally explained in the following terms. First, human beings are simply impatient, that is, they tend to display "time preference" because they are bedeviled by what is termed the "risk of death" syndrome. The preconception is that present consumption benefits will always be preferred to future gratifications because of a generalized fear of "dying tomorrow." In other words, members of the present generation may feel that they will not live long enough to enjoy the benefits to be derived from postponing consumption. This is partly explained by the fact that the life course of humans is irrevocably molded by the somatic vulnerability to aging, illness, and eventual death.

In a fundamental sense, this reality can be interpreted to mean that the present generation should ignore the problem of environmental degradation or collapse, since there can be no good reason for sacrifices to be made in order to keep the human race going any longer than is necessary. From this perspective, extending its duration merely implies that a few more million people will be born only to die anyway. Second, based on the assumption that capital is productive a given amount of resources available at present can be expected to generate a greater amount of income and production in the future. Under the circumstances, a typical investor will be willing to pay more than, say, (x) dollars in the future in order to acquire the same (x) dollars worth of resources now. The guiding rule is that profitability, or the "internal rate of return" on an investment, should exceed some notional rate of interest – usually termed the "discount rate." The latter is the rate of interest that would have to be paid on a loan taken out to finance a development project.

The discount rate is at the heart of decisions about private investment. The main rule-of-thumb is that the "discounted" or "present value" of all net benefits or financial returns should be positive. In other words, discounting involves the treatment of time in valuing the relevant benefits and costs. Since those associated with an investment are normally dispersed through time, they have to be adjusted to their present values for purposes of meaningful interpretation. In general, the discount rate can be interpreted as the ruling notional interest rate in the economy, or a measure of society's time preference. As such, it tends to influence the choice of alternative macroeconomic policy measures, the funding of development projects by multilateral lending agencies, and the rate at which natural resources such as minerals and forests are exploited (Markandya and Pearce 1990).

A low discount rate tends to favor sustainability, and vice versa. Economists are generally prone to favor high discount rates. The higher the discount rate, the lower is the present value of future production and the less is the inclination to surrender present consumption in order to sustain production in the future. This implies that investments with potentially high long-term benefits will be discouraged, while those with potentially high long-term costs may be encouraged. The preference for high discount rates also entails that renewable resources will be harvested more intensively and non-renewable ones will be exhausted at a much faster rate. The former include living resources (plants and animals) and certain other natural resources (for example, soil and water) that can create and sustain life. By contrast, non-renewable resources such as fossil fuels and minerals are not self-renewing.

While some renewable resources can be recycled, non-renewable ones cannot. Once the existing stock of non-renewable resources is depleted, the environmental resources on which posterity must depend for its survival will be irreversibly changed. The problem for sustainable development surrounds the added burden that will be placed on future generations, in the sense that they will have to subsist on a reduced availability of certain critical resources. Their relative abundance continues to provide a major condition for the standard of living and prosperity of the present generation.

One clear lesson is that economics and ecology must march in tandem. This is emphasized in the evolutionary or ecological conception of nature. It views all animal life, including humans and their communities, as evolving through dynamic spatio-temporal processes. A basic preconception is that all natural, economic and socio-cultural values have arisen out of the same underlying processes, with humans and other species becoming actors or interveners within nature. Hence, human life is intrinsic to nature and the human-ecology dialectic is grounded in historical and dynamic forces that continually shape the proclivities of nature and human communities to vigorously carry on into an indefinite future.

Correlatively, Waddington (1977) suggests that interpretation of the human-ecology dialectic should rely on evolutionary and adaptive processes geared toward preservation of system flows, or keeping them altering in the same way as they have been behaving in the past. His concept of *homeorhesis*, or "evolutionary stability," highlights an organic type of human-ecology symbiosis that renders systems behavior less subject to cancerous outcomes. The materialist trajectory has resulted in human beings setting purposive goals to which natural systems are expected to adjust. In some instances, this promises to significantly enhance human welfare, at least in the short run. However, this path is also fraught with dangers. These arise because, through a lack of sufficient symbiotic understanding, human actions may actually push environmental systems away from their stable paths, thereby precipitating a mode of collapse.

In similar vein, Lovelock (1979, 1988) has advanced the "Gaia hypothesis," which stresses the imperative of a continuous evolutionary sequence to maintain symbiosis between human life and the biophysical environment. The guiding premise is that the earth is a self-regulating system that is able to maintain the climate, atmosphere, soil, and ocean composition in a stable balance favorable to human life. This process is named after the Greek goddess "Earth." Conventional scientific thinking leads us to believe that as planetary conditions change, life evolves to fit them, or dies. The Gaia hypothesis suggests that it is not precisely the inability to adapt that might trigger environmental collapse, but rather a failure to play by the "rules of the game." As Lovelock emphasizes, Gaia would be ruthless in eliminating species that make no contribution toward maintenance of the global ecosystem and its fitness for life.

The perspective of evolutionary symbiosis is apposite to a belief in "strong sustainability." Ecologists who subscribe to this thesis view human survival as being inherently linked to the health of the natural world, and contend that environmental limits cannot be compromised. More generally, environmentalists typically perceive sustainability as being coterminous with "*sustainable* growth." In other words, more emphasis is placed on the negative consequences of resource mismanagement over the longer run, and therefore on the need to conserve or preserve the life-sustenance properties of nature. We return to this subject in the final part of this chapter.

What are known as "eco-fundamentalists" stand at the extreme end of the ideological spectrum. They repudiate conventional economic and conservationist views on the grounds that only deep changes in human relationships with nature can ensure survival of the species. Included in their midst are disparate groups such as (i) deep ecologists or "ecocentrists" who believe that society is determined by ecological conditions; (ii) "speciesists" who revere nature as holy and plants/other animals as equal to humans; (iii) "eco-feminists" who uphold feminist qualities of nature, and view the "rape of Mother Earth" as a reflection of male domination; and (iv) "green economists" and eco-political analysts who emphasize politico-economic factors, harmony of resources and the poor, and advocate radical structural reforms and changes in values. Their claim is that the allocation and distribution of resources at the global, regional, and local levels should be governed by appropriate moral principles. As stated by the Group of Green Economists (1992, 15),

> equal opportunity, distribution of wealth and sustainable develop-
> ment, global justice and the protection of nature can only be a-
> chieved if economic goals are embedded in an integrated complex
> of ethically motivated international agreements and treaties.

In this context, the issue of sustainability should be located in the larger context of North-South relations. While many politicians and policymakers in LDCs have been forced to conform to pressures from Northern lending agencies and eco-fundamentalists, they normally oppose environmental policies since these are viewed as anathema to rapid economic development For example, the *Kyoto Conference on Global Warming* revealed that a most difficult obstacle surrounds the need to reconcile global curbs on fossil fuels to limit greenhouse gases with the efforts of poor nations to develop their industries. Germane to this is a contention that LDCs need more time to build their economies through greater reliance on fossil fuels, just as industrial nations have done for over 150 years.

At the same time poverty groups in LDCs are rarely involved in the mainstream of the environmental movement. This remains true even though they are directly affected by resource problems. The pertinent question then becomes: sustainability for *whom* or *what*? In this regard, the sustainability issue has become most pressing for poor people. The dilemma is that, like mainstream economists, they are precisely the ones who favor high discount rates. The paradoxical situation arises because their survival needs require an intensive consumption of available resources in the short run. It goes without saying that they are under constant pressure to eke out bare levels of subsistence from the relatively limited supply of natural resources. But this very orientation results in the kind of environmental degradation, for example, deforestation and soil erosion, that produce negative spillover effects and heighten the suffering of marginalized groups.

This predicament was vocalized by the late Indira Gandhi, India's Prime Minister, at the 1972 Stockholm Conference on the Environment in the following terms:

> We do not wish to impoverish the environment any further and yet
> we cannot for a moment forget the grim poverty of large numbers
> of people. Are not poverty and need the greatest polluters? .... How

can we speak to those who live in villages and in slums about keeping the oceans, the rivers, and the air clean when their lives are contaminated at the source? *The environment cannot be improved in conditions of poverty.* [Reported in the *Bulletin of Atomic Scientists*, 1972; emphasis added].

The *World Commission on Environment and Development* (Brundtland) also emphasized the intrinsic evil inherent in poverty and that a world in which it is endemic will always to prone to ecological disasters. As stated in its influential report *The Common Future* (1987, 81),

sustainable development requires meeting the basic needs of all and extending to all the opportunity to fulfill their aspirations for a better life. Meeting essential needs requires not only a new era of growth for nations in which the majority are poor, but an assurance that those poor get their fair share of the resources required to sustain that growth.

However, the growth-oriented option runs the risk of generating further resource depletion and even environmental collapse in LDCs if accumulation of reproducible capital takes place at the expense of equity, distributive justice, and other humanitarian ends. As the Commission fully recognizes, poor countries will remain transfixed on the horns of a dilemma unless a vision of *restructuring growth* is melded with the pursuit of environmental integrity.

The Birthright Approach: Balancing Economic and Environmental Interests

Under the dominant economic perspective of sustainability, all forms of resource use are subsumed under the umbrella of capital theory. Hence sustainability is linked to a perceived need to maintain the overall capital base of the economy, and linking this to the requirements of present versus future generations. The overall implication is that natural resource availability can be maintained or enhanced through increased investment in and/or conservation of supplies. The interpretive thrust rests implicitly on the concept of a production function in which output growth is characterized as a return to various inputs, including natural resources, physical assets, human capital, and technology. The contribution of natural resources tends to be ignored or underestimated due to the historically entrenched assumption, albeit implicit, that they are immutable and hence beyond the control of human allocative decisions.

A crucial reason is that the environmental services provided by natural resources do not usually flow through standard market transactions, so that their asset values are non-appropriable. The conventional economic calculus used to evaluate outcomes of economic decisions is predicated on an asymmetry between the measurement of natural resources vis-à-vis other productive assets. Fixed capital formation and physical assets such as buildings and equipment are valued as wealth-creating capital and, as they depreciate, are written off against the value of production or income. The same is not true for the valuation of natural resources, that is, any deterioration of their value or decrease in their future production potential is not charged off against current earnings or production.

The conventional failure to depreciate natural resource assets typically results in an overstatement of the benefits accruing from material economic growth and current consumption, leading to a concomitant undervaluation of natural resource conservation and environmental integrity. The overall implication for sustainable development is that a country's measured income or rate of economic growth may rise steadily as its natural resource base disappears. This can occur, for example, if in the pursuit of maximum economic growth and returns to private investors it exhausts its non-renewable natural resources, deforests its land, depletes Its stock of biotic species, pollutes the air, or otherwise despoliates its beaches (Repetto 1986, 1989). Of course, such a reckless abandon depicts the extreme position, since most countries are now sensitized to the need for conservation.

Germane to this is a need to reinterpret sustainability based on a recognition that a given country's socio-economic surplus is created and cumulatively enhanced through the coherent use of all its natural resource assets — natural, physical, and human. In other words, sustainability should be linked to multifaceted processes whereby new wealth can be created and maintained. The creation of new wealth entails generation of what is called "genuine savings," which is the residual of production less depreciation of produced assets, and drawing down of natural resource assets (World Bank 1995b). There is also a need to take account of the "saving" of human resources that can be potentially realized through broad-based investments in people — in terms of education, health, nutrition, and other forms of human capital.

Table 8.3: Sources of Wealth by Region (percentage of total)

	Human Resources	Produced Assets	Natural Capital
World	64	16	20
High-income Countries	67	16	17
Developing Countries			
Sub-Saharan Africa	31	17	52
India and China	73	18	9
Other Asia	75	13	12
Latin America & Caribbean	50	15	35
Middle East and North Africa	39	29	32
Eastern Europe	41	16	43

Source: World Bank (1995b)

Table 8.3 provides estimates of three broad sources of wealth by region for 192 countries. First, natural capital, even when limited to items that are usually accorded commercial value, is a larger asset component than produced assets for about 50 percent of the countries. Second, human capital generally accounts for a larger share of wealth than produced assets. This is correlated with the fact that labor earnings account for the lion's share of income per person in the majority of countries. Third, and as would be expected, there are significant differences in the composition of wealth between the more and less developed sectors of the world. With under 17 percent of the world's population, the richer countries boast nearly 80 percent of global wealth.

Given the three broad types of resources, an important question arises about interactions among new wealth creation, savings, and investment. Its resolution can help to throw light on the prospects for reducing macroeconomic imbalances and improving environmental integrity. In this context, it is first necessary to distinguish between two concepts of saving. In conventional national income accounting, saving is defined as a residual or difference between aggregate production (national output or GNP) and aggregative consumption or expenditure. By contrast, what may be termed "authentic" or "genuine" saving, while itself a residual based on aggregate production less consumption, must also take account of the following three elements: (i) the depletion of natural capital assets; (ii) depreciation of produced or human-made assets; and (iii) any human resource saving realized from investment in education and training, health and nutrition, especially of disadvantaged people. The relationships can be summarized in a simple equation, as follows:

$$S_a = GNP - D_n - D_p + H$$

where

S_a	= authentic or genuine saving
GNP	= gross national product or aggregate output
C	= aggregate consumption or expenditure
D_n	= depletion of natural capital or assets
D_p	= depreciation of produced or human-made assets
H	= human resource savings realized from investments in education and training, health, nutrition, etc.

In essence, the relationship expresses what may be termed a "birthright approach" to development. The overall implication is that countries which utilize their natural resource assets prudently are likely to end up with much more wealth because of the payoffs that can potentially accrue from complementary investments in human and social development. By contrast, those that are wont to squander the income earned from selling oil, minerals, gold, diamonds, timber, and other natural resources such as "beaches" are essentially "dissaving" and will have to face the dire consequences for their future development. While most regions in the less developed sector of the world have been depleting their natural capital, the investment in people undertaken by East Asian countries has paid handsome dividends. At the same time, many natural-resource-rich countries in Africa and Latin America remain in the doldrums because of an inability or unwillingness to convert the proceeds from exploitation and sale of natural resource assets into concomitant investments in people. The rich nations that purchase these natural resources have skillfully complemented them with human capital built up from their own education systems and the continuous inflow of immigrants.

In conclusion, the following broad messages may be gleaned from the "birthright" perspective. First, a country may deplete its natural resources as long as this contributes to sustainable human development in the form of complementary investments in human, social, and infrastructural resources. Where proceeds from the sale of natural resources are utilized in this manner, future generations would be guaranteed at least the same opportunities as the present one. Hence the prospects for achieving humanitarian goals of intergenerational efficiency and equity will be enhanced. Second, this balanced strategy also highlights a major bone of contention between economic vis-à-vis environmental fundamentalists. The former are wont to emphasize the critical importance of conventional forms of savings and investment as catalysts to economic growth; the latter tend to interpret the same processes in terms of the need for stringent resource conservation.

The birthright perspective is anchored on the imperative of making the growth process more environmentally friendly. It is predicated on a revised trajectory of *organic* or *qualitative* growth based on a symbiotic relationship between human development potentials and the requirements of environmental integrity. At both national and international levels, this requires internal restructuring in order to restore real interdependencies among their constituent parts. As alluded to earlier, attainment of goal-oriented human futures based on optimal synergy in the human-ecology dialectic requires transformation of both horizontal and vertical relationships. Horizontal restructuring is predicated on drastic changes in human and societal goals, values, and norms. Vertical changes would involve complementary alterations in the deep structure of global economic relations via reorientation of consumption patterns and redistribution of financial resources, but with sensible use and renewal of environmental resources.

In the final reckoning, the possibilities for achieving sustainable development hinge on the power of those who make decisions about the management of the biophysical environment. This entails a need for complementary actions and institutions to engineer change. *Agenda 21*, the concluding document of the 1992 *United Nations Conference on Environment and Development* (the "Earth Summit") emphasized the need for restructuring of the decision-making process so that environmental and socio-economic issues are fully integrated and broader public participation is assured. As stated in Section 8.2 of the report:

> Prevailing systems of decision making in many countries tend to separate economic, social and environmental factors at the policy, planning and management levels. This influences the actions of all groups in society, including governments, industry and individuals,

and has important implications for the efficiency and sustainability
of development. An adjustment or even a fundamental reshaping of
decision making, in the light of country-specific conditions may be
necessary if environment and development is to be put a the center
of economic and political decision making, in effect achieving full
integration of these factors.

It goes without saying that efforts aimed at restructuring the decision-
making process cannot be divorced from the larger context defining the
global political economy of environmental management, governance,
or stewardship. As emphasized in chapter 5, this represents the overarching arena or modus vivendi in which conflicts over power,
dominance, wealth, resistance, and accountability are ultimately played
out and perhaps resolved. Germane to this is a fundamental premise, or
longstanding belief, that the differential power relations underlying the
major institutions of the world order, such as markets and states, may
be ecologically dysfunctional. This suggests that they are not only a
primary cause of the human-ecological crisis, but also constitute
formidable stumbling blocks to its resolution.

In particular, perceptions about state power and correlative
notions about sovereignty, adequacy, and authority, have played a
critical role in the debate. It bears the hallmark of the historically
dominant neo-realist perspective in which states are construed as unitary actors pursuing their own interests through interactions that are
guided primarily by considerations of material power. Among other
things, the debate on state realism has been devoid of concerted efforts
to expand the international agenda to include issues pertaining to
environmental integrity, equity, and obligations of stewardship of the
earth's life-supporting systems. The overriding issue has centered
around the polarity inherent in state responsibility vis-à-vis global
environmental governance.

The problematique was aptly stated by the World Commission on
Environment and Development in the following aphorism: "the earth is
one but we are not" (1987, 27). At one level, the capacity of the state to
respond effectively to environmental challenges through independent
action is continuously circumscribed by the inexorable forces of globalization and deterritorization. At another level, misgivings have
surfaced about the state's ability to secure environmental sustainability
for its citizens, defend them against extra-territorial threats, and
implement multilateral environmental agreements based on universal

norms. While most states may pay lip service to such norms, the majority tend to attach greater significance to their national sovereignty and authority. This is particularly true for the sensitivities of small and relatively weak states which fear the potential "environmental imperialism" that may be perpetrated by powerful states whose priorities are different from those of LDCs.

The sovereign responsibilities and obligations of states have been set forth in three international documents: the Stockholm Declaration on the Human Environment (1972); the RIO Declaration emanating from the UN Conference on Environment and Development (UNCED 1972); and the World Charter for Nature, approved as a UN General Assembly resolution in 1982. Both Principle 21 of the Stockholm Declaration and Principle 2 of the RIO Declaration identically state that "States have the sovereign right to exploit their own resources pursuant to their own environmental policies, and the responsibility to ensure that activities within their jurisdiction or control do not cause damage to the environment of other States or of areas beyond the limits of national jurisdiction." Paragraph 22 of the World Charter for Nature articulates the same normative standard in slightly different terms: "[t]aking fully into account the sovereignty of States over their natural resources, each State shall give effect to the provisions of the present Charter through its competent organs and in co-operation with other States."

The Stockholm/RIO injunction is predicated on the cosmopolitan rule that while states, as actors in a global community, have a right to develop their own resources as they deem fit, they are also responsible for avoiding damage to the environment of others or the global commons. The neighborhood and community standards were not only adumbrated in the World Charter for Nature, but restated as a *principle of common differentiated responsibility* by UNCED and in the UN convention on climate change. In terms of their implications for a more progressive decision-making environment, the normative standards are not simply rules for promoting managerial efficiency and effectiveness, but rather reflect cosmopolitan values that often run counter to the interests of elites and governments in LDCs. We return to this subject in the next chapter where the ramifications of "cosmopolitan morality" vis-à-vis the "morality of states" are further explored.

Chapter 9

The Moral Imperative

> A human being exists inescapably in a space of ethical questions;
> she or he cannot avoid assessing herself or himself in relation to
> some standards. To escape all standards would not be liberation,
> but a terrifying lapse into total disorientation. It would be to suffer
> the ultimate crisis of identity.... I tell who I am by situating myself
> in some sort of social, professional, familial space. But the kind of
> identity that is crucial to having a coherent sense of self is one that
> relates us to ethical space.
>
> Charles Taylor (1991)

An intimate relationship undoubtedly exists between the "human" and
the "ethical" or "moral." Thus, the appraisal of human life and
development potentials cannot be divorced from systems of normative
beliefs, life-and-world visions, and value standards that perennially
guide human conduct and behavior. Since morality constitutes a
characteristic feature of human nature, value or ethical neutrality

becomes an anathema to the quest for genuine or humanitarian development. Values tend to intrude at every point into our beliefs and actions, and are therefore central to the maintenance of society, culture, and human existence itself. As the quotation above suggests, an endemic facet of life is that human beings always have a sense of self that situates us in "ethical space."

This reflects moral characterizations, descriptions, and situated experiences that locate us relative to essential needs, standards of excellence, and obligations that we cannot simply repudiate. They mirror the intrinsic and dynamic nature of our moral valuations, or what Sen (1988) calls "value-endogeneity." This encapsulates any type of normative, evaluative, or prescriptive experience, in fact everything that gives meaning to life. It traverses judgments not only of what is "good," but also what is "right," or a concern for the well-being of other human beings – the conditions that must be satisfied if the actions of individuals are to be justifiable to others who may be affected by them. In the contemporary world order, the need to heed such "moral imperatives" has been particularly critical for at least two reasons.

One is rooted in a perception of a mortal danger facing humankind. While it is deeply entrenched in human history and in an imperfect social order, the danger is of global proportions, immediate, and intensifying. Most easily perceived and widely debated are its overt manifestations such as inequality, poverty, war, genetic damage, and resource depletion. But these are physical signs of a far more complex system of institutional and individual habits, attitudes, and beliefs that debase the overall quality of life. They include, inter alia, diverse ways in which different people perceive their rights of ownership, security, and freedom; how they form moral, social, and political values; as well as the stated and assumed rights and responsibilities among individuals and between citizens and their institutions.

Second, and on a related basis, the heated debate being waged in all capitals of the world over narcotics, crime, health care, poverty, and the welfare state raises a basic question whether contemporary human and social problems stem primarily from economic factors (for example, a lack of money or economic opportunity) or from a breakdown of individual and collective values. The nature of the answer is by no means clear-cut, and depends on the interplay of interpretation, ideology, and moral standards. Some commentators argue that the problem can be traced to misdirected values or a lack of them, so that "throwing more money" at it would be ineffective. Given the ubiquity of budget deficits and resource scarcity, the major task, it is claimed, becomes a moral one. If this is true, changes are needed in the value-orientations undergirding pertinent cultures to reflect enduring human attributes such as integrity, self-discipline, and personal responsibility. Such values, it is opined, are essential for guaranteeing psychological and social health. While others may not be averse to such claims, they insist that money and opportunity do play a critical role in shaping values and behavior. However, the strict money-values dichotomy may lead to a cul-de-sac, with arguments used as masks for different ideological persuasions. Since it is a "chicken or egg" problem, absolutist claims may overstate the case by trying to achieve too rigid a separation between economics and values. The two realms overlap because genuine moral discourse takes place at several levels of the debate on authentic or humanitarian development: in terms of the nature of desirable ends, specific criteria identifying them in real situations, clusters of means that are proportional to the ends to be achieved, and the individual means considered separately (Goulet 1978; David 1988).

Moral criteria are endogenous to the choice of both ends and means. The choice is rooted in ancient normative questions about human well-being, including the following: (i) what is the relationship between material goods and the good life? (ii) what constitutes a just, cooperative, and pleasant society, that is, one based on reasonable pluralism and where everyone accepts the same basic principles of political, social, and economic justice? and (iii) what kind of world is truly desirable (the creative utopian vision) vis-à-vis what is possible (pragmatic, practical, or feasible options)?

While morality may be intrinsic to, or constitutive of, human nature, there is still considerable disagreement about the nature of answers to such questions. This stems in part from problems surrounding the defensibility of alternative moral claims. From time immemorial, there have been a number of competing ethical systems and principles to which people give allegiance. These help to shape their lives, explain the presence of good or evil, and are often enshrined in a series of fundamental rules that subscribers utilize to make decisions about what they ought to do. Some derive their substance from ancient or traditional religious and philosophical teachings, while others are more modern and draw their normative orientations from utilitarianism, norms of efficiency, conceptions of rights and justice, and principles of libertarianism.

In his book *After Virtue*, the philosopher Alasdair MacIntyre interprets the situation in terms of what he perceives as a moral confusion facing humankind. Readers are asked to imagine a society in which there were competing moral systems to which people adhered. They are further asked to imagine that this society had been subjected to a flood, or "moral deluge," in which all that remained of these moral systems were a few islands merely peeping up above a sea of chaos. Since they were no longer connected to one another in an agreed-upon or consensual mainland, any debates about them would be rootless and often interminable. The reason is that participants would be talking from different fundamental premises, which even those who believed in them would be unable to locate or articulate.

The moral of the story is that we not only live in an imagined society of competing moral and ethical demands, but also one in which surviving fragments and memories of strong ethical systems have been drowned in disconnected islands of relativism and irrelevance. For many people throughout the globe, the only time they realize that they live under competing ethical systems is when they are faced with a crisis in which one set of values enjoins them to do X, another set Y, and yet another set that both X and Y are irrelevant to Z, or what really matters.

Utilitarianism: Search for Individual Happiness

In intellectual history, what is known as the "consequentialist" variant of ethical theory has become the most prominent. It views the good to be brought about as externally related to the right action. In other words, actions are deemed to be right if they bring about good consequences. The most widely acclaimed example is utilitarianism. It emerged as a systematic moral system during the 18th and 19th centuries, but has maintained a dominant place in modern debates on economic and social policy. Utilitarianism has two faces. On the one hand, it is a doctrine about the rightness of actions or policies. This condition is satisfied if they produce the best possible results for the majority of people in society. On the other hand, it projects a philosophy of the good, or the nature of consequences. In the eyes of some scholars, utilitarianism is the only reasonable criterion of justice in a secular society because it purports "to offer a criterion of neutrality among competing conceptions of the good life in a particularistic and antagonistic world" (Welch 1989, 268).

As indicated in the previous chapter, the evolution of human consciousness about self has marched in tandem with particular perspectives of human nature, for example, as being elaborated entirely out of forces acting upon it, including instinctual drives and experience. In the context of utilitarianism, one influential version of this perspective has come to be known as the Pleasure Principle: people act so as to maximize pleasure and minimize pain. Jeremy Bentham (1789) is credited with originally advancing a number of basic propositions about human beings as seekers of pleasure.

He considered the happiness of society as the *summum bonum*, or "highest good." Happiness, or total utility, was equated with the net value of all pleasures and pains. It was also assumed that pleasures differed only in amount, or in terms of intensity, duration, and the probability of occurring. In other words, "pushpin [pinball] is as good as poetry" as long as it generates equal pleasure. Moreover, the following Benthamite postulates have formed the bedrock of utilitarianism and modern social theory: (i) the welfare of the individual should be the primary end of moral action; (ii) each individual ought to "count for one and no more than one;" and (iii) the object of social action is to promote "the greatest good of the greatest number," that is, maximize general utility.

Hence, primary emphasis was placed on the psychological, subjective, or hedonistic dimensions of pleasure or happiness, or the concept of utility as a sensation that can be experienced. In modern variants of utilitarianism, the content of utility has shifted from maximum pleasure, satisfaction, or happiness to desire fulfillment, or some kind of representation of a person's choice behavior (Harsanyi 1977). An implicit moral world has been created out of the universe of autonomous individuals, with each perceived as a self-seeking locus of all choice. As noted earlier, individualized choice has been made coterminous with personal liberty, and a concomitantly jaundiced imagery has emerged about the prospects for collective choice and social action. As shown in Chapter 2, this perspective has come to exert a lasting influence on the evolution of modern economics, its imperialist tendency, and liberal/libertarian preconceptions.

Contextually, modern forms of utilitarian evaluation hinge on three requirements: *consequentialism* (alluded to earlier), *welfarism*, and *sum-ranking* (Sen and Williams 1982). Welfarism connotes the common practice, implicit in economic arguments, of defining the good or rightness of a given state of affairs solely in terms of the maximization of utilities or preferences. No direct attention is paid to norms such as fulfillment of rights, duties, responsibilities, and obligations. When welfarism is combined with consequentialism, the moral rule is that any action should be judged by the consequent state of affairs or results (because of consequentialism) and the utilities inherent in that state (influence of welfarism) [Sen 1999, 59]. In similar vein, sum-ranking states that the ethical value of a situation is simply the sum of individual utilities contained in it. Common to both welfarism and sum-ranking is a perspective of rational action in which the power of legitimization devolves on the process of choice, and not on what is actually chosen.

The utilitarian tradition raises several issues that are central to our understanding of the moral bases of development. One concerns the principle of utility itself, and the related idea of human happiness implicit in the felicific calculus. In the first place, all pleasures are not of the same quality and happiness is not the only desirable human goal or condition of existence that is intrinsically good. The hedonistic vision does not adequately recognize the complexity of human nature. In this regard, John Stuart Mill, a prominent utilitarian, chided Bentham for neglecting the "whole unanalyzed experience of the human race." His eloquent statement on this subject is well worth quoting at length. As he continues ([1838] 1962, 100-101):

> Man is never recognized by him [Bentham] as being capable of pursuing spiritual perfection as an end; of desiring for its own sake, the conformity of his own character to the standard of excellence, without hope for good or fear of evil from other source than his own consciousness...
>
> Nor is it only the moral part of man's nature, in the strict sense of the term – the desire of perfection or the feeling of an approving or an accusing conscience – that he overlooks; he but faintly recognizes, as a fact in human nature, the pursuit of any other ideal end for its own sake. The sense of *honor* and personal dignity – that feeling of personal exaltation and degradation which acts independently of other people's opinion, or even in defiance of it; the love of *beauty* the passion of the artist; the love of order, of congruity, of consistency in all things and conformity to their end; the love of *power*, not in the limited form of power over other human beings, but abstract power, the power of making our

> volitions effectual; the love of *action*, the thirst for movement and
> activity, a principle scarcely of less influence in human life than its
> opposite, the love of ease. [emphasis in original].

There is also the commonsense moral judgment that it is always better
to relieve suffering than directly promote pleasure. Even if it is accepted that pleasure is something of human value, a pertinent question is
how it should be compared with the innumerable human goods that
people treasure: for example, truth, knowledge, freedom, and equality
(Moore 1903). The hedonist response is that pleasure is the only
intrinsic good and all other valued things are only means or extrinsic
goods. From this perspective, knowledge is valued in an instrumental
sense because it can be used to produce much pleasure in life, and/or
because we obtain pleasure from the very act of acquiring knowledge.
In similar vein, freedom and good health are construed as mere means
of achieving the good life, that is, in terms of the resultant pleasure and
happiness generated.

   This interpretation is apposite to the discussion in Chapter 3 of
the instrumental-intrinsic dichotomy, or the Kantian distinction
between constitutive vis-à-vis regulated phenomena or behavior. In the
overall context of humanitarian development, the state of "being
happy" cannot be meaningfully divorced from the overall quality of
life people succeed in living. The full evaluation must rely on further
information about the reasons people are made to feel happy, for
example, the influence of religious, socio-cultural, political, and
intellectual factors (Sen et al. 1988). However, the utilitarian approach
concentrates almost exclusively on mental attributes (pleasure,
happiness, and desires), so that psychological conditioning and
adaptive attitudes are accorded a pivotal role in determining individual
well-being. This life-and-world vision is not only unfair to persons
facing persistent inequalities, but it also rules out interpersonal
comparisons of well-being and deprivation.

   Similar concerns arise over what are perceived to be the perni-
cious implications of a particularly narrow psychological assumption
about human motivation and behavior. One is that the satisfaction of
hedonic pleasures may prove to be harmful to individuals themselves,
others, and society at large. The larger consequences of pleasure-seeking activities wholly and partially motivated by personal preferences
and choices have been well documented. Relevant examples include
the negative spillover effects or external diseconomies associated with

behavioral practices such as alcohol and drug abuse, driving auto-mobiles, cutting down trees, anti-semitism, and race-baiting under systems of apartheid and Jim Crow.

Sociologists and like-minded social theorists often complain that the "methodological individualism" undergirding the utilitarian program is incapable of generating useful insights into social life. As a quintessentail individualist doctrine, it does not attribute sufficient constitutive power to social forces, or the tendency for individual desires, aspirations, and actions to be constantly defined, shaped, and constrained by social structures. In a fundamental sense, being-in-the-world and the pursuit of goal-oriented human futures are concerned with the promotion of collective human welfare, social cooperation, and community involvement. In thinking about what courses of action to pursue, people are normally prone to assess their wants and needs not just in terms of individual motivations, but often take account of the interests of others. More often than not, alternatives are evaluated on the basis of previous commitments, obligations, and responsibilities.

This is at variance with a preconception based on "duty-free" action, exclusive reliance on a choice-theoretic ontology, or forms of behavior based on individual utility maximization, since such perspectives fail to ask pertinent reflexive questions about the benefits of self-servingness. The utilitarian belief that the ends justify the means implies that people do not necessarily have certain duties or moral obligations they should pursue as a matter of principle, rather than because of the consequences that are likely to ensue. Hence, actions such as telling the truth or being honest in one's dealings with others are not deemed to be worthy or appropriate in their own right, but as dependent on whether they maximize the common good (Downie 1989).

A further question can be raised about the precise definition of notions such as the "common good," and therefore the nature of consequences and how they should be evaluated. The principle of sum-ranking implies that appraisal of consequences in terms of the "greatest good of the greatest number" justifies actions tending to promote the greatest aggregate good. But, notions such as the "greatest good of the greatest number" and the "greatest aggregate good" lack sufficient specificity and tend to leave us in a limbo about the collectivities to which the best consequences refer. While the standard interpretation is in terms of the "majority" in society, the reference could also be to people in general, interest groups, the family, or community. This is not a matter of mere semantics, but carries important implications for the consequences of policy actions. The latter usually involve delicate intertemporal choices about resource allocation, intergenerational equity, and distributive justice.

For example, if a government has a limited amount of funds to spend on providing public schooling, among the possible options it may face are the following. It may allocate the available resources so as to produce the greatest degree of improvement in the existing stock of school facilities, or try to produce the greatest improvement in such facilities for the greatest number of children, including the very large numbers yet unborn. If the former option is chosen, a larger proportion of the available funds will be channeled toward improving a relatively limited number of facilities; if the latter course is pursued, relatively smaller amounts of money will be spent on providing a larger number of schools. In actuality, the choices may not be as clearcut as the example suggests, since they involve multiple decisions with overlapping and indeterminate consequences.

Besides problems with evaluating intended and unintended consequences, the utilitarian ethic tends to ignore inequalities in the distribution of happiness and other correlates of human welfare. Only total utility matters, no matter how unequally distributed. The idea of maximizing the common good (based on the "greatest good of the greatest number") apparently sanctions the notion of an unequal distribution of the good because it leaves the existing pattern of distribution more or less unchanged. Hence prevailing patterns of inequality are likely to persist. This conflicts with people's basic intuitions about distributive justice since it would allow punishment of the innocent or suffering of the poor if this were perceived to improve the general welfare.

In essence, utilitarianism rests on a preconception that efforts devoted toward maximizing the well-being of the "majority" are ethically superior to actions based on egalitarian principles such as equality of opportunity. This means that the basic rights of certain groups, such as ethnic minorities and women, will be ignored or violated if they are perceived to stand in the way of the "common good," "general will," or "national interest." Utilitarianism does not accept the principle of basic human rights. Its ontology rests on an implicit belief that society has no obligations to carry out mandates of human development. This is at odds with the life-and-world vision promoted in this book, which advocates a philosophy of life based on notions such as rights, justice, equality, and freedom.

Egalitarianism: Justice, Equality, and Rights

Even an ardent utilitarian like John Stuart Mill believed that justice and rights-based standards should be viewed as distinct aspects of morality because they involve the idea of people receiving fair rewards or entitlements as a matter of right. For him, calling something a person's right means that he or she has a claim on society to protect it by every possible means. Correlatively, justice was conceived as a requirement that all persons be allowed to possess those goods which society determines they should have. It reflects a pattern of distribution that maximizes the common good, that is, a relatively high degree of equality in the distribution of goods. Deontologists go beyond Mill's revisionism. They contend that certain actions or states of affairs are inherently just, right, and obligatory, regardless of their consequences.

Justice and Equality

Justice operates as a set of appeals or claims based on precepts that are denoted by terms such as merit, need, rights, fairness, equality, and equity (Arthur and Shaw 1991). Whatever the form of legitimization, all such claims tend to impose obligations of action, and sometimes even sacrifice, on behalf of individuals and groups deemed to be unfairly harmed or deprived. The claims are especially significant when socio-economic and political processes demonstrably produce unfair advantages for some individuals and groups and unfair disadvantages for others. Ideally, justice requires that all persons should be treated as moral equals. Hence, injustice in the sense of unfairness occurs when like cases are not treated equally. However, the term "equality" has many different meanings, and the alternative connotations are not always commensurable (Coleman 1989).

The historically dominant conception is one of "natural," "ontological," or "absolute" equality. This sometimes goes under the rubric of "equality of persons." The principle of absolute equality derives its universal appeal from the primordial belief and widely accepted preconception about the original equality of all human beings – "all men [persons] are created equal." It carries the normative injunction that all human beings should be treated equally unless very good reason can be marshaled to justify unequal treatment. In other words, any claim of "justice" based on inequality shifts the burden of proof to those advocating unequal treatment. Absolute equality also suggests that all persons should share equally in the overall benefits and achievements of society. But, the principle suffers from the drawback that the utopian ideal of perfect equality may be highly unrealistic and self-serving.

In actuality, many calls for absolute equality are disguises of real demands for privilege, that is, they tend to be motivated by pure self-interest. A more popular notion of equality rests on the claim that all persons should be given equal chances in the socio-economic system. This idea of "equality of opportunity" is based on the precept that the processes through which people come to occupy offices or positions in society should be fair, affording an equal chance to all its members. Under a third principle – "equality of condition" – people's life chances are made equal through legislation. A special case of this is "equality before the law," which implies equal treatment by legal and related authorities. There is a close affinity between equality of opportunity and condition because unequal access to offices in society often leads to visible forms of inequality – for example, in income, wealth, employment, and education. As a consequence, promoting both forms of equality often requires some measure of state intervention and "affirmative action." This is to ensure that inequalities are not systematically transmitted across generations, and so that children will be guaranteed life chances and opportunities that are totally unaffected by inequalities existing among their parents.

A fourth principle is "equality of outcomes" or results, for example, equality in the distribution of goods and services. Sir Isaiah Berlin (1961, 131) provides a very authoritative statement of the natural principle involved in the equality of results, as follows:

> No reason need to be given for ... an equal distribution of benefits for that is 'natural,' self-evidently right, and just, and needs no justification, since it is in some sense conceived as self justified.... The assumption is that equality needs no reasons, only inequality does so; that uniformity, symmetry ... need not be specifically accounted for, whereas differences, unsystematic behavior, changes in conduct, need explanation and, as a rule, justification.

The caveat should be added that neither a respect for equality nor the requirement of equal treatment of persons necessarily guarantees an egalitarian distribution of goods and services. It all depends on the decision rules that are followed. Under the economist's decision rule, for example, equality of outcomes is predicated on a distribution based on people's preferences and tastes, that is, the outcome is deemed to be fair if each person gets what he or she wants. This criterion is problematic because preferences and tastes are not fixed or given, but formed in diverse ways, for example, through social conditioning. Further, some individual preferences may be totally harmful both to the persons concerned and others. Hence, there is no overriding reason to expect preference-based decisions, as revealed in the marketplace, to generate equality of outcomes or results.

The criterion of "distribution according to contribution" is sometimes invoked to justify equality of outcomes. It states that "he or she who contributes the most should get the most." But, a basic problem surrounds the meaning or definition of "contribution." The standard economic argument is that the competitive market pays contributors of factors of production (for example, laborers, capitalists, and managers) the value of their respective contributions to total production or output. The process is viewed as a harmonious one in which benefits are distributed equitably to all economic classes and income groups. The pursuit of market efficiency is expected to result in all individuals and groups gaining according to their inputs into the generation of final output. Theoretical support is usually provided by the marginal productivity theory of distribution, which simply states that you are allowed to take out or receive the value of what you put into the production process.

As a consequence, it is argued, there is no need to tamper in any way with the manner in which the market distributes economic prizes. Under the circumstances, any attempt to enforce absolute equality in the pattern of income or wealth distribution will lead to an unnecessary loss of economic efficiency and growth. Some of the most ardent supporters of the competitive market reject this claim, while others with a different ideological persuasion argue that the market is inherently unjust. They cite as evidence the fact that the structure and functioning of markets throughout the globe continuously reveal a host of inefficiencies and failures. The historical experience of market capitalism provides ample evidence that bigger economic gains are normally appropriated by more fortunate economic cadres on the basis of power, ownership and control of resources, and the like. The end result has been an unequal distribution of basic rights and opportunities, and a compromising of democratic values of human decency and self-respect.

It is an incontrovertible fact that the socio-economic ethos of a society usually establishes certain "rules of the game" for determining acceptable distributional outcomes or results. As elaborated in the previous chapter, the preferred corpus of rules usually emanate from his-

torical patterns of social organization, socialization, and cultural conditioning. Hence, existing inequalities may be accepted as just, or may
result from extant norms and ideologies, even when they are openly
opportunistic or biased. Once the rules of the game are internalized,
any type of distributional outcome, be it egalitarian or inequitable, is
permissible.

While there may be a range of possible outcomes on which
citizens agree or disagree, it may be difficult to arrive at a just form of
distribution when there is pervasive conflict in society or a lack of social and political consensus. When this occurs, there will be a tendency
to distribute according to the maxim: "to them that hath shall be
given." Government policies on labor markets and inheritance
sometimes lend an abetting hand to such situations. The overall
conclusion is that while the human quest for equality and fair
distribution will not die, it can be likened to a chimera, or continuous
search for the "Holy Grail" or "Arch of the Covenant."

Moral Rules: Universality and Fairness

In his *Groundwork of the Metaphysics of Morals*, Immanuel Kant
contends that the moral worth of an action or state of affairs lies "not in
the purpose to be attained by it, but in the maxim in accordance with
which it is decided upon" ([1785] 1948, 13). The success or failure of
people in achieving their ends does not depend on their actions alone,
which cannot be judged as good or bad, right or wrong, by merely taking into account the states of affairs they actually bring about. While
the ends and purposes of a moral agent's actions are important, Kant
argues, they should be accorded priority only because moral action is
something that is performed for its own sake, and not primarily for the
results it is supposed to ensure. This deontological perspective is one
of the foremost antidotes to utilitarianism.

In the Kantian schema, moral duty or the imperative of morality
is commanded "categorically." This requires that human agents
sacrifice their own personal happiness, satisfaction, or desires rather
than violate the *Categorical Imperative* mentioned in Chapter 2. The
latter is a kind of rule that mandates the type of action independently of
the desired (utilitarian) end. Hence, the unique obligatoriness of moral
rules lies in their unrestricted universality and independence from any
facts or circumstances of human nature. From this perspective, there is
only one *Categorical Imperative* from which all specific moral duties

are derived: "Act only on that maxim which you can will to be a universal law."

What is known as the "universalizability criterion" implies that the maxim governs my own actions and those of others facing similar circumstances. If the "moral law" applies without distinction to all rational beings, it follows that they should be treated as equally entitled to rights under it, that is, as ends in themselves and never as mere means to my own ends. The general statement of the *Categorical Imperative*, therefore, is that no person's ends should be systematically subordinated to those of others. In other words, people should be treated as beings of intrinsic worth, or in accordance with a universal law that is applicable to all human beings.

In modern times, one of the most prominent responses to utilitarianism is provided by John Rawls's egalitarian or contractarian theory of justice. As stated in his tour-de-force *The Theory of Justice* (1971), "justice is the first virtue of all institutions" and is primarily concerned with the distribution of rights and duties in society. As noted earlier, it can be said to operate as a set of appeals or claims for the distribution of burdens and benefits based on overlapping notions of rights and fairness, or the elemental fact that "all persons are morally equal." The Rawlsian theory envisages the basic principles of justice as being chosen by free and rational individuals who are concerned with their own interests, but are willing to cooperate with others.

According to Rawls,

> the guiding idea is that the principles of justice for the basic structure of society are the object of the original agreement. They are the principles that free and rational persons concerned to further their own interests would accept in the initial position of equality as defining the fundamental terms of their association (1971, 11).

This "original position" is delimited by a "veil of ignorance," which implies that a hypothetical contract is agreed upon in a situation where all parties are impartial and share a common worldview. The original position is explained by the idealistic vision underlying the theory, which interprets the real or non-ideal world through the lens of an ideal world structured by a social contract. Accordingly, the primary goal of society becomes one of apportioning basic rights, obligations, and socio-economic benefits in the fairest manner possible. While Rawls seems to have in mind a society with a relatively rich resource, capital, and political base, the social contract is also relevant to countries at all levels of development.

Three principles emerge from the original position: (i) the "maximin" principle – "each person is to have an equal right to the most extensive basic liberty compatible with a similar liberty for others;" (ii) the "difference" principle – "social and economic inequalities are to be arranged so that they are both (a) to the greatest benefit of the least advantaged and (b) attached to offices and positions open to all under fair equality of opportunity;" and (iii) as a corollary, the "primary goods" of society should be distributed equally, except in those cases where their unequal distribution would benefit its least advantaged members. Such primary goods are defined as "things it is supposed a rational man wants, [such as] rights, liberties and opportunities" (1971, 60, 83, 92).

They include equal liberties and a structure of income and wealth that would permit a just distribution of goods and services considered essential for the exercise of freedom. As we have argued, the latter inheres in the fulfillment of human needs, human motivation, and especially people's capabilities to conduct worthwhile lives. This idea was originally adumbrated in the "Aristotelian Principle," which states that human beings can only fulfill themselves by continually refining their talents in the direction of perpetually increasing subtlety and complexity. Nobel Laureate Amartya Sen (1988, 1999) has taken it one stage further by focusing on individual functionings or achievements as an important aspect of the production process. His vision of development is defined in terms of the expansion of people's entitlements and capabilities, the former giving life sustenance and the latter generating freedom. Enhancement of entitlements and capabilities for all peoples depends on factors such as the ability to sell labor, the prices of commodities, the spatial distribution of resources, power relations in society, and what individuals can extract from the state.

In the latter context, the Rawlsian principle espousing equal liberties presupposes a socio-economic system or "background institutions" that afford equal participation for all individuals and groups. The underlying principle is one that characterizes the culture of a modern democratic society in terms of a "political conception of justice" or "justice as fairness." Such a conception is thought to enable citizens to cite "what are publicly recognized among them as valid and sufficient reasons singled out by the concept itself" so that:

society's main institutions and how they fit together into one
system of social cooperation can be assessed in the same way by
each citizen, whatever the citizen's social position or more
particular interests (Rawls 1993, 9).

Rawls advances three "facts" about the political culture of modern democratic society in support of his thesis that "justice as fairness"
should be interpreted as a political conception. One is "reasonable
pluralism," or a plurality "of incompatible yet reasonably comprehensive doctrines." The latter pertain to conceptions of what is of value
in human life, ideals of personal character, friendship, familial and
associational relationships, and other rules that inform our conduct and
life as a whole. Religious belief systems such as Christianity, Judaism,
Islam, Hinduism, and Confucianism provide some of the best examples
of such comprehensive doctrines. A second "fact" is that "reasonable
disagreement" is an intrinsic part of modern democratic life. Since a
fulfilled life can be lived in a multiplicity of ways, there is no universally agreed method of moral assessment or ranking. One comprehensive religious, moral, or philosophical doctrine can only be maintained
through the oppressive power of the state.

Finally, the longevity of the political conception of justice in a
particular environment depends on the extent to which it is "willingly
and freely supported by at least a substantial majority of its politically
active citizens" (1993, 38). Hence, a combination of the fact that there
is no single comprehensive doctrine that forms the basis of political
regulation without oppressive state power and the intractable character
of dissensus within modern democracy tends to suggest that any conception of justice must necessarily rely on an overlapping consensus of
moral and other doctrines.

Libertarianism and Entitlements

The emphasis placed on equality of opportunity in the Rawlsian
schema entails that background institutions in society should ensure
that all persons receive their just rewards. When this happens, people
will be strongly motivated to produce more and everyone will benefit.
Such an outcome will be realized if all participants have an equal
chance of receiving the extra rewards from their productive efforts. If
the system results in certain people receiving less, such an inequality
would be unjust because it involves sacrificing some so that others may

profit. This outcome exemplifies a major bone of contention between the egalitarian and libertarian perspectives of morality and justice.

Libertarian critics contend that justice is not only one ideal among many, such as equality and democracy, but that it frequently conflicts with others, such as freedom. In this context, Nobel Laureate Friedrich Hayek (1960) has argued that utilitarian and egalitarian notions of justice can lead to illegitimate forms of coercion, and are therefore anathema to the ideals of freedom and liberty. The reason is that they purportedly constitute *patterned principles* of justice. The general libertarian claim is that if society seriously pursues a patterned ideal of justice, it would inevitably impose a uniform pattern. This in turn will ultimately lead to unwarranted forms of government regulation and coercion.

Robert Nozick (1974) also contends that there is a conflict between the patterned ideal of justice and the ideal of freedom to exchange or transfer goods without excessive government interference. His argument rests on the broader premise that conventions of the real world should essentially serve as a basis for determining the norms of distributive justice. Such conventions, it is claimed, did not originate from ideal patterns or social contracts, but are rather a byproduct of the forces of historical evolution. The latter are thought to define people's entitlements, which they would have provided for themselves and others through their own efforts.

The historical argument is that groups of people in society have come together for common purposes and that the bonds of association have enabled them to develop diverse conventions or customs to govern their many relationships. Hence, people tend to rely more on history rather than reason to demonstrate the relationship between society and justice. In particular, it is claimed that in no society was there an initial distribution of goods or resources in the sense of a strict or deliberate parceling out of rights and benefits. The people who came together, at least in Western society, had diverse kinds of resources and talents. Some were well endowed, while others boasted very little or no resource holdings. As an extrapolation of this argument, the claim is that personal wealth or merit has no significance for these initial holdings. Furthermore, this state of affairs needs no moral justification, no matter how randomly the Deity might have dealt out the goods in the world.

Various theories have been used to account for the origins of private property. For example, John Locke's theory of property rights posits that the world has been bequeathed to humankind and that people have a right to own and control those resources which they have created from their own labor. Contextually, the libertarian perspective places tremendous emphasis on the natural liberty of people to acquire, use, and transfer private property rights. To the extent that people are endowed differentially with talents, abilities, and inclinations in these respects, some are likely to benefit more than others. Therefore, it is argued, if attempts are made to prevent individuals from securing this sort of superiority, the natural liberty of people will be tampered with. If individuals can claim exclusive rights to certain bundles of goods and resources, so must groups of individuals be able to enjoy their possession of common goods and resources, even though this will occur at the expense of excluding other groups from the pertinent benefits. Thus, the historical principles are supposed to apply to diverse collectivities, including nation states.

The claim, therefore, is that people are entitled to the holdings they have acquired through their own efforts. Under the circumstances, interference with the exchange of such freely acquired holdings cannot be considered an act of justice, but as involving the suppression of liberty. Those who argue for redistribution must be able to demonstrate that some or all of these holdings were improperly acquired; otherwise, they would themselves be supporting infringement of moral rules by depriving others of the freedom to use and dispose of their resources as they choose. According to Nozick (1974, 163):

> No end-state principle or distributional pattern principle of justice can be continuously realized without continuous interference with people's lives. Any favored pattern would be transformed into one unfavored by the principle, by people choosing to act in various ways, e.g., by people exchanging goods and services with other people, or giving things to other people, things the transferrers are entitled to under the favored distributional pattern. To maintain a pattern one must either continuously interfere to stop people from transferring resources as they wish to, or continually (or periodically) interfere to take from some persons resources that others for some reason choose to transfer to them.

In this context, Nozick has proposed a theory of morality and justice based on three components: (i) an account of how the holdings were acquired in the first place; (ii) rules governing transfer of such holdings: and (iii) principles for rectifying unjust transfers. From this perspective, entitlements or ownership rights are presumed to exist if they came about by legitimate means, defined in the following terms. First, such ownership rights can legitimately pass from one person to another via inheritance. Second, they can be considered just if the holdings were acquired through free and voluntary exchange or gifts. Given these prerequisites, the libertarian claim is that people are *entitled* to their wealth and other resource holdings whether or not they desire or deserve them.

Hence, they have no obligation to assist those who are less fortunate. In the event that they choose to help others, it should be on an entirely voluntary basis, and not through coercion or government intervention in the redistributive process. But, such interference may be justified in those instances where it can be shown that the present distribution of holdings came about by illegitimate means such as force, theft, fraud, plunder, exploitation, and other injustices in the original pattern of distribution. The emphasis is on procedural fairness, or the historical conditions by which a pattern of distribution came about. Accordingly, it becomes ethically sufficient for a particular distribution to be procedurally fair, irrespective of its precise nature. In other words, it is irrelevant whether the distribution adequately reflects the personal or collective goals undergirding the humanitarian imperative.

In summary, supporters of a libertarian moral stance tend to opt for the ideal of freedom and liberty, thereby rejecting end-state or egalitarian ideals of justice, and the corpus of intrinsic ethical values pertaining to equality of opportunity and human self-worth. This carries tremendous implications for government decision-making and its role in the development process. It suggests that the pertinent decision rules should be neutral, so that legislation by the state should not take from some groups and redistribute to others. Rather the rules should be in place to enable individuals to organize and better themselves, and not explicitly accord special advantages to some over others. It is evident that such a policy perspective rules out a particular role for the state which has become enshrined in modern forms of governance, that is, redistribution of income from rich to poor as a means of improving the general welfare or common good.

The argument that nothing should be done about inequality in income and wealth distribution has been rationalized on the following grounds:

we cannot .... identify equity and efficiency as the sole ends of social welfare .... Other ends such as "liberty" are also valued.... [I]f redistribution entails costs in terms of other social ends which are equally valued, it would be foolish to disregard them and concentrate solely on the strictly 'economic ends' (Lal 1983, 89).

This fundamentalist claim essentially suggests that no matter how significant the human welfare gains that are likely to accrue from redistributive policies, even a modicum of liberty is never worth trading or sacrificing. As argued in this book, however, the authenticity of the development process depends as much on the individualistic and market-based allocative or efficiency goals stressed in orthodox neo-classical economics, as on the benevolent hand of the state and its sensitivity to distributive justice and social efficiency.

Correlatively, deontologists, or supporters of the rights-based moral stance, urge that while the ideal of liberty remains important, it should not necessarily take precedence over the patterned ideals of justice. The claim is that justice in the patterned sense lays the human or social foundation for other significant types of freedom to which the great masses of people throughout the globe do not have access. Such freedoms are associated with genuine opportunity, people's ability to cultivate tastes on their own, pursue disinterested knowledge, associate, move about, and express themselves. In terms of human existence itself, such freedoms are ontologically prior to the freedom to transfer material goods and resources. While they cannot always be legislated into existence, it becomes the duty of enlightened individuals and governments, where appropriate, to create enabling environments for the full development and nurturing of such fundamental freedoms.

The principles of libertarian morality tend to favor certain groups and social classes, for example, those who already own and have unlimited access to resources. Given this reality, when distributional patterns are arbitrated primarily through voluntary arrangements, the bigger economic prizes tend to be appropriated by such groups on the basis of power and unequal ownership and control of resources. The visible result, alluded to earlier, has been cumulative inequality in the distribution of economic rights and opportunities. Under the circumstances, it comes as no surprise that basic values pertaining to freedom, equality, full employment, poverty eradication, and basic human needs fulfillment tend to be ignored or compromised.

An important chapter in this debate has been written by scholars who advocate a perspective based on a conception of the *moral economy*. For example, in his book of the same name, John Powelson (2000) emphasizes the need for an economic culture based on a morality that endogenizes humanitarian imperatives, such as: paying fair wages; preserving the environment; hiring without racial, gender, class, and other prejudices; and ensuring that everyone has access to basic social services. Such an economic morality rests on two basic premises. First, it is consonant with ethical behavior according to certain relatively high standards defined by the citizenry at large. Second, it must command consensus of all people affected. As Powelson (2000, 8) remarks:

> The moral economy is some future world, decades or centuries away, projected from trends that are centuries long. It is a defined culture, including ways of determining prices, wages, money supply, property and law, and methods of preserving the environment and caring for the poor. It will have ancillary effects on education, religion, and interpersonal trust...
>
> Despite its emphasis on freedom, the moral economy is one of social control. However, controls are not imposed by governments that determine how society ought to be run and then pass laws to make it run that way. Rather, they are negotiated by citizens groups... The moral economy goes beyond democracy to a society of negotiation and compassion, characteristics grounded in popular will and understanding more than in governments requiring citizens to behave in ways not normal to their psyche.

A focal point is that the moral economy is based on an array of power-diffusion processes, and occupies a middle ground between naked libertarianism at one end of the spectrum and statism at the other. As indicated earlier, libertarianism rests on an ideological preconception that government interference with an economy should cease altogether, leaving regulatory and charitable functions to the market and other private agencies. Statism is predicated on widespread interventionism, or a dirigiste orientation whereby government "taxes, subsidies, and regulates" with the expressed purpose of guiding people toward its own desired form of economic organization. The moral economy is somewhat coterminous with the idea of a "well-ordered society," that is, one in which people operate as free and equal persons.

Its basic structure is defined by a fair system of social cooperation across generations (Rawls 1999, 2001). This means that political, economic, and social institutions coalesce into one system assigning rights, duties, responsibilities, and obligations.

Cosmopolitanism: Search for Global Distributive Justice

The principles of morality and distributive justice are based on an implicit assumption that the individual person is the primary moral subject and therefore the appropriate unit of analysis. However, the sociosphere is made up of international regimes, nation states, and other institutions that are interlocked in various dimensions of interdependence, dependence, and differential power relationships. The diverse forms of association have tremendous implications not only for individual behavior within and across nations, but also raise intricate issues about the grounds, spatio-temporal or otherwise, on which appeals to morality and justice should be arbitrated – individual, national, or cosmopolitan.

Some of the pertinent issues include: (i) the justness of a world order in which the defining principles of morality and justice are to be shifted from traditional political, legal, and economic requirements to the prerequisites of an international moral discourse; (ii) how the presumed moral obligation of the rich to help the poor both within and across national borders can be justified; and (iii) changes that can be effected in the basic principles of morality and justice as a result of conflicting interests of nation states vis-à-vis a perceptible global community of nations and peoples subscribing to universal principles of the right and the good. Germane to this is the burning question whether humankind can be said to constitute a global community in the relevant sense, or whether the duties, responsibilities, and obligations of humanitarian development are essentially delimited by national geographical boundaries.

The enduring view, alluded to in Chapter 5, is that nation states and not persons should be considered the lynchpin of morality and justice. The claim is that complexity of economic exchanges, social interactions, and other forms of cooperation and conflict at the national level are basic to any form and understanding of morality. This perspective boasts a very long tradition of intellectual support, ranging from the early idealist or positivist views of Machiavelli, Hobbes, and Hegel to modern liberal-positivist perorations of Nardin (1983) and Keohane (1964). The guiding preconception is that morality and justice stop at the water's edge. In other words, nation states are conceived as discrete or morally autonomous entities, which cannot be attributed with the slightest intention of subscribing to universal or cosmopolitan principles of the right and the good.

This is the starting point for the modern liberal-realist thesis about the "morality of states." The basic proposition is that nation states, as politically sovereign entities, represent the primary mechanism for collective decision-making in the world order. Correlatively, their political institutions can be used to articulate concerns of citizens about morality, justice, and fairness. Even though government policies invariably reflect the sectional interests of ruling elites and other power brokers, it is argued, it does not necessarily follow that the citizenry at large would lightly jettison the entrenched belief in the superordinate role of national autonomy. Such sentiments enable nation states to protect what they usually project as national self-interests within the global comity of nations. The overall conclusion is that, whatever their ideological orientations, all nation states are endowed with the freedom of maneuver to pursue their own precepts, rules, and procedures pertaining to morality, justice, and human betterment.

By contrast, the cosmopolitan life-and-world perspective does not attribute any deep moral significance to the *de jure* autonomy of nation states. It posits that their internal affairs should be subject to external and universal moral scrutiny. The main protagonists, such as Beitz (1979, 1983), criticize the morality of states doctrine on the grounds that individual persons are the primary moral agents in ethical theory; therefore, a special justification has to be given for refusal to apply this principle in the arena of global political economy. Contextually, "cosmopolitan morality" encompasses the ethical principles that should guide the behavior of, and relations among, members of a global or universal community in which national boundaries have only a purely geographical or derivative significance.

The implications can be addressed by looking again at the question whether the rich minority in the world can still be said to have any significant moral obligations to help the poor majority, and the ethical rules or standards that should guide such redistribution. Contrary to the morality of states doctrine, the guiding principle behind cosmopolitan morality is equality among individual persons, even though visible inequities and inequalities may persist among nation states and national economies. The guiding preconception is that all persons should be accorded equal moral worth irrespective of their countries of origin, citizenship, and other ascriptive characteristics. The moral case for redistribution can then be arbitrated on libertarian, utilitarian or conesquentialist, or egalitarian or rights-based grounds.

At one end of the normative spectrum lies what we may term *cosmopolitan libertarianism*, which has been dubbed "entitlement valid for all substance I own now – 'evasion' for short" (Sen 1981b, 478). The underlying ethic rests on a conservative belief that all persons in the world are entitled to the present set of resources they happen to own or control. This implies that the status quo does not need any further justification, while any proposals for change do. Hence, there is no good reason to tamper in any way with the manner in which the sociosphere distributes benefits and burdens. As a corollary, the implicit assumption is that a global order left on its own would ultimately generate a Panglossian "best of all possible worlds."

One counter-argument is that due to past injustices, for example, slavery, imperialism, colonial exploitation, Hitlerite holocaust, and the like, some groups of people may be entitled to compensation in the form of reparations and related forms of "affirmative action" at the international level. Accordingly, international transfers from rich to poor can be defended on the grounds that they constitute a proxy for reparations, or an important mechanism for rectifying past unjust transfers from poor to rich. The moral premise is that descendants of those who reaped unjust benefits have an obligation to make restitution to the offsprings of the deprived. However, this response raises a number of knotty questions. One concerns the extent to which past generations were in fact guilty of exploitation. Even if it is assumed that they were, and taking into account the costs of past injustices, a more important question is whether the present generation of beneficiaries is obliged to pay compensation for past ills in which they did not participate, and for which they cannot be held accountable.

One answer to this dilemma is that the favored position of the present generation in the North is partly a result of conceivably illegitimate acts perpetrated in the past, so that its members do not fully deserve their relatively favored economic status. Even if it is agreed that compensation should be paid, an intractable question remains about its quantity and form – for example, outright grants, concessional aid, and should it be paid to governments or directly to individuals or groups? Furthermore, should there be any restrictions on how the funds are utilized? Such questions must remain unanswered.

Second, an alternative perspective of global morality can be grounded on utilitarian principles. Such a *cosmopolitan utilitarianism* would rely on the goal of attaining the "greatest happiness of the greatest number" in the world or "aggregate world welfare" as well as perceptions about global welfare in terms of the expected consequences of redistribution. The implications depend on how such concepts are interpreted. It becomes a highly demanding standard if they are taken to mean an unlimited obligation to help all disadvantaged individuals and groups in the world. However, if the standard simply refers to the "majority," it is likely that most target groups would be captured in the safety net, even though the interests of certain innocent minorities may be compromised.

The case for redistribution based on utilitarianism can also rely on the economic concept of "diminishing marginal utility of income." The assumption is that the average poor person values small additions to income more (has a higher marginal utility of income) than the average rich person. If this is true, a dollar redistributed from rich to poor persons adds more to aggregate human welfare than it detracts from it. In other words, poor people in the South are likely to gain more than taxpayers in the North would lose. Hence, aggregate world welfare would be augmented. On consequentialist grounds, an important prerequisite is for the system of resource transfer and use to exhibit some degree of transparency, that is, knowledge that the transfer will directly benefit intended target groups. Even if a kleptocracy prevails, flexible schemes for monitoring and evaluation can be introduced without posing any threats to the national sovereignty of countries in which beneficiaries reside.

At a third level, the concern shifts to the properties of *cosmopolitan egalitarianism*, which many scholars believe constitutes the essence of global redistributive justice. At least three consensual research programs can be used to illustrate this point. The foundations are traceable to the political writings of Immanuel Kant who saw "domestic" and "international" progress as two sides of the same coin. He introduced the concept of "cosmopolitan right" based on the claim that "peoples of the earth have entered in varying degrees into a universal community, and it has developed to the point where a violation of rights in one part of the world is felt everywhere (*Political Writings* 1970, 107-108). Hence, rights and obligations transcend the bonds established among fellow nationals or between a state and its citizens, but extend to outsiders.

The point of emphasis is that the traditional scope of the law of nations should be extended to include the transnational rights of individuals. The fundamental Kantian thesis is that in order to establish universal justice and perpetual peace, that is, provide conditions for universal human freedom, it is necessary to institutionalize a cosmopolitan or humanitarian law that enshrines the rights of world citizens alongside those of national publics and sovereign states, thereby establishing a sociosphere encompassing a universal community governed by the rule of law. The principles of the cosmopolitan ethic suggest that justice invariably cuts across diverse levels of economic, social, and political life, and that the whole of humanity constitutes a "single moral universe."

Members of the modern school of what is called "critical international theory" have extended the Kantian framework to analyze the possibility of undoing the tenets of state-centrism and promoting more emancipatory forms of community within a more embracing cosmopolitan structure. For example, Neufeld (1995) articulates the cosmopolitan ethic in terms of mapping the Greek *polis* on to the global sphere, the idea being that freedom and equality can be expanded to all human beings. From this perspective, the sovereign state becomes a "limited moral community" that promotes particularism and breeds alienation, greed, insecurity, conflict, war, and related forms of ill-being. In similar vein, Linklater (1998) views the modern state as a product of a "totalizing project" that combines various monopoly powers: the right to monopolize the legitimate means of violence over claimed territory; the exclusive right to tax; the right to demand undivided political allegiance; the sole legal authority in the adjudication of disputes among citizens; and the sole right of representation in international law.

Hence, he highlights the need for a cosmopolitan ethos that is grounded in a "community of humanity," while recognizing the importance of transnational, regional, national, and sub-national entities. The idea is to overcome the "moral deficits" inherent in global capitalism and the system of sovereign states and promote "moral progress" or enlargement of the sphere of freedom and equality through the creation of appropriate institutions. In Linklater's eyes, such moral progress is not coterminous with an eternal moral truth or universal conception of the good life. Rather, it entails a hermeneutic process of interpreting and reinterpreting received moral values – universalistic and particularistic – whenever they smack of exclusion. In other words, moral progress signifies

> the widening of the circle of those who have rights to participate in dialogue and the commitment that norms cannot be regarded as universally valid unless they have, or could command, the consent of all those who stand to be affected by them (Linklater 1998, 96).

This dialogical approach is in the tradition of the "discourse ethics" or proposals for "decentering of moral viewpoints" advanced by Jurgen Habermas (1998). From this perspective, moral progress takes place when the nexus among state sovereignty, citizenship, and nationalism is successively dismantled and replaced by freer forms of political association or an emancipatory conversation in which national strife, economic inequality, gender exclusion, and racial discrimination are eradicated. Hence, the cosmopolitan reinterpretation rests on an imperative of establishing principles, norms, and institutional arrangements that can form the basis of a consent-oriented, deliberative, and inclusive dialogue, or a moral framework for resolving political, social, and economic issues.

From a somewhat different but related angle, Rawls (1999) advances a notion of a "Law of the Peoples," which extends the political conception of "justice as fairness" to the international arena. While all of the details would take us too far a field, the implications can be appraised by utilizing Rawlsian concepts such as the "veil of ignorance" and "social contract" to make the moral case for global redistribution. The question can then be asked how people, stripped of their nationalities or not knowing their respective places in the system of global stratification, would perceive the structure of sociospheric relationships. Would they, for example, approve of the present structure as governed by, say, the IMF, World Bank, and WTO? For reasons advanced in Chapter 2, one can hazard a guess that from the "original position" most people will call for a new human order based on an entirely different set of principles, norms, and procedures, that is, significant structural reforms reflecting universal values of democracy, equality, equity, and freedom.

Cosmopolitan egalitarianism can also be evaluated on the basis of Rawls's "maximin" and "difference" principles. In the former case, the relevant guiding standard becomes the equal distribution of liberties or the "primary goods" which undergird the pursuit of humanitarian development. Extrapolation of the difference principle suggests a need to concentrate relief efforts on the poorest or "least advantaged" persons in the world. Moreover, a strict application of rights-based principles would entail a denial of loans, gifts and other resource transfers to governments and countries with a record of violations, such as abuses of human rights and environmental degradation, or which otherwise are wont to promote global public bads such as predatory wars and terrorism.

On the more positive side, the norms and principles of global egalitarianism are synergistic with the values articulated in the United Nations *Millennium Declaration* of September 2000 and the comcomitant Millennium Development Goals. The Declaration recognizes that while individual societies have separate responsibilities, they also have a shared or collective responsibility to uphold the principles of humanitarian development, such as freedom, equality, equity, solidarity, tolerance and respect for nature. Accordingly, the Millennium Development Goals are viewed as broad, but specific, initiatives in the "road map" towards implementation of the Declaration. They encapsulate eight areas of responsibility and targets to be achieved by 2015:

- *Eradication of extreme poverty and hunger* - reducing by half the proportion of people living on less than a dollar a day; and similar reduction in the proportion of people who suffer from hunger.
- *Achievement of universal primary education* - ensuring that all boys and girls complete a full course of primary schooling.
- *Promotion of gender equality and empowerment of women* - eliminating gender disparity in primary and secondary education preferably by 2005, and at all levels by 2015.
- *Reduction of child mortality* - reducing by two thirds the mortality rate of children under five.
- *Improvement of maternal health* - reducing by three quarters the maternal mortality ratio.
- *Combating HIV/AIDS, malaria and other diseases* - halting and beginning to reverse the spread of HIV/AIDS and incidence of malaria and other major diseases.
- *Ensuring environmental sustainability* - by integrating the principles of sustainable development into country policies

and programs; reversing the loss of environmental resources; reducing by half the proportion of people without sustained access to safe drinking water; and, achieving significant improvement in the lives of at least 100 million slum-dwellers by 2020.

- *Crafting a global partnership for development* - through (i) further developing an open trading and financial system that is rule-based, predictable and non-discriminatory, including a commitment to good governance, development and poverty reduction - nationally and internationally; (ii) addressing the special needs of the least developed countries, including tariff- and quota-free access for their exports; enhanced debt relief for heavily indebted poor countries; cancellation of official bilateral debt; and more generous development assistance for countries committed to poverty reduction; (iii) addressing the special needs of landlocked and small island developing States; (iv) dealing comprehensively with developing countries' debt problems through national and international measures to make debt sustainable in the long term; (v) developing decent and productive work for youth; (vi) providing access to affordable essential drugs in developing countries; and (vii) making available the benefits of new technologies - especially information and communications technologies.

Chapter 10

The Right to Development

> The better life, once a decent minimum has been reached, is largely
> a matter of people getting along with each other and not fouling
> their own fairly well upholstered nests.... Freedom of movement,
> freedom to express ideas, a feeling of security, and, in general, a
> reasonable bill of rights are surely involved in creating the
> conditions [for] the better, more satisfying, and more constructive
> life.
>
> Wendell Gordon (1973)

The rights-based or egalitarian perspective of morality projects a vision
of the natural right of all human beings to share and participate equally
in the design of Institutions based on an overlapping consensus. Correlatively, people can be said to possess a universal "right to development" by virtue of their common status as human beings who are endowed with capabilities to make plans, enforce shared rules, and ap-

portion justice (Dworkin 1978). The right to development is grounded in a preconception that every human being should live a free and worthy life in his or her community. This connotes a "right to life," or the capability to aspire to an increasingly better quality of existence. Hence, all individuals and groups should be afforded an equal opportunity to participate in, contribute to, and benefit from the fruits of material progress.

The right to development is a fundamental human right that lies at the intersection of the entire gamut of economic, social, cultural, political, and civil rights highlighted in this chapter. It is a focal point of Articles of 1, 55, and 56 of the United Nations *Charter*, which emphasizes the joint responsibility of member states to promote development, social progress, and respect for human rights. Such themes are also adumbrated in several normative resolutions adopted by the United Nations and its specialized agencies. For example, the 1986 United Nations *Declaration on the Right to Development* affirms that "the human person is the central subject of development and should be the active participant and beneficiary of the right to development." A recurrent theme has centered around the collective responsibility of the global community to ensure attainment of an adequate standard of living necessary for enjoyment of equal rights and fundamental freedoms throughout the world.

Various resolutions of the Human Rights Commission also stress the duty of all member states and the global community jointly and severally to create the conditions necessary for realization of the right to development. The 1993 *World Conference on Human Rights* not only reaffirmed this right, but also reiterated that "the human person is the central subject of development." It was also emphasized that "while development facilitates the enjoyment of all human rights, the lack of development cannot be invoked to justify the abridgement of internationally recognized human rights." Hence, a relatively low level of development should not be used as an excuse for denying citizens of a country their basic rights, and in particular, as a justification for political and other forms of oppression. While it is evident that poverty and social exclusion do constitute violations of human dignity, their incidence does not absolve governments from the duty of designing programs guaranteeing human rights, while fostering effective citizen participation in decisions governing fulfillment of needs, capabilities, and aspirations.

Universals Versus Particulars

The fundamental goals and processes of humanitarian development are inextricably intertwined with principles guaranteeing the provisioning of basic rights – economic, social, cultural, civic or civil, and political. Over the centuries, these principles have come to reflect forms of citizenship that provide people with access to rights and powers in most established societies (Marshall 1964). The economic and social categories denote the rights of all people to a certain minimum standard of living, economic welfare, and social security. Cultural rights pertain to the ability of each society to design and enforce its own norms and standards about how its citizens may or may not achieve their goals. Civic or civil rights refer essentially to legal rights, while the political dimension stresses the right of every person to participate in the exercise of political power, or more directly in the practice of politics.

These broad categories of "first generation" rights are both indivisible and interdependent. For example, enjoyment of economic, social, and cultural rights is a *sine qua non* for the enjoyment of political rights. At the same time, abridgement of civil and political rights militates against enjoyment of social, cultural, and economic rights. A distinction is also sometimes drawn between "individual" and "collective" rights (Macpherson 1987). The former are supposed to be enjoyed by all persons irrespective of social class, gender, ethnicity, religion, age and political affiliation. By contrast, collective rights are normally claimed by subordinated cultural minorities such as Native Americans and Aborigines in Australia. In this context, 1993 World Conference on Human Rights focused attention not only on the plight of individuals, but also on the undesirable conditions facing specific groups at risk: women and girls; national, religious, ethnic, and linguistic minorities; disabled persons; children; indigenous peoples; refugees and internally displaced persons; migrants and other vulnerable groups.

The major historical and logical conflicts among the broad categories of rights can be traced to the peculiar evolution of international laws and corresponding changes in modes of interpretation. In particular, human rights law was initially developed as a part of the constitutional codes of individual nation states. The perception was that its substance and enforcement were primarily concerned with relations among nation states, an area historically regarded as a domestic matter. The first set of bills of fundamental rights emerged in the

French Declaration of the Rights of Man and the Citizen in 1789, and in the declarations of the North American colonies at the time of their independence. From the very inception, however, a major bone of contention arose over the "human" versus the "rights" dimension of the equation. For example, the historical debate on the French Declaration has demonstrated that while it specified the actual constitution of valued rights, there was not sufficient clarity about the individuals or groups who were entitled to them (Hunt 1996).

Along similar lines, Chirot (1994) poses the question: who is considered human or subhuman? Its import lies in the historical tendency for tyrants and dictators to dehumanize entire groups of people. The process of human rights empowerment shows that large numbers of people have become collective "non-persons" who have been treated inhumanely and deprived of their rights. The worst kinds of abuses, Chirot opines, have occurred when authoritarian regimes implicitly categorize certain groups as "subhuman," not so much because of what they are perceived to have done but more because of who they are. The upshot of the argument is that there has been considerable divergence between the philosophical and prescriptive dimensions of human rights on the one hand vis-à-vis the historical realities surrounding their enforcement, on the other. The same is true for related notions such as freedom (Patterson 1991).

Through the more general lens of Western thought and practice, the ideal notion of economic justice was predicated on equality in the distribution of rights. This preconception was grounded in the classical or Enlightenment view of a good society, which espoused two broad principles: equal incomes and equal rights. It was expected that the economic and political institutions of capitalism would guarantee equal incomes and privileges for all members of society. Economic justice was to be arbitrated through the rules governing the operation of free markets, while equality was to be guaranteed by the principles of democracy (Okun 1975). But, humanitarian skeptics point out that capitalism and free markets do not necessarily guarantee equality, and democracy in the sense of absolute majority rule - is not always consistent with human rights. The record suggests that unconstrained majorities can impose inordinate burdens on minorities, for example, through propagation of overtly racist policies, denial of legal equality to women, or suppression of opposition voices.

While issues about the "tyranny of the majority" remain with us, the immediate concern is more with the evolution of "universal" human rights. Their contemporary fundamentals, especially the economic and social variety, did not enter into international law until the Second World War. The resulting atrocities led to a realization that international security, peace, and progress could only be guaranteed through universal enforcement and protection of such rights (Forsythe 1977). The United Nations emerged in this context, and pursuant to Article 66 of its Charter, a Commission on Human Rights was established in 1946 to give precision to the scope and content of human rights. It drafted a *Universal Declaration of Human Rights*, which was proclaimed by the General Assembly on December 10, 1948 as a *de facto* code of universal human rights, even though it was merely termed a "declaration." It consists of thirty Articles highlighting basic rights and freedoms to which people are entitled without discrimination. Several supporting covenants and conventions have subsequently defined and further codified the contexts of these rights. Table 10.1 lists the major human rights agreements for ease of reference.

Thus, the United Nations Charter, through the Universal Declaration, to subsequent International settlements have been responsible for enunciating a set of intrinsic rights that all established societies have a moral obligation to bring about, guarantee, and protect. Our common humanity and the very fact that we live in an interdependent world tend to establish the need for shared standards of human dignity and embracement of the fundamental rights of all humankind. In concert with the humanitarian development perspective, they should not be interpreted as abstract or metaphysical constructs, but rather as concrete human goals to be progressively achieved. The enforcement of some categories (positive rights) calls for positive action, while others involve refraining from certain types of action (negative rights).

Whatever the actual constitution of individual categories of rights, fundamentalists argue, they should be construed as mutually reinforcing elements of a composite that is guided by universal standards guaranteeing not only political, civil, and religious liberties, but also optimal human welfare through social and economic protections such as job security, access to health, education, and social security. As shown, in Table 10.2, the comprehensive vision is mirrored in what is nowadays termed an International Bill of Rights, which encapsulates the major provisions of the Universal Declaration of Human Rights (D) and two international covenants it engendered (International Covenants on Civil and Political Rights (C) and Economic, Social, and Cultural rights (E)).

Table 10.1: International Human Rights Agreements

Charter of the United Nations (1945)
United Nations Commission on Human Rights (1946)
Universal Declaration of Human Rights (1948)
Convention on the Prevention and Punishment of the Crime of Genocide (1948)
European Convention on Human Rights (1950)
Convention Relating to the Status of Refugees (1951)
Convention on the Political Rights of Women (1952)
Convention on the Status of Stateless Persons (1954)
Convention Abolishing Slavery (1956)
ILO Convention on the Abolition of Forced Labor (1957)
Convention on Consent to Marriage (1962)
Convention on the Elimination of Racial Discrimination (1965)
International Covenants on Economic, Social, and Cultural Rights/ Civil and Political Rights (1966)
Convention on the Suppression and Punishment of the Crime of Apartheid (1973)
Convention on the Elimination of all Forms of Discrimination against Women (1979)
Convention against Torture and other Cruel, Inhuman or Degrading Treatment or Punishment (1984)
Convention on the Rights of the Child (1989)
International Criminal Tribunal for Ex-Yugoslavia (1993)
International Criminal Tribunal for Rwanda (1994)

Source: United Nations.

The past fifty years or more have witnessed a very intensive debate between protagonists who share a common belief about the nature of humans and society vis-à-vis others subscribing to a more relativistic mode of interpretation. The latter stress the need to recognize how the substantive concepts have emerged and changed over time. One variant of the argument is that no uniform or monolithic standards and criteria can be used to assess disparate cultural contexts – for example, global versus regional, Western versus Asian, or liberal versus socialist regimes. The strongest claim is that the very concept of

Table 10.2: International Bill of Human Rights

Rights to:	Document/ Article*
- Life	D3, C6
- Liberty and security of person	D3, C9
- Freedom from slavery and servitude	D4, C8
- Freedom from Torture or cruel, inhuman or degrading treatment or punishment	D5, C7
- Equality before the law	D6, C16
- Equal Protection under the law	D7, C14, C26
- Freedom from arbitrary arrest and detention	D9, C9
- Fair trial by an independent and impartial tribunal	D10, C14
- Presumption of Innocence	D11, C15
- Inviolability of home, family, and privacy	D12, C17
- Freedom of movement and residence	D13, C12
- Seek asylum from persecution	D14
- Nationality	D15
- Marry and found a family	D16, C23, E10
- Own property	D17
- Freedom of peaceful assembly and association	D20, C21, C22
- Vote and participate in government	D21, C25
- Social Security	D22, E9
- Work, form, and join trade unions	D23, C22, E8
- Rest and Leisure	D24, E7
- Food, clothing, and housing	D25, E11
- Health care and social services	D25, E12
- Special protections for children	D25, E10, C24
- Education	D26, E13, E14
- Participation in cultural life of the community	D27, E15
- Self-determination	C1, E1
- Humane treatment when detained or imprisoned	C10
- Protection against arbitrary expulsion of aliens	C13
- Protection against advocacy of racial or religious hatred	C20
- Protection of minority culture	C27

Source: Author

universal human rights is a product of Western civilization and individualism. Hence, any attempt to impose human rights on other societies is a form of cultural imperialism. Such arguments are being increasingly championed by Islamic fundamentalists and exponents of Asian values based on Confucianism, Hinduism, Taoism, Shintoism, and the like.

For example, China subscribes to a notion of what may be termed "particularistic" human rights, the rationale being that so-called universal human rights are not only an infringement of national sovereignty, but are really a matter of domestic rather than international concern. It may be commented that the very idea of particularistic human rights is contradictory. Human rights would not be "human" if certain individuals or groups were denied them. This is not meant to deny that their enforcement should always be sensitive to diverse regional and cultural differences. But, the perspective of cultural relativism also draws support from noted Western political scientists such as Samuel P. Huntington (1993), who predicts that culture rather than ideology will become the most potent causal force generating conflicts, or the "clash of civilizations."

Huntington claims that Western ideas such as individualism, liberalism, constitutionalism, human rights, equality, liberty, the rule of law, democracy, free markets, and separation of church and state often have little resonance in Islamic, Hindu, Confucian, Buddhist, or "orthodox" cultures. Western attempts to propagate such ideas have produced a reaction against "human rights imperialism" and a concomitant reaffirmation of indigenous values. Huntington's prognostication is certainly correct in the sense that all societies now pay attention to cultural values and domestic appurtenances when confronting perceptibly international or "universal" standards imposed from outside. However, the implicit assumption that prevailing cultural patterns are more or less sedimented and will inevitably be the source of conflicts is open to question. Historically, cultural differences and the rivalry emanating from their interactions have frequently brought creative changes at both national and international levels. A useful example is Japanese confrontation with Western civilizations during the mid-19th century. This allowed the country to progressively open its door to external influences, which provided an essential catalyst in its subsequent Industrialization. Moreover, the violent clash of civilizations is more likely to result from one civilization trying to dominate others and/or a failure to transform systems of inequality (Rubenstein and Crocker 1994).

The fact that human rights are firmly entrenched in Western civilization is not sufficient ground to deny their universal status. It can be argued that the human rights concept is based on an "overlapping consensus," or values shared across cultures. These "transcultural universals" encapsulate a respect for the sanctity of life and human dignity, a tolerance of differences among peoples, and a desire for freedom, equality, fairness, order, and stability. Across cultures, there is no uniform or monolithic set of Western, Asian, or Islamic values, as the case may be. While the world is made up of varying degrees of multiculturalism, there may be more "unity in diversity" than meets the naked eye.

There is also a lingering proclivity to compartmentalize rights, rank them in hierarchical order, and even separate them across generations. This is reflected in the debate about the relative status of so-called "first generation" rights such as freedom and equality vis-à-vis "second" and "third" generation ones such as those pertaining to women, the biophysical environment, and the right to (economic) development (see Steiner and Alston 1996; Shute and Hurley 1993; and Van Ness 1999). This is exemplified by the "full belly" or "bread first" thesis, or the claim that promotion and enforcement of civil and political rights can be postponed until economic needs (economic and social rights) are fulfilled. One biblical variation on this theme is implicit in Moses's admonition to the Israelites that "man doth not live by bread only."

In modern times, on the contrary, many authoritarian regimes and "development dictatorships" adopted a philosophy that a full belly was more valuable than political liberty, democracy, and a free press. On the one hand, the record suggests that huge economic costs have to be borne by regimes that deliberately suppress civil and political rights. In general, they have failed to generate the economic rewards that were promised. On the other hand, the spectacular economic growth experienced during the 1970s and 1980s by Hong Kong, Singapore, South Korea, Taiwan, and perhaps Chile is sometimes used to support the argument that LDCs could achieve some measure of material prosperity based on a market-oriented development path propped up by authoritarian rule. The full list of provisions contained in the International Bill of Rights reflects the organic goals of human development, which is also grounded in the principle that human rights are universal, indivisible, and derive their substance from the dignity of the human person. People cannot fully exercise the freedoms inherent in their civil, political, and cultural rights if they are destitute, impoverished, or face other forms of economic debilitation. The provision of adequate levels of food, shelter, education, medical care and other wherewithals of human well-being cannot be divorced from the imperative of establishing a decent, fair, and ultimately free society. The argument may be taken one stage further by exploring the need for fair labor standards and the protection of workers' rights.

Workers' Rights and Labor Security

Labor market institutions play a pivotal role in employment creation, determining the structure of earnings, and therefore in achieving equitable and fair outcomes in the real world. Unlike the textbook model of factor and commodity markets, they directly affect the living standards of workers and their families because the majority of households largely depend on income from work for their well-being. When the domestic economy falters, labor must bear the brunt of the shock because, unlike capital, it is not internationally mobile and invariably stays at home. In recent times, the problem has been exacerbated by the falling demand for labor in almost all episodes of structural adjustment. No country has been able to escape the resultant employment losses and decline in real wages.

Unfortunately, the new international division of labor inherent in globalization of the world economy, with its highly mobile capital, almost instantaneous communication, and spirited even cut-throat competition, has put a downward pressure on workers' wages, working conditions, labor standards, and the rights of workers in every part of the world. Labor laws have been thrown out of the window, unions have lost their strength, and many employers now have the right to hire and fire workers as an incentive to increase investment. There is also a growing preference for casual and temporary workers who now have to work harder and longer in order to fulfill their basic needs. On an overall basis, therefore, there has been an erosion of labor's influence despite the fact that it has to bear the brunt of adjustment costs and is still expected to play a responsible role as social partner in the development process.

As discussed in Chapter 6, the wage bargaining process has been increasingly governed by a cost-cutting assumption on the part of powerful employers and exporters. This is supported by the notion of labor market flexibility and a "distortionist" theoretical perspective of labor relations. The latter posits that trade union activity, traditional forms of collective bargaining, government regulation of wages, and the imposition of fair labor standards represent pervasive examples of policy-induced distortions that raise labor costs, militate against flexibility, and slow up the economic and trade liberalization process. While unions are attributed with positive qualities in terms of their potential contribution to productivity and equity, more emphasis is placed on the negative effects of their monopoly power on other groups such as employers, consumers, and unorganized workers.

In contrast to the distortionist approach, the "contextualist" perspective views the labor market as a social institution, and collective bargaining as a mechanism facilitating achievement of societal goals (Freeman 1992; Solow 1990). This is supported by the rights-based philosophy of the United Nations and its specialized agencies, especially the ILO. To illustrate, the Universal Declaration of Human Rights contains a number of provisions specifically relating to workers' rights. For example, Article 20 declares: Everyone has the right to freedom of peaceful assembly and association. Article 23 contains the following provisions: (1) Everyone has the right to work, to free choice of employment, to just and favorable conditions of work, and to protection against unemployment; (2) Everyone, without discrimination, has the right to equal pay for equal work; (3) Everyone who works has the right to just and favorable remuneration ensuring for himself and his family an existence worthy of human dignity, and supplemented, if necessary, by other means of social protection; and (4) Everyone has the right to form and join trade unions for the protection of his interests. Many other Articles of the Universal Declaration are concerned with workers' rights, for example, protection of children, freedom of opinion and expression, protection against arbitrary arrest, and prohibitions against torture.

These and other provisions are grounded in the preconception that labor market intervention is beneficial, and that where efficiency criteria conflict with the social protection of labor, the latter course should be chosen. This philosophy also informs the policies of the ILO – a tripartite labor-business-government agency – that promotes fair labor practices, including the protection of minors, freedom of assembly, and abolition of discrimination. As the ILO declares,

> countries which are members of the ILO are presumed to accept
> the value judgment that free collective bargaining between

employers and autonomous pluralistic trade unions is the best method of determining terms and conditions of employment. *Access to such mechanisms is regarded as a basic human right.* Therefore, governments are expected to introduce legislative provisions to encourage the development of trade unions and free collective bargaining (ILO 1990, 39; emphasis added).

The ILO's "Core" human rights conventions are summarized in Table 10.3 for ease of reference. These, together with its Declaration on the Fundamental Principles and Rights at Work are deemed to constitute five "core worker rights," even if legislatures of member countries have not ratified ILO Conventions pertaining to these rights: (i) freedom of association; (ii) effective recognition of the right to collective bargaining; (iii) elimination of all forms of forced or compulsory labor; (iv) effective abolition of child labor; and (v) elimination of discrimination in respect to employment and occupation. Organized labor is considered the principal mechanism of collective bargaining to determine wages and working conditions. But, governments have an important role to play in setting the rules defining the rights of workers, trade unions, and employers; the conditions of collective bargaining; and the system for settling disputes. Governments are also expected to intervene directly in labor markets -

Table 10.3: ILO Human Rights (Core) Conventions

No. 29 Forced Labor Convention (1930): Requires the suppression of forced or compulsory labor in all forms. Certain exceptions are permitted, such as military service, convict labor properly supervised, emergencies such as wars, fires, earthquakes...

No. 87 Freedom of Association and Protection of the Right to Organize Convention (1948): establishes the right of all workers and employers to form and join organizations of their own choosing without prior authorization, and lays down a series of guarantees for the functioning of organizations without interference by the public authorities.

No. 98 Right to Organize and Collective Bargaining Convention (1949): Provides for protection against anti-union discrimination, for protection of workers' and employers' organizations against acts of interference by each other, and for measures to promote collective bargaining.

No. 100 Equal Remuneration Convention (1951): Calls for equal pay and benefits for men and women for work of equal value.

No. 105 Abolition of Forced Labor Convention (1957): Prohibits the use of any form of forced or compulsory labor as a means of political coercion or education, punishment for the expression of political or ideological views, workforce mobilization, labor discipline, punishment for participation in strikes, or discrimination.

No. 111 Discrimination (Employment and Occupation) Convention (1958): Calls for a national policy to eliminate discrimination in access to employment, training and working conditions, on grounds of race, color, sex, religion, political opinion, national extraction or social origin and to promote equality of opportunity and treatment.

No. 138 Minimum Age Convention (1973): Aims at the abolition of child labor, stipulating that the minimum age for admission to employment shall not be less than the age of completion of compulsory schooling.

Source: ILO

to achieve specific socio-economic goals: for example, protection of women, children, and other minority groups; setting minimum wages; and legislation on safety and health standards in the workplace.

In some countries, the earnings of select categories of workers such as women, girls, children, and migrants are so low that they typify "exploitation wages" or "slave labor." This raises a question about the effects of minimum wage policies. The conventional economic wisdom is that too high a minimum wage not only prevents wages generally from being set at market-clearing levels, but also establishes a floor under the wage distribution profile. The effect, it is claimed, is to price low-skilled and younger workers out of the formal labor market. According to one study,

> inasmuch as minimum wage and other regulations discourage formal employment by increasing wage and non-wage costs, they hurt the poor who aspire to formal employment. Hence it is difficult to argue for minimum wages in low- and middle-income countries on equity grounds (World Bank 1995a, 75).

From a rights-based perspective, it can be countered that appropriate application of minimum wage legislation can help to raise earnings of poor and disadvantaged groups at little or no cost to employment creation. The minimum wage tends to set the floor to the wage structure below which it becomes socially unacceptable and economically unjust for labor to cooperate fully in building a viable economy and decent society. No iron-clad generalizations can be made about the positive or negative economic effects of minimum wages, since specific outcomes ultimately depend on the structural and institutional contexts of individual countries, as defined by the labor market structure, levels at which minimum wages are set, and the ability of the state to enforce them. Furthermore, legal minimum wages are so low and labor standards so weakly enforced in many poor countries that any putative distortionary effects are virtually non-existent.

The increasing deregulation of the economy in Africa, Asia, Latin America and the Caribbean has led to a deterioration of wages and labor standards for the following four reasons, inter alia: weak trade union bargaining power; deliberate attempts to abandon minimum wage policies due to the onslaught of structural adjustment and globalization; removal of social safety nets; and accelerated inflation. As a result, new cadres of unprotected workers – veritable "reserve armies" or "labor reservoirs" – have emerged in the urban informal and rural sectors. Since the environment for public policy has been transformed by exogenous forces, national governments find it increasingly difficult to cushion workers against the adverse effects of economic dislocations. Besides the disciplinary effects of world markets on public expenditures, the state's ability to raise tax revenues has been diminished, leading to a curtailment of expenditure on health, education, housing, and other social services. In many countries, such trends continue to inhibit the use of growth-oriented macroeconomic policies to improve job prospects and wages of workers.

The general problem relates to the distribution of burdens and benefits across different segments of society. While this is primarily an issue about social legitimacy and justice, it also has implications for society's capacity to generate the human resources necessary for equitable growth. The paradox is that the global forces of adjustment have apparently given rise to economic hardship, which increases deprivation and heightens inequality. The consequent human damage, in terms of people's capabilities and future life chances, is most severe for those who are least prepared to bear it. Thus, shifting the cost of economic adjustment to workers and society's most vulnerable, or those with the least resistance, flies in the face of sustainable human development and protection of basic needs.

This calls for a new rights-based development ethic in which rules governing employment and earnings reflect the principles of social legitimacy. It entails universal standards guaranteeing jobs that pay more than the minimum wage and providing necessary protection for labor. Forging a feasible social compact requires that trade unions, employers, and other participants in the labor market are transformed from being antagonistic players of a game toward becoming representative and cooperative social partners. This imperative was at the heart of the protests by labor and environmental groups at the Seattle meetings 6f the WTO in 1999. A major bone of contention was whether labor standards should be linked to WTO trade rules. It touches on some critical aspects of labor rights, their enforcement, and the responsibilities of North-South protagonists.

Northern trade unionists and politicians have long argued that trade should be used as a lever for countries to practice minimum standards of decency. But skepticism has surfaced about the real or hidden intent, that is, whether advocacy of a link between trade liberalization and labor standards is motivated more by self-interests of the rich North rather than by altruistic or moral feelings toward the poor South. American and European trade unions contend that low wages and labor standards in the South create "unfair" competition by luring investments away from rich to poor countries. The counter-argument is that low wages, a reflection of lower levels of development, are a primary factor in the international competitive advantage of LDCs. They also believe that the attempt to link trade and labor standards is no more than a ploy for increased protectionism by rich nations.

In the eyes of the WTO, labor standards are the domain of the ILO whose *Declaration on Fundamental Principles and Rights at Work* obliges its members "to respect, to promote and realize" the seven ILO conventions defining "core" labor standards. The ILO does not link trade and labor standards; indeed, its Declaration stresses that labor standards should not be used for protectionist purposes. The real question concerns whether or how they will be enforced. It is envisaged that public opinion will become an important mechanism in goading governments to comply with their commitments. In this regard, the *International Confederation of Free Trade Unions* (ICFTU) – a Brussels-based club of 206 union federations from 141 countries –

hopes that, in the absence of world government, moral suasion can be used to get the world committed to labor standards. It wants to see WTO membership made conditional on the observance of core labor standards certified by the ILO.

The available evidence suggests that there is no strong link between observance of core labor standards and trade flows, so LDC exporters are unlikely to be harmed much if they adopted the ILO conventions. By the same token, it seems that workers in rich countries have little to fear from competition with the downtrodden in LDCs. While this may be reassuring, it does not necessarily mean that use of trade measures to enforce labor standards is a good idea. As we have argued, there is nothing wrong with the intentions behind the standards. People of good will would agree that slavery, child labor, other forms of bonded labor, and imprisonment of trade unionists should not be sanctioned. But enforcement of standards may not always produce the desired effect. If trade unions are recognized, wages in unionized sectors might rise but employment might fall. The displaced workers might be pushed into jobs that pay less than they earned before. It should be remembered, however, that the lion's share of labor in LDCs, especially in agriculture, remains unorganized. This is not because their rights, such as collective bargaining and freedom of association, are denied but more because it best suits their ethos and condition.

Engenderment of Human Rights

It goes without saying that the adequate functioning of labor markets and other institutions requires some perception of fairness on the part of their main constituents and society as a whole. In this regard, workers' rights and the broader right to development are inextricably linked to the imperative of "women's rights as human rights." "Human development, if not engendered, is endangered" (UNDP 1995, 1). A recursive relationship may be posited between women's rights and authentic development. The latter will be impossible without the full emancipation of women, and vice-versa. This requires a clear commitment to universal norms and standards of gender equality. As noted earlier, one of the major purposes of the United Nations Charter was to define and protect the rights and freedoms of every human being regardless of race, sex, language or religion. The *Preamble* to the Charter affirms the equal rights of men and women, a faith in fundamental human rights, and the dignity and worth of the human person.

The Universal Declaration of Human Rights and supporting international conventions also affirmed that women should participate equally in economic, social, and political development, contribute equally to such development, and share equally in improved conditions of life. The 1979 Convention on the Elimination of All Forms of Discrimination Against Women covered the broad categories of indivisible rights, and in 1980 became what is viewed as the women's international human rights treaty. As mentioned earlier, the United Nations also defined development as a human rights issue in its 1986 Declaration on the Right to Development. It states that "the right to development is an alienable human right by virtue of which every human person and all peoples are entitled to participate in, contribute to, and enjoy economic, social, cultural and political development."

The entire issue of women's rights should be interpreted as a part of longstanding attempts to "mainstream" gender into the development conversation, or integrate women into the development paradigm. The ensuing debate has witnessed successive shifts (paradigmatic) in the intellectual and political focus of the discourse – from early "welfarist" ideas about women's roles as "mothers," through "women in development" (WID), "women and development" (WAD), and "gender and Development" (GAD) to "Development Alternatives with Women for a New Era" (DAWN). These perspectives have been variously influenced by the rise of Western feminism and its quest for a good and just life for both women and men. Feminist schools of thought and research programs tend to perform what may be viewed as a "radical hermeneutics," or progressive mode of reinterpretation, that attempts to appropriate or modify other philosophies of life as a means of coming to grips with issues arising from women's confrontation with injustices and inequality. Hence, the *interpretive turns* are grounded in alternative preconceptions about the centrality of women to human life and development, or what constitutes a just social and economic order.

Contextually, the quest for women's liberation can also be interpreted through the lens of the "discourse ethics" alluded to in the previous chapter. To reiterate, it does not project the idea of an undifferentiated humanity, but accepts feminist and related arguments that the particularity of "concrete others" should be recognized, respected, and perhaps celebrated. The overall idea centers around eradication of unjust forms of exclusion and the promotion of freedom and equality through overlapping and intersecting *communities of dialogue* (class-based, racial, ethnic, religious, feminist, and the like). Such conversations would "enable multiple political authorities to develop, and to endeavor to bring harmony through dialogue to the great diversity of ethical spheres which stretches from the local community to the transnational area" (Linklater 1998, 45).

Prior to the emergence of WID, the orientation of development thought and policy was in terms of women as "better mothers," thereby reinforcing their traditional gender roles within the family. Given the reproductive focus, development projects concentrated on family planning, nutrition, literacy and related areas that promised to improve women's welfare. During the early 1970s, it was recognized that women were not merely mothers who were passively affected by development in general and family planning programs in particular; they were also active agents of change in key aspects of production and economic development. Hence, their inimitable contributions could be enhanced by more gender-sensitive programs and projects. This change in orientation ushered in the WID perspective, which placed more emphasis on women's productive roles.

The integration of women into the development process was legitimized in terms of their equal productivity to men. They were presented as decision-makers and active production agents rather than as mere passive or needy beneficiaries of development (Boserup 1970). While it attempted to bring women into the mainstream, WID was essentially rooted in the ruling development paradigm of the day and its philosophical preconceptions. The potential benefits of increased productivity were implicitly linked to individualism and market-based efficiency, which were central elements of the "growth-oriented" philosophy of development. The prevailing orthodoxy or "global consensus" was essentially driven by a gender-neutral theory of modernization. Its basic preconception was that women would advance through a "trickle down" process of incremental change.

The WID perspective was anchored in a very limited conception of equality or justice. Since its primary focus was on "merit" and individual achievement (implicit in notions such as economic growth, productivity, and efficiency), very little attention was paid to other "claims" that emphasize women's intrinsic moral worth as human beings. As it turned out, the econocentric WID discourse carried tremendous rhetorical and utilitarian appeal for influential economists and development officials in the North; but women in the South were essentially cast as passive recipients and implementers of programs and projects emanating from aid donors. Furthermore, given its homogenizing tendency, WID virtually ignored differences in interests among women belonging to diverse classes, ethnic groups, cultures, and societies.

The philosophical thrust of WAD was an outgrowth of several meliorist strands of the political economy of development that emerged during the mid-1970s: growth with redistribution or equity; basic needs; and poverty alleviation (David 1997a). As a result, WAD overtook WID at a time when the development debate was coming to grips with failures of the "trickle-down" approach and new people-centered perspectives were taking shape. The focus on equity (as opposed to efficiency) became most popular during the 1975-1985 period, and attempts to adopt it were catapulted by the United Nations Decade for Women. Achievement of gender equity was predicated on women receiving their fair share of the benefits of development in the form of higher incomes, greater access to resources, better education, health, and similar achievements. This orientation was supported by a needs-based argument for justice. As emphasized in the previous chapter, it entails that a society cannot be just if it treats the weakest and poorest members without compassion.

The argument for equity was supported by an "anti-poverty" approach to poor men and women. The latter made the feminist agenda less threatening to economists, male bureaucrats, and implementers who were resistant to feminist incursions into the bureaucracy. In the eyes of Buvinic (1983), the anti-poverty program was a "toned-down" version of the equity approach. In other words, it was interpreted more as a reaction to male resistance to fundamental claims for gender equality and justice, and therefore as a strategic tactic to enhance the feminist agenda. Given this instrumental approach, the WAD perspective failed to address the multifaceted and structural factors responsible for the marginalization of women, such as war and civil conflict, rapid urbanization, environmental degradation, and the social relations of gender itself.

During the 1980s and 1990s, the GAD perspective emerged as a means of capturing the holistic meanings undergirding women's lives. Primary emphasis was placed on the social realities shaping views on sex, and the corresponding assignment of specific roles, responsibilities, and expectations of both men and women. This shift was interpreted through the lens of "gender," which connotes the socially constructed and culturally variable roles that men and women play in their daily lives (Elson 1991). Contextually, gender refers to the historically structured relation of inequality between men and women, as manifested in the domestic household unit, markets, and political systems. Hence, engenderment was predicated on the imperative of fostering a "gender-based analysis" and its integration into development thought and policy (Moser 1993).

Like WAD, the GAD perspective consists of multiple discourses about women's social praxis. As noted in Chapter 7, one crucial element concerns the general and daily processes inherent in human reproduction, such as rearing of children, nursing the sick, and caring for other dependents and senior citizens. The argument is that any genuine interpretation of human development must necessarily be based on effective ways of fully integrating such "domestic labor" or "reproductive work" into the overall processes of production. This requires a transformation of historically sedimented relations of gender inequality, and the concomitant empowerment of women. While the idea of empowerment always lurked in the minds of WID protagonists, primary emphasis was placed on *status,* as distinct from its more intrinsic and dynamic counterpart – *power.* Insofar as empowerment was accorded any significance, it was limited to women's increased access to income-earning work and related opportunities provided for them by development agencies and through greater participation in the market.

This was a far cry from an organic concept of *self-empowerment,* which denotes women's capability of gaining more autonomy and control over their lives, becoming more self-reliant as active agents in their own development, exercising their choices, and setting their own agendas. The self-empowerment concept is grounded, albeit implicitly, in a philosophy of "development as liberation" or the pursuit of effective freedom. Income-earning opportunities are important, but they are not on the same footing as the "human agency" of women or their ability to exercise the full range of possible options through democratization, popular participation, and enforcement of human rights. Hence, the full engenderment of human development entails that barriers to the attainment of equal rights be identified and progressively eliminated. It is not merely sufficient for such initiatives to be consistent with national laws and development priorities. They must also conform to universality recognized human rights and cosmopolitan values.

Finally, DAWN was created during the mid-1980s by a network of women from the South who wanted to distantiate themselves from what they perceived as a white, middle class, feminist paradigm originating from the North. They challenged the WID research program on the grounds that women in the South did not necessarily want to be integrated into mainstream development models. In their eyes, such conceptual systems not only contained gender and class biases, but the capital accumulation processes underlying them were neither neutral nor benign, that is, they are inherently hierarchical and polarizing (Sen and Grown 1988). They recognized that their subjugation was multidimensional – based on the cumulative interplay of sex, class, race, and their subordinate position in the global hierarchy. Hence, strategies for the full empowerment of women can only be successful through simultaneous action in all these domains. This involves an egalitarian development trajectory based on concerted resistance to hierarchies and inculcation of positive values such as cooperation, sharing, accountability, and commitment to peace. These were to be operationalized through consciousness-raising at the political level and popular education in the workplace, home, and community.

Human Rights Programming

An intractable problematique has always surrounded human rights programming. This relates to practical issues of enforcement, promotion, and protection. The glaring gap between international aspirations for the enjoyment of human rights vis-à-vis what are perceived to be widespread violations poses an ongoing challenge at both global and national levels. Closing the gap requires concerted and credible actions in several interrelated avenues: identification and elimination of the root causes of conflicts and violations, including the panoply of economic, cultural, political, and legal barriers to the full realization of equal rights; implementation of provisions guaranteeing the right to development; fostering and ensuring a greater respect for universal human rights; and, at the most basic level, improving the daily life of the individual – worker, woman, young person, girl-child, and so on.

An endemic source of conflict stems from the fact that many powerful sectors of interest continue to approach the issue from their own narrow and iron-clad ideological perspectives about what is desirable and practically feasible. For example, some political scientists and philosophers still harbor strong misgivings about the logical defensibility of human rights. In general, hard-nosed economists, industrialists, transnational corporations, and politicians tend to be skeptical because of a fear that human rights enforcement may have negative effects on national economic growth, private profitability, market efficiency, and international competitiveness, as the case may be. By contrast, most trade unions, women's groups, human rights organizations, and NGOs usually advocate vigorous enforcement of human rights principles.

Another complicating factor is that many poor countries do not boast a strong tradition of human rights enforcement, promotion, and protection. While the majority has constitutions, institutions, and other instruments subscribing to the broad principles of universal human rights, they are poorly enforced and in some cases openly flouted. For example, the Convention on Elimination of All Forms of Discrimination Against Women still remains one of the most widely disregarded international treaties, with some signatories ignoring provisions that are perceived to conflict with their customary laws. A case in point was the unanimous decision by the Zimbabwe Supreme Court in 1999 to overrule or challenge every law relating women's rights in the country.

The ruling was that Vienna Magaya could not inherit her father's estate, even though Zimbabwean laws and international treaties supported her claim. The Court gave the estate to her half-brother. The decision made explicit reference to the deep-seated roots of patriarchy in Africa. The judges opined that the "nature of African society" relegates women to a lesser status, especially in the home. In their eyes, a woman should not be considered an adult within the family, but only as a "junior male." One justice went so far as to say that Zimbabwe's 1982 Majority Age Act, which said that women over 18 could be treated as minors, had been interpreted "too widely" and had accorded women "rights they never had under customary law." Thus, they were stripped of almost all the rights they had gained over the past two generations.

Even if it is assumed that there is a "separation of powers" between the judicial and executive branches of government, the Zimbabwean case clearly demonstrates the influence of cultural relativism and the conflict that can arise between requirements of international human rights law and national sovereignty. The sensitive nature of human rights law is that it challenges the way in which governments exercise power and authority over their citizens. The difficulty is that nation states assiduously guard their national sovereignty, but must simultaneously submit to international scrutiny and reluctantly accept restrictions on their domestic behavior (Manasian 1998). In many cases, international conventions and treaties are not backed up by the political will of national governments, so that they sometimes become smokescreens for the perpetuation of human rights abuses.

The reconciliation of international standards with national purposes implies establishment of coherent frameworks of principles, objectives, legislation, and procedures for monitoring and evaluation at the domestic level. This implies the design of appropriate human rights yardsticks as goals to be attained, or performance criteria against which the success of development policies, strategies, and projects can be appraised. Such a guideline takes on added significance when account is taken of the widespread incongruity between human rights norms on the one hand and the goals of many development programs and projects, on the other. Contextually, the United Nations Committee on Economic, Social, and Cultural Rights drew attention to the fact that

> development cooperation activities do not automatically contribute
> to the promotion of [human rights]. Many activities undertaken in
> the name of 'development' have subsequently been recognized as
> ill-conceived and even counterproductive in human rights terms
> (UNHCR 1990, 87).

Examples of the incompatibility between human rights norms and conventional development activities are a legion. They include: (i) abridgement of the freedom of residence and cultural rights due to mass relocations stemming from large hydroelectric and irrigation projects; (ii) unemployment caused by the introduction of labor-displacing and capital-intensive technologies; (iii) employment retrenchment and wage cuts attendant upon structural adjustment programs; (iv) limitations placed on the basic right to a minimum level of education, health care, and nutrition due to mandated cuts in social sector spending; and (v) the tendency to turn a blind eye to international labor standards pertaining to free collective bargaining, trade unions, rates of pay, child labor, health, safety, and environmental laws.

In the final analysis, the most effective means for protection and promotion of human rights require a synergistic interplay of both national commitment and international obligation. Since human rights are universal in scope and have a global connotation, the relevant standards should apply equally to all actors, including transnational corporations (TNCs), aid donors, and recipients of development finance. Among other things, this calls for a new path of accountability whereby North-South sectors of interest openly bind themselves to adhere not only to the provisions of international agreements in general, but also to specific areas such as enforcement of fair labor standards. Concrete meaning and relevance can be given to accountability through formulation and execution of additional incentives for compliance on the one hand, and disincentives for arbitrary or willful noncompliance, on the other.

A few recent developments promise to ensure a greater degree of public commitment, transparency, and accountability. First, about 36 corporations such as Chevron, General Motors, and Proctor and Gamble have agreed to abide by the so-called "Sullivan principles" which set standards for corporate social responsibility. Second, governments of 20 OECD countries have ratified new guidelines for safeguarding labor and environmental standards by TNCs. Third, and in the wake of this development, 50 of the world's largest TNCs have signed a "global compact" under the auspices of the United Nations, committing them to support free trade unions, abolish child labor, and protect the environment. The list includes several firms, such as Nike and Royal Dutch Shell, which were targets of protesters at Seattle.

The UN's global compact with the private sector to promote human rights and raise labor and environmental standards seems to represent a new normative framework or progressive agenda for reform of the ground rules that inform the current global institutional architecture. The underlying premise is that the global public good should take precedence over the private interests of financial capital and profitability of free markets. Apposite to our discussion of "marketization" in chapter 11, the implications for human rights are based on a recognition that the present global system does not treat all participants equally and in a fair and just manner. Markets apparently operate with double standards. Powerful industrialists from rich nations are allowed the benefit of the doubt even when they stray from the straight and narrow path of market fundamentalism. Hence a key normative goal of the reformist agenda is to mitigate the market vulnerabilities of weaker members of the system.

In a quasi-theoretical sense, the global compact is also consistent with those research programs of the "post-Washington consensus" that advocate globalization of the original Keynesian vision or compact for supranational controls over global finance and markets. The evolution of Keynesianism was predicated on a bargain between market capitalism and the state that was designed to ensure the survival of open liberalism and free markets, but tempered by mechanisms that would prevent repetition of the Great Depression and provide compensatory support systems for the most dispossessed. Historically, the Keynesian compact not only reflected the extant state of economic theory but was also an exercise in normative political economy. In today's world, it reflects a necessity to return to an economic morality that transcends the naked individualism that has apparently wrought havoc on the global economic order. In other words, the revisionist ethic would allow the private sector to operate successfully and profitably while providing adequate social protection for vulnerable participants.

Part Four

Institutional Transformation

Chapter 11

State, Market, and People

> The disenchantment with politics has fed market fundamentalism
> and the rise of market fundamentalism has, in turn, contributed to
> the failure of politics. One of the great defects of the global capital-
> ist system is that it has allowed the market mechanism and the
> profit motive to penetrate into fields of activity where they do not
> properly belong.
>
> George Soros (1998)

The saliency of any institutional order is inherently linked to
conditions necessary for fostering a civic community undergirded by
strong state-market-civil society relations. There is no guarantee that
civic virtue will correspond to the distribution of wealth, power, and
competencies in society. Hence, the normative principle to be extolled
and defended is the *social rule of law* which, as Sen (1990) reminds us,
is an achievement of humankind's social conscience. This is predicated

on a new framework of *political morality* that subscribes to the basic principles of representative government and social democracy. These include, inter alia, institutional pluralism based on local dimensions of social interchange and systems of knowledge; respect for constitutional norms; and endorsement of people-friendly policies and programs based on explicit and implicit contractual obligations among government, markets, people, and their communities.

The Political Conjuncture

In the final reckoning, authentic or sustainable human development results from a political process rather than from mere technical efficiency or technological change. It is the political system or conjuncture that ultimately defines the environment in which development agendas are set and executed. By enabling or disabling human choices among alternative goals and by arbitrating among divergent sectors of interest, it mirrors a constant interplay of power relationships, ideological confrontations, and bargaining strategies. Thus, possibilities for matching humanitarian ends and means are intimately bound up with the nature of political management, the resourcefulness of the political leadership, and its ability to make delicate political calculations, build interest coalitions, and strike effective compromises.

In every human society, the political conjuncture reflects differential struggles for power among individuals and groups in relation not only to their own interests but also to the more general regulation and orientation of collective life. In this sense, every society can be said to have a distinctive political apparatus within which such struggles normally take place and are mediated. The underlying framework typically consists of a corpus of rules and practices – well-established or rudimentary, formal or informal – involving contestations among different possible courses of action, and is usually subject to change. In this context, two broad perspectives of political philosophy are typically invoked to explain the relationship between politics and the constitution of society. One juxtaposes the autonomy vis-à-vis independence of political forces. The other juxtaposes the importance of stability and integration in the determination of values against mutability, contradiction, and the use of force as pre-eminent features of societies.

The fundamentalist view, traceable to Aristotle, is that the study of human beings and their development potentials must begin with an investigation of the *regime* under which they live (Codevilla 1997). At one level, this perspective raises an issue about the theoretical link between the notion of a "regime" and humanitarian ends such as "virtue" and "the good life." While a regime has something to do with the formulation and execution of policies, it transcends the more limited notion of government machinery. For Aristotle, each regime sets the standards of "virtue" for those who live under it. It tends to project, explicitly or implicitly, what it means to be a virtuous human being. Since it is a team sport and not an individual activity, such virtuous living requires a community of accountability and support.

At the more practical level, the issue relates to the possibilities of improving the conditions of life. A basic proposition is that each historical and contemporary form of government has differentially affected the capabilities of people living under it to enjoy economic prosperity, civic freedom, family and spiritual life, and in terms of generating various forms of military power and violence. Diverse political systems have emerged within the largely separate political histories encountered in different regions of the world. However, the historical growth and internal differentiation of societies have been accompanied by certain more or less uniform patterns: an increase in the scale of government; escalation in the degree of political intervention in the conduct of economic and social life; a growth of bureaucratic administration; and formation and consolidation of the predominant political unit – the nation state.

Correlatively, evolution of thinking about the autonomy of politics has been marked by attempts to differentiate between the "political," "social," and other spheres of life, or in terms of contrasts between the "state" and "civil society." The classic formulations of Hegel, Marx, de Tocqueville, elite theorists such as Mosca and Pareto, and Weber may be used to throw some further light on this dichotomy. For example, Hegel viewed the state as a higher universal in which the contradictions of civil society, such as the interrelated growth of wealth and poverty, could be resolved. By contrast, Marx conceived the state as a dependent element of a total social process in which motive forces emanating from the economic sphere generate the contradiction between wealth and poverty, and hence class polarization.

Alexis de Tocqueville also emphasized the independent effectiveness of politics and saw the need for a "new science of politics," which would be concerned with the development of democracy and formation of "modern" society (in contrast to the *ancien regime*) in

France, England, and the United States. He wrote in the spirit of Aristotle when he began his study of democracy in America. In his eyes, virtually everything in the American way of life, including what Americans believed a good human being to be, could be explained by political equality and their belief in the justice of equality. The importance of independent political forces was later elaborated in the neo-Machiavellian elitist theories of Mosca and Pareto, but from an entirely different perspective. This was rooted in the "realist" tradition of thought, which views power, authority, and domination as universal and ineradicable characteristics of all human societies (Lukes 1978).

Mosca explained this phenomenon in terms of the superior power that an organized minority always possesses in relation to the unorganized majority. As he stated (1896, 50):

> in all societies – from societies that are very meagerly developed and have barely attained the dawnings of civilization, down to the most advanced and powerful societies – two classes of people appear – a class that rules and a class that is ruled. The first class, always the less numerous, performs all political functions, monopolizes power and enjoys the advantages that power brings, whereas the second, the more numerous class, is directed and controlled by the first, in a manner that is now more or less legal, now more or less arbitrary and violent.

In Mosca's schema, the sharp antithesis is reduced with the march of democracy, which lessens the gap in power between rulers and ruled.

Pareto also considered elitist rule to be a universal and unalterable fact of social life. Like other realists he tried to debunk what were viewed as liberal illusions about asymmetric power relations by pointing to control, inequality, dependence, and authority by imposition as inevitable features of both democratic and socialist societies. Contextually, he looked askance at "the humanitarian who swoons over a passage of Rousseau," the "socialist who swears by the word of Marx and Engels," and the "devout democrat who bows reverent head and submits judgment and will to the oracles of suffrage, universal or limited, or what is worse to the pronouncements of parliaments and legislatures." He continues that

> [a]ll governments use force and all assert that they are founded on reason. In fact, whether universal suffrage prevails or not, it is always an oligarchy that governs, finding ways to give to 'the will of

the people' the expression which the few desire (Pareto [1915-19] 1963, 585, 2244).

Max Weber also attributed some measure of autonomy to politics in his conception of the state bureaucracy as the dominating force in societal relations. Like Marx and elite theorists, Weber accepted the universality of domination and the corresponding power of organized minorities. In this context, he identified three "pure types" of authority: legal-rational, traditional, and charismatic. *Legal-rational authority* involves obedience to formal rules that have been established by regular or public procedures. By contrast, *traditional authority* pertains to the acceptance of rules embodying custom and ancient practice. Under *charismatic authority*, commands are obeyed because followers or disciples believe in the extraordinary character of leaders, whose authority is presumed to transcend customary or existing practices. These forms of authority provide the ideological bases for the legitimacy conferred on political leaders via the beliefs of their followers. While any one type of authority may predominate in a given structure of vertical relationships, "the forms of domination occurring in historical reality constitute combinations, mixtures, adaptations, or modifications of these 'pure' types" (Weber 1968, 954).

From a Weberian perspective, the development process has been associated with a kind of political rationalization that is marked by a decline in traditional forms of legitimacy and the replacement of charismatic leadership by the "state machine." For society as a whole, the governing dynamic has inhered in a continuous spread of bureaucracy and state control. The notion of "rationalization" forms part of Weber's interpretation of capitalist society as an "iron cage" in which individuals, stripped of moral value, would be increasingly subjected to government surveillance and bureaucratic regulation. Like Marx's concept of alienation, the idea of rationalization connotes separation of the individual from family and community, as well as his or her subordination to political, legal, and economic regulation at the level of the work-place, school, and state.

The modern problem of legitimacy is essentially one of political representation or consent, that is, the focus is on which individuals are legitimately entitled to wield political power. In Weber's schema, any regime with minimum acceptance as a *de facto* government has some basis of legitimacy even If its authority largely depends on force. However, he thought that the state could not be legitimated by any absolute standards based on natural law. The modern state typically displays a "legitimization deficit" because its operations are usually extended beyond the scope of public consent. As explored later in this chapter, Weberian notions such as legitimization "deficits" and "crises" lie at the heart of misgivings about the role of the state in promoting authentic development.

Over time, the problem surrounding the relationship between the "political" and other spheres of life has come to be conceived in much more complex terms, with more emphasis placed on reciprocal influences and historical changes. One variation on this theme is an outgrowth of systems theory, which views political institutions as only one element of a total system moving toward equilibrium. The corresponding image of society is one of an integrated system maintained by complementary relationships among various elements or subsystems, with outcomes ultimately resting on a common set of values. The focus is on the notion of a "stable" or viable democracy. Its existence in a particular society is thought to depend primarily on certain values held by the citizenry, that is, an underlying consensus or common value system (Barry 1970), A basic preconception is that such a democratic political system has reached a more or less mature stage of development, and therefore can be contrasted with others, such as totalitarianism, dictatorship, or "unstable" democracy.

This perspective has been propounded as part of the same general model of "modernization" in which development is viewed as largely a process whereby traditional or agrarian societies are gradually adapted to conditions of life, institutions, and value-orientations of industrial nations. Accordingly, political modernization involves development of key institutions – political parties, parliaments, franchise and secret ballots – which support participatory decision-making. Huntington (1968) has pointed to the many pathological but temporary phases preceding the transition from traditional to modern society or the advent of stable democracy as an integrating force. He starts with the proposition that "the most important political distinction among countries concerns ... their degree of government," and then proceeds to distinguish between countries "whose politics embodies consensus, community, legitimacy, organization, stability" vis-à-vis those displaying the opposite – political fragmentation, intense ethnic and class conflicts, rioting, and violence.

From the above perspective, stability is interpreted as the highest political virtue, which is purportedly exemplified by the politics of democratic industrial nations. Over the past three decades, such ideas have come to lose their potency on account of the intractable problems posed by political crises throughout the globe. As a consequence, there is a renewed interest in alternative models which take as a point of departure the tensions, contradictions, and conflicts existent in all social systems. Such interpretations treat the maintenance of order and stability as only a temporary or partial resolution of various deep-seated antagonisms.

In the case of LDCs, such traumatic outcomes are reflected in a "sociology of politics" in which politicians, supporting cadres of top civil servants, leading policymakers, and dominant classes maintain control of the decision-making environment by structuring bargaining conditions that crystallize their power and influence and attenuate those of other groups who are less fortunate. More often than not, the policy positions of candidates for political office or elected officials are governed by special interest coalitions that contribute campaign funds or lobby as a means of guaranteeing specific programs and developmental outcomes. Hence, a wedge is often driven between the prescriptions of economists and other technical experts on the one hand, and the actual practice of politics, on the other.

Political environments dominated by lawyers, landowners, businessmen, psephologists, political party ideologues, and even soldiers are usually guided by their own or preferred frameworks of endogenous decision-making, bargaining, systems of logic, and visions of the future (Stiglitz 1998a). In extreme cases, the situation has been characterized as "neo-patrimonialism" or "personal rule" – an environment in which the political requirement of regime and personal survival often contradicts the very economic policies and practices needed to guarantee material progress and sustained human development.

Reconstituting Government: The Developmental State

While there are alternative theories of the state, the intractable problem is why different activist states with command over more or less similar instruments of control and discretionary power have ended up along dissimilar paths of humanitarian development. Relatively few are traveling along the road of becoming effective "developmental states." The larger majority remain "regulatory" or even "obstructionist" (Bardhan 1988). The developmental state is defined not so much by the size of the government apparatus, but more by its quality, effectiveness, and legitimacy. The issue is addressed at four related levels: (i) the linkage between the "hard state" and development; (ii) the nature of state-civil society relations; (iii) the requirements of "endogenous" politico-economic management; and (iv) devolution of state power (Chapter 12).

Historically, one influential perspective of the state has concerned its ability to rely on social discipline or society's tolerance for varying degrees of compulsion. Accordingly, what is known as "softness" of the state in LDCs was construed as a problematic absence of an appropriate framework for planning. Writing in the context of South Asian development, Gunnar Myrdal (1968, 895-96) remarked:

> When we characterize countries as "soft states" we mean that, throughout the region, national governments require extraordinarily little of their citizens. There are few obligations either to do things in the interest of the community or to avoid actions opposed to that interest. Even those obligations that do exist are enforced inadequately if at all. This low level of social discipline is one of the most fundamental differences between the South Asian countries today and Western countries at the beginning of their industrialization.

It may be commented that this perspective does not come to grips with significant differences in political structure that "permit a more or less authoritarian stance by governments in a given cultural context" (Toye 1987, 101). In many instances, what may appear to be "softness" actually represents responsiveness of the state to public assertiveness and vocal demands for a more reliable flow of public goods and services (Drèze and Sen 1989). More generally, for over three decades increased public action has enabled many countries to register favorable performances in terms of both macroeconomic growth and human development. The experiences of the four small East Asian countries – Hong Kong, Singapore, South Korea, and Taiwan – are commonly cited in this regard (Wade 1990).

However, the unwillingness or inability of governments to fulfill their obligations to the community can be interpreted as a failure of the political legitimization process. How a polity is legitimized depends, inter alia, on concerted steps taken to socialize political life, integrate citizens into the process, and reconcile special interests with the general will to develop. This connotes legitimization by *symbolic* means, or a process of convincing the electorate that the government is working for the common good. By contrast, legitimization by *material* means entails a situation in which the government machinery is associated with access to special funds, or "buying" of votes. It promotes "values" that encourage "clan" relationships and a deliberate confusion of private welfare with the public purse.

State-Civil Society Interactions

In the above context, patterns of state-civil society interaction are expected to play a pivotal role in defining the openness of the political system, improving public sector performance, and ensuring optimal involvement of the people in the development process. Openness is exemplified by a relatively large number of political organizations, public and private agencies, and autonomous interest groups. This is coterminous with a definition of civil society as consisting of disparate intermediate and interacting institutions that provide the constitutional bases of humanitarian development. The heterogeneous groupings may range from relatively simple organizational structures at the local level to more complex national and global networks. Ideally, the organs of civil society are supposed to guarantee a relatively high degree of ideational competition about the net benefits to be realized from alternative development paths or styles. But the experiences of many LDCs and transitional economies in Eastern Europe provide ample evidence that it is a very fragile and vulnerable edifice to be constructed, reconstituted, and repaired. It is often built on shifting sands, and its permanence cannot be always assured.

At any given moment, civil society can be transformed into an un-civil, distorted, anarchical, and despotic system teetering on the brink of a Hobbesian "state-of-nature" situation in which life is "poor, solitary, nasty, brutish, and short." At a more optimistic and salutary level, the vibrancy of civil society is a function of the democratic process. From an institutionalist perspective, democracy is not just a system of political parties, elections, and taking turns at exercising largely arbitrary power. Rather, it is akin to an institutional order which, as emphasized earlier (Chapter 2), is predicated on cumulative causal processes and relations among institutions forming a holistic matrix. This allows for public assembly and "voice" by all members of society, appeals or claims to justice based on equal moral worth rather than patronage and clientism, and open guarantees of individual and institutional freedom based on the same abstract norms or rules of the game rather than on influence peddling and personal contacts. The focal point is on how most people are socialized into democracy by acquiring power and other resources through collective action. The pertinent processes of interaction inhere in the fact that representativeness and openness constitute the very essence of democracy.

The goals of humanitarian development are unreachable except through an open political process that guarantees democratic forms of participation in civil society by all citizens who share a strong commitment to solving common problems. This point cannot be overemphasized because considerable uneasiness has surfaced about the rise of "illiberal" democracies in many parts of Africa, Asia, Latin America, and Eastern Europe. Many of these regimes cannot be said to be fully democratic when judged by universal criteria such as transparency, the rule of law, accountability, sustainable development, and meeting the needs of the people. There is also a more general concern that many government officials and development practitioners have been working in ways that derail the essential advocacy functions of civil society organs, resulting in false expectations and a waste of resources.

The tenor of the argument so far is that the state-civil society nexus is an essential pivot in the institutional dynamics of human betterment. While the nature of civil society tends to influence the state or political system, the other side of the coin is that the state also needs civil society to attain its objectives. Its capacity to formulate and execute policies and programs hinges on the degree of synergy that can be forged with organs of civil society and the steps taken to reinforce them. Patterns of state-civil society interaction tend to vary, depending on whether the state's behavior is benevolent or hostile. An illustration is provided in Table 11.1 which shows five stages depicting a wide spectrum of conditions to be satisfied if the state is to operate at lower (hostile) and higher (benevolent) thresholds. The lowest stage is one of a hostile state that does not tolerate independent civil activity and where the threshold is defined by a *de facto* right of non-state actors to establish autonomous institutions. A second stage is slightly better. The state accepts independent activity but remains aloof and does not provide much space for civil society to function.

Table 11.1: State Treatment of Civil Activity

Stage 1	The state does not tolerate civil activity	**Hostile State**
Threshold	*De facto* right to form autonomous organizations	
Stage 2	The state accepts autonomous organization, but does not provide a space for it	
Threshold	State withdrawal, opening up a space for independent activity	
State 3	A space for independent activity exists, but the practice of governance does not promote autonomous organizations	
Threshold	Favorable institutional structures	
Stage 4	The state provides favorable structures but no active support	
Threshold	Active state programs in support of civil society	
Stage 5	The state actively promotes autonomous organization	**Benevolent State**

Source: Hadenius and Uggla (1996, 1629)

Favorable institutional structures emerge during a third stage, more space is allowed for independent activity, but government practices do not necessarily promote autonomous organs of civil society. This environment is by and large maintained during a fourth stage in which more enabling structures emerge, but with very little active support by the state for civil society. A fifth stage exemplifies the ideal situation in which there is optimal synergy between objectives of the state and those of civil society and people's organizations.

Realization of this outcome comes close to the ideal of emancipatory politics, or an institutional structure reflecting alignments of public and private interests at different levels. This is consonant with our creative utopian vision of what may be termed *non-partisan community self-determination*. It is a political mode of empowerment reflecting society's relations of full partnership with the state. The overall implication is that when people participate in politics, it is more empowering for them to do so as active members of "political institutions" rather than as mere tools of "political parties," that is, as liberated human agents with power bases located in multiple sites and processes. Such a transition is predicated on the imperative of transforming the historically sedimented, partisan, and largely imported model of political economy (top down, national, bureaucratic) toward a more democratic, non-partisan (bottom up, local, communitarian) mode based on full democracy.

The experience suggests that national political parties are necessary for country-wide representatives to emerge, but only as servants of the people, their non-partisan community structures, and local institutions. The modality of politics inherent in the model of community self-government constitutes a first step toward empowering the masses through effective engagement in the fundamentals of humanitarian development. A guiding premise is that social pluralism would lead to political pluralism and the dispersion of power.

Endogenous Politico-economic Management and Development Policy

The imperative of establishing a developmental state based on strong state-civil society linkages, community self-government, and mechanisms for consensus building should be located in the much broader context of "endogenous politico-economic management." As shown in Figure 11.1, other essential ingredients include: the political leadership and will to create and nurture an appropriate development milieu; and an adequate substructure of intellectual and ideological conviction as a basis for the emergence of a new development consciousness and full expression of felt needs at the local level.   The extended list is by no means exhaustive, and a question remains as to how a minimal corpus of such requirements can be met in all LDCs. What remains true, however, is that the nature of a society and its developmental orientation tend to be closely correlated with the types of people it permits to hold high office and exercise political power.

This very fact highlights an endemic and vicious circle that lurks in the path of authentic or humanitarian development. On the one hand, a given country will not be able to produce a development-oriented leadership in the absence of an appropriate socio-cultural milieu. On the other hand, a political elite that lacks interest in broad-based development will not generate the organic changes needed to promote this end. It is a truism that humanitarian development will not take place in

Figure 11.1: Political Context of Development

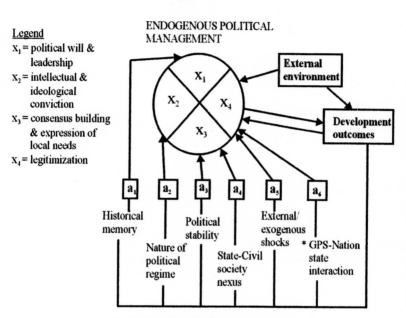

Legend
x_1 = political will &
    leadership
x_2 = intellectual &
    ideological
    conviction
x_3 = consensus building
    & expression of
    local needs
x_4 = legitimization

ENDOGENOUS POLITICAL
MANAGEMENT

X_1

X_2 X_4

X_3

External
environment

Development
outcomes

a_1 a_2 a_3 a_4 a_5 a_6

Historical
memory

Political
stability

External/
exogenous
shocks

Nature of
political
regime

State-Civil
society
nexus

* GPS-Nation
state
interaction

* Global Public Sector (GPS),
  including IMF, World Bank, WTO,
  and UN.

countries where the political leadership is not sufficiently committed to it. In some cases, a society may produce a development-minded political elite that is not prepared to give its support to the requisite economic and social policies. Examples abound in LDCs where ostensibly "reformist" or "progressive" governments prove unable to introduce truly effective reforms. While the people may want a particular pattern of development and the government they elect may reflect their wishes, this is a far cry from the will to formulate, enforce, and implement policies and programs designed to effect meaningful change.

Besides the problem posed by a lack of political commitment and will, the real trouble with reformist governments often lies in the fact that they are often undecided about the means by which reforms should be executed. Not only must imported systems be adjusted to local conditions, but existing institutions and values have to be dovetailed into the incoming ideology. This raises a crucial question about the role of ideological and intellectual conviction in moving the development process along. In the case of industrial countries, Rostow has provided an explanation in terms of the potency of "reactive nationalism," which was a bulwark against ideological insurgency from abroad. In his eyes, the economic history of all countries, especially Europe, explains in varying degrees "the primacy of reactive nationalism over other motives that have led nations to modernize their economies." Furthermore, it was only at a later stage that nationalistic reaction "merge[d] with the interests of others who, for reasons of profit, domestic power or status – or whatever – [were] prepared to act or press for modernization of the economy" (Rostow 1971, 24, 62).

While such ideological forces were instrumental in the early development of Japan, they have not produced determinate results in the majority of LDCs. During the early days of their political independence, most countries subscribed to a national development ideology geared toward enhancing national economic power. In recent times, however, there has been a lack of congruence between the rhetoric of national self-determination and the record of authentic developmental achievement. This is explained by the differential impacts of both exogenous and domestic factors. In the former case, much of what is deemed to be an appropriate development ideology emanates from abroad, leaving most countries with very little room for maneuver. But failure of the internal process of political legitimization must shoulder much of the blame.

There is still a need to establish an enabling environment necessary for creating a critical mass of development-oriented cadres with a
clear vision of the future. The reference here is to "popular" or "plural"
elites as distinct from traditional rulers, tribal chiefs, or village head-
men. While the latter group still has an important role to play,
emphasis is placed on the former because they are purportedly capable
of understanding the deep meaning of humanitarian development in a
changing world order, alternative people-centered paths toward
attaining it and its ultimate acceptability in terms of local norms and
value systems. We hasten to add that the reference to popular or plural
elites is not meant to suggest that change is a function of elitist rule.
Rather, the idea can be interpreted as an extrapolation of Pareto's
concept of elite differentiation mentioned earlier. From this
perspective, one can separate "non-elites" from "governing elites" (the
traditional ruling class) and "non-governing elites" (the new breed of
potential leaders).

They constitute a critical mass of intellectual, managerial, and
new political leaders who, arguably, personify the values, interests, and
aspirations of fellow citizens and can empathize with them. Their strategic role becomes even more critical in an institutional and public policy environment where community leadership and organizational skill
are scarce and time is of the essence. How such a leadership emerges
and is nurtured is an open question and still remains a matter of debate
and judgment. However, it potentially constitutes an essential ingredient in human resource substrata of the developmental state.

Its effectiveness ultimately hinges on the appropriateness and
quality of professional advice, informed judgments about alternative
goal-oriented human futures, and the extent to which these can be
translated into symbiotic decisions and action programs. To reiterate,
the challenges are multifaceted, and include: (i) guaranteeing sustained
improvements in the material conditions of living as a means of fulfilling the physiological and psychic needs of the population; (ii)
ensuring justice and fairness in the distribution of material benefits;
(iii) engineering a process of accumulation based on the need to create
wealth, augment economic capacity, and make poverty groups more
productive through ownership of and better access to assets and resources; and (iv) maximizing the spread effects by ensuring that the
process is expanded to all localities and groups through creation and
consolidation of optimal linkages and appropriate channels of
communication.

While the idea of national development planning has lost its popularity and is now in the doldrums, this humanistic trajectory calls for a policy process capable of projecting a long-term perspective based on multi-period plans. Since few, if any, problems are solved for all time, planning and decision-making should become iterative activities that rely not only on the correction of mistakes but also expertise and experience. The critical task lies in crafting an institutional environment based on the coordinated wisdom of political leaders, intellectual and managerial cadres, and the social consciousness of citizens. This wide net is required for at least two crucial reasons. First, futuristic options and plans should not be formulated in a crisis mode. Second, the policymaking process is typically defined by varying degrees of uncertainty and indeterminacy, or what is essentially a giant "coefficient of ignorance." The methods used to effect change are equally significant as the tangible results expected. For example, a change that is apparently "progressive" or "humanistic" on the surface may actually alienate citizens and further distort their interests if the preferred mechanisms of implementation are accompanied by, say, more government control of their lives and increased bureaucracy.

Collective decisions and coordination by the developmental state are particularly necessary for the provision of public goods. The obvious reason is that achievement of humanitarian goals may require significant increases in at least two critical public expenditure ratios; the *public allocation ratio*, defined as the proportion of government spending for infrastructure, health, education and other basic services; and the *social priority ratio*, that is, the proportion of public allocation devoted to critical areas such as elementary and vocational education, primary health care, child immunization, nutrition, and youth development. Hence, an enlightened development policy targeted toward provisioning of an optimal mix of public goods may require an actual increase in the size of the state apparatus rather than its minimalization. But, such goods have to be provided in a cost-effective and equitable manner. The contemporary neo-classical preoccupation with the rent-seeking behavior of the state, privatization, and marketization seems to have diverted attention away from a primordial argument in development economics that a minimal threshold of public investment in basic infrastructure and social overhead capital is a *sine qua non* for civilized life and the "big push" toward sustainable human development.

In conclusion, the argument for a reconstituted role for the developmental state is not necessarily inconsistent with the widely discussed principles of "good governance" such as transparency and accountability. In principle, the state can perform its functions of coordination, indicative planning, and people-centered development without sacrificing efficiency and openness, and ensuring that its activities do not lead to an overexpansion of the bureaucracy and parastatal organizations. What is undesirable, however, is a situation in which the state merely becomes a neo-liberal "nightwatchman" that is merely responsible for law and order, as well as national defense.

Marketization of Society

However, new rules of the game reflect a deistic glorification of markets and a concomitant need to delimit the role of the state. A religion of the market has now superseded that of the state, and what was once asked of the latter is now being required of the former, thereby exacerbating their natural roles. While no government can appropriate the role of an omnipotent God-giver who plans private lives and doles out happiness, the pertinent question becomes whether the market can take over the public role of assuring the social efficiency and protection necessary to meet the needs of the general public and disadvantaged groups.

Scholars and other commentators with divergent ideological beliefs and persuasions posit that the rush toward *marketization of society* throughout the globe may result in a self-defeating, ineffective, and even de-civilizing exercise just as would be the case of a purely state-orchestrated style of development. At one end of the ideological spectrum, even avid sympathizers with the market mechanism now think that it should not be allowed to assume such a position of overwhelming importance. For example, the money manager and philanthropist George Soros (1998) perceives this development as endangering the open society and ushering in a "crisis of global capitalism." He argues that the functioning of capitalism during the 1960s was rather benign, but that the intensification of competition since then has generated a large number of processes whereby market values now drive out all others.

In his eyes, a transactional culture, or one in which contractual relationships rule the roost, is replacing one that valued very lasting relationships among individuals. The paradox is that while the economic sphere is now global in scope, most political and social institutions remain bound to nation states. John Gray (1998), a progressive social scientist boasting an ideological orientation different from that of Soros, advances the thesis that the "grand conspiracy" to promote free markets throughout the globe is likely to produce a host of devastating consequences: destruction of the bourgeoisie; mass unemployment; an undermining of traditional institutions; and possibly war as nation states compete for diminishing resources. In particular, Gray argues, nation states now have less freedom of maneuver because of the influence of the "casino of currency speculators." Furthermore, it has become increasingly difficult for the state to cushion workers against the adverse effects of economic dislocation resulting from the inexorable exposure to market forces. The irony is that the need for social protection has increased at the very time that the conditions created by global markets have transformed the environment for public policy.

Whether or not one believes in "conspiracy theory," it is evident that the state-market dichotomy is overdrawn. There are few countries where a clear and unambiguous distinction can be drawn between enterprises that are strictly in the private domain and those that are not. In many cases, the private sector does not necessarily perform better than its public partner. In certain countries such as India where the private sector is relatively well developed, its ability to manage even unsophisticated enterprises, for example, textiles, leaves much to be desired. Hence, the implicit assumption that only private markets can be efficient has not been corroborated. Furthermore, the widespread belief that an inverse relationship exists between economic performance and the size of the public sector needs revision.

Such considerations raise a crucial question whether a preordained or homogenized market model can be imposed on all countries. Measures of market efficiency and profitability do not always provide a clear enough indication of performance in the development arena where the yardsticks are social efficiency and human welfare. Attainment of such ends requires the popular choice of priorities and societal goals, and an ongoing evaluation of how these goals are being met. Such a process requires a thorough national and social assessment of the benefits and burdens of marketization, or a continuous scrutiny of the entire balance sheet. For example, the social efficiency of an agricultural development project should encapsulate not only considerations of strict microeconomic efficiency and private profitability at the farm level, but also their effects on the ecological system, levels of employment and wages, the nutritional quality of products, their affordability, and so on.

Even if marketization were to result in improved efficiency of resource utilization, no firm conclusion can be drawn about the desirability of this improvement unless it can be shown that the efficiency gains promise to enhance social benefits and these are distributed in a manner that is satisfactory to society as a whole. Thus, the social acceptability of some particular act of marketization cannot be judged on purely ideological or abstract economic grounds, but more in terms of humanitarian value standards. As we have emphasized, one preminent set of people-centered norms inheres in the primordial principle of equal or moral self-worth. This reflects the historically recognized principle that free markets depend on fairness, trust, and integrity among participants engaged in voluntary exchange.

Contextually, what should be avoided at all cost is a type of societal organization in which the market becomes an adversarial disciplinary system which, in its crudest form, uses economic need as a constant whip to keep people working at substandard wages, and condones a milieu in which the power of money becomes a tool to impose punitive levels of unemployment while doling out excessively lavish rewards on business managers, CEOs, and owners of capital. By contrast, a more "people-friendly" market model is one in which problems of government regulation, finance, management, and labor are intermeshed into a more cooperative web of mutual obligation and support. The fostering of such an environment implies that employment will then become a basic conduit or outlet for social participation and creative expression, resulting in pride and personal satisfaction.

Such a model is suggested in the UNDP's *Human Development Report 1993*, which outlines the fundamentals of what it terms a "more pragmatic partnership between market efficiency and social compass-sion." The overall objective is to design a system that will enable markets to maintain their dynamism while serving people's interests. In this regard, Table 11.2 identifies sets of preconditions, conditions, corrective actions, and social safety nets that are deemed necessary for markets to serve humanitarian ends rather than people merely serving markets. But, even this "egalitarian" alternative raises a number of critical issues: the social and ethical roles that can be attributed to markets; the nature of the criteria themselves, and the extent to which they constitute a viable, socially acceptable, and sustainable strategy for hu-

manitarian development; and the specific types of institutional innovation envisaged, for example, the nature and degree of government coordination that will be needed to smooth the difficult path of structural
change.

In the first place, formal markets are not known for their "social
compassion." The general challenge concerns the kind of social
responsibility that can effectively link ethical conduct with commercial
benefit. While the dust has not yet settled on this debate, of some relevance is the United Nations "global compact" which challenges business leaders to inculcate a set of cosmopolitan values and principles
into their corporate practices in order to give globalization a human
face. The compact is based on nine principles drawn from the
Universal Declaration on Human Rights, the ILO's fundamental
principles on labor rights, and the corpus of environmental and
development principles drawn from the Earth Summit held at Rio de
Janeiro in 1992.

It is also supported by the OECD guidelines setting standards for
overseas investment policies by multinational enterprises. In this
context, the Internet has moved to the center of the battleground for
corporate social responsibility.

Implementation of the relevant standards would require increased
global cooperation and coordination around what is perceived as a cosmopolitan guidance system. This is the best that can be expected in the
absence of a supranational authority with relevant enforcement powers.
But, many analysts and influential corporate executives continue to
argue that no tinkering with the international system is required because Adam Smith's *Invisible Hand* will inevitably coordinate the discrete or independent decisions of individuals, free markets, nations,
and other institutions. The well-known assumption is that their
competitive and uncoordinated decisions are much more likely to
generate better results in human terms. As emphasized in Chapter 9,
the libertariansque moral or normative premise is that all persons and
collectivities are "entitled" to the bundles of resources they happen to
own and/or control. Hence, there is no good reason to tamper in any
way with the market distribution of benefits and burdens. This
argument essentially dismisses claims for global and national
restructuring based on egalitarian, rights-based, principles or a
cosmopolitan morality.

At another level, commentators such as the Chilean economist
Hernando de Soto (2000) contend that the real difference between rich

Table 11.2: Public Policy for People-friendly Markets

1. Preconditions
- Adequate investment in the education, health and skills of people to prepare them for the market
- An equitable distribution of assets, particularly land in poor agrarian societies
- Extension of credit to the poor
- Access to information, particularly about the range of market opportunities
- Adequate physical infrastructure, especially roads, electricity and telecommunications, and adequate support for research & development (R&D)
- A legal framework to protect property rights
- No barriers to entry, irrespective of race, religion, sex or ethnic origin
- A liberal trade regime, supported by the dismantling of trade barriers, but with protection for entrepreneurs in LDCs

2. Accompanying conditions
- A stable macroeconomic environment, especially ensuring steadiness in domestic prices and external currency values
- A comprehensive incentive system, with correct price signals, a fair tax regime and adequate rewards for work and enterprise
- Freedom from arbitrary government controls and regulations

3. Corrective Actions
- Protection of competition, through antimonopoly laws and safeguards against financial malpractices
- Protection of consumers, especially through drug regulations, safety and hygiene standards and honest advertising
- Protection of special groups, particularly women, children and ethnic minorities
- Protection of the environment, particularly through incentive systems and by banning pollution or making polluters pay

4. Social Safety Nets
- Adequate arrangements to look after temporary victims of market forces to bring them back into the markets, primarily through human investment, worker retraining and access to credit opportunities – as well as more permanent support for groups such as the disabled and aged.

and poor nations is that the former have markets and the latter do not. Christ is reported to have thrown merchants out of the temple some 2000 years ago. Historically, vibrant markets and trade long existed on the African continent. In Latin America, people were avidly conducting market transactions long before Columbus reached the New World. Through the lens of history, therefore, the real difference between rich and poor countries has something to do with the manner in which transactions are conducted, how things are exchanged, and the nature of property rights. In fact, the view that the market is better at managing resources hinges on an implicit assumption about the structure of property rights and related incentives for productive efficiency. This requires some concept of an expanded market based on legal entitlements and other mechanisms for enforcing contracts. As previously emphasized, the establishment of efficient markets requires an appropriate institutional base.

It is in this sense that many LDCs are still far back on the road toward establishing the requisite institutional framework for efficient markets to emerge and flourish, not to mention egalitarian ones. Market-friendly protagonists, facilitators, and enlightened policymakers are often caught up in dysfunctional structures and processes that place definite limits on what can be realistically achieved. Across the less developed sector of the world, some of the major and persistent constraints include: highly concentrated systems of land ownership and insecure tenurial arrangements; the absence of or relatively undeveloped nature of complementary capital, labor, and insurance markets; low levels of human resource development; and a most glaring lack of appropriate social safety nets.

While the myriad preconditions and conditions necessary for creation of people-friendly markets can be construed as a pragmatic minimum, the entire process of transition may prove to be too traumatic, tortuous, and disruptive for the fragile structures of many LDCs. It must remain an open question whether the citizenry of most countries will be able or willing to pay the price. Among other things, they will be required to internalize the imported cultural norms of what Kuttner (1997) calls "turbo-charged" market capitalism. In any event, the success or failure of the transitional path will ultimately depend on the nature of complementary adjustments that can be forged in the structure of state-market-community relations.

As we have mentioned, and counterintuitively, the process of adjustment may actually require a more visible hand of the state in establishing and nurturing an enabling market-oriented environment rather than exclusive reliance on the evolutionary possibilities suggested by Adam Smith's Invisible Hand. But, a morally and politically bankrupt state structure is unlikely to provide the kind of long-range vision, political wisdom, and selfless forms of leadership that can potentially build up institutional capabilities necessary for promoting alternative goal-oriented human futures. It goes without saying that a rotten body politic can be expected to harbor the kind of "crony capitalism" evident in many LDCs rather than the more "popular capitalism" that is required for people-friendly markets to become a reality and flourish.

Chapter 12

Development From Below

> If devolved community provides status based on our place in the order of things, involved community offers us the chance to find meaning based in our unique contributions to purposes larger than ourselves and our immediate families. [This is] vital, not only to our mental health but also to our physical well-being.
>
> Frances Lappé and Paul Du Bois (1995)

A central question surrounding developmental management is related to its "directionality:" is it more appropriate to start from the top of the national structure and direct efforts downwards, or vice-versa? Most governments in LDCs remain overcentralized, and based on an imported bureaucratic structure of organization. In this "view from the top," state bureaucracies are not only centrally managed and financed, but their diverse functions and activities normally reflect programs that issue from the national political directorate. This style of decision-making and rulership is sometimes so highly centralized that there is a visible lack of community participation or active involvement of intermediate institutions. Such rigid systems are often perceived as impersonal, arrogant, unsympathetic, and ineffective by the majority of people at the local level or grassroots.

Bureaucracies in LDCs, especially in Africa, are unproductive for several related reasons. First, the highly centralized and hierarchical structures imposed by colonial powers left ensuing public administrations with a tradition of legalistic and unresponsive practices. Second, bureaucrats are wont to maintain conservative tendencies when change threatens established power structures and demands a mastery of new tasks. Third, the civil service routinely acts as an informal network of alliances based on family, ethnic loyalties, and so forth. Fourth, bureaucrats are often too undisciplined to implement policies with precision.

Such a pattern of governance and developmental management has proven to be particularly inappropriate and dysfunctional in societies with considerable ethnic and cultural diversity, and where people constantly resist dictates from the center. While state bureaucracies do provide a variety of services to the general public, they find it extremely difficult to adapt programs to the needs of specific groups at risk or those in need of social protection and to changes in such needs. They include poor, unemployed, landless, illiterate, or otherwise marginalized cadres. A new development milieu based on the communal will to power is more conducive to dialogical acts, interpersonal communication, and a willingness of powerful state bureaucracies to "listen" and "learn." At the same time, people in general will become more aware of, and can better understand, the sources of both their powerlessness and capabilities, and begin to chart their own destinies.

Self-Reliance, Decentralization and Devolution

Given the dismal failure of a development delivery system based on a "top down" orientation, ordinary citizens now want and are expected to assume responsibilities for their own self-development based on dialogue or conversation, resource mobilization, and institutional inclusiveness. Hence, a new urgency, significance, and respectability is attributed to the relatively old concept of "development from below" (Hicks 1961; David 1973; Chambers 1997). Its basic preconception is that for authenticity and success development efforts must be innovative, locally conceived and initiated, and grounded in a clear understanding of the local political economy. The legitimacy of a central government ultimately depends on its responsiveness to the demands and felt needs of people at the grassroots.

This inheres in its ability and willingness to create and nurture an environment in which public officials and agencies devote themselves to national and local development needs rather than doggedly follow the conventional practice of suppressing popular dissent or turning a blind eye to it. This calls for an institutional order that can effectively deal with situations requiring flexibility and creativity. As illustrated in Figure 12.1, the policy environment should promote people-centered goals and priorities based on integrated efforts at the national, regional, local, and individual levels. A guiding principle is that the policymaking and planning system should allow for optimal coordination of the component parts in accordance with these goals and priorities. This is consistent with a mode of "consistency planning," which implies that national development efforts should be integrated at several programmatic but highly decentralized levels that are oriented toward specific local conditions.

Ideally, this requires a constitutional distribution of authority and responsibilities among central, regional, district, and village institutions based on deconcentration and devolution of power. It goes beyond a mere juridical structure of governance, but is rather predicated on transformation of the total system so that practices of self-government can become a reality. In the final analysis, however, decentralization can only be sustained by a fair and equitable political economy that is characterized by transparency, accountability, and distributive justice. Germane to this is an issue concerning the relative merits/demerits of deconcentration vis-à-vis devolution, or the extent to which levels of self-determination allow for full participation.

Deconcentration signifies the assignment of responsibilities to field agencies and personnel, but with very little or no sharing of power. In federal states such as Malaysia, India, and Brazil, it has permitted certain centrally-sponsored programs to flourish under a variety of circumstances. This pattern of decentralization involves supplementing professional staff by an increased use of paraprofessionals as a means of reducing administrative and operational costs. This approach has been very effective in programs for preventive medicine, nutrition, and

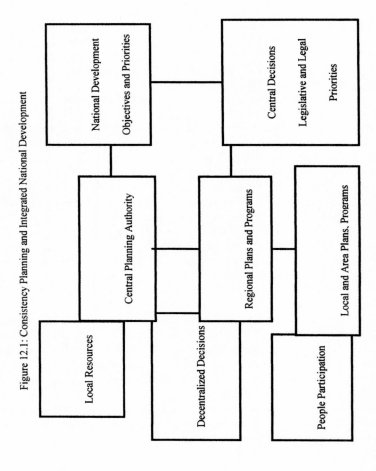

Figure 12.1: Consistency Planning and Integrated National Development

non-formal education. While they are trained and supervised by professsional personnel from the center, paraprofessionals are often selected by the communities they serve. Even though their formal education may be limited, they can be trained in specific skills required to provide services that would otherwise be unavailable, or at a cost local communities can afford. Their outreach to the wider public and ability to empathize with local people tend to permit a more responsive delivery of development services. More reliable feedbacks are also provided to the center than are normally available from the hierarchical structure of bureaucratic elites.

It is always difficult to redistribute power within public bureaucracies. The "devolution" alternative involves a transfer of power and authority from the central government to local government units. There is more extensive sharing of authority in one or more of the following significant senses: formulation of policies and programs; administering projects and running enterprises; and allocation of expenditure as well as raising revenue. While it is generally recognized that legally accountable local government units can perform developmental functions without imposing severe burdens on the central bureaucracy, the debate on development remains devoid of any comprehensive interpretation of their critical role.

Where they have been allowed to function, local government authorities have demonstrated responsiveness to local influence, accountability to local publics, as well as an ability to organize and interact with those at the bottom rungs of society. However, the tradition of popular sovereignty has been considerably fragmented and weakened in the majority of LDCs. The situation continues to be exacerbated by the inordinate influence and onslaught of macroeconomic adjustment programs emanating from Washington and national capitals. Yet adequate restructuring at the local level can bring substantial benefits in terms of the formulation, execution, and delivery of development services. Such positive effects can be significant especially where there are complex multisectoral mixes of activities requiring proper integration and timing. At the same time, managerial input at the local level may infuse the development process with the flexibility needed to modify programs as local parameters and constraints become better understood or as circumstances change.

The combination of authority, responsibility, and accountability focused at the local level can foster a mentality that is better attuned toward so-called community "ownership" of development programs, and lead to much more active and salutary promotional efforts than otherwise. An intractable problem, however, is that any serious attempt at devolution would necessarily involve financial and fiscal reforms that are anathema to the conventional wisdom informing macroeconomic management, centralized budgeting, and fiscal discipline. In this regard, many government propagandists and other detractors are wont to harp on the attendant costs. The standard argument is that more local autonomy would result in a duplication of government functions and inestimable expenses for building and maintenance of additional administrative infrastructure. But such costs are unavoidable, and to some extent represent the price that has to be paid in a holistic drive toward decentralization.

Substantial net benefits can accrue from adequate levels of fiscal decentralization and a reconstituted financial architecture at the local level. Among other things, this would require: (i) more cost-effective subsidies from the center plus greater authority for local governments to collect revenues and impose taxes; and (ii) a gradual building up of the capacity of local authorities to increasingly provide "matching" contributions for financing various services. Examples include raw materials for building and road construction; and pro-rated payments of salaries of teachers, the police, paraprofessionals, health care workers, and similar cadres.

Return to Community

When local governments and authorities are transformed from being mere administrative appendages of central state power to more autonomous and effective developmental institutions, they become facilitators of the devolution process. But, their creative and dynamic role should be interpreted as an integral part of community self-development. Contextually, eradication of the real insecurities afflicting diverse groups of people throughout the globe is predicated on the imperative of building an integrative community, or communities of communities, based on symbiotic interactions among individual motivations and actions, group behavior, and the more embracing social order. This involves cooperative relations among people, promotion of consensual values, and a subscription to common rules governing people's conduct toward one another. The fundamental objective inheres in the need to enhance people's sense of belongingness by expanding the arena of participation, social cooperation, and civic engagement through a better articulation of shared values and cultural norms.

The communitarian option guarantees "social acceptability" and adds legitimacy to the overall development process. The crucial implication is that humanitarian ideals cannot be achieved unless adequate weight is given to specific goals such as equity and participatory democracy. The transitional path becomes unacceptable when people and their communities are not sufficiently involved, or it results in further impoverishment, inequities, oppression of powerless groups, as well as other forms of alienation and displacement. Hence the communal and social acceptability standards are grounded in principles of economic justice, fairness, and equality of opportunity. Supporting policy aims include activating the rural sector, increasing access of poverty groups to resources, and guaranteeing productive and remunerative employment.

In some circles, the development transition continues to be interpreted in terms of an "end of community." This is based on the historically dominant perspective of community as a uniquely "traditional" form of social organization or relationship to be contrasted with more "modern" forms of life – as exemplified by the impersonal, rationalized, urbanized, and hierarchical structures of industrial society. The dichotomy is a holdover from the 19th century when the idea of community was equated with rural and pre-industrial conditions as distinct from what were perceived to be their more destructive urban counterparts. The cohesive relationships of kinship and organic ties of rural societies were thought to be dissolved by the modernization process, and concomitant forms of individualism, increased division of labor, and competitiveness.

In the contemporary world order, the imperative of a return to community as both a transformative means and end of authentic development has been buttressed by at least three dimensions of theory and social praxis underlying the creative utopian vision. In general, the communitarian option is an essential antidote or corrective to four prominent ideologies about the satisfactory or good life: that human beings live almost exclusively in the political sphere of differential power relations; through individual work efforts ("by the sweat of thy brow, thou shalt eat bread"); by the inexorable working of the invisible hand of the competitive market; and through heavy reliance on the benevolent hand of the state (Walzer 1983).

In the more developed sector of the world, the communitarian movement has been calling for a rejection of individualism and a concomitant renewal of a sense of community. For example, it is pointed out that the United States began as a known group of religious communities, or as a nation of "rugged conformists" rather than one of "rugged individualists" (Fukuyama 1995). During the 1840s, Alexis de Tocqueville viewed as an essential feature of American democracy the tendency for "Americans of all ages, all conditions, and all dispositions to constantly form associations," which came in all shapes and sizes – "religious, moral, serious, futile, general or restricted, enormous or diminutive." Modern communitarians now bemoan the increasing tendency for de Tocqueville's original thesis to be disproved.

As one leading scholar states,

> [u]nless the retreat to ego is overcome and community institutions reconstituted, the levels of conflicts and frustrations will rise, and the limited energy channeled to shared concerns will make for an ineffectual 'can't do' society, continued deterioration, and, even, ultimately, the possibility of destruction (Etzione 1983, 186).

Swindler and others (1997) comment on the increasing withdrawal or exclusion of entire groups of Americans from seeing themselves as members of communities, reflecting the possibility that institutional life may be in shambles. From another angle, Lasch (1995) points to a decline in civic responsibility, which he blames on the restlessness of new mobile elites. These so-called "cosmocrats" are thought to constitute "perhaps the most meritocratic ruling class the world has seen, yet they are often as worryingly disconnected from local communities as the companies they work for" (Micklethwait and Wooldridge 2000, xxii). In similar vein, Putnam (2000) has advanced the "solitary bowler" thesis – "people are going bowling by themselves," even though ten-pin bowling remains an extremely social activity. He views this as the most whimsical and disconfiting evidence of a decline of social capital, or a fall-off of Americans willing to join voluntary associations or groups of all kinds.

Hence, the upsurge of the communitarian ethic is supported by a life-and-world vision that variously extols the virtues of "trust," "social capital," "civil society," or some vaguer bond of solidarity considered essential for sustained economic and human development, social peace and democracy.   On a related basis, large numbers of people throughout the globe have long recognized, and are increasingly asserting, the importance of local and cultural life-giving forces – belongingness, caring, sharing, and membership of communities. In the wake of concerted encroachments by inexorable external forces and apparently soulless international institutions, community attachments are considered real for most people in LDCs, if not for mainstream economists who deal in abstractions and are prone to interpret reality from a distance.

The humanitarian development paradigm is anchored on a basic preconception that only societies comprising layers of humanistic institutions are fit for human beings to inhabit. The concept of community is central to our understanding of the ability of such societies to promote goal-oriented human futures. In this regard, the fostering of appropriate communal relations can be viewed as both an endogenous process (instrumental means) and humanitarian goal (intrinsic or constitutive end) of authentic development. In a general sense, community consists of persons who are internally related to and can identify with one another on the basis of norms, ethical codes, and behavioral expectations constituting a form of life (Cohen 1985). The latter is defined by the unity, identity, and meaning it embodies in terms of belief systems and culture.

Contextually, members of a given group tend to share certain identifiable characteristics. They have something in common, an attribute that distinguishes them from other putative groups. Hence, the idea of community is relational, that is, it is predicated on the simultaneous existence of similarity and difference. In this regard, two broad perspectives of life may be used to delimit the boundaries of a community. In the more restricted sense, it connotes specialized groups of people, such as religious, business, scientific, and academic groups who propagate particular worldviews or cultural practices. A more comprehensive form of life is consonant with the interpretation of community as something that is symbolically constructed, that is, a system of shared values and common understandings.

This reflects the "integrative power" of community, or its ability to promote the common good based on love, benevolence, social cooperation, and voluntary action (Boulding 1973b). When people work together through communal efforts, a virtuous circle is created whereby socially responsible individual action builds community, enlarges personal freedom, generates more social cooperation, and so on *ad infinitum*. Germane to this is the distinction between "devolved" and "involved" community mentioned in the quotation at the beginning of this chapter. The devolved community is historically given, that is, it constitutes relationships such as family and place that are handed down to any given group. In this sense, a community is governed by inherited codes of conduct, consensual rules, exchanges based on diffuse types of obligations guaranteed by friendship and respect, and modes of conflict resolution that are implicit rather than explicit. The involved community builds on its historically devolved parent by strengthening yearnings for identity, belongingness, autonomy, and participatory democracy. This adds a new dimension to the community-development nexus. It is not static or "given," but deliberately created to meet different but equally significant human needs over time. The new levels of consciousness tend to produce "win-win" outcomes by enhancing opportunities for self-expression and self-exploration, social learning through honest communication with others, and effective forms of community problem-solving.

Such liberating behaviors and expectations constitute what is termed the "communal will to power" (Daly and Cobb 1989). It is based on a particular form of freedom – making new proposals and suggesting new avenues that can potentially expand people's choices and options. This differs from the usual situation in which changes are forced upon members of a community through external pressures and manipulation. Hence, the emancipatory form of communal power tends to give more "voice" to others, expand their freedom, enhance their personhood, and build community. The process is given a further fillip by the receptive dimension of power, which tends to reduce alienation and anomie in two mutually reinforcing ways. It enables a "person-in-community" to incorporate the thoughts and feelings of others into his or her selfhood. At the same time, it empowers others because they come to feel that their views are heard and taken seriously. As the sense of community deepens, people are able to use their shared power to achieve collective goals that are usually outside the pale of individual action.

At the pragmatic level of policymaking and institutional development, the communal will-to-power reflects the positive roles played by diverse organizations occupying the space between the state and private sector. They not only constitute a circle championing programs of community development, but are also enablers of a process whereby people in provinces, districts, and villages have become involved in improving their personal lives by establishing their own priorities in the context of existing realities. Thailand's Five Star Partnership Program provides a notable exemplar of the integration and coordination of communal efforts. On the one hand, the model demonstrates how state bureaucracies can become more democratic, thereby allowing civil society to evolve on the basis of partnership and participation. On the other hand, it calls for new and creative roles for local people's organizations.

As focal points for initiating and sustaining involvement and empowerment of people, they reflect the strategic role of an animated "Third Sector" in effecting optimal synergy between national development goals and the needs, motivations, and aspirations of the masses at the grassroots. This communal sector encompasses a multifaceted array of intermediate and pluralistic entities combining the virtues of autonomy and private enterprise with community building and social responsiveness. Its membership spans cooperatives, labor unions, religious communities, fraternal orders, women's organizations, farmers associations. Parent Teachers Associations, self-help groups, and a variety of other private voluntary organizations (PVOs) – all accountable to the interests of members and people at large. The longevity of these diverse organs is testimony to the fact that all societies contain both endemic communitarian and market-based structures.

Some elements of material life rely on voluntary exchange and personal advantage, while others are more oriented toward sustaining self and others in the larger community. But the "market-community" dualism has become problematic in a world where many facets of community are being increasingly threatened, transformed, and dominated by market forces. Yet, a dialectical relationship exists between the two spheres. As a source of empowerment and commensality of participants, the community does not allocate shares on the basis of economic logic, that is, by calculating marginal costs and benefits to individuals. While communities must now bow to market principles, the competitive market itself relies on communal practices such as pure gifts, charity, and altruism (Gudeman 1996). This remains true even though such practices may represent no more than a temporary suspension of individualism and self-interest or a fleeting commitment to community.

Moreover, markets in the real world cannot function effectively without a stream of public goods guaranteed under communal support systems, such as social security schemes, education, health, and welfare programs. At the same time, the community must also leave sufficient space for individual development. The idea of a "person-in-community" signifies that voluntary cooperation among individuals complements rather than displaces community. The upshot of the argument is that in a global environment in which the private sector is expected to play an expanded role in the development process, the Third Sector of communal relations and people's organizations should be considered its institutional bedrock. It is precisely at the local community level that disparate economic, social, political, and related structural changes are likely to produce a profound and lasting effect (Esman and Uphoff 1984).

The constituent organizations usually function at minimal cost to the central government. Their members and volunteers typically display a strong dedication to the poor, flexibility in responding to changing traditions and needs, and a willingness to cater to the needs of clienteles not normally reached by local offices and field stations of central government agencies. However, their resources are meager and scale of operations disproportionately small in relation to national priorities and needs. Over the years, some external support has been flowing to this sector, especially since it directly addresses the needs of marginalized groups. Involvement of foreign NGOs has sometimes helped to mitigate resource constraint and uncertainty, but too visible an external presence has been known to introduce elements of suspicion that militate against their effectiveness in dealing with politically sensitive groups.

In the final analysis, what matters most for the capacity to empower people at the middle and bottom rungs of society is not so much the size of their organizations, but more importantly, the extent to which their survival skills and mechanisms can be enhanced and protected. In many instances, local communities have had no alternative but to fend for themselves, since they could no longer expect to build a better life and future through exclusive reliance on national governments, planning agencies, or foreign aid. This has usually entailed efforts to build their own survival economies. This recourse to so-called collective self-reliance perhaps demonstrates the creative utopianism that is implicit in "barefoot economics" (Max-Neef 1982) and "development as liberation" (Goulet 1979; Gran 1983). The optimistic missive for authentic development is that communal solutions of the right kind, i.e., based on "involved community," can meld idealistic visions and practical outcomes.

Correlatively, collective self-reliance at the grassroots is eminently capable of generating an emancipatory conversation about humanitarian development for at least three reasons. First, both smaller local communities and national societies in which they are embedded are liberated from the rigors of material deprivation and human insecurity. Second, villagers and other groups at the bottom are afforded an opportunity to define their own needs, as well as formulate, execute, evaluate, and monitor their own development plans and projects. Among other things, this is likely to enhance their chances of earning sustainable livelihoods, heighten their development consciousness, and provide them with improved knowledge about self-government and organizational effectiveness. Moreover, the entire process of local capacity building and the corresponding raising of self-confidence are likely to cumulate over time, generating more and more pressure for sustainable changes in the overall quality of life and human well-being.

Finally, the confluence of community activism, supportive government, and humanitarian policies by aid donors have helped to increase sensitivity about the many complex factors purporting to explain the success of community participation. Table 12.1 provides a checklist of perceived benefits. For example, community provisioning has become a common feature of local water and sanitation systems, small-scale infrastructure such as feeder roads, distribution canals for irrigation, and maintenance of local drainage systems. In such cases, community action has required involvement of users in decision-making, setting priorities for expenditure, and ensuring an agreed sharing of costs and benefits of services (World Bank 1994, 9).

Given perceptions about government complacency concerning the need for adequate supplies of clean water, hundreds of communities, especially women's groups, have tried to overcome the problem of fetching water over long distances by building permanent reservoirs and low-cost irrigation channels. In this regard, evaluations of rural water supply projects in Africa, Asia, and Latin America reveal that successful outcomes tend to be positively correlated with beneficiary participation in their design and execution. Isham et al. (1995) report that full community involvement has made a positive contribution to the proportion of water systems in satisfactory condition, the percentage of the target population reached, and environmental benefits. Furthermore, communal processes have resulted in increased access to and control of water resources, acquisition of new organizational skills, and strengthening of community groups undertaking other development efforts.

Table 12.1: Benefits of Community Involvement

- Empowerment of the poor and disadvantaged through increased access to resources, ownership and control of the means of development, and reduction of gaps in power and knowledge.
- Increased relevance and appropriateness of policies, processes, and outcomes of development efforts to human needs.
- Increased equity and solidarity by involving marginalized and poor people in development efforts, and strengthening their capabilities.
- Enhanced commitment to and "ownership" of policies, programs, and projects, as well as willingness to share costs and sustain benefits.
- Greater social energy, understanding, efficiency, and better planning based on concerns and knowledge of a wide range of constituents and stakeholders at the local level.
- More synergy among humanitarian goals, physical investments, and human resource development.
- Greater transparency, accountability, and improved institutional performance.
- Better information flows and coordination with local etiology, allowing the development process to function more smoothly.
- Enlarged potential for conflict resolution through greater inclusiveness and bringing together of individuals and groups with divergent priorities, interests, and needs.

Source: Author.

Community action has also played a catalytic role in the improvement of basic social services such as health, nutrition, family planning, and education. Communal organizations have become major conduits of a variety of creative credit programs that now flourish in different parts of the world. Historically, many potential entrepreneurs have faced tremendous difficulties in gaining access to financial services that would enable them to establish small-scale enterprises to create income and jobs. The obvious reason is that commercial banks and other financial intermediaries prefer to deal with larger businesses in urban areas. The upsurge of financial self-help organizations has not only helped to blunt the edges of this constraint, but continues to generate and nurture the impetus toward greater collective financial self-reliance.

View from the Countryside

Despite concerted onslaughts, intended or unintended, by forces of modernization, globalization, and macroeconomic adjustment, rural places or the countryside still remain the most important repositories of communal life, participation, and the normative vision of development. Germane to this tenacity is the fact that people tend to be alienated from institutions embodying cultures that are different from their own, or otherwise perceived to be at odds with the shared norms they have internalized in their own way of life and identity. The norms are usually acquired through processes of socialization or the means by which cultural patterns – values, beliefs, language, and other symbols – are internalized. Socialization helps to guarantee stable and secure patterns of interpersonal relationships, and bears a primary responsibility for legitimizing and reproducing the communal or social order (Berger and Luckmann 1967).

Over the course of their lives, people come to internalize practices such as cooperation and reciprocity through village life, communal living, education and social learning, role modeling, and by experiencing the rewards and sanctions attached to normative behavior. Hence, they participate collectively in shaping the larger groupings to which they belong because of a feeling of identity with contemporaries, past generations who participated in their form of life, and future generations who will inherit it. But skepticism remains rife over the possibilities of utilizing indigenous rural formations or rules of the game as catalysts of sustainable human development. To some extent, this is reminiscent of Karl Marx's original comment about the "idiocy of the countryside," or "backwardness" of countryfolk.

One misgiving is based on the argument that attempts to use such mechanisms to change the very values of which they are guardians may actually reinforce dysfunctional traditional values. But efforts can always be made within the prevailing socio-cultural milieu to link human development programs to traditional values. This can be achieved by "symbolically" assigning institutions to the former realm if they are synergistic with the latter. The undesirable and impracticable alternative is to go against the grain of the normative foundations of a community by, for example, using coercive or largely imported measures to impose an institutional base and form of development based on cultural discontinuity.

At one level, there is a need to link institutional change to the local cultural etiology (indigenous systems of thinking) and related forms of knowledge, communication, and information. Indigenous forms of knowledge are often more holistic than their scientific counterparts because they are relatively free of the tunnel vision implicit in the monodisciplinary orientation. Traditional systems of communication and information are important mechanisms for reaching people via messages about new technologies, agricultural credit, modern health practices, family planning, and so on. When they are ignored, such networks may transmit messages that undermine, oppose, and even derail development programs. While specific forms may vary from country to country, the missive is that the informational substructure should be adapted to local cultural norms or "webs of significance" that have been accepted in the countryside and informal places for generations.

In the above context, the possibility of effecting synergy between modern formal institutions and indigenous social formations and value systems is implicit in the variety of intermediate, "middle rung," or "socializing" institutions that have sprung up in village communities. They not only traverse the economic sphere, but also the political, religious, and other dimensions of the social system. While rooted in the local culture, they provide viable links between past and future, central government and village, as well as between external aid agencies and disadvantaged groups in need of social protection. While maintaining the dominance of traditional values, such hybrid institutions have become essential conduits for the transformation of non-economic activities into economic ones. Walking this tightrope has enabled some communities to balance the apparently contradictory forces of tradition and modernity in such a way that social equilibrium is not disturbed even in a situation of rapid social and cultural change.

Historically, some of the most active grassroots movements and institutions have been observed on the Asian continent. The most widely reported is the Indian self-help movement, which is rooted in Mahatma Gandhi's early pioneering work on village development. The Gandhian self-help tradition has burgeoned into innumerable local development groups and independent community organizations that nowadays wage a constant battle for human development based on promotion of social welfare, economic enterprise, appropriate technology, environmental protection, and the like. Some widely acclaimed success stories include: (i) the Self-employed Women's Association (SEWA), consisting of poor women and illiterate villagers who have been able to improve their living standards substantially through political action and self-help; (ii) the sugar cooperatives in Maharastra state; (iii) the Amul Dairy Cooperatives in Gujarat – the birthplace of Mahatma Gandhi; and (iv) the Community Forest Movement – "Chipko" – which has evolved from "embracing trees" to natural resource management or "eco-development" (Shiva 1994; Kasmin 2000).

In Sri Lanka, millions of people have been engaged in the *Sarvodaya Shramadana* movement, which combines Gandhian teachings with Buddhist precepts of social action ("Sarvodaya" means "village awakening" and "Shramadana" "the gift of labor"). These principles are operationalized through massive working parties and village feasts. They have become effective media of social interchange in which people engage in emancipatory dialogues based on "listening," "learning," and "speaking" (Macy 1985). They give their labor voluntarily to community projects in health, education, crafts, road construction, and cooperative credit. The Sarvodaya Credit Scheme is a prominent example of financial mobilization at the grassroots. The Sarvodaya center in each village helps to establish societies whose members are required to go through a rigorous training period and join a compulsory savings scheme. The accumulated funds are then used as collateral for loans to village societies which relend to individual members for diverse projects.

Bangladesh, one of the world's poorest countries, has emerged as a leader when judged by the activities of its NGOs and local development. They number about 20,000 and operate in 66,000 villages, providing small-scale agricultural development, literacy, health care, and other basic social services much more efficiently than the central government. Organizations such as the Bangladesh Rural Development Committee (BRAC), Proshika, the Association for Social Advancement (ASA), and the Grameen Bank are some of the biggest and well-respected community action groups in the world. They have been collectively responsible for a reduction in absolute poverty in the country from 59 percent in 1991-92 to around 53 percent during the late 1990s.

Such examples of group solidarity demonstrate how human agents have been successful in devising social institutions to cope with environments defined by high risks and limited liquid assets. Besides providing insurance and intergenerational transfers, such mechanisms have also been instrumental in solving problems of agricultural subsistence and management of common property resources. Societies could effectively regulate their use because husbandry of such resources takes place in the larger socio-cultural context of frequent interaction, observation, and sociability. People living in the countryside tend to accept a significant level of mutual dependence and obligation. This is normally asserted through various consensual rules of allocation and distribution that are designed to provide a basic level of subsistence for all members of the community. The primary motivation is to guarantee survival in the face of uncertainty about the supply of food and other basic necessities. The resultant "subsistence ethic" reflects values and social relations that help to mitigate hardship in the worst of times.

Rural communities are more like "moral economies" than market economies because the rules of village life tend to produce moral outcomes. Historically, such rules have imposed an obligation on members to protect the subsistence needs of the less fortunate and the community at large from the costs of inequality through a process of consensual decision-making and by allocating burdens according to means. As a result, such collectivities should not be viewed as mere associations of rural producers, but more as "cultural units" boasting a strong sense of identity and subscribing to an all-inclusive moral code. Layers of behavioral norms and rules of compliance help to sustain a variety of insurance arrangements that lower information costs and reduce moral hazard. Non-contractual systems of reciprocity encourage people to meet their obligations, even when there are no explicit or formal laws to enforce them. Integrated systems of intra-group or mutual insurance normally protect people against unemployment, crop failures, illness, and bad luck.

The primary point of intersection inheres in the historically entrenched family structure, which is the basic institution or cohesive force in communal life. Being born into a family and having to subscribe to its cultural rules are somewhat akin to an insurance scheme. The family is a source of economic and other support in any type of circumstance. It also functions as a business unit in which individual and collective resources are marshaled to meet consumption and investment needs. In essence, the family represents a corporate body whose goals are rooted in an "economy of affection" rather than in the market-oriented values such as profit maximization (Hyden 1986).

In Africa, for instance, the economy of affection is exemplified by traditional systems of income distribution, which are based on the ever-presence of the extended family and rules governing the communal sharing of wealth. These reflect cooperative relations of production, open access to kinfolk, and a refusal to accept a state of joblessness. Such attitudes have taken on added significance in an environment where rapid population growth in rural areas, out-migration, the failure of urban industrialization, and the rigors of structural adjustment have produced various forms of unemployment. Under the circumstances, the rural household, extended family, and community remain the institutions that guarantee some sense of human or social security. They collectively act as employers "of last resort" for those who might have failed in the formal employment market.

The institutional endogeneity of the family structure is also exemplified by rules governing kinship and lineage systems. There are costs to individual families of belonging to extended lineages and benefits derived from spreading risks in environments marked by high economic and ecological variability. Studies on the Luo and Kikuyu in Kenya, Bambara of Mali, and East African pastoralists clearly demonstrate that different lineage groups are wont to create different types of property rights and access to intergenerational income flows. For example, the broad-based lineage structure of the Luo group in Kenya enables individuals to spread risk.

> They can disperse their cattle to family members located in contrasting settings; drought in any particular area is therefore likely to affect but a small portion of the individual's herd. They can gain access to gardens in different ecological zones... The lineage form of property rights thus provides insurance (Bates 1990, 158).

Collier and Gunning (1999) also summarize research showing how the costs of moral hazard and adverse selection are lowered in alternative ecological settings. The semi-arid lowland areas are climatically risky and have a relatively low population density. People living in the lowlands invest in lineage groups because they provide a form of insurance, access to geographically dispersed crops and livestock, and tend to reduce the covariance of returns on assets of the respective groups. By contrast, groups living in the highlands, for example, the Kikuyu tea and coffee farmers in Kenya, have less need for insurance because rainfall patterns are more reliable. Hence, they have developed private property rights.

Finally, cultural regularities and variations observed in rural life should be juxtaposed against the perceived rationality of *homo oeconomicus rusticus* ("rural economic man") or what often goes under the rubric of "peasant rationality." On the one hand, it is believed that people in the countryside, especially subsistence farmers, are conservative in their value orientations. The early orthodox consensus was that they are usually bound by tradition, and therefore cannot be induced to change their ways through market incentives designed to increase agricultural output, and adoption of new technologies and cultural practices. On the other hand, rural producers are thought to display much more individualism and profit-seeking tendencies than is often supposed. As Popkin (1979, 30-31) remarks, the peasant or small farmer "is a rational problem-solver, with a sense of both his own interests and a need to bargain with others to achieve mutually acceptable outcomes."

This is linked to a perception that peasant farming is highly efficient, negating the need for appeal to traditional cultural values as an explanation of behavioral patterns. The theoretical argument is that responses to price and profit incentives are universal, and therefore do not differ across countries or regions of a country (Schultz 1964, 1980). The implication is that the behavior of farmers in both modern and traditional institutional settings is substantively rational, that is, the "rational" producer tends to allocate resources efficiently in order to maximize output gains and profits. In the world of neo-classical economics, rationality is interpreted in the very narrow sense of price and profit responsiveness. Hence, the behavior of all economic agents is explained by relying on conventional assumptions such as perfect foresight, certainty, and relatively stable relationships among prices, inputs, and outputs. This interpretation strips the rural producer of all personal and collective cultural traits that may have a bearing on the decision-making process. As previously mentioned, these include the socio-economic characteristics of villages, farming households, families, kinship, and lineage systems.

What is known from observations *in situ* of rural households and production structures is that decisions are almost always based on uncertainty and a lack of information from the center. They know little or nothing about the macroeconomic picture, face uncertainty about the behavior of input relative to output prices, and are usually at a disadvantage when attempting to obtain information about future trends in prices. Subsistence farmers are always sceptical about the advice received from the central government, and live in a world that is generally antagonistic to the state apparatus (David and David 1995). Furthermore, they constantly face uncertainty about natural factors such as the weather, rainfall patterns, and the incidence of pests, crop diseases, and so on.

Under the circumstances, it is reasonable to argue that relevant decisions are not substantively rational, but rely on the more limited or procedural rationality that usually guides "satisficing" forms of behavior. In this context, John Adams uses a concept of "demirationality" to capture the "shadowy and uncertain contours" defining the environment in which small farmers operate. As he states,

> the principle of economic gain must operate in a complex context in which peasant security, prestige, the place and continuity of the family, and future hopes are all constantly at stake; where information is scarce and unreliable and risks abundant; where general and uncontrollable factors intrude before, during, and after any decision is taken (Adams 1986, 279).

Therefore, the rural landscape is defined by rules of the game in which behaviors and expectations are conditioned by the persistence of cultural values and entrenched attitudes to farming, approaches to work, and the tradeoff between efficiency and equity. The small-scale agriculturist may reject so-called "modern inputs" such as high-yielding varieties of seeds (HYVs), fertilizers, and pesticides because his or her criterion of choice is based on reproducibility rather than mere increased output or the highest returns to investments. Throughout the less developed sector of the world, many small farmers resist the advances of capitalist agriculture and defend the moral fabric of their communities against what are perceived as alien values of individualism, materialism, and acquisitiveness. The foremost concern remains continued survival over the longer run rather than maximizing short-term physical and monetary gains. For good or evil, the allocation of labor (in terms of the designated roles for men, women, and children) continues to follow what may be termed the "law of subsistence," that is, production of use-values.

Epilogue
From Bottom to Top

Humanitarian, authentic, or people-centered development bears a mutually reinforcing, interlocking, and recursive relationship with other global public goods such as peace, sustainability, and justice. A universally accepted precept, particularly relevant to today's troubled international environment, is that a peaceful society or sociosphere is a *sine qua non* for human well-being. At the same time, sustainable human development is also a necessary precondition for peace, which provides the most lasting context in which human beings can flourish. It is hardly worth sustaining an economy or society that at any moment can be made completely chaotic by war, violence, or terrorism. In similar vein, doubts can be raised about the wisdom of sustaining an inherently unjust, oppressive, society or world order. Moreover, it would be foolhardy to hanker after a just society that is not peaceful, viable, technologically sustainable, or socially acceptable.

The foundations of a sustainable human order inhere in an emancipatory conversation that is structured around enduring person-to-person, person-to-society, person-to-nature, and society-to-socio-sphere relationships. The challenge for the new millennium lies in building a human guidance system, or normative compact, based on optimal synergy among individual aspirations, community activism, market transactions, government activities, and "communities of communities" reaching right up to the United Nations and beyond. In theory and practice, this calls for a "back-to-forth" dynamic of processual change in which local micro-processes and national economic orders are simultaneously "decoupled" from and "embed-ded" in overarching supranational relationships.

This entails a dialectical process of change in which the development discourse is pushed in two directions at the same time. One is predicated on the idea that creation of relatively stable and self-sufficient local communities is by and large preferable to global integration into a single and homogeneous market. But, this should not be construed as a call for an alternative utopia or perfect society. Rather, it forms part of a more embracing humanitarian plea for symbiotic regimes based on wholesome, decent, and pleasant lives. The "bottom up" approach is not coterminous with autarchy, but is consonant with an expanded notion of "assisted self-help" or a reshaping of decision-making based on meaningful partnership. What is envisaged is a coordinated process whereby people are assisted to develop and manage their own resources through networks of local communities, grassroots organizations, NGOs, governments, and aid donors.

In the latter context, complementary changes will be needed "from bottom to top," that is, in the structure and functioning of supranational institutions and corresponding philosophies governing trade, aid, and finance. A critical task inheres in redefining the role of the global public sector (GPS) and its constituent organs, such as the United Nations (UN) system and the Bretton Woods institutions (BWIs) – the IMF, World Bank, and WTO. In its original Charter, the UN was charged with two broad but related mandates. It was expected to become the lynchpin of global economic management, and was given the responsibility of channeling development aid to poor "emerging nations" – a "Marshall Plan for the Third World." From the very inception, however, a dichotomous relationship was established and concretized between two more or less autonomous subsystems of the overarching suprasystem.

The BWIs appropriated the responsibility of what was perceived as the "hard core" of development: the provenance of money, finance, and currencies; and economic strategy, trade, and balance payments. Other agencies of the UN system were allocated the "soft" underbelly: peacekeeping, emergencies, food security, health, education, and environment. Over the years, this division of labor has solidified. The BWIs have maintained their ascendant and preeminent position due to the differential impacts of power politics, ideology, and financial prowess. At the same time, the UN has been constantly perceived as a counter-revolutionary deviant from the straight and narrow path of the dominant neo-liberal paradigm or "Washington consensus."

Even more telling, this attitude has translated into a lack of political and financial support for the UN, resulting in a vicious circle in which inadequate support and the unequal distribution of resources between the two subsystems have tended to cumulate over time. This has culminated in an impasse in which there is adequate finance, but very little democracy in the BWIs, and democracy but no finance in the UN. Furthermore, the jaundiced milieu remains one in which poor countries have very little or no confidence in the weighted voting system of the BWIs, because creditor nations of the industrial North control the overwhelming majority of the votes. On the other hand, the rich nations have very little confidence in the UN, which is still considered a veritable "talking shop."

A widespread feeling is that the BWIs have failed to implement their mandate of overseeing the management of global capital and instituting a system that would bring sustained economic progress, full employment, stable prices and exchange rates, and beneficial conditions of trade. Hence, the new movement for global justice has been calling for a substantial revision of the Bretton Woods policy paradigm as a means of making it more synergistic with the aspirations of the majority of humanity for a better quality of life and equal opportunity to participate in the market system. Inherent in this revisionism, or emerging "post-Washington consensus," is the imperative of imbuing the lending programs of the IMF and World Bank with a new perspective based on pluralism of interpretive and policy models rather than dogged reliance on a uniform, and arguably outmoded, economistic model of stabilization and adjustment.

In other words, this requires a retreat from the entrenched proclivity of imposing onerous conditionalities based on devaluation, belt-tightening, and deregulation irrespective of the humanitarian needs of borrowing countries. The proposed paradigm shift is from a preoccupation with economic rationality toward emphasis on the extent to which debtor nations manage to achieve actual performance based on human and social indicators. The BWIs may also need to revisit their original Articles of Agreement, which projected a system that would enable countries to adjust their external payments without resort to deflation or curbs on domestic spending and human welfare. The vision of John Maynard Keynes, a primary architect of the Bretton Woods system, is apposite to this claim. He presented a case for a set of institutions of a "purely technical and non-political character." As stated in a note of April 1943 (reprinted in his *Collected Economic Writings*, Vol. 26):

> We need a central institution of a purely technical and non-political character, to aid and support other international institutions concerned with planning and regulation of the world's economic life. More generally, we need a means of reassurance to a troubled world, by which any country whose own affairs are conducted with due prudence is relieved of anxiety for causes which are not of its own making, concerning its ability to meet its international liabilities.

In the case of the UN system per se, since it remains the foremost supranational vanguard of the global public good, justice, and cosmopolitan value standards, a crucial need still exists for strengthening its financial base as a means of enhancing its support for humanitarian development. In this context, *Our Global Neighborhood* (1995), the report of the Commission on Global Governance, projects a grand vision of "global civil society" through creation of a new Economic Security Council. Besides providing global leadership on human security, it would be concerned with the overall state of the world economy and promotion of sustainable human development. One of its major tasks would be to ensure consistency among the policy goals of international organizations. At the same time, it would help to promote a consensus-building dialogue among international actors about evolution of the global economic system, while providing a reinvigorated forum for the new forces in the world economy, including regional organizations, the private sector, and civil society.

Bibliography

Adams, Edwin. *A Society Fit for Human Beings*. Albany, NY: State University of New York Press, 1997.

Adams, John. "Peasant Rationality: Individuals, Groups, Cultures," *World Development*, vol. 14 (1986), pp. 273-82.

Adorno, T., and M. Horkheimer. *Dialectic and the Enlightenment*. New York: Herder and Herder, 1972.

Ake, Claude. *Democracy and Development in Africa*. Washington, DC: Brookings Institution, 1996.

Amin, Samir. *Accumulation on a World Scale*. New York: Monthly Review Press, 1974.

_____. *Uneven Development*. New York: Monthly Review Press, 1976.

_____. *Maldevelopment*. London: Zed Books, 1990.

Argyle, Michael. *The Psychology of Happiness*. London: Methuen, 1987.

Arthur, J. and W. Shaw. *Justice and Economic Distribution*. Englewood Cliffs, NJ: Prentice Hall, 1991.

Bardhan, Pranab. "Alternative Approaches to Development Economics," in H. Chenery and T.N. Srinivasan, eds. *Handbook of Development Economics*, Vol. 1, Amsterdam: North Holland, 1988, pp. 39-71.

_____. *Economic Theory and Agrarian Institutions*. Oxford: Oxford University Press, 1989.

_____. "Distributive Conflicts, Collective Action, and Institutional Economics," in G. Meier and J. Stiglitz, eds. *Frontiers of Development Economics*. New York: Oxford University Press, 2001, 269-90

Barry, Brian. *Sociologists, Economists and Democracy*. London: Collier-Macmillan, 1970.

Bates, Robert. "Contra Contractarianism: Some Reflections on the New Institutionalism," *Politics and Society*, vol. 16 (1988), pp. 387-401.

_____. "Capital, Kinship and Conflict: The Structuring Influence of Capital in Kinship Societies," *Canadian Journal of African Studies*, vol. 24 (1990), pp. 151-64.

Bauer, Peter. *Equality, the Third World and Economic Delusion*. London: Weidenfeld and Nicolson, 1981.

Becker, Gary. *The Economic Approach to Human Behavior*. Chicago: University of Chicago Press, 1976.

Beitz, Charles. "Global Egalitarianism: Can We Make A Case?" *Dissent*, vol. 26 (1979), pp. 59-68.

_____. "Cosmopolitan Ideals and National Sentiment," *Journal of Philosophy*, vol. 80 (1983), pp. 591-600.

Ben-Porath, Y. "The F-Connection: Families, Friends, Firms, and Organization of Exchange," *Population and Development Review*, vol. 6 (1990), pp. 1-29.

Bentham, Jeremy. *An Introduction to the Principles of Morals and Legislation*. London: Athlone Press, 1970[1789].

Berger, P. and T. Luckmann. *The Social Construction of Reality*. New York: Anchor Books, 1967.

Berlin, Isaiah. "Equality," in F. Olafson, ed. *Justice and Social Policy*. Englewood Cliffs, NJ: Prentice Hall, 1961.

_____. *Four Essays on Liberty*. Oxford: Oxford University Press, 1969.

Bernstein, Richard. *Beyond Objectivism and Relativism*. Philadelphia, PA: University of Pennsylvania Press, 1988.

Bhatnagar, G. and A. Williams. *Participatory Development and the World Bank*. Washington, DC: The World Bank, 1994.

Biggs, T. and P. Srivasta. "Structural Aspects of Manufacturing in Sub-Saharan Africa," *World Bank Discussion Paper No. 346*. Washington, DC: The World Bank, 1996.

Bohman, James. *New Philosophy of Social Science*. Cambridge, MA: MIT Press, 1991.

Boserup, Ester. *Women's Role in Economic Development*. New York: St. Martin's Press, 1970.

Boulding, Kenneth. *The Economy of Love and Fear*. Belmont, CA: Wadsworth Publishing Co., 1973a.

_____. "Equality and Conflict," *Annals of the American Academy of Political and Social Science*, vol. 409 (1973b), pp. 1-8.

Bouvier, L., H. Shyrock, and H. Henderson. *International Migration*. Washington, DC: Population Reference Bureau, 1977.

Brown, D. *Human Universals*. Philadelphia, PA: Temple University Press, 1991.

Bruton, Henry. *On the Search for Well-Being*. Ann Arbor, MI: University of Michigan Press, 1997.

Bryant, Ralph. *International Financial Intermediation*. Washington, DC: Brookings Institution, 1987.

Buchanan, James. *Liberty, State and Market.* New York: New York University Press, 1986.

Bury, J. *The Idea of Progress.* London: Macmillan, 1920.

Buvinic, M. "Women's Issues in Third World Poverty: A Policy Analysis," in M. Buvinic, M. Lycette, and W. McGreevy, eds. *Women and Poverty in the Third World.* Baltimore, MD: Johns Hopkins University Press, 1983, pp. 14-31.

_____. "Projects for Women in the Third World: Explaining their Missing Behavior," *World Development,* vol. 14 (1986), pp. 653-64.

Caldwell, Bruce. "Clarifying Popper," *Journal of Economic Literature,* vol. 29 (1991), pp. 1-33.

Cantril, Hadley. *The Pattern of Human Concerns.* New Brunswick, NJ: Rutgers University Press, 1965.

Castells, Manuel. "The Informational Economy and the New International Division of Labor," in M. Carnoy et al., eds. *The New Global Economy in the Information Age.* University Park, PA: Pennsylvania State University Press, 1993.

Castells, Manuel, and Alejandro Portes. "World Underneath," in A. Portes et al., eds. *The Informal Economy.* Baltimore, MD: Johns Hopkins University Press, 1989.

Chambers, Robert. 1983. *Rural Development.* London: Longmans.

_____. *Whose Reality Counts: Putting the Last First.* London: Intermediate Technology Publications, 1997.

Chenery, Hollis. "A Structural Approach to Development Policy," *American Economic Review,* vol. 65 (1975), pp. 310-16.

Cheung, Stephen. "Economic Organization and Transaction Costs," in J. Eatwell, M. Milgate, and P. Newman, eds. *The New Palgrave: Allocation, Information, and Markets.* New York: Norton, 1989, pp. 77-82.

Chirot, D. *Modern Tyrants.* Princeton, NJ: Princeton University Press, 1994.

Codevilla, A. *The Character of Nations.* New York: Basic Books, 1997.

Cohen, A. *The Symbolic Construction of Community.* London: Tavistock Publications, 1985.

Cole, Ken. *Understanding Economics.* London: Pluto Press, 1995

Coleman, James. "Equality," in J. Eatwell, M. Milgate, and P. Newman, eds. *The New Palgrave: Social Economics.* New York: Norton, 1989, pp. 49-57.

_____. *Foundations of Social Theory*. Cambridge, MA: Harvard University Press, 1990.

Collier, P., and J. Gunning. "Explaining African Performance," *Journal of Economic Literature*, vol. 37 (1999), pp. 64-111.

Cornia, G., R. Jolly, and F. Stewart. *Adjustment with a Human Face*. London: Oxford University Press, 1987.

Crook, John. *The Evolution of Human Consciousness*. Oxford: Oxford University Press, 1980.

Daly, Herman, and John Cobb, Jr. *For the Common Good*. Boston, MA: Beacon Press, 1989.

Dasgupta, Partha. *An Inquiry into Well-being and Destitution*. Oxford: Clarendon Press, 1993.

David, Wilfred. "Development from Below: Aspects of Local Government and Finance in a Developing Economy," in W. David, ed. *Public Finance, Planning, and Economic Development: Essays in Honor of Ursula Hicks*. London: Macmillan, 1973.

_____. *The IMF Policy Paradigm*. New York: Praeger, 1985.

_____. *Conflicting Paradigms in the Economics of Developing Nations*. New York: Praeger, 1986.

_____. *Political Economy of Economic Policy*. New York: Praeger, 1988.

_____. *The Conversation of Economic Development*. New York: M.E. Sharpe, 1997a.

_____. "The Washington Consensus and Prospects for Authentic Development in the Caribbean," in R. Palmer, ed. *Repositioning of US-Caribbean Relations in the New World Order*. Westport, CT: Praeger, 1997b.

David, Wilfred, and Peggy David. "Resolving the African Development Cachexia: Empowerment of the People," in F. Shams, ed. *State and Society in Africa*, Lanham, MD: University Press of America, 1995.

Davidson, Paul. *Money and the Real World*. London: Macmillan, 1978.

_____. "Post Keynesian Economics: Solving the Crisis in Economic Theory." *The Public Interest*, Special Edition (1980), pp. 151-73.

DeBreu, Gerard. *Theory of Value*. New Haven, CT: Yale University Press, 1959.

_____. "The Mathematization of Economic Theory," *American Economic Review*, 81(1991), pp. 1-7.

de Soto, Hernando. *Another Path*. New York: Harper and Row, 1989.

_____. *The Mystery of Capital*. New York: Basic Books, 2000.

de Tocqueville, Alexis. *Democracy in America*. London: Oxford University Press, 1946.

de Waal, Francis. *Peacemaking Among Primates*. Cambridge, MA: Harvard University Press, 1989.

_____. *Good Natured: The Origins of Right and Wrong in Humans and Other Animals*. Cambridge, MA: Harvard University Press, 1996.

Dewey, John. *The Quest for Certainty*. New York; Minton, Balch, and Co., 1929.

Diamond, Jared. *Guns, Germ, and Steel*. New York: Norton, 1999.

Domar, Evsey. "The Causes of Slavery and Serfdom: A Hypothesis," *Journal of Economic History*, vol. 30 (1970), pp. 18-32.

Donahue, T. "International Labor Standards: The Perspective of Labor," in US Department of Labor. *International Labor Standards and Global Economic Integration: Proceedings of Symposium*. Washington, DC: US Department of Labor, 1994.

Downie, Robert. "Moral Philosophy," in J. Eatwell, M. Milgate, and P. Newman, eds. *The New Palgrave: The Invisible Hand*. New York: Norton, 1989, pp. 213-22.

Dreze, Jean, and Amartya Sen. *Hunger and Public Action*. Oxford: Clarendon Press, 1989.

Dummett, Michael. *On Immigration and Refugees*. London: Routledge, 2001.

Durning, Alan. "Action at the Grassroots," *Worldwatch Paper No. 88*. Washington, DC: Worldwatch Institute, 1989.

_____. *How Much Is Enough*. London: Earthscan, 1992.

Dworkin, Ronald. *Taking Rights Seriously*. London: Gerald Duckworth, 1978.

Easterly, William. *The Middle Class Consensus and Economic Development*. Washington, DC: The World Bank (processed), 2000.

Elson, D., ed. *Male Bias in the Development Process*. Manchester, UK: Manchester University Press, 1991.

Elster, Jon. *The Cement of Society*. Cambridge: Cambridge University Press, 1989.

Engels, Friedrich. *The Origins of Family, Private Property and the State*. New York: International Publishers, 1972 [1884].

Esman, Milton. *Management Decisions of Development*. West Hartford, CT: Kumarian Press, 1991.

Esman, Milton, and Norman Uphoff. *Local Organizations*. Ithaca, NY: Cornell University Press, 1984.

Etzione, Amitai. *The Immodest Agenda*. New York: McGraw Hill, 1983.

_____. *The Spirit of Community*. New York: Crown, 1993.

Evans, Peter. *Embedded Autonomy*. Princeton, NJ: Princeton University Press, 1995.

Fieldhouse, David. *Black Africa 1945-1960*. London: Alien and Unwin, 1986.

Forsythe, David. *Humanitarian Politics*. Baltimore, MD: Johns Hopkins University Press, 1977.

Frank, Andre Gunder. *Capitalism and Underdevelopment in Latin America*. New York: Monthly Review Press, 1967.

_____. *Crisis in the Third World*. London: Heinemann, 1981.

Freeman, A., R. Haveman, and A. Kneese. *The Economics of Environmental Policy*. New York: Wiley, 1973.

Freeman, Richard. "Labor Market Institutions and Policies: Help or Hindrance to Development?" in World Bank. *Proceedings of the World Bank Annual Conference on Development Economics*. Washington, DC: The World Bank, 1992, 117-44.

Fukuyama, Francis. *The End of History and the Last Man*. New York: Free Press, 1991.

_____. *Trust*. New York: Free Press, 1995.

Furtado, Celso. *Development and Underdevelopment*. Berkeley, CA: University of California Press 1965.

_____. *Accumulation and Development*. Oxford: Martin Robertson, 1983.

Gadamer, Hans-Georg. "The Problem of Historical Consciousness," in P. Rabinow and W. Sullivan, eds. *Interpretive Social Science: A Reader*. Berkeley, CA: University of California Press, 1979.

Galbraith, John Kenneth. *The Affluent Society*. Boston, MA: Houghton Mifflin, 1958.

GATT [General Agreement on Tariffs and Trade]. *Analysis of the Proposed Uruguay Round Agreement, with Particular Emphasis on Aspects of Interest to Developing Countries*. Geneva: GATT Secretariat, 1993.

Geertz, Clifford. "The Rotating Credit Association: A 'Middle Rung' in Development." *Economic Development and Cultural Change*, vol. 10 (1962), pp. 240-63.

_____. *The Interpretation of Cultures*. New York: Basic Books, 1973.

Georgescu-Roegen, Nicholas. *The Entropy Law and Economic Process*. Cambridge, MA: Harvard University Press, 1971.

Gerschenkron, Alexander. *Economic Backwardness in Historical Perspective*. Cambridge, MA: Harvard University Press, 1962.

Giddens, Anthony. *Critical Problems in Social Theory*. Berkeley, CA: University of California Press, 1979.

_____. *The Constitution of Society*. Cambridge: Polity Press, 1984.

_____. "Structuration Theory: Past, Present, and Future," in C. Bryant and D. Nary, eds. *Theory of Structuration*. London: Routledge, 1991, pp. 201-21.

_____. *Runaway World*. London: Profile Books, 2002.

Gilpin, Robert. *War and Change in World Politics*. Cambridge: Cambridge University Press, 1981.

_____. *The Political Economy of International Relations*. Princeton, NJ: Princeton University Press, 1987.

Goldin, I., O. Knudsen, and D. van der Mensbrugghe. *Trade Liberalization: Global Economic Implications*. Paris: OECD, 1993.

Goode, William. "Individual Choice and Social Order," in J. Short, Jr., ed. *The Social Fabric*. Berkeley, CA: Sage, 1986.

Gordon, Wendell. *Economics from an Institutional Viewpoint*. Austin, TX: University of Texas Press, 1973.

Goulet, Denis. *The Cruel Choice*. New York: Atheneum, 1978.

_____. "Development as Liberation: Policy Lessons from Case Studies," *World Development*, vol. 7 (1979), pp. 556-66.

Gran, Guy. *Development by People*. New York: Praeger, 1983.

Granovetter, M. "Economic Action and Social Structure: A Theory of Embeddedness," *American Journal of Sociology*, vol. 91 (1985), pp. 481-510.

Gray, John. *False Dawn: The Delusion of Global Capitalism*. London: Granta Books, 1998.

Greif, Avner. "Institutions and International Trade: Lessons from the Commercial Revolution," *American Economic Review*, 82 (1992), pp. 128-33.

Grene, Marjorie. "Martin Heidegger," *Encyclopaedia of Philosophy*, vol. 3&4 (1967), pp. 459-65.

Griffin, J. *Well-Being*. Oxford: Clarendon Press, 1986.

Grindle, Merilee. "In Quest of the Political: The Political Economy of Development Policymaking," in G. Meier and J. Stiglitz, eds.

Frontiers of Development Economics. New York: Oxford University Press, 2001, pp. 345-80.

Group of Green Economists. *Ecological Economics.* London: Zed Books, 1992.

GTZ [German Agency for Technical Cooperation]. *Beyond the Toolkit.* Eschborn: GTZ, 1998.

Gudeman. S. "Sketches, Qualms, and Other Thoughts on Intellectual Property Rights," in S. Brush and S. Stabinsky, eds. *Valuing Local Knowledge.* Washington, DC: Island Press, 1996, pp. 102-21.

Habermas, Jurgen. *Knowledge and Human Interests.* Boston, MA: Beacon Press, 1973.

_____. "Reason and the Rationalization of Society," in *The Theory of Communicative Action*, Vol. 1. Boston, MA: Beacon Press, 1984.

_____. "Lifeworld and System," in *The Theory of Communicative Action*, Vol. 2. Boston, MA: Beacon Press, 1987.

_____. *Justification and Application.* Cambridge: Polity Press, 1993.

_____. *The Inclusion of the Other.* Cambridge: Polity Press, 1998.

Hadenius, A., and F. Uggla. "Making Civil Society Work, Promoting Democratic Development: What States and Donors Do?" *World Development*, vol. 24 (1996), pp. 1621-39.

Haq, Mahbub ul. *Reflections on Human Development.* New York:Oxford University Press, 1995.

Hardin, Russell. *Collective Action.* Baltimore, MD: Johns Hopkins University Press, 1982.

Harsanyi, J. *Essays on Ethics, Social Behavior, and Scientific Explanation.* Dordrecht: Reidel, 1977.

Hayek, Friedrich. *The Constitution of Liberty.* London: Routledge, 1960.

_____. "The Mirage of Social Justice," in *Law, Legislation, and Liberty.* Vol. 2. Chicago: University of Chicago Press, 1976.

Hayter, Teresa. *Open Borders.* London: Pluto Press, 2001.

Hazen, R., and M. Singer. *The Unanswered Questions at the Frontiers of Science.* New York: Anchor/Doubleday, 1997.

Herrick, B., and C. Kindleberger. *Economic Development.* New York: McGraw Hill, 1983.

Hicks, John. *A Theory of Economic History.* Oxford: Clarendon Press, 1969

Hicks, Ursula. *Development from Below.* Oxford: Oxford University Press, 1961.

Higgins, Benjamin. "Economic Development and Cultural Change: Seamless Web or Patchwork Quilt?" in M. Nash, ed. *Essays in Economic Development and Cultural Change in Honor of Bert F. Hoselitz.* Chicago: University of Chicago Press, 1977.

Hirsch, Fred. *The Social Limits to Growth.* Cambridge, MA: Harvard University Press, 1976.

Hirschleifer, Jack. "Expanding the Domain of Economics," *American Economic Review,* vol. 75 (1985), pp. 53-68.

Hirschman, Albert. *Exit, Voice, and Loyalty.* Cambridge, MA: Harvard University Press, 1970.

_____. *A Bias for Hope.* New Haven, CT: Yale University Press, 1971.

_____. *Essays in Trespassing.* Cambridge: Cambridge University Press, 1981.

_____. *Getting Along Collectively.* Oxford: Pergamon Press, 1984a.

_____. "Against Parsimony: Three Easy Ways of Complicating Some Categories of Economic Discourse," *American Economic Review,* vol. 74 (1984b), pp. 89-96.

_____. *Rival Views of Market Society.* Cambridge, MA: Harvard University Press, 1992.

Hoff, K., A. Braverman, and J. Stiglitz., eds. *Economics of Rural Organizations.* New York: Oxford University Press, 1993.

Hopkins, Anthony. "The World Bank in Africa: Historical Reflections on the African Present," *World Development,* vol. 14 (1986), pp. 1473-87.

Horkheimer, Max. *The Eclipse of Reason.* London: Oxford University Press, 1947.

_____. *Critique of Instrumental Reason.* New York: Seabury Press, 1974.

_____. *Critical Theory: Select Essays.* New York: Herder and Herder, 1982.

Hunt, Lynn. *The French Revolution and Human Rights.* New York: St. Martin's Press, 1996.

Huntington, Samuel. *Political Order in Changing Societies.* New Haven, CT: Yale University Press, 1968.

_____. "The Clash of Civilizations," *Foreign Affairs,* vol. 72 (1993), pp. 22-49.

Huntington, Samuel, and Joan Nelson. *No Easy Choice.* Cambridge, MA: Harvard University Press, 1986.

Hyden, Goran. *Beyond Ujamaa in Tanzania.* London: Heinemann, 1980.

_____. "African Social Structure and Economic Development," in R. Berg and J. Whitaker, eds. *Strategies for African Development*. Berkeley, CA: University of California Press, 1986, pp. 52-80.

IFAD [International Fund for Agricultural Development]. *The State of World Rural Poverty*. Rome: IFAD, 1992.

ILO [International Labor Organization]. *Wages, Labor and their Impact on Adjustment, Employment, and Growth*. Geneva: ILO, 1990.

_____. *Multinationals and Employment*. Geneva: ILO, 1993.

_____. *World Employment 1996/97*. Geneva: ILO, 1997.

_____. *Child Labor in Africa*. Geneva: ILO, 1998a.

_____. *Promoting Gender Equality at Work*. Geneva: ILO, 1998b.

_____. *World Employment Report 1998/99*. Geneva: ILO, I999a.

_____. *New Challenges for Employment Policy*. Geneva: ILO, 1999b.

Inter-American Development Bank. *Facing Up to Inequality in Latin America*. Baltimore, MD: Johns Hopkins University Press, 1998.

Isham, I., D. Nayaran, and L. Pritchett. "Does Participation Improve Performance?: Establishing Causation with Subjective Data," *World Bank Economic Review*, vol. 92 (1995), pp. 175-200.

James, William. *Pragmatism*. Cambridge, MA: Harvard University Press, 1907.

Kant, Immanuel. *Groundwork of the Metaphysics of Morals*. London: Hutchison, 1948 [1785].

_____. *Kant's Political Writings*. Cambridge: Cambridge University Press, 1970.

Kaplan, Robert. "The Coming Anarchy," *The Atlantic Monthly*, February 1994, pp. 44-76.

Kazmin, A. "Gandhi and the Milk of Indian Self-Reliance," *Financial Times*, August 24, 2000, p. 8.

Keohane, Robert. *After Hegemony*. Princeton, NJ: Princeton University Press, 1984.

Keohane, Bobert, and Joesph Nye, Jr. *Power and Interdependence*. Boston, MA: Scott Foresman, 1989.

Keynes, John Maynard. *The General Theory of Employment, Interest and Money*. London: Macmillan, 1936.

_____. "Shaping the Post-War World: Bretton Woods and Reparations," in D. Moggridge, ed. *The Collected Writings of John Maynard Keynes*, Vol. 26. London: Macmillan, 1980.

Kindleberger, Charles. *The International Economic Order*. Cambridge, MA: MIT Press, 1988.

Kornai, Janos. *Anti-Equilibrium*. Amsterdam: North Holland, 1971.

Krasner, Stephen. *International Regimes*. Ithaca, NY: Cornell University Press, 1984.

Krueger, Anne. "Government Failure in Development," *Journal of Economic Perspectives*, vol. 4 (1990), pp. 9-23.

Kuhn, Thomas. *The Structure of Scientific Revolutions*. Chicago: University of Chicago Press, 1970.

Kuttner, Robert. *Everything for Sale*. New York: Knopf, 1997.

Kuznets, Simon. *Modern Economic Growth*. New Haven, CT: Yale University Press, 1966.

Lakatos, Imré. "Falsification and the Methodology of Scientific Research Programmes," in I. Lakatos and A. Musgrave, eds. *Criticism and the Growth of Knowledge*. Cambridge: Cambridge University Press, 1976, pp. 91-196.

Lal, Deepak. *The Poverty of Development Economics*. London: Institute of International Affairs, 1983.

____. *Unintended Consequences*. Cambridge, MA: MIT Press, 1999.

Landes, David. "Why Are We So Rich and They So Poor?" *American Economic Review*, vol. 80 (1990), pp. 1-13.

____. *The Wealth and Poverty of Nations*. New York: Norton, 1998.

Lange, Oskar. *Wholes and Parts*. Oxford: Pergamon Press, 1965.

Lappe, F., and P. Dubois. "From Devolved to Involved Community," in *Annual Report of the Johnson Foundation*. Minneapolis, MN: The Johnson Foundation. 1995, pp. 7-10.

Lasch, CHristopher. *The Revolt of the Elites and the Betrayal of Democracy*. New York: Norton, 1995.

Lastarria-Cornheil, S. "The Impact of Privatization on Gender and Property Rights in Africa," *World Development*, vol. 25 (1997), pp. 1317-33.

Latsis, Spiro. *Method and Appraisal in Economics*. Cambridge: Cambridge University Press, 1976.

Levins, R., and R. Lewontin. *The Dialectical Biologist*. Cambridge, MA: Harvard University Press, 1985.

Lewis, W. Arthur. *The Theory of Economic Growth*. London: Alien and Unwin, 1955.

Linklater, Andrew. *The Transformation of Political Community*. Cambridge: Polity Press, 1998.

Lipton, Michael. "Editorial: Poverty - Are There Holes in the Consensus?" *World Development*, vol. 25 (1997), pp. 1003-1007.

List, Friedrich. *The National System of Political Economy*. London: Longman, Green, 1904 [1841].

Loevinger, June. *Ego Development*. San Francisco, CA: Jossey Bass, 1976.

Loury, Glen. "A Dynamic Theory of Social Income Differences," in P. Wallace and A. Lamond, eds. *Women, Minorities and Employment Discrimination*. Lexington, MA: Lexington Books, 1977.

_____. "Discrimination in the Post-Civil Rights Era: Beyond Market Interactions," *Journal of Economic Perspectives*, vol. 12 (1998) pp. 117-26.

Lovelock, James. *Gaia*. Oxford: Oxford University Press, 1979.

_____. *The Ages of Gaia*. Oxford: Oxford University Press, 1988.

Lukes, Steven. "Power and Authority," in T. Bottomore and R. Nisbet, eds. *A History of Sociological Analysis*. New York: Basic Books, 1978, pp. 633-76.

MacIntyre, Alasdair. *After Virtue*. Notre Dame, IN: University of Notre Dame Press, 1981.

Macpherson, C.B. *The Rise and Fall of Economic Justice and Other Essays*. Oxford: Oxford University Press, 1987.

Macy, J. *Dharma and Development*. West Hartford, CT: Kumarian Press, 1985.

Maddison, Angus. *Monitoring the World Economy, 1820-1992*. Paris: OECD Development Center, 1995.

Manasian, David. "A Survey of Human Rights." *The Economist*, December 5, No. 62 (1998), pp. 1-16.

Marcuse, H. *One-Dimensional Man*. Boston, MA: Beacon Press, 1964.

_____. *Negations*. Boston, MA: Beacon.Press, 1968.

Markandya, A., and D. Pearce. "Development, the Environment, and the Social Discount Rate," *The World Bank Research Observer*, vol. 6 (1991), pp. 137-52.

Marshall, T.H. *Class, Citizenship and Social Development*. New York: Doubleday, 1964.

Maruyama, M. "Toward Human Futuristics: Trans-epistemic Process." *Dialectica*, vol. 26 (1972), pp. 156-83.

_____. "Logic, Cultures and Individuals," *The UNESCO Courier*, vol. 10 (1996), pp. 31-35.

Maslow, Abraham. *Motivation and Personality*. New York: Harper and Row, 1954.

_____. *Toward a Psychology of Being*. New York: Van Nostrand, 1962.

Mason, E., and R. Asher. *The World Bank Since Bretton Woods.* Washington, DC: Brookings Institution, 1973.

Max-Neef, Manfred. *From Outside Looking In: The Experiences in Barefoot Economics.* Uppsala: Dag Hammarskjold Foundation, 1982.

Mearsheimer, John. *The Tragedy of Great Power Politics.* New York: Norton, 2001.

Meier, G., and J. Stiglitz., eds. *Frontiers in Development Economics.* New York: Oxford University Press, 2001.

Merton, R. *The Sociology of Science.* Chicago: University of Chicago Press, 1973.

Micklethwait, J., and A. Wooldridge. *A Future Perfect.* New York: Crown, 2000.

Milanovic, Branco. *Income Inequality and Poverty during the Transition from Planned to Market Economy.* Washington, DC: The World Bank, 1998.

Moore, Barrington. *Social Origins of Dictatorship and Democracy.* Boston, MA: Beacon Press, 1966.

Moore, G.E. *Principia Ethica.* Cambridge: Cambridge University Press, 1903.

Morgenstern, Oskar. "Thirteen Critical Points in Contemporary Economic Theory: An Interpretation," *Journal of Economic Literature*, vol. 10 (1972), pp. 1163-89.

Morishima, Michio. *Why Japan Has Succeeded?* Cambridge: Cambridge University Press, 1982.

Mosca, G. *The Ruling Class.* New York: McGraw Hill, 1939 [1896].

Moser, Carolyn. *Gender Planning and Development Theory, Practice and Training.* London: Routledge, 1993.

Myrdal, Gunnar. *Asian Drama.* New York: Pantheon, 1968.

Nair, Kusum. *Blossoms in the Dust.* New York: Praeger, 1966.

____. *The Lonely Farrow.* Ann Arbor, MI: University of Michigan Press, 1969.

____. *In Defense of the Irrational Peasant.* Chicago: University of Chicago Press, 1979.

Nardin, Terry. *Law, Morality and the Relations of States.* Princeton, NJ: Princeton University Press, 1983.

National Research Council. *The New Americans.* Washington, DC: National Academy Press, 1997.

Neufeld, Mark. *The Restructuring of International Relations.* Cambridge: Cambridge University Press, 1995.

North, Douglass. *Structure and Change in Economic History*. New York: Norton, 1981

_____. *Institutions, Institutional Change and Economic Development*. Cambridge: Cambridge University Press, 1990.

_____. "Institutions," *Journal of Economic Perspectives*, vol. 5 (1991), pp. 97-112.

Nozick, Robert. *Anarchy, State, and Utopia*. New York: Basic Books, 1974.

Nussbaum, Martha. *Fragility of Goodness*. Cambridge: Cambridge University Press, 1986.

Nye, Joseph. *The Paradox of American Power*. New York: Oxford University Press, 2002.

Odum, E. *Fundamentals of Ecology*. Philadelphia, PA: Saunders College Publishing, 1971.

OECD [Organization of Economic Cooperation and Development]. *Open Markets Matter*. Paris: OECD, 1998.

Okun, Arthur. *Equality and Efficiency: The Big Trade-Off.* Washington, DC: Brookings Institution, 1975.

Olson, Mancur. *The Logic of Collective Action*. Cambridge, MA: Harvard University Press, 1965.

_____. *The Rise and Decline of Nations*. New Haven, CT: Yale University Press, 1982.

_____. "Collective Action," in J. Eatwell, M. Milgate, and P. Newman, eds. *The New Palgrave; The Invisible Hand*. New York: Norton, 1989, pp. 61-69.

Pagden, A. *Peoples and Empires*. New York: Modern Library, 2001.

Pareto, V. *The Mind and Society*. New York: Dover, 1963.

Passmore, John. *The Perfectibility of Man*. London: Duckworth, 1970.

Patel, S. "Can the Intellectual Property Rights System Serve the Interests of Indigenous Knowledge?" in S. Brush and D. Stabinsky, eds. *Valuing Local Knowledge*. Washington, DC: Island Press, 1996, pp. 305-22.

Patterson, Orlando. *Freedom and the Making of Western Culture*. New York: Basic Books, 1991.

Pogge, Thomas. *Realizing Rawls*. Ithaca, NY: Cornell University Press, 1989.

Polanyi, Karl. *The Great Transformation*. Boston, MA: Beacon Press, 1944.

Popkin, S. *The Rational Peasant*. Berkeley, CA: University of California Press, 1979.

Popper, Karl. *The Logic of Scientific Discovery*. New York: Harper and Row, 1959.
____. *Conjectures and Refutations*. New York: Basic Books, 1962.
____. *Objective Knowledge*. Oxford: Clarendon Press, 1972.
Porter, Michael. *The Competitive Advantage of Nations*. New York: Free Press, 1990.
Powelson, John. *The Moral Economy*. Ann Arbor, MI: University of Michigan Press, 2000.
Pred, Allan. "Out of Bounds and Undisciplined: Social Inquiry and the Current Moment of Danger," *Social Research*, vol. 82 (1995) pp. 1065-91.
Putnam, Robert. *Making Democracy Work*. Princeton, NJ: Princeton University Press, 1993.
____. *Bowling Alone*. New York: Basic Books, 2000.
Ranis, G., F. Stewart, and A. Ramirez. "Economic Growth and Human Development," *World Development*, vol. 28 (2000), pp. 197-215.
Rawls, John. *A Theory of Justice*. Cambridge, MA: Harvard University Press, 1971.
____. *Political Liberalism*. New York: Columbia University Press, 1993
____. *The Law of Peoples*. Cambridge, MA: Harvard University Press, 1999.
____. *Justice as Fairness: A Restatement*. [Ed. E. Kelly]. Cambridge, MA: Harvard University Press, 2001.
Repetto, Robert. *World Enough and Time*. New Haven, CT: Yale University Press, 1986.
Repetto, Robert., ed. *The Global Possible*. New Haven, CT: Yale University Press, 1995.
Rifkin, Jeremy. *The End of Work*. New York: Putnam, 1995.
Rorty, Richard. *Objectivism, Relativism and Truth*. Cambridge: Cambridge University Press, 1991.
Rose. S. *Lifelines*. London: Allen Lane, 1997.
Ross, W. D. ed., *The Works of Aristotle Translated into English*. Oxford: Oxford University Press, 1925.
Rostow, W. W. *The Stages of Economic Growth*. Cambridge: Cambridge University Press, 1960.
____. *Politics and the Stages of Growth*. Cambridge: Cambridge University Press, 1971.
____. *Theories of Economic Growth from David Hume to the Present*. New York: Oxford University Press, 1990.

342 Bibliography

Rubenstein, R., and P. Crocker. "Challenging Huntington," *Foreign Policy*, vol. 96 (1994), pp. 113-28.

Samuelson, Paul. *Foundations of Economic Analysis*. Cambridge, MA: Harvard University Press, 1983.

Sartre, Jean-Paul. "Introduction," in Frantz Fanon. *Wretched of the Earth*. New York: Grove Weidenfeld, 1961.

Schultz, Theodore. *Transforming Traditional Agriculture*. New Haven, CT: Yale University Press, 1964.

_____. "Nobel Lecture: The Economics of Being Poor," *Journal of Political Economy*, vol. 88 (1980), pp. 639-51.

Schutz, Alfred. *The Phenomenology of the Social World*. Evanston, IL: Northwestern University Press, 1962.

Scitovsky, Tibor. *The Joyless Economy*. Oxford: Oxford University Press, 1976.

Scott, James. *Seeing Like a State*. New Haven, CT: Yale University Press, 1997.

Seabrook, J. *Victims of Development*. London: Verso, 1993.

Seers, Dudley. *The Political Economy of Nationalism*. Oxford University Press, 1983.

Sen, Amartya. *Poverty and Famines*. Oxford: Clarendon Press, 1981a.

_____. "Ethical Issues in Income Distribution: National and International," in S. Grassman and E. Lundberg, eds. *World Economic Order: Past and Present*. New York: St. Martin's Press, 1981b, pp. 464-93.

_____. "Economics of the Family," in A. Sen. *Resources, Values and Development*. Cambridge, MA: Harvard University Press, 1983.

_____. *Commodities and Capabilities*. Amsterdam: North Holland, 1985.

_____. "Gender and Cooperative Conflict," *WIDER Working Paper No. 18*. Helsinki: WIDER, 1987.

_____. "The Concept of Development," in H. Chenery and T.N. Srinivasan, eds. *Handbook of Development Economics*, Vol. 1. Amsterdam: North Holland, 1988, pp. 9-26.

_____. "Development as Capability Expansion," *Journal of Development Planning*, vol. 19 (1989), pp. 41-48.

_____. *On Ethics and Economics*. Oxford: Blackwell, 1990.

_____. *Development as Freedom*. New York: Knopf, 1999.

Sen, Amartya, and Bernard Williams, eds. *Utilitarianism and Beyond*. Cambridge: Cambridge University Press, 1982.

Sen, Amartya., et al. *The Standard of Living.* [Ed. G. Hawthorn]. Cambridge: Cambridge University Press, 1988.

Sen, G., and C. Grown. *Development, Crises and Alternative Visions.* London: Earthscan, 1988.

Shackle, George. *Epistemics and Economics.* Cambridge: Cambridge University Press, 1972.

Shiva, Vandana. *Close to Home.* Philadelphia: PA: New Society Publishers, 1994.

Shute, S., and S. Hurley., eds. *On Human Rights: The Oxford Amnesty Lectures.* New York: Basic Books, 1993.

Sidanius, J., and F. Pratto. *Social Dominance.* Cambridge: Cambridge University Press, 1999.

Siggi, M. *Economic Society in Islam.* Lahore: Kazi Publishers, 1970 [1939].

Simon, Herbert. "Rationality as a Process and Product of Thought," *American Economic Review*, vol. 68 (1978), pp. 1-16.

Smith, Adam. *Theory of Moral Sentiments.* Oxford: Clarendon Press, 1974 [1759].

____. *An Inquiry into the Nature and Causes of the Wealth of Nations.* Oxford: Clarendon Press, 1976 [1776].

Solow, Robert. *The Labor Market as a Social Institution.* Oxford: Blackwell, 1990.

Soros, George. *The Crisis of Global Capitalism.* New York: Public Affairs, 1998.

Standing, Guy. "Globalization, Labor Flexibility and Insecurity: The Era of Market Regulation," *European Journal of Industrial Relations*, vol. 3 (1997), pp. 7-37.

____. *Beyond the New Paternalism.* New York: Verso, 2000.

Standing, Guy, and Viktor Tokman., eds. *Towards Social Adjustment.* Geneva: ILO, 1991.

Steiner, H. "Entitlements," in J. Eatwell, M. Milgate, and P. Newman, eds. *The New Palgrave: Social Economics.* New York: Norton, 1989, pp. 40-44.

Steiner, H., and P. Alston. *International Human Rights in Context.* Oxford: Clarendon Press, 1996.

Stenhouse, David. *The Evolution of Intelligence.* London: Allen and Unwin, 1974.

Stewart, Frances. *Adjustment and Poverty.* London: Routledge, 1995.

Stiefel, M. *A Voice for the Excluded.* London: Zed Books, 1994.

Stiglitz, J. "Economic Organization, Information, and Development," in H. Chenery and T.N. Srinivasan, eds. *Handbook of Development Economics*, Vol. 1. Amsterdam: North Holland, 1988, pp. 93-160.

____. "Markets, Market Failure, and Development," *American Economic Review*, vol. 79 (1989), pp. 197-203.

____. "The Private Uses of Public Interests: Incentives and Institutions," *Journal of Economic Perspectives*, vol. 12 (1998a), pp. 1-22.

____. "More Instruments and Broader Goals: Moving Towards the Post-Washington Consensus," *WIDER Annual Lecture*, January 7, Helsinki: WIDER, 1998b.

____. *Globalization and its Discontents*. New York: Norton, 2002.

Streeten, Paul. "Introduction" in Gunnar Myrdal. *Value and Social Theory*. New York: Harper and Row, 1958

____. "International Cooperation," in H. Chenery and T.N. Srinivasan, eds. *Handbook of Development Economics*, Vol. 1. Amsterdam: North Holland, 1988.

____. *Thinking about Development*. Cambridge: Cambridge University Press, 1995.

Swindler, Ann. et al. *Habits of the Heart*. Berkeley, CA: University of California Press, 1997.

Taylor, Charles. "The Dialogical Self," in D. Hiley, J. Bohman, and R. Shusterman, eds. *The Interpretive Turn*. Ithaca, NY: Cornell University Press, 1991.

Tendler, J., and S. Freedheim. "Trusting in a Rentseeking World: Health and Environment Transformed in Northeast Brazil," *World Development*, vol. 22 (1994), pp. 1771-92.

Thomlinson, R. *Population Dynamics*. New York: Random House, 1965.

Timbergen, Jan. *RIO: Reshaping the International Order*. New York: Dutton, 1976.

Tinker, Irene. *Persistent Inequalities*. Oxford: Oxford University Press, 1990.

Toulmin, Stephen. *Cosmopolis*. Chicago: University of Chicago Press, 1990.

Toye, John. *Dilemmas of Development*. Oxford: Blackwell, 1987.

Ullman-Margalit, E. *The Emergence of Norms*. Oxford: Oxford University Press, 1977.

UN [United Nations]. *The International Dimensions of the Right to Development as a Human Right.* New York: UN, 1979.

____. *Agenda 21, UNCED Concluding Document.* New York: UN, 1992.

____. *The Vienna Declaration and Program of Action.* New York: UN, 1993.

UNCTAD [United Nations Conference of Trade and Development]. *Structural Adjustment and Poverty Alleviation.* Document PA/7. Geneva: UNCTAD, 1994.

____. *World Investment Report.* Geneva: UNCTAD, 1997.

____. *World Investment Report.* Geneva: UNCTAD, 1998.

____. *World Investment Report.* Geneva: UNCTAD, 2002.

UNDP [United Nations Development Programme]. *Human Development Report 1992.* New York: Oxford University Press, 1992.

____. *Human Development Report 1993.* New York: Oxford University Press, 1993.

____. *Human Development Report 1994.* New York: Oxford University Press, 1994.

____. *Human Development Report 1995.* New York: Oxford University Press, 1995.

____. *Human Development Report 1996.* New York: Oxford University Press, 1996.

____. *Human Development Report 1997.* New York: Oxford University Press, 1997.

____. *Human Development Report 1998.* New York: Oxford University Press, 1998.

____. *Human Development Report 1999.* New York: Oxford University Press, 1999.

UNECA [United Nations Economic Commission for Africa]. *African Alternative Framework to Structural Adjustment and Economic Recovery.* Addis Ababa: UNECA, 1989.

UNESCO [United Nations Education, Scientific, and Cultural Organization]. *Declaration of MONDIACULT: World Conference on Cultural Policies.* Paris: UNESCO, 1982.

____. *The Cultural Dimension of Development.* Paris: UNESCO, 1994.

UNFPA [United Nations Population Fund]. *Population and Development.* New York: UNFPA, 1991

____. *The State of the World Population 1998.* New York: UNFPA, 1998.

_____. *The State of the World Population 1999*. New York: UNFPA, 1999.

UN, General Assembly. *Declaration on the Right to Development.* New York: UN, 1986.

UNHCR [United Nations Commission on Human Rights]. *Global Consultation on the Right to Development as a Human Right.* Document E/CN.4/9/Rev. New York: UNHCR, 1990.

UNICEF [United Nations Children's Fund]. *The State of the World's Children 1999*. New York: Oxford University Press, 1998.

Uphoff, Norman. "Assisted Self-Reliance: Working With, Rather than For, the Poor," in J. Lewis et al., eds. *Strengthening the Poor: What Have We Learned?* New Brunswick, NJ: Transaction Books, 1988.

_____. *Learning from Gal Oya*. Ithaca, NY: Cornell University Press, 1992.

_____. "Grassroots Organizations and NGOs in Rural Development: Opportunities with Diminishing States and Expanding Markets," *World Development*, vol. 21 (1993), pp. 607-22.

Valette, J. "Larry Summer's War Against the Earth," *Counter Punch* at http://www. counterpunch.org/summers.html, 1992.

Van Arcadie, Brian. "The Role of Institutions in Economic Development," in World Bank. *Proceedings of the World Bank Annual Conference on Development Economics 1989.* Washington, DC: The World Bank, 1989.

Van Ness, P., ed. *Debating Human Rights*. London: Routledge, 1999.

Veblen, Thorstein. *The Theory of the Leisure Class*. New York: Kelley, 1965 [1899].

Wachtel, Paul. *Poverty and Affluence*. Philadelphia, PA: New Society Publishers, 1989.

Waddington, C. *Tools for Thought*. London: Jonathan Cape, 1977.

Wade, Robert. *Governing the Market*. Princeton, NJ: Princeton University Press, 1990.

_____. "Global Inequality," *The Economist*, April 28 (2001), pp. 72-74.

Wallerstein, Immanuel. *The Modern World System*. New York: Academic Press, 2001 [1974].

_____. *The Capitalist World Economy*. Cambridge: Cambridge University Press, 1979.

Walzer, Michael. *Spheres of Justice*. New York; Basic Books, 1983.

Ward, Barbara. *The Rich Nations and the Poor Nations*. New York: Norton, 1962.

Warnock, M., ed. *John Stuart Mill: Utilitarianism, On Liberty, Essay on Bentham.* Cleveland, OH: World Publishing Co., 1962.

Weber, Max. *Economy and Society.* New York: Bedminster Press, 1968 [1922].

____. *The Methodology of the Social Sciences.* Glencoe, IL: Free Press, 1949.

Welch, C. "Utilitarianism," in J. Eatwell, M. Milgate, and P. Newman, eds. *The New Palgrave: The Invisible Hand.* New York: Norton, 1989.

Whitehead, Alfred North. *Science and the Modern World.* New York: Macmillan, 1925.

____. *Process and Reason.* New York: Harper, 1929.

Williams, Bernard. *Ethics and the Limits of Philosophy.* London: Fontana/Collins, 1985.

Williamson, John. *Latin American Adjustment: How Much Has Happened?* Washington, DC: Institute for International Economics, 1990.

Williamson, Oliver. *Markets and Hierarchies.* New York: Free Press, 1975.

____. *The Economic Institutions of Capitalism.* New York: Free Press, 1985.

World Bank. *World Development Report 1990: Poverty.* New York: Oxford University Press, 1990.

____. *Third Report on Adjustment Lending.* Washington, DC: The World Bank, 1992a.

____. *Poverty Reduction Handbook and Operational Directive.* Washington, DC: The World Bank, 1992b.

____. *World Development Report 1994: Infrastructure.* New York: Oxford University Press, 1994.

____. *World Development Report 1995: Workers in an Integrating World.* New York: Oxford University Press, 1995a.

____. *Monitoring Environmental Progress.* Washington, DC: The World Bank, 1995b.

____. *Toward Greater Gender Equality: The Role of Public Policy.* Washington, DC: The World Bank, 1995c.

____. *Global Development Finance.* Washington, DC: The World Bank, 1997a.

____. *World Development Indicators.* Washington, DC: The World Bank, 1997b.

_____. *Global Development Indicators*. Washington, DC: The World Bank, 1998a.

_____. *Global Economic Prospects and the Developing Countries*. Washington, DC: The World Bank, 1998b.

_____. *World Development Report 1999: Knowledge for Development*. New York: Oxford University Press, 1999.

_____. *World Development Report 2003: Sustainable Development in a Dynamic World*. New York: Oxford University Press, 2003.

World Commission on Environment and Development. *The Common Future*. New York: Oxford University Press, 1987.

Worster, D. *Nature's Economy*. Cambridge: Cambridge University Press, 1985.

Zeidin, Theodore. *The Ultimate History of Humanity*. Oxford: Oxford University Press, 1997.

Zinam, Oleg. "Quality of Life, Quality of the Individual, Technology and Development," *American Journal of Economics and Sociology*, vol. 48 (1983), pp. 55-68.

Index

children, 53, 176, 251, 262
Chile, 258
China, 15-16, 40, 105, 128, 136,
    140, 173, 256
Christianity, 15, 55, 234
civil society, 285-89
class relations, ix, 20, 55, 57, 64,
    69, 81, 144, 166, 184, 194,
    239, 251, 266, 269, 279, 283
Cobb, Charles, 33, 36, 310
Cole, Ken, 8
Coleman, James, 40, 68, 228
collective bargaining, 69, 260,
    265, 272
collective self-reliance, 313
colonialism, 23, 92, 103, 173, 243,
    302
community, 32, 60, 117, 226, 244,
    270, 281, 383, 306-15
    and participatory develop-
    ment, 68, 164, 180, 198,
    200, 301
    self-determination, 288, 291
    See also participation;
empowerment
competition, 34, 67, 96, 124, 131-
    32, 270, 307
    See also market(s)
conditionality, 109, 113, 117, 141,
    325
conflict, x, 24, 43, 46, 100, 130,
    169, 191, 245, 268, 270, 283
    household, 175-76
    systemic, 69-73
Confucianism, 15, 56, 234, 256
consequentialism 224
consumption, 27-28, 65, 102, 215,
    319
    conspicuous, 126, 197
    development nexus, 129, 192-
    97
conversation, ix, 90-93, 131, 183,
    266, 302, 313, 323
cooperation, x, 42-43, 132, 191,

cooperation (*continued*) 296
    global, 63, 66, 298
    household, 175-76, 233
    social, 226, 240, 263, 310, 315
corruption, 24, 34, 93
critical theory, 85-90
culture, 60, 64, 88, 91, 103, 220,
    231, 240, 256, 309, 316, 319
    American, 104-5
    diversity, 17, 302
    domination, 62, 71-92, 197
cumulative causation, 168, 313

Daly, Herman, 33, 36, 310
Debreu, Gerard, 31
debt, 68, 109, 112, 141-43, 139,
    170
decentralization, 79, 302-6
democracy, 54, 73, 201, 240, 247,
    258, 280, 286
    unstable and illiberal, 282, 286
    and community, 288, 307
    in international institutions,
    324-25
deontology, 232, 239
deregulation, 3, 24, 130, 262, 325
Descartes, René, 81-83
desertification, 203
de Soto, Hernando, 296
determinism, 14-17, 37
de Tocqueville, Alexis, 279-80,
    308
devaluation, 116, 325
development, 4, 19-23
    authentic, 111, 18, 52, 56, 69,
    118,134, 191, 247, 282, 289,
    307, 309, 313
    human/humanitarian, 7, 13,
    20, 24, 51-54, 195, 238, 241,
    247, 263, 285, 289
    sustainable, 99, 180, 177, 180,
    192, 263, 284, 293, 309, 326,
    and human security, 53, 81-82,
    99, 113, 120, 177, 182-83,

and human security
(*continued*) 189, 249
de Waal, Francis, 186
dialectics, 83, 88, 323
dialogue, ix, 59, 94-95, 246, 266,
    302, 317, 326
Diamond, Jared, 15
discounting, 208-9
discourse ethics, 87-88, 255, 266
displaced persons, 151
division of labor, 143-46, 171,
    173
Domar, Evsey, 70
Downie, Robert, 226
Dreze, Jean, 285
DuBois, Paul, 301
Dummett, Michael, 153
Durning, Alan, 196
Dworkin, Ronald, 250

Earth Summit, 217, 296
East Asia, 109, 122, 126, 133,
    138, 142, 144, 151, 216, 285
Easterly, William, 69
Eastern Europe, 17, 162, 285, 296
economic growth, ix, 4, 14, 20,
    37, 46, 52-53, 62, 112, 126,
    137, 193, 195, 267, 270
    efficiency criteria, 27-29, 41,
    43, 53, 263, 295
    efficiency/equity tradeoff, 44,
    46, 322
    and underdevelopment, 124-
    25, 129, 141-42, 161, 207, 213
    See also development;
    poverty; unemployment
education, 46, 53, 73, 129, 140,
    166-7, 177, 188, 192, 214,
    229, 240, 263, 293, 312, 324
    role in development, 216, 254,
    272
    and women, 173-75, 267, 270
    See also human needs
elites, 200, 291-2, 308

Elster, Jon, 84
employment, x, 4, 24, 54, 70, 113,
    137, 295-6, 307
    full, 108, 121, 142, 146, 180,
    193, 229, 239, 325
    See also unemployment
empowerment, x, 53, 62, 269,
    288, 311
Engels, Friedrich, 172
Enlightenment, 13,15, 55, 252
environment (biophysical), 60, 62,
    117, 192, 239, 295, 315, 324
    degradation of, 18-19, 28-9,
    53, 194, 203, 247, 268
    sustainability, 202-217
epistemology, 6, 8, 36, 50, 54
    idealist-essentialist, 81-83
    realist-existentialist, 83-87
    See also knowledge
equality, 55, 62, 225, 228-31, 239,
    247, 252
    of opportunity, 96, 229, 235,
    238, 250, 307
    See also inequality; freedom;
    justice
equity, 4, 62, 113, 192, 201, 216,
    227, 262, 267
Esman, Milton, 312
ethnicity, 1x, 39, 55, 57, 66, 69,
    166, 184, 251, 266, 283
Etzione, Amitai, 308
Europe, ix, 15, 37, 40, 102, 105,
    109, 120, 151
Europeans, 13, 14, 20, 131, 150,
    194
European Union, 63, 105, 122
exchange rates, 136, 325
exploitation, 169, 178, 193, 238,
    243
export pessimism, 122-23

feminism, 105, 266
Fieldhouse, David, 23
financial liberalization, 27, 130,

South Korea, 128, 133, 258, 285
speculation, 33, 134, 294
Sri Lanka, 16, 150, 317
stakeholders, 59, 198, 314
state(s), 130-31, 235, 238, 240
    and civil society, 285-88
    hard versus soft, 284-85
    minimal, 240, 293
Stewart, Frances, 54, 115
Stiglitz, Joseph, 43, 116, 283
stratification, 107, 130, 147, 157,
    246
Streeten, Paul, 36, 46, 53, 160
structural adjustment, 113-14,
    263, 272, 305,
    social cost of, 117
    and underdevelopment, 115-
    17, 146, 164-65, 259-60
    See also IMF; World Bank
structural change, 20-22, 38, 69,
    71-73
Summers, Lawrence, 28-29
Swedish International
    Development Agency (SIDA),
    201
Swindler, Ann, 308
systems theory, 282

Taiwan, 133, 258, 285
Taylor, Charles, 219
technology, 13, 16, 21, 29, 46, 51,
    67, 72, 126, 132, 147, 166,
    213
    change, 15, 22, 36, 64, 123,
    316
    labor-displacing effects, 145,
    272
    transfers of, 121, 123, 132,
    136
Tendler, Judith, 69
terrorism, ix, 17, 131, 151, 184,
    247, 323
Thailand, 128, 136, 311
Timbergen, Jan, 101

Toulmin, Stephen, 80
Toye, John, 284
trade, 103, 118, 122, 188, 324
    comparative advantage, 119,
    144
    free and open, 24, 27, 119,
    130, 134
    and labor standards, 264-65
    terms of, 109, 122
trade unions, 259, 271, 273
transaction costs, 41-42
transdisciplinarity, xi, 79-85, 118,
    193
transnational corporations
    (TNCs),
    viii, 23, 63, 101, 104, 105,
    120, 125, 127, 134, 136, 142,
    266, 270, 272
transnational relations, 26, 106
trust, 41, 117, 134, 240, 295, 309
Turkey, 136, 155

ul Haq, Mahbub, 164
unemployment, 37, 46, 53, 129,
    137, 166, 272, 319
United Nations (UN), 107, 120,
    173, 194, 253, 259, 265, 296,
    323, 324
United Nations Children's Fund
    (UNICEF), 115, 164
United Nations Conference on
    Trade and Development
    (UNCTAD), 106, 137
United Nations Development
    Programme (UNDP), 49, 99,
    124, 126, 127, 134, 143, 157,
    159, 164, 192, 265, 296
United Nations Population Fund
    (UNFPA), 166, 167
United States, 23, 108-109, 122,
    127, 142, 194
    democracy, 280, 308
    hard and soft power, 103-4
    immigration, 151, 155-56

United States Agency for
International Development
(USAID), 201
Universal Declaration on Human
Rights, 129, 254, 259, 265,
296
universalism, 12, 16, 26, 84, 247,
256
Uphoff, Norman, 68, 312
urbanization, 179, 268, 307, 319
41
urban informal sector, 19, 145-47,
167
utilitarianism, 222-28, 267
utility, 30, 48, 222, 226

values, 6, 9, 14, 21, 26, 36, 79,
132, 282, 310
cosmopolitan, 50, 56, 241-47,
269, 296
human, 60, 88-89, 198, 220
versus money, 220-21
and structures, 71-73
Western, 6, 12-16, 25, 106
Veblen, Thorstein, 196
Venezuela, viii, 136
violence, 4, 158, 165, 184, 278-
279, 283, 323

Wachtel, Paul, 196
Wade, Robert, 126-27, 284
wages, 34, 65, 69, 193, 239,
272, 295
cost-cutting assumption, 143-
44, 259
minimum wage policies, 262-
63

Wallerstein, Immanuel, 20
Walzer, Michael, 307
Ward, Barbara, 3
Washington consensus, 108, 113,
136, 324
Weber, Max, 36, 193, 279, 281
welfarism, 224, 266
Whitehead, Alfred North, 37, 55,
150
Williams, Bernard, 55, 224
Williamson, John, 113
Williamson, Oliver, 42
Wolfensohn, James, 117
women, 39, 53, 66, 70, 144, 147,
167, 192, 193, 252, 262
See also gender; rights
Women and Development
(WAD), 266, 267
Women in Development (WID),
266, 267-68
World Bank, viii, 28-29, 41, 63,
107, 109-110, 156, 173, 214,
246
approach to poverty, 124, 159,
162, 164
and debt relief, 139-41
role in community
and development, 198, 313-14
World Trade Organization
(WTO), viii, 41, 63,
118-24, 246, 263, 324

youth, 53, 293
See also children

Zeldin, Theodore, 18
Zimbabwe, 271

About The Author

Wilfred L. David D.Phil (University of Oxford) is a distinguished international scholar, philosopher, and economist. He is currently a senior graduate professor of economics and African studies at Howard University, Washington, DC. He previously held academic appointments at Fisk and Vanderbilt Universities, Brooklyn College of the City University of New York, and the University of Delaware.

Dr. David, a former economic adviser to the President and government of Guyana, has also served as a staff member and consultant at the World Bank. In addition, he has held consultantships in development policy with the United States Agency for International Development (USAID) and the United Nations Conference on Trade and Development (UNCTAD).

In 1998, he was voted as one of the most productive Ph.D faculty mentors by the Graduate School at Howard University. He was also a Senior Fulbright Scholar, Brookings Economic Policy Fellow, and George Webb Medley Scholar at the University of Oxford.

His numerous other books and monographs include: *The Conversation of Economic Development* (1997); *Political Economy of Economic Policy* (1988); *Conflicting Paradigms in the Economics of Developing Nations* (1986); *The IMF Paradigm* (1985); *Public Finance, Planning, and Economic Development* (1974); and *The Economics of Racial Discontent* (1972). He is also the author of a large number of chapters in other books, official reports, and journal articles.